Transforming the Irvine Ranch

From citrus trees to spring breakers, *Transforming the Irvine Ranch* tells the story of Orange County's metamorphosis from 93,000 acres of farmland into an iconic Southern California landscape of beaches and modern architecture. Drawing on decades of archival research and their own years at the famed Irvine Company, the authors bring a collection of colorful characters responsible for the transformation to life, including:

- Ray Watson, whose nearly century-long life took him from an Oakland boarding house to the Irvine and Walt Disney Company boardrooms
- Joan Irvine Smith, a much-married heiress who waged war against the US government and the Irvine Foundation's reactionary board and won
- William Pereira, the visionary architect whose work became synonymous with the LA cityscape.

Spanning the history of modern California from its Gold Rush past to the late 1970s, *Transforming the Irvine Ranch* chronicles a storied family's largely successful attempts to remake their corner of the vast Irvine Ranch in its own image.

H. Pike Oliver has worked on real estate development strategies and master-planned communities since the early 1970s, including nearly eight years at the Irvine Company. He was born and raised in the San Francisco Bay Area and resided in the City of Irvine for 15 years. As the founder and sole proprietor of URBANEXUS, Oliver works on advancing equitable and sustainable real estate development and natural lands management. He is also an affiliate instructor at the Runstad Department of Real Estate at the University of Washington. Earlier in his career, Oliver worked for public agencies including the California Governor's Office of Planning and Research where he was a principal contributor to An Urban Strategy for California. Prior to relocating to Seattle in 2013, he taught real estate development at Cornell University and directed the undergraduate program in urban and regional studies. He is a member of the Urban Land Institute, the American Planning Association, and a founder and emeritus member of the California Planning Roundtable. Oliver is a graduate of the urban studies and planning program at San Francisco State University and earned a master's degree in urban planning at UCLA.

C. Michael Stockstill received a degree in journalism from Humboldt State University in 1971. After a year as a legislative staff member in the California Assembly, he worked as a reporter and editor in Orange County before joining the Irvine Company in 1978. During his 13-year career there, he helped formulate and implement strategy for major planning and policy issues, including a multi-year effort to pass a half-cent sales tax for local transportation improvements. Stockstill also worked for the Transportation Corridor Agencies, which built the first toll roads in modern California history, CalOptima, Southern California Edison, and as a public affairs consultant. Stockstill moved to Irvine in 1975 and was active in local government, youth sports, and education while raising a family there. Now retired, he lives in Irvine. He has written for national magazines including *Planning* and *Parks and Recreation*.

The American Real Estate Society (ARES) Real Estate Thought Leadership Collection

Expertly curated by ARES leadership in partnership with Routledge, Taylor & Francis, the ARES Real Estate Thought Leadership Collection showcases cutting-edge scholarly research, practice-oriented textbooks, professional references, case studies, and other applications of research to everyday professional practice. Aimed at researchers, faculty, and industry practitioners, this portfolio of real estate resources is distinguished by scholarship, quality, and impact.

Transforming the Irvine Ranch: Joan Irvine, William Pereira, Ray Watson, and the Big Plan
H. Pike Oliver and C. Michael Stockstill

Transforming the Irvine Ranch

Joan Irvine, William Pereira,
Ray Watson, and the Big Plan

H. Pike Oliver
C. Michael Stockstill

Routledge
Taylor & Francis Group

NEW YORK AND LONDON

American Real Estate Society

Cover image: Photo used by permission of the Regents of the University of California

First published 2022
by Routledge
605 Third Avenue, New York, NY 10158

and by Routledge
4 Park Square, Milton Park, Abingdon, Oxon, OX14 4RN

Routledge is an imprint of the Taylor & Francis Group, an informa business

Library of Congress Cataloging-in-Publication Data
A catalog record for this title has been requested

ISBN: 9781032128016 (hbk)
ISBN: 9781032127835 (pbk)
ISBN: 9781003226291 (ebk)

DOI: 10.1201/9781003226291

Typeset in Goudy
by KnowledgeWorks Global Ltd.

Visit the companion website at: https://www.thebigplanbook.com/

Pike Oliver dedicates this book to his spouse, Rosemarie, for her support, and to all the Irvine Company alumni as well as John Reps and Tom Sills who encouraged sharing this story.

Mike Stockstill dedicates this book to his wife, Colleen, for her love and inspiration, and to Mason, Caroline and Theo, Patrick, Rachel and Zinnia, and Stephanie and Daniel.

Contents

About the American Real Estate Society

The American Real Estate Society (ARES) is a leading producer of real estate research worldwide, with the mission of facilitating disciplinary innovation and knowledge exchange between real estate academy and industry constituents. Founded in 1985, ARES is a 501 (c)(3) nonprofit association comprised of academic and professional real estate thought leaders from the United States and around the world. The society is dedicated to the advancement of real estate knowledge, education, and outreach, and to bridging the gap between real estate thought and practice.

ARES Publications

The American Real Estate Society promotes the global dissemination of research representing the forefront of critical thought in real estate, with findings applicable to all areas of industry, policy, education, and practice. ARES publishes a broad range of real estate topics within an international scope, including finance, economics, investment, business, development, housing, sustainability, and environmental and urban studies. ARES publications provide insider access to the latest high-level real estate research, case studies, reports, analyses, pedagogies, and reviews. These constitute an up-to-the-minute resource of interest and relevance to business decisionmakers, academic researchers and educators, industry professionals, and emerging real estate leaders.

ARES publishes six, peer-reviewed, academic journals in partnership with Routledge, Taylor & Francis that provide relevant and timely research of interest to real estate academics and practitioners worldwide: The *Journal of Real Estate Research* (JRER), *Journal of Housing Research* (JHR), *Journal of Real Estate Literature* (JREL), *Journal of Real Estate Portfolio Management* (JREPM), *Journal of Real Estate Practice and Education* (JREPE), and *Journal of Sustainable Real Estate* (JOSRE). For more information visit: https://www.aresnet.org/page/ARES-Journal-Info#rjer

Conference

ARES hosts an academic and professional conference each spring in a unique travel destination that attracts real estate researchers from around the globe. The event features formal paper presentations, panels and roundtables, exhibitions, and social and networking events.

Membership

Membership in ARES includes the subscription to the journals, discounted conference registration, and many other benefits. For more information visit: https://www.aresnet.org/page/Benefits.

American Real Estate Society

Acknowledgments

Indigenous Peoples

The authors acknowledge the Indigenous peoples whose ancestral homeland includes the Irvine Ranch. These lands were never ceded or deeded during or following the Spanish occupation that began in 1769.

Upon gaining independence from Spain in 1822, Mexico claimed what was then known as Alta California but offered no compensation to Indigenous peoples. And in 1848 the United States formally annexed and paid $15 million for the Mexican Cession that included the land that became the State of California in 1850. No financial or other compensation was offered to Indigenous tribes or individuals.

Between 1864 and 1868, James Irvine and his partners acquired two Mexican land grants and a portion of a Spanish land grant. These men later acquired several adjacent tracts. In 1876, James Irvine acquired his partners' interests and obtained sole control of the land that became the Irvine Ranch. Indigenous peoples received no compensation from these transactions.

Libraries and Librarians

This history could not have been written without the assistance of research librarians in California and elsewhere, as well as managers of oral histories. Their efforts were made extremely difficult due to the COVID-19 pandemic, which for months inhibited or at times prevented access to important materials. We remain in their debt and sincerely appreciate their help:

- Briscoe Center for American History of the University of Texas at Austin
- Claremont Graduate University Library—Ashley Larson, Susan Hampson, and Dr. Joanna Poblete
- Langson Library Special Collections of the University of California at Irvine Libraries—Derek Quezada
- LAWRENCE B. DEGRAFF CENTER FOR ORAL AND PUBLIC HISTORY, California State University Fullerton—Natalie Garcia
- Orange County Archives, Santa Ana, CA—Chris Jepsen

- Regional Oral History Office of the Bancroft Library at the University of California at Berkeley—Martin Meeker
- Walter Reuther Library, Wayne State University, Detroit, MI.

We are also indebted to Don Howard and the staff of the James Irvine Foundation for allowing access to records of the foundation.

Individuals

The following individuals generously shared their personal memories of the Irvine Ranch, Irvine Company, Irvine Foundation, City of Irvine, and UC Irvine with the authors:

- Philip Bettencourt
- Midge Mason Browning
- Daniel Beals
- John Burton
- Martin Brower
- Richard Cannon
- Rick Cermak
- Robert Dannenbrink Jr., FAICP, AIA
- Ted Dienstfrey
- Lanny Eberling
- Carol Flynn
- Warren Fix
- Douglas Gfeller
- Keith Greer
- Carlyle Hall
- Kathy Watson Godwin
- David Kerrigan
- Dave Kuhn
- Judith Larson
- Judy and Wesley Marx
- John Martin
- Michael Meyer
- Douglas Mirell
- Don Moe
- Douglas Neff
- Todd Nicholson
- David Neish
- Thomas Nielsen
- Mark Palmer
- Rhonda Priestly
- Pamela Privett
- Richard Reese
- Steve Ross
- Robert Schout
- Sally Anne Sheridan
- Bill Stinger
- Timothy Strader
- Al Treviño
- William Watt
- Scott Wood

Special Research and Editing Assistance

- Jon Aries
- Michael Bissell
- Leslie Bonkowski
- Yana Bridle
- Richard Demerjian
- Kristan James
- Naphtali Knox
- Russell Queen
- Craig Reem
- Larry Sample
- Mary Susa
- Joycelyn Tetel
- Gary Weber

Maps and Illustrations

- Original hand-drawn maps by Robert Dannenbrink Jr., FAICP, AIA
- Digital map editing by Jason Baesel

Special Thanks to Jim Sleeper

The late Jim Sleeper wrote and researched extensively on Orange County history. The authors delved deeply into Sleeper's records related to the Irvine Ranch and family. We found in his files one particularly poignant and, for us, inspirational note that Sleeper wrote in 1984 to Athalie Clarke:

> I read so much about the Company but little about its past anymore. I miss the family name in the business (even the family spats). At least the Irvines sounded like real people…it's a shame that a good history of the ranch up to the Bren period couldn't have been written…something approximating the facts, and a little more personal and less PR-ish.

Jim, wherever you may be, we hope this book fulfills your wish.

Notes to Readers

The Irvine Family

James Irvine II, the patriarch, known as **JI**. He was the son of the ranch's founder, his father, **James Irvine I**.

James Irvine II had three children, **James Jr.** (also known as **Jase**), **Kathryn**, and **Myford**. His first wife was **Frances**, his second **Katherine**, also known as Big Kate.

James Jr. married **Athalie Richardson**. Together they had a daughter, Athalie Irvine, who at age 4 declared that her name would be Joan. She was known as **Joan Irvine** the rest of her life.

James Jr. died of tuberculosis at age 42. Kathryn died shortly after childbirth, age 26. Myford died by his own hand at age 60.

James Irvine II died at age 79 in 1947.

Key Organizations and Associated Individuals

The principal individuals involved in transforming the Irvine Ranch and the five firms or institutions with which they were affiliated are:

The James Irvine Foundation

Formed by James Irvine II in 1937, its two most important members were **N. Loyall McLaren**, a San Francisco accountant and business executive, and **Arthur J. McFadden**, an Orange County farmer and business executive.

The Irvine Company

The Irvine Company was incorporated in West Virginia in 1894 by James Irvine II. He served as its first president. After his death in 1947, his son Myford became president, followed by A.J. McFadden.

Charles Thomas became Irvine Company president in 1960; **William R. Mason** succeeded him in 1966 and served until his death in 1973.

Ray Watson came to the Irvine Company in 1960 as a planner and rose to become president in 1973, serving until 1977.

University of California Irvine

Clark Kerr was the president of the University of California. **Daniel Aldrich** was the founding chancellor of UC Irvine. **William Pereira**, an architect and planner, led the campus site search and designed the land plans for UC Irvine and the initial community of Irvine as well as the first overall master plan for the Irvine Ranch.

Taubman-Allen-Bren-Irvine

In 1977, investors from Detroit, New York, and Orange County formed a company to acquire shares of the Irvine Company. The principals were: **Charles Allen**, a New York investment banker; **A. Alfred Taubman**, a retail magnate; **Max Fisher**, a businessman and philanthropist; **Milton Petrie**, a retailer and philanthropist; and **Henry Ford II**, businessman in the automotive industry; **Joan Irvine Smith**, granddaughter of James Irvine II; **Howard Marguleas**, an agricultural expert; and **Donald Bren**, an Orange County homebuilder.

Persons Referenced

- Ken Agid—Irvine Company marketing executive
- Daniel Aldrich—First chancellor at UC Irvine
- Jean Aldrich—Wife of Daniel Aldrich and founding member of UCI Town and Gown
- Joseph Alioto—Mayor of the City of San Francisco
- Charles Allen Jr.—New York investment banker and member of consortium that purchased Irvine Company
- Herbert Allen—Son of Charles Allen Jr. Investment banker with Allen and Company
- Art Anthony—City of Irvine councilmember
- Brad Atwood—UCI vice-chancellor
- Al Auer—Irvine Company executive
- Robert Badham—Member of the California State Assembly, Member of the United State House of Representatives
- Richard Baisden—Dean of University Extension, UC Irvine
- Gerson Bakar—Apartment developer
- Claude Ballard—Executive at Prudential Insurance Company
- William Banowsky—President, Pepperdine University
- Robert Battin—Member, Orange County Board of Supervisors
- Daniel "Dan" Beals—Irvine Company human resources executive
- Marian Bergeson—Member of the California Assembly, State Senate and Board of Supervisors
- Harry Bergh—Retired county planning director
- Phillip Berry—Sierra Club attorney and activist
- Philip Bettencourt—Irvine Company public affairs executive

- Jack Bevash—Urban planner at the Pereira firm and his own firm
- Arnold Binder—Psychologist and UC Irvine professor
- Paul Brady—Assistant city manager, City of Irvine
- Donald L. Bren—Current sole owner of the Irvine Company, member of the consortium that purchased Irvine Company in 1977
- Margaret Martin Brock—Republican activist
- Martin Brower—Irvine Company director of public relations and author of a book about the Irvine Company
- Edmund G. "Pat" Brown—Governor of California
- Edmund G. "Jerry" Brown Jr.—Governor of California
- Dean Buchinger—Vice president of Irvine Company Agriculture Division
- Walter Burroughs—Publisher of the *Daily Pilot* newspaper
- Richard D. Burt—Third husband of Joan Irvine
- John Burton—City of Irvine councilmember
- Donald Cameron—Irvine Company director of planning
- France Campbell—Founding member of UC Irvine Town and Gown
- Richard Cannon—Irvine Company executive, president of the Irvine Industrial Complex
- Dennis Carpenter—State senator
- Edward (Ed) Carter—UC Regent, James Irvine Foundation Trustee, retailing magnate
- Ronald (Ron) Caspers—Member, Orange County Board of Supervisors
- Dorothy Chandler—UC Regent
- Guy Claire—Attorney, Gibson Dunn and Crutcher
- Ralph Clark—Member, Orange County Board of Supervisors
- Athalie Irvine Clarke—Wife of James Irvine Jr., mother of Joan Irvine
- Judge Thurmond Clarke—Third husband of Athalie Irvine
- Frederick "Chip" Cleary—Publicist for Joan Irvine Smith
- Eldridge Cleaver—Black Panther Party leader
- William Coblentz—Regent of the University of California
- Mickey Cohen—Los Angeles mobster with alleged ties to Myford Irvine
- Jerry Collins—Irvine Company director of public relations
- Hunt Conrad—Irvine Company lobbyist in Sacramento
- Ross Cortese—Developer of Leisure World, later incorporated as City of Laguna Woods
- L. E. Cox—First vice chancellor for business affairs at UC Irvine
- Robert F. Dannenbrink Jr.—FAICP, AIA Irvine Company planner
- Angela Davis—Professor and activist
- Don Dennis—Editor of *Irvine World News*
- Ephraim Diamond—CEO of Cadillac Fairview
- Ralph Diedrich—Member, Orange County Board of Supervisors
- Ted Dienstfrey—Irvine Company aide to Ray Watson
- James Dilley—Founder of the Laguna Greenbelt
- Paul Dinsmore—Trustee, James Irvine Foundation
- Morris Doyle—Trustee and president of the James Irvine Foundation

- Lanny Eberling—Irvine Company vice president of finance and board member of the Irvine Ranch Water District
- Dwight D. Eisenhower—President of the United States
- James E. Erickson—City attorney for the City of Irvine
- Joseph Escherick—Architect and initial designer of Promontory Point Apartments
- Robert Evans—UC Assistant Vice President
- Cecil M. "Cye" Featherly—Member, Orange County Board of Supervisors
- Gilbert (Gil) W. Ferguson—Irvine Company vice president of public affairs, member of California Assembly
- William Ficker—America's Cup yachtsman and Newport Beach activist
- Robert Finch—Lieutenant Governor of California
- William M. Fischbach—First mayor of the City of Irvine
- Max Fisher—Industrialist and member of consortium that purchased the Irvine Company in 1977
- Warren Fix—Irvine Company vice president of finance and board member of the Irvine Ranch Water District
- John Simon "Si" Fluor—President of Fluor Corporation and trustee of the James Irvine Foundation
- J. Robert "Bob" Fluor—President of Fluor Corporation
- Carol Flynn—City clerk, City of Irvine
- Henry Ford II—President of Ford Motor Company, member of consortium that purchased the Irvine Company in 1977
- Howard Friedman—Attorney for Joan Irvine Smith
- Jean Wood Fuller—Republican activist and president of the Federated Women's Clubs of California
- Keith Gaede—Husband of Linda Irvine
- Linda Irvine Gaede—Daughter of Myford and Thelma Irvine
- Frank Gehry—Architect who designed apartments for the Irvine Company
- Robert Gentry—UC Irvine associate dean of students and mayor of the City of Laguna Beach
- Frosty Gerard—Founding member of UC Irvine Town and Gown
- William Geyer—California legislative staffer and later Irvine Company adviser and lobbyist
- Douglas (Doug) Gfeller—Irvine Company project manager for the Village of Woodbridge
- James Glavas—City of Newport Beach chief of police
- Kathy Watson Godwin—Daughter of Ray Watson
- John Gottlieb—Real estate investor
- W.F. Graves—Founding director of the Irvine Ranch Water District
- Barbara Gray—Writer and historian
- Loren Griset—Mayor of the City of Santa Ana
- C.Z Guest—Friend of Joan Irvine Smith
- Donald Haines—Owner of an architectural firm where Ray Watson worked

- Carlyle Hall—Lawyer and founder of the Center for Law in the Public Interest
- Fred Harber—Political consultant
- James Harrington—First director of administrative services for the City of Irvine
- George Hart—Developer of Corona del Mar
- Elinor Raas Heller—Regent of the University of California
- William Bradford (Brad) Hellis—General manager of the Irvine Ranch
- Ivan Hinderaker—UC Irvine vice chancellor
- Andrew Hinshaw—Orange County assessor and member of Congress
- Patricia Hitt—Republican activist and assistance secretary of HEW
- Max C. Hoeptner—Founding director of the Irvine Ranch Water District
- James R. Hoffa—President of the Teamsters union
- Ebenezer Howard—English planner, father of the Garden City movement
- Frank Hughes—Irvine Company executive
- Gary Hunt—Employee of the Donald Bren Company and later the Irvine Company
- Samuel Hurwitz—Lawyer from Orange, CA
- Athalie A. Irvine (Smith)—Daughter of James Irvine Jr., granddaughter of JI
- Frances Plum Irvine—First wife of James Irvine II
- James Irvine I—First owner of the Irvine Ranch
- James Irvine II (JI)—Son of James Irvine I, inherited the Irvine Ranch 1886
- James Irvine Jr. (Jase)—First son of James Irvine II
- Katherine Brown White Irvine (Big Kate)—Second wife of James Irvine II
- Madelaine Irvine—First wife of James Irvine Jr. (Jase)
- Myford "Mike" Irvine—Second son of James Irvine II
- Allan Jacobs—Planning director for the City of San Francisco
- George Jeffrey—Member, Orange County Board of Supervisors
- Charles Johnson—Executive at Wells Fargo Bank
- Scott Johnson—Architect at William Pereira and Associates
- Lyndon B. Johnson—President of the United States
- Edward Jones—Deputy assessor for Orange County in the early 1960s
- Heinz Kaiser—Orange County supervisor
- Jeanne Keevil—Editor of *Irvine World News*
- Clark Kerr—President of the University of California
- Jerry Kobrin—Marketing executive for Lion Country Safari
- C.K. Krauss—Irvine Ranch general manager
- Peter Kremer—Irvine Company president, 1977–1982
- Adam Krivatsy—San Francisco planner
- David (Dave) Kuhn—Irvine Company executive
- Benjamin Lambert—Owner of Eastdil Realty, advisor to the Taubman–Allen consortium
- James Langenheim—Pereira–Luckman employee
- Howard Lawson—Developer and university campus advocate

- George Leidal—Reporter for the *Daily Pilot*
- Kathryn Irvine Lilliard—Daughter of James Irvine II
- Art Linkletter—TV personality and housing developer in the Village of University Park
- Jack Lockhart—Campus facilities technician at UC Irvine
- Olive Lorentzon—Mother of Ray Watson
- Charles Luckman—Owner of architectural and planning firm, partner of William Pereira
- William Lund—Partner with Ray Watson in Newport Development Company
- Kevin Lynch—Urban planner and author
- Michael Manahan—Irvine Company community relations executive
- Howard Marguleas—Agriculturalist, member of consortium that purchased Irvine Ranch
- John Martin—Irvine Company employee and owner of a market research firm
- Wesley Marx—Environmental author and activist and spouse of Judy Marx
- Judy Marx—Community activist and spouse of Wesley Marx
- William R. Mason—President of the Irvine Company 1966–1973
- Leo T. McCarthy—Speaker of the California Assembly
- Samuel McCulloch—Dean of Humanities at UCI and book author
- George McDonald—Editor of *Irvine World News*
- Arthur J. McFadden—James Irvine Foundation trustee, president of the Irvine Company, 1959–1960
- Norman Loyall McLaren (N. Loyall)—Trustee of the James Irvine II Foundation, Irvine Company board member
- Michael (Mike) Meyer—Executive at the Kenneth Leventhal accounting firm
- Wilber Mills—Chairman of the Ways and Means Committee of the House of Representatives
- Douglas Mirell—Los Angeles attorney
- Thomas H. Mitchell—Second husband of Athalie Irvine Clarke
- Willis Mitchell—Founding director of the Irvine Ranch Water District
- Leonard Moffitt—Campus community planner at UC Irvine, 1962-1965
- Brent Muchow—First director of public works for the City of Irvine
- John Murdy—State senator
- Tom Murphine—Managing editor of the *Daily Pilot*
- John Murphy—Irvine Company marketing executive
- Richard Neutra—Acclaimed California architect
- John Newman—Irvine Company board member
- Todd Nicholson—First executive director of Greater Irvine Industrial League
- Richard Nixon—President of the United States
- Stanley (Stan) Ott—Irvine Company director of planning
- Paul Palmer—Developer and university campus advocate in the late 1950s
- John Parker—Marketing consultant

- John William Wright Patman—Member of the United States House of Representatives
- Richard Patterson—City engineer for the City of Newport Beach
- Edwin (Ed) Pauley—Regent of the University of California
- Jack Peltason—Chancellor of UC Irvine
- Suzanne Peltason—Wife of Jack Peltason
- Russell S. Penniman III—Second husband of Joan Irvine
- Russell S. Penniman IV—Second son of Joan Irvine
- Hal Pereira—Brother of William Pereira
- William L. Pereira—Architect and urban planner
- Milton Petrie—Retailing entrepreneur and member of consortium that purchased Irvine Company 1977
- Fern Pirkle—Founder of Friends of the Irvine Coast
- Hugh Plumb—Orange County assessor
- Walter Pollard—Founding director of the Irvine Ranch Water District
- Ed Portmann—Irvine Company public relations executive
- Brick Power—UC alumnus who assisted Walter Burroughs and Joan Irvine
- Howard Privett—Attorney for the James Irvine Foundation
- Pamela Privett—Daughter of Howard Privett
- Gabrielle Pryor—City of Irvine councilmember
- E. Ray Quigley—City of Irvine councilmember; director, Irvine Ranch Water District
- Henry Quigley—City of Irvine councilmember
- George Rasmussen—Founding director of the Irvine Ranch Water District
- Jack Raub—Consulting civil engineer
- Ronald Reagan—President of the United States and governor of California
- Jay Reed—Fluor Corporation executive
- Richard Reese—Irvine Company vice president of planning
- Roger Revelle—President of the Scripps Institute
- Frances Robinson—Environmental activist and wife of Frank Robinson
- Frank Robinson—Environmental activist and husband of Francis Robinson
- James Rouse—Founder of the new town of Columbia, MD
- Ken Sampson—County of Orange employee
- James Scarborough—Irvine Company attorney and trustee of the James Irvine Foundation
- John Schmitz—California State senator and member of Congress
- Robert Schout—Marketing executive for the Taubman Company
- Ray Serrano—Irvine Company cowboy
- Robert H. Shelton—Newport Beach City manager, Irvine Company vice president of government relations
- Harry Shuster—Developer of Lion Country Safari
- David Sills—City of Irvine councilmember and mayor
- Norton Simon—Regent of the University of California
- Robert E. Simon—Founder of the New Town of Reston, Virginia
- Jim Sleeper—Irvine Company historian and author

- Don Smith—Irvine Company planner
- Morton Wistar "Cappy" Smith—Fourth husband of Joan Irvine Smith
- Morton Smith III—Third son of Joan Irvine Smith
- William French Smith—UC Regent
- William H. Spaulding—Trustee of the James Irvine Foundation
- William Spurgeon—Irvine Company executive
- James Steele—Professor of Architecture at the University of Southern California and author of a book on William Pereira
- William Steinkraus—American horseman and Olympic medal winner
- Horace Stevens—Investor in the San Joaquin Investment Corporation
- Roger Stevens—New York developer who advised the Irvine Company
- Bill Stinger—Architect at William L. Pereira & Associates
- Timothy (Tim) Strader—Attorney for Irvine pro-incorporation organizers
- Deyan Sudjic—Urban planner and author
- Bruce Sumner—Member of California Assembly, Superior Court judge
- Charles L. Swinden—First husband of Joan Irvine
- James (Jim) Irvine Swinden—First son of Joan Irvine
- A. Alfred Taubman—Retail magnate and member of the consortium that purchased the Irvine Company in 1977
- James Taylor—Irvine Company government relations executive
- Allen Temko—Architecture critic
- Jim Teffer—City planning director of the City of Santa Ana
- Charles Thomas—President of the Irvine Company, 1960–1966
- Carl Thornton—City manager of the City of Santa Ana
- Al Treviño—Irvine Company planner
- James Utt—U.S. congressman
- Rawleigh Warner—President of Mobil Oil
- Willis Warner—Member, Orange County Board of Supervisors
- Doris Watson—Sister of Ray Watson
- Elsa Watson—Wife of Ray Watson
- Leslie Watson—Father of Ray Watson
- Raymond L. (Ray) Watson—President of the Irvine Company, 1973–1977; Chairman of the Board Walt Disney Enterprises
- William Watt—Irvine Company vice president of multifamily housing
- John Wayne—Actor, resident of Newport Beach
- Robert West—Irvine City councilmember
- William White III—Stepson of Myford Irvine
- Thomas (Tom) Wilck—Irvine Company vice president of public affairs
- Paul Revere Williams—Architect
- William "Bill" Williams—Irvine Company vice president of agriculture
- Fred Williamson—Member of the California Assembly, author of the Williamson Act
- Thomas Wolff—Irvine Company industrial development executive
- Gin Wong—Architect at William Pereira and Associates

- Scott Wood—UCI public relations executive
- William (Bill) Woollett, Jr.—First City manager of the City of Irvine
- Lyndol Young—Attorney for Joan Irvine Smith
- Basil "Bill" Vardoulis—Irvine City councilmember

Chronology of Key Events

1864   With three partners, James Irvine acquires, for $18,000, the 50,0000-acre Rancho San Joaquin that had been granted to Jose Sepulveda by the Mexican Government

1866   James Irvine and his partners acquire, for $7,000, the 47,227-acre Rancho Lomas de Santiago from William Wolfskill who had acquired that property from the original grantee Don Teodosio Yorba in 1860

1868   As a debt settlement, James Irvine and his partners are awarded a 3,800-acre portion of the Rancho Santiago de Santa Ana, which bordered the northwestern boundaries of both Rancho San Joaquin and Rancho Lomas de Santiago

1876   After acquiring additional adjacent tracts that brought the ranch to over 100,000 acres, James Irvine buys out the half interest of his partners for $150,000 and forms the Irvine Ranch

1886   James Irvine dies

1887   The trustees of James Irvine's estate offer the ranch for sale but due to bidding confusion cancel the sale. Following a lawsuit by one of the bidders, the Superior Court of Los Angeles throw out both bids and the trustees are unsuccessful in seeking other purchasers over the next several years

1893   At age 25, James Irvine II comes into full control of the Irvine Ranch and dropping "Jr." from his name and calling himself "JI," weds Frances Anita Plum of San Francisco

1894   JI incorporates the Irvine Ranch in West Virginia as the Irvine Company and becomes its first president

1902   JI offers the ranch or any portion of it for sale and by 1906 sells less than 2,000 acres, including some coastal property. Thereafter he abandons all thought of selling the Irvine Ranch as a whole

1906   JI and family (wife Anita Plum Irvine, sons James Irvine Jr., Myford Irvine and daughter Kathryn) move to Orange County following the San Francisco earthquake, and build a home near the center of the 100,000-plus-acre property

1929   James Irvine Jr. marries Athalie Richardson

1933   Athalie Anita Irvine (Joan) born to James Irvine Jr. and Athalie Irvine

1935   James Irvine Jr. dies of complications of tuberculosis at age 42

1937   JI forms James Irvine Foundation and endows it with 54 per cent of Irvine Company stock plus cash and property

1947   JI dies while fishing in Montana. His only surviving son, Myford Irvine, is named president of the Irvine Company

1950s   During the 1950s, the Irvine Company develops, primarily with Macco Corporation, several residential neighborhoods in and adjacent to the City of Newport Beach as well as the Irvine Coast Country Club, the first golf course on the ranch

1953   Boy Scouts of America hold national Jamboree on the Irvine Ranch

1957   Joan Irvine joins the Board of Directors of the Irvine Company and the University of California begins a search for a new campus in Southern California and retains the firm of Luckman and Pereira to assist in the effort

1959   Myford Irvine dies from gunshot wounds—death is ruled a suicide and Joan Irvine thwarts a deal preventing the Irvine Company ceding control of development of the Irvine Ranch to a joint venture with a New York City based firm

1960   William L. Pereira and Associates prepares a master plan for a 10,000-acre university community that the Irvine Company submits to the University of California and then a 35,000-acre plan for the southern sector of the Irvine Ranch

   Ray Watson joins Irvine Company as a planner

   Charles Thomas is recruited as president of the Irvine Company

   Irvine Ranch Water District is formed

   Irvine Company offers, for one dollar, 990 acres to University of California for a new campus that becomes the University of California, Irvine (UCI)

1961   William L. Pereira & Associates submits to the Irvine Company a master plan that encompasses the entire ranch

1964   UC Irvine Dedication Ceremony; Eastbluff developed

   UC Irvine acquires 510-acres of the Inclusion Area from the Irvine Company at a discounted price, bringing the campus acreage to 1,500 acres

1965   UC Irvine opens

1966   William R. Mason elected president of the Irvine Company

1967   Newport Center and Fashion Island open

1968   University Park developed in the future City of Irvine, followed by Turtle Rock

1969   Tax Reform Act of 1969 signed into law in Washington DC

1971   City of Irvine incorporated

1972   Coastal Act passed as an initiative by California voters

1973   William Mason dies; Ray Watson elected president of the Irvine Company

1975   James Irvine Foundation begins negotiations to sell Irvine Company stock

1976   Village of Woodbridge opens with at least 10,000 persons in attendance

1977   Public bidding war for Irvine Company stock held by James Irvine Foundation ensues and a consortium led by Alfred Taubman, Allen and Company, Joan Irvine Smith, and Donald Bren win the contest and take control of the Irvine Company

1977   Ray Watson and two other senior executives resign from the Irvine Company.

Additional Resources

The authors maintain on the Internet additional information about the transformation of the Irvine Ranch, including maps and charts. These materials may be accessed without additional charge at https://thebigplanbook.com

Preface

Ray Watson often mentioned to friends and Irvine Company employees that he was going to write "the book"—his recollections and interpretations of the key events he and others at the Irvine Company experienced during the years the company planned and developed the City of Irvine. Few other people had such insight and knowledge of the subject; Watson worked at the Irvine Company for 17 years, rising from a junior planner to president.

Watson wrote six chapters of his book. He also gave a lengthy oral history to the Bancroft Library at UC Berkeley, to UC Irvine professor Samuel McCulloch, and corresponded with several academics and planners, critiquing and commenting on their works relative to Irvine.

Unfortunately, Watson never completed his book. The authors of *Transforming the Irvine Ranch* undertook its research and writing out of respect for the vision he set out to chronicle, and the inspiration he provided to us and to hundreds of others in Orange County who knew him personally or professionally.

The book draws on six main sources. The first are the writings and oral history of Ray Watson. The second are excerpts from books, oral histories, and newspaper and magazine articles that chronicle the period from 1937 to 1977 and events relating to the Irvine Ranch. Prominent among these books are Joan Irvine Smith's autobiography, "A California Woman's Story"; Martin Brower's "The Irvine Ranch, a Place for People"; "The Irvine Ranch" by Robert Glass Cleland, updated by Robert V. Hein; "California Rich" by Robert Birmingham; "Threshold Resistance" by Alfred Taubman; "William Pereira" by James Steele; and "Twice in a Lifetime" by Charles Luckman. Third are government accounts documenting the Tax Reform Act of 1969 and records of the Irvine Ranch Water District. Fourth are minutes of the James Irvine Foundation. Fifth are interviews with individuals who worked for the Irvine Company directly or indirectly. Sixth are the personal recollections of the authors.

The book is largely written in chronological fashion, but there are exceptions where the subject matter lends itself to greater explanation at the point it occurs in the text. A list of key figures and a condensed chronology of events are provided in the *Notes to Readers*.

H. Pike Oliver and C. Michael Stockstill
June 2022

Introduction
The Land

> The entrances to California are enchanting…if you enter the golden land
> through the attractive green valleys of Southern California, you find them rich
> in orange orchards and blessed with a mild, gentle air.
>
> *Happy Days in Southern California* by Fredrick Hastings Rindge, 1898

If a planner, builder, or architect set out to discover the most favorable landscape upon which to locate a new city, is it possible anywhere was superior to the Irvine Ranch?

Thousands of acres are found in the vital center of an immense valley that seems flat, but with an imperceptible slope allowing runoff from infrequent rains to drain slowly into two large natural creeks. Mile after mile of such land means there are virtually no natural barriers to construction, and only minimal needs for localized drainage. Roads, water pipes, and sewers can be aligned to fall neatly into place.

Hillsides to the west slope gently, their geological foundations sturdy and firm, resistant to slides, perfect for creation of lots for new homes, row upon row, nearly all with stunning views.

At the opposite side of the great valley, another range of rolling hills, equally well suited to nest homes and schools into neighborhoods. The two elevations also form a pleasing symmetry, enveloping the center of the future city in natural borders.

And just over the edge of the western range, the greatest gift any California land can bestow: coastal shores facing the Pacific Ocean. From the ridgeline, canyons descend to the shore, their narrow bottoms lined with tangled, leafy sycamores, roots searching the soil for winter's runoff. The hills dotted with oaks and scrub brush amid rocky outcroppings, creating a landscape that begs for the painter's eye.

Two magnificent bays anchor the southern edge of the miles of beaches that play out beneath the cliffs, calm and pristine, unchanged since the days native Indians gathered abalone and mussels from the rocky shores.

DOI: 10.1201/9781003226291-1

At the northern boundary of the ranch coast, the land met the sea in a marshy bay, attracting thousands of migratory birds, the perfect location for a man-made harbor and seaside homes and businesses.

However enticing the landscape may have become years in the future, it is unlikely James Irvine I and his three partners envisioned anything other than crops, orchards, and grazing land when they first surveyed the two adjoining Mexican land grant ranchos they purchased in 1864 and 1866, and the portion of an adjacent Spanish land grant rancho that they acquired in 1868. The only missing element from the serene landscape was year-round running water—that would have to be drilled for and stored.

In 1876, Irvine bought out his partners for $150,000 and owned it all. And the land would all pass to his son, James Irvine II, who would spend a lifetime as steward of 110,000 acres, setting the stage for its dramatic transformation. The vision that guided James Irvine II's management of his vast property was rooted in the soil where his crops and citrus trees grew; no streets, shopping centers, or homes filled his dreams.

It would be a young generation of visionaries that led the Irvine Ranch into a modern era and a new and potentially risky strategy of transformation.

At the heart of their story is Joan Irvine Smith. The granddaughter of James Irvine II received 20 per cent of his shares in the Irvine Company upon his death in 1947. Just 14 at the time, Smith grew into a beautiful, willful, and intelligent young woman who considered her inheritance not just a gift, but her birthright to control the ranch her grandfather had ruled like a modern monarch. Her life would be defined by multiple marriages, extraordinary wealth, and decades of legal and business conflict that welled up from her burning desire to emulate James Irvine II's ownership of the Irvine Ranch.

Towering over the landscape in the role of philosopher/king was William Pereira. Handsome, charismatic, and blessed with the talent to translate his architectural dreams and designs into structure and form, Pereira would parlay a modest assignment to site a new campus for the University of California into a lifetime connection to the New Town that he helped to plan and nurture on the Irvine Ranch.

While Pereira's mind swirled with lofty images for campus and community, it fell to a group of young planners to turn the drawings and blueprints into physical form. One planner in particular stood out as someone who could lead, inspire, and, critically, convince politicians and community members that the Irvine Company's plans would enrich their lives. Ray Watson was an architect by training, but had immersed himself in the teachings of modern psychologists, leading to a holistic approach to planning and development that made the Irvine Company communities he and others would build so unique.

The lives of Pereira, Watson, and Joan Irvine Smith intersected in 1960 as the University of California set out to build new campuses in Southern California. Smith had seen the success the Janss family enjoyed after donating land in Los Angeles for the UCLA campus and reaping the rewards of adjacent development of homes and commercial real estate. But the trustees of the James Irvine Foundation, who controlled the Irvine Company by virtue of majority stock holdings, were hesitant. Smith became prodder, cheerleader, and nemesis to the aging men ("the old bozos" as she called them) until—with Pereira whispering in the wings—a deal was struck.

Locating University of California Irvine on 1,000 acres of the Irvine Ranch became the anchor for the planning and development of what would become the most successful New Town in the United States. Led by Watson and his compatriots, innovations in the creation of communities—greenbelts, underground utilities, generous and well landscaped setbacks, all tied together with a distinctive design—sprouted from the fields and orchards of Irvine. In Newport Beach, similar new villages took shape, as well as the company's first major commercial and retail centers. Massive industrial complexes at opposite ends of the ranch would follow, as would planning for four miles of untouched coastal property along the Pacific Ocean. The Irvine Company was on its way to becoming one of the most valuable real estate empires in the nation.

In 1969, Congress enacted the Tax Reform Act of 1969, which required the James Irvine Foundation to sell the majority of its Irvine Company stock. And two years later, Irvine residents voted to incorporate the City of Irvine. Joan Irvine Smith welcomed the new federal law, correctly seeing it as her path to finally grasp control of the Irvine Company after decades of tumultuous boardroom battles and litigation. In the end, after a rancorous bidding war, she gained a share of the company ownership but never achieved the dominance she yearned for.

The citizen leaders of Irvine had learned well the lesson of a planned community, enacting a general plan for the new city that reflected the one created by the Irvine Company, but promising that public opinion and direction would ultimately prevail. The maturing communities, especially the Village of Woodbridge, burnished the reputation of the Irvine Ranch as the centerpiece of New Town planning and development. Visitors from all over the nation and the world traveled to Orange County to view the fruits of the planner's labors first hand.

It all happened in just two decades. Joan Irvine Smith—only half-jokingly—compared her life to the television prime time soap opera *Dynasty*. Ray Watson received honors from professional organizations and in his time as company president, won the undying devotion and respect of the employees he led. William Pereira became an icon of modern architecture and planning, working on projects around the globe. Along with hundreds of other men and women, they transformed the Irvine Ranch.

1 A Decade of Determination

Irvine Ranch Assemblage in 1899

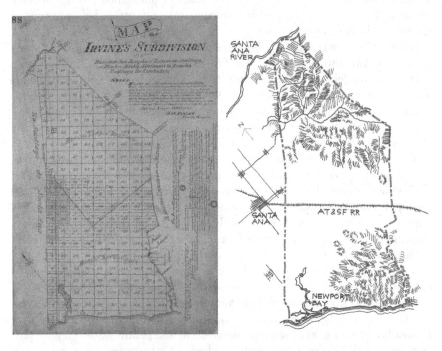

Figure 1.1 In 1899, the Irvine Ranch consisted of approximately 110,000 acres, stretching 22 miles northeast from the Pacific Ocean to the Santa Ana River.

The image on the left is the 1899 survey prepared by S.H. Finley (courtesy OC Archives) and the image on the right was hand drawn for the authors by Robert Dannenbrink, Jr.in June 2021 and digitally edited by Jason Baesel in July 2021.

The hand drawn map highlights the geography of the property, with the foothills framing the central section, and the rugged mountainous area where the ranch boundaries taper to the Santa Ana River.

DOI: 10.1201/9781003226291-2

Since 1864, when James Irvine and three partners began acquiring land in Southern California, the Irvine Ranch had contended with drought, crop failures, an armed standoff with the Southern Pacific Railroad, and countless conflicts with humans and nature.

But just ten years—from 1937 to 1947—were perhaps the most consequential in shaping the future of the ranch.

It was in 1937 that James Irvine's son, James Irvine II, who was best known as "JI," established the James Irvine Foundation, endowed it with cash, real estate holdings, and, most important, shares of the Irvine Company. JI's decision to vest control of his ranching empire in the foundation after his death irretrievably charted the course for future development of the ranch into a New Town.[1]

The impact of World War II in the middle of that decade would also shape the destiny of the ranch both during and after the conflict.

In 1943, the federal government identified 2,400 acres of fog-free flatlands at the base of the Lomas de Santiago foothills at the eastern edge of the ranch as the perfect site for an airfield. Marine Corps Air Station El Toro, named for the tiny community that abutted it, was quickly constructed to train hundreds of Navy and Marine pilots headed to the war in the Pacific. And in 1944, the government approved funds to double its size.

On the western side of the ranch, near Tustin, another 1,600 acres of property was also taken by the Navy and turned into a dirigible base. The blimp hangars, hastily but soundly built, remain to this day on the site of the former base, which like El Toro, was retired from service in the early 1990s.

JI rarely sold land—it must have been a terrible blow to part with even just 4 per cent of his property. But he did not fret long. He took the funds paid to him by the government for the unexpected land sales to purchase the 100,000-acre Flying D Ranch in Montana, where he raised cattle and angled for trout on the Madison and Gallatin Rivers. It was there on August 24, 1947, Irvine keeled over while fishing, dead from an apparent heart attack. He was 79.

Irvine's estate was valued at just under $15 million; estate taxes reduced it to $9.9 million—in 2022 dollars about $124.8 million.

At the close of the decade, the James Irvine Foundation, by the terms of Irvine's will, would hold most of the Irvine Company stock and thus control of the company. (Family members held the rest.)

One motivation for creation of the foundation was the untimely death of his son, James Irvine Jr., known as "Jase," who died at age 42 from tuberculosis. Multiple reports indicate Irvine was grooming Jase to run the ranch. His death left his brother, Myford, as the only other male heir, but Myford loved music more than farming and was considered by JI as ill-suited to assume the leadership role at the ranch.

The foundation board was selected by Irvine. The original members were Myford Irvine, Katherine Irvine (JI's wife), W.H. Spaulding, A.J. McFadden, N. Loyall McLaren, James Scarborough, and Paul Dinsmore.

Figure 1.2 James (JI) Irvine, II, ca 1912.

(Courtesy of James Irvine Foundation)

The foundation was established and headquartered in San Francisco, where the Irvine family owned commercial real estate and a family residence. Other than the family members and Irvine Company legal counsel, Scarborough, McLaren, and McFadden were sterling members of California's business establishment. McLaren had been a member of the Federal Reserve Bank and worked at a successful accounting firm in San Francisco. More important, McLaren had been advising JI for nearly 30 years on tax and investment issues. McFadden, an Orange County resident, had extensive knowledge in agriculture, and Dinsmore and Spaulding were attorneys. Spaulding died in 1944 and was replaced on the foundation board by Brad Hellis, the general manager of the ranch.

From the time he established the foundation until his death ten years later, Irvine made regular donations of cash, real estate, and shares of Irvine Company stock to the foundation, which made its first grant of $1,000 in 1938, then made increasingly larger gifts and donations as Irvine's contributions increased the value of its investments and income.

Immediately following Irvine's death, the foundation board named Myford Irvine as president of the Irvine Company.

The company's principal business at the time was agriculture and livestock. Citrus abounded, as did lima beans and other specialty crops.

Orange County was now on a new course. The war brought thousands of newcomers to California to arm America and defeat fascism, as well as soldiers and

Figure 1.3 N. Loyall McLaren (ca 1970), the guiding force behind the James Irvine Foundation.

(Bancroft Library at the University of California, Berkeley)

Figure 1.4 James (JI) Irvine, II in the later years of his life.

(James Irvine Foundation)

Figure 1.5 Myford Irvine in the 1950s.

(Orange County Public Libraries)

sailors stationed or trained all over the state. GI Joe and Rosie the Riveter got married and wanted to settle down.

The county population was 130,700 in 1940; ten years later it was 216,200, and by the mid-1950s it had doubled. And in the next five years the population almost doubled again to 703,000 in 1960. New residential communities like Garden Grove sprung up seemingly overnight. Established small towns like Huntington Beach and Costa Mesa spread out into the flat landscape, where building a three-bedroom ranch house could be accomplished as fast as carpenters and plasterers could be hired.[2]

The Irvine Foundation and Irvine Company recognized that a tide of humanity would soon crash upon the western boundaries of the ranch. Real estate developers and their agents were already making offers, including one from local attorney Samuel Hurwitz, who proposed on behalf of an unidentified "syndicate" to buy the Irvine Company shares from the foundation for $60 million. Another developer from New York proposed a 70/30 partnership that would leave the foundation in charge while ceding planning and building expertise to the new partner.[3]

Other forces of change were gathering, including the powerful University of California. The Irvine Company no longer needed people whose skills were limited to planting and harvesting. The future demanded expertise in engineering, finance, management, and urban planning. The people they would hire—especially one named Ray Watson—would shape that future.

Notes

1. "History," The James Irvine Foundation, accessed May 4, 2021. www.irvine.org/about-us/history/.
2. "Population.us," Orange County population, accessed November 7, 2021. https://population.us/County/ca/orange-county/.
3. "Tax-Exempt Foundations and Charitable Trusts: Their Impact on Our Economy. (Fifth Installment) Subcommittee Chairman's Report to Subcommittee No. 1, Select Committee on Small Business, House of Representatives, 90th Congress. April 28, 1967," 94 and 1087.

2 A Planner's Path
Early Life, Education, and Real Work

Ray Watson's career was shaped in large part by an uncertain childhood, followed by an awakening to the possibilities of planning on a large scale in the years after his graduation from the University of California as an architect.

He was born in Seattle on October 4, 1926, to a mother of Norwegian extraction, Olive Lorentzon, and a father, Leslie, who was Scots Irish. He had an older sister, Doris, also born in Seattle.

His mother was a schoolteacher, his father a carpenter. They lived in Greenwood; a low-lying neighborhood once known as the Woodland Bog. In one of his written remembrances, Watson recalled that the family, "...took the streetcar to town and the Pike Street farmer's market when it really was a farmer's market."[1]

The family enjoyed a normal life until the day they were celebrating Doris' third birthday. Olive collapsed, the victim of a stroke. She fell into a coma and died three months later, just 33 years old. Watson recalls that the trauma of his mother's death sent his father into a deep depression and eventually a nervous breakdown.

A year later, the Depression overwhelmed the national economy, leaving the Watson family dependent on relatives. It was the start of a period of instability for young Ray, shuttling from grandparent to grandparent, to aunts and uncles. Ray remembers the family moving from one small apartment to another as his father looked for work.

Ray and his sister lived with his maternal grandfather and great-aunt in Seattle for just over two years; in retrospect, he said, it was apparent that this father and grandmother couldn't take care of them.

His father recovered to the point that he found work constructing state park buildings, and with Ray's grandmother opened a boardinghouse in Oakland. Ray and his sister left school in Seattle mid-term to return to their father and move into an old Victorian house at 2769 Telegraph Avenue.

Oakland was a prosperous city of around 220,000 people until the Depression; its port was one of the busiest on the West Coast, and its population was homogenous, almost 97 per cent white. A three-bedroom home sold for $7,150, and there were stylish Art Deco designed houses scattered among more substantial dwellings in the hills.

DOI: 10.1201/9781003226291-3

But the economic downturn sent the city, like the rest of the state and nation, into a spiral. Soon a homeless encampment appeared in a yard where oversized sewer pipes were stored. Residents called it Miseryville, the newspapers dubbed it Pipe City. Oakland limped through the next few years until World War II activated the shipyards and jobs became plentiful. Oakland's demographics began to change rapidly as Black workers streamed into the shipyards; a large public housing project was built to accommodate them.[2]

As Ray Watson was entering college, growing pains and labor unrest swept into Oakland. In December of 1946, he would have experienced a three-day general strike organized by unions targeting clerks in a downtown department store. Longshoreman's union president, Harry Bridges, provided moral (and probably financial) support to the strike.[3]

Ray's father was fortunate to find work during the Depression but was gone five days a week on the job. "He came home Friday evening and left again on Sunday afternoon."[4] Except for the summer of 1939, when the elder Watson worked on a project in San Francisco, his itinerant work schedule left Ray's grandmother as his most consistent adult role model.

Watson's memories of life in the boardinghouse made a strong impression; he mentioned it in speeches and conversations for the rest of his life. In his (2005) oral history, Watson recalled that:

> The people who lived there, well, they were hard of luck. They couldn't live anywhere else, but I didn't know that then. My grandmother, who was into her seventies, she's running this house all by herself, and one of her obligations—she didn't cook meals for (the boarders), but she did their sheets and towels, without a washing machine. So that means a scrub board in the bathtub. I can remember her to this day scrubbing those sheets.[5]

Ray and his sister worked too, sweeping carpets on the stairs manually and polishing the handrails. Their pay was 10 cents a week.

During the school year the Watson children lived in Oakland, but for summer vacation they traveled to Seattle to stay with their grandfather and great-aunt. Watson recalled vivid and warm memories of a large extended family of Norwegian-Americans enjoying outdoor activities including fishing in Puget Sound, picnicking, and socializing.

Oakland, however, was an experience tinged with some sadness for Watson.

Because the family moved often, he never had any neighborhood roots—a place where there were friends to play with.

Nor was there much time for the rites of a boy's teenage years—a pickup baseball or basketball game or hanging out in the neighborhood with peers. Watson's memories are largely of working, around the boardinghouse to put the laundry out to dry (a washing machine had been obtained by then), two paper routes, and during the summer, a job in a cannery (his salary was likely 15 cents an hour, based on historical reports): "I worked 12-hour days, six days a week. I felt rich."[6]

The residents of his grandmother's boardinghouse ranged from people who drifted in and out to one or two stable tenants who were there for years.

One tenant was particularly vivid in Watson's memory: Miss Miller. She was a single woman who sometimes took Ray to the movies, a nice person in his recollection.

But Miss Miller's stay at the boardinghouse ended in tragedy: a jilted boyfriend abducted her when she returned from work, took her across town to a motel, shot her, and then shot himself. Watson and his grandmother found out about her fate when a reporter showed up at their door inquiring for a photo of the unfortunate young woman.

Watson remembers high school as a place exclusively for study. With his after-school hours taken up with labor, there was no time for sports or dances. His friendships were with other boys in classes, especially in math, where he demonstrated strength in understanding and solving algebra equations.

Woven into Watson's recollections of childhood and his young adulthood was the growing sense of self confidence and early maturity enforced by his circumstances. Summer trips to Seattle, for instance, were either arranged with adults driving there who would take a brother and sister along, or on a bus, and later the train, where a pair of teenagers had to switch trains in Portland to continue to their destination. "So, if you add it all up—the relationship with the roomers, taking care of ourselves, getting the confidence." This led to the feeling that, "… no, we don't need any help."[7]

Watson left high school early to enlist in the Army Air Corps, a decision, he said, based largely on the desire to avoid the infantry (too dangerous) and the Navy (prone to seasickness). Shipped out first to Montana and then to flight school in Texas, his military service turned out to be a positive experience: luck, timing, and serendipity combined to give him the ability to access the GI Bill for education after the war and no overseas service, combat or otherwise.

(At his memorial service, one of Watson's sons recalled that his father kept a photo of himself in uniform displayed in the hall of their home, occasionally pointing to it and commenting wryly, "that was a lean, mean, fighting machine.")

His military service ended, Watson returned to Oakland, moved back in with his grandmother, and applied for financial assistance under the GI Bill, which to a frugal young man accustomed to hard work was quite generous, paying for classes, books, and $65 per month for living expenses.

Commuting to City College in San Francisco, Watson found that he had met many of the general education requirements because of his studies as a cadet in the Army Air Corps (where he qualified as a pilot and navigator). It allowed him to indulge a recurring theme from his memories of that time: curiosity about why people behaved the way they did, in all aspects of life.

Watson began to read extensively in the field of psychology, delving into Carl Jung after reading "Essays on Morality" by Philip Wylie, an author he refers to repeatedly in his oral history. He also was coming to terms with his thoughts about faith and religion, determining for himself that the existence of God was not critical to him personally, while acknowledging that religion was a critical part of civilization, and that as far as he was concerned, every religion was equal to another.

While musing on these philosophical issues, Watson also pondered the mundane question of choosing his academic major at UC Berkeley. The fame and prestige of the campus a few blocks away from his home was lost on Watson at the time—he selected it because it was convenient, and he could still live with his grandmother while attending.

For a while, Watson toyed with the idea of studying to be a psychiatrist, but soon determined that multiple years of study would tax his patience and bank account. He was also uncomfortable with the prospect of treating people who were sick.

Maintaining his intellectual curiosity about human motivations, Watson took a variety of classes in subjects like economics, genetics, and sociology. He eventually drifted to architecture, influenced in varying degrees by the fact that his father built structures, and watching the Bay Bridge under construction as a teenager, he was impressed by the magnitude of the undertaking. He was also adept at math, a good match for the curriculum.

As Watson settled into architectural classes, he learned that it was a fertile time for the subject. The classic Beaux Arts School was being challenged by a new generation of design thinkers like Walter Gropius. But for Watson, issues of design, materials, colors—the architect's basic tools—were giving way to his interest in architecture as the foundation for planning and building entire communities:

> While other architects are thinking about a particular building, I'm thinking about the entire physical, political, and social community. I think it had a lot to do with my interest in Jung, as it has to do with my interest in life, the kind of world I grew up in, and that if you're going to build a living community it takes more than the physical form. It's the political and societal parts of a community that ultimately transform the sense of place we architects concentrate on to form a sense of community.[8]

After finishing his four-year degree in architecture at Berkeley, Watson looked for practical experience. He found a job with a small architectural firm in Visalia in California's Central Valley, worked there for a year, then returned to Berkeley to start a two-year graduate program in City and Regional Planning and Architecture.

Within a few months of study, he joined four other students in a project that would reinforce the decision to make community planning his emphasis.

A favorite professor had a contact at Lafayette, one of the growing suburban communities east of the hills behind Berkeley and Oakland. Watson and 12 other students in the graduate school were given a six-month assignment to write an interim master plan for the community.

Watson became chair of the group, working on the economic base of the plan. Watson didn't know what an economic base was and had to learn a whole new vocabulary. It forced him to see that the buildings architects design within a community are what is physically seen, but are only part of what makes up the community.

Watson pored himself into the assignment and ended up designing a shopping center to provide the city with revenue as his part of the overall master plan.

The experience was very fulfilling, Watson recalled, and almost immediately led to a similar assignment with the City of Stockton and a connection with that city's planner that would ultimately send him to Orange County. In this case, the assignment was two-fold: a land use study, essentially walking through the town going door to door and mapping the structures along the way, and designing a civic center, evaluating the land around the existing city hall to expand it into a more comprehensive site.

A professor at Berkeley, Jack Kent, had been impressed with a presentation Watson had made and recommended him to Stan Ott, the Stockton planning director.

Ott offered Watson the assignment, which he took on the condition that it last no more than three months; Watson was eager to start a one-year job with a licensed architect so he could take his own license test—the city job wouldn't count.

So, with two classmates, Watson decamped to the YMCA in Stockton and began work.

For the civic center assignment, he came up with a concept to extend a road and build a bridge from the city hall to the University of the Pacific, the private school that lent some degree of sophistication to the otherwise gritty, working-class city.

Watson had to contend with planning commissioners who were concerned about building a bridge that would connect the Skid Row side of the river to city hall. His egalitarian upbringing found a voice with the commissioners:

> You know, it isn't just Skid Row, it's not undesirable. These people are just poor, they are not undesirable. Include them in your city. Let them benefit from the civic center you are creating. Isn't the civic center supposed to be for everyone?[9]

After completing the Stockton assignment, Watson passed the license test and found his first permanent job with a small firm in the city, Coro and Wang. Calling it his apprenticeship as an architect, he worked the basics, learning the rudiments of going from design into documents specifications and working drawings.

Watson was a young man on the move. Just in passing in his oral history, he noted he was a member of the Active 20/30 Club and was on the city of Stockton's building code board of appeals.

Active 20/30 was an organization designed to give young men an opportunity to have a more active part in the affairs of their community. The tenets of the group must have appealed to Watson: Enthusiasm, Goodwill, Progress, and the signature phrase it embraced (probably not original, but meaningful nonetheless), "… a man is never so tall as when he stoops to help a child."[10]

Watson cited his membership in 20/30 and his position on the appeals board in a cold call letter he sent to architect Donald Haines, whose firm had won a bid to design a building in Stockton. Watson proposed to open an office for the firm in town—it had offices in San Francisco and San Jose, but not in the Central Valley. Haines interviewed Watson, liked what he saw, and in 1955 Watson opened the Stockton office.

His tenure at the Haines firm gave Watson the chance to mature as a manager and, more important, to discover in himself an ability to connect with clients and public officials as an advocate.

His view of himself, until then, as recounted in his oral history was:

> I'll be in the back room. You go out there and get the work. I'll be back here doing the design and the working drawings, and you bother with the clients. And suddenly I am thrust into an environment in which that's what I am doing, and I was comfortable at doing it. So, it changed my self-image to.... somebody who said, 'you know, I am very comfortable in terms of meeting and convincing people.'[11]

Watson soon found himself dealing directly with clients, including school districts, where to assure that an assignment would be funded, the architects and contractors joined school boards and citizens in crafting and funding local campaigns to pass school bonds. (Dealing with multiple districts reinforced Watson's opinion later at the Irvine Company to press for a single unified school district where the new city of Irvine would be built).

Working for churches, Watson preferred the Catholics to Lutherans; the former had an archbishop who made the calls, the latter formed committees.

These were fulfilling years for Watson, personally and professionally. He had met and married his wife Elsa and they had started a family. He was left largely on his own to manage the Stockton office and found increasing comfort in his judgments:

> I felt quite satisfied in that phase of my career, in terms of what we produced. None of it was what I would call award winning architecture ... but it was good, competent work. It was early in my career, and I was gaining confidence.[12]

Recalling an internal budgeting system, he developed for the office, he said, "... I didn't learn that from business school—it just seemed the right thing to do, to me."[13]

Watson was also expanding his network. The Haines firm teamed up with famous California architect Richard Neutra on a military housing project at Lemoore Naval Air Station. On a call with Neutra to discuss the project budget, Watson found that he and Neutra shared an interest in Carl Jung.

Watson and his young family had moved to San Francisco when Haines consolidated the firm into a single office. Before long, Watson had become the manager, overseeing a staff of 20. Finding life in the Outer Sunset district of San Francisco a bit too urban or perhaps simply too foggy, the Watsons moved to Sunnyvale, purchasing a modern Joseph Eichler home.

Watson was having lunch with a client in San Francisco when he ran into Stan Ott, the former Stockton planning director. Ott had something he wanted to discuss with Watson—a place in Southern California called the Irvine Ranch.

Location of the Irvine Ranch in Southern California

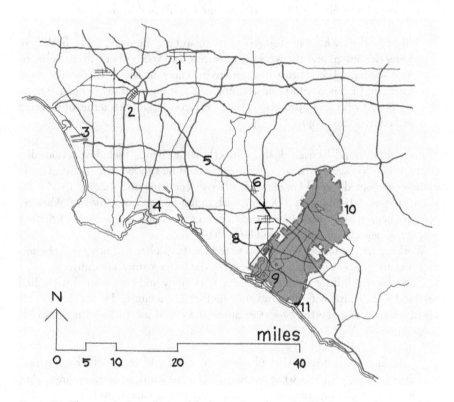

Figure 2.1 The exterior boundaries of the Irvine Ranch as of 1960 are outlined on a modern map of major roadways and cities in Southern California.

1) Pasadena, 2) downtown Los Angeles, 3) Los Angeles International Airport (LAX), 4) Long Beach, 5) Santa Ana Freeway (I-5), 6) Anaheim (Disneyland), 7) Santa Ana, 8) San Diego Freeway (I-405), 9) Newport Beach, 10) Santa Ana Mountains and Cleveland National Forest, 11) Laguna Beach.

Image hand drawn by Robert Dannenbrink, Jr., FAICP in June 2021 and digitally edited by Jason Baesel in July 2021.

Notes

1. Raymond L. Watson, *Material for an Unpublished Manuscript on Irvine* (Raymond L. Watson Papers [MS.R.120]. Special Collections and Archives of the UC Irvine Libraries, 2006) unpaginated.
2. Alexis Madrigal, "Pipe City," Oakland Museum of California, August 10, 2013. https://museumca.org/story/pipe-city.

3. "We Called It a Work Holiday: The 1946 Oakland General Strike," Digital Collections: California Labor Federation, AFL-CIO: Proceedings and publications, accessed November 14, 2020. https://irle.berkeley.edu/digital-collection/oakland/.

4. Raymond L. Watson and Ann Lage, *Planning and Developing the New Town of Irvine California, 1960–2003: Irvine Company President, 1973–1977, Walt Disney Company Chairman, 1983–1984* (Regional Oral History Office, the Bancroft Library, University of California, Berkeley, 2005) 7.

5. Watson and Lage, *Planning and Developing*, 7

6. Watson and Lage, *Planning and Developing*, 12

7. Watson and Lage, *Planning and Developing*, 19.

8. Watson and Lage, *Planning and Developing*, 42.

9. Watson and Lage, *Planning and Developing*, 48.

10. "The History of Active 20-30 US & Canada." Active 20-30 United States and Canada®, accessed February 6, 2022, www.active20-30.org/history-us-canada.

11. Watson and Lage, *Planning and Developing*, 74.

12. Watson and Lage, *Planning and Developing*, 77.

13. Watson and Lage, *Planning and Developing*, 77.

3 Ray Arrives at a Company on the Brink of Change

Ray Watson's fateful encounter with Stan Ott took place at one of California's most exclusive and storied private clubs—the influential Bohemian Club.[1]

The Bohemian Club building, located just below Nob Hill at Taylor and Post Streets in San Francisco, is a three-story brick edifice, fringed with ivy. A bas-relief of an owl with the club motto, "Weaving Spiders Come Not Here," is affixed to one side.[2]

The interior was decorated with Persian rugs, statuary, and wood paneling. A Maxwell Parrish-inspired mural hung over the bar, photos, and artworks in the Cartoon Room. All in all, the perfect picture of a men's club whose members reflect the upper echelons of San Francisco business and commerce. A business lunch at the Bohemian Club was and is an elegant experience.

Lunch at the Irvine Company, where Watson would locate a few months later, was decidedly different. Here is how he described it in his oral history:

> They would serve lunch to the agricultural workers in one room, but they had a long, thin room that by 1960 had become the executive dining room. The kitchen would serve the food to everyone…family style. There was no menu.
>
> Each of us when we came to work there, got a clothespin, which held a napkin. It had our name written on it. It would be put down at our place on this long table, … the years I spent going to lunch there, aside from trying to avoid eating too much … you could gain a lot of weight quickly. I would normally just have a piece of cheese and an apple … but other people would eat all the mashed potatoes and the meat and the vegetables and the soup, the whole thing.[3]

The rooms Watson described were in trailers adjacent to the Irvine family mansion, which by then had been turned into the offices of the Irvine Company. The mansion was two stories, built in a Victorian style of white wood, surrounded by a large porch. Set back from the street, visitors entered formally through an iron gate and down a long driveway planted with tall palms (the entrance was from Irvine Avenue, which has since been re-routed and now runs behind the mansion).

There was a bunkhouse for agricultural workers; Watson stayed there the first few days of his employment.

DOI: 10.1201/9781003226291-4

Figure 3.1 Raymond L. Watson in 1978. He worked for the Irvine Company from 1960 to 1977, starting out as a planner and rising to become president in 1973.

Figure 3.2 Irvine Family "mansion" served as the headquarters of the Irvine Company during the first half of the 1960s.

(Orange County Archives)

The mansion/headquarters and the few buildings around it were about half a mile from the city limits of Tustin, and another four miles from the county seat of Santa Ana. Warren Fix, who also worked at the mansion as a young employee, recalled that there was a "town man" on the company staff who was tasked with driving into Santa Ana for office supplies and to do the banking.

The surrounding area was almost entirely planted in citrus orchards, all the way to the border of the Marine Corps Air Station El Toro four miles to the southeast. Newport Beach was about 12 miles southwest. The remote location reflected what the Irvine Company was at the time: an agricultural empire on the cusp of dramatic change.

After their brief discussion at the Bohemian Club, Watson and Ott met a few days later at Watson's home in Sunnyvale. Ott described the opportunity: a new town to be built around a new campus of the University of California. Ott had been hired to lead the planning department—he proposed that Watson become his assistant.

Watson and his young family had moved into their new home a few months earlier. He wrestled with the potential to succeed Donald Haines at his architecture firm against the idea of,

> ... suddenly a company's got 93,000 acres, and that's a career. You don't have to worry about the next job. And the idea of building a new town for a young architect, even though I didn't know what that meant at the time. And they made me feel I was needed down there.
>
> So, I finally talked to my wife, and incredible person that she is, she says, 'whatever you want.' She never quarreled, never argued. I'm sure she cried that night.[4]

The Irvine Company had made the watershed decision to hold the huge property instead of selling it off piecemeal, which had been the standard for most development in Southern California up until then. Committed to create a New Town, the company had soon realized existing management and staff didn't have the education for such a task. The result was a rapid recruitment of engineers and planners like Watson. According to Watson, everyone came into the new job with an attitude that they would learn together and tackle the immense challenge as a team.

Watson gave notice at the Haines firm in June and spent the summer relaxing and readying his house for sale. Arriving at the rural Irvine Company headquarters just after Labor Day, 1960, he reflected on the formidable opportunity before him.

The next day Watson reported to work and found that Ott had been fired.

Watson learned that company executives had received negative feedback about Ott from local planning departments—the very people the company would need permission from to proceed with the development envisioned for the ranch. The decision was made not to burden the incoming president of the Irvine Company (Charles Thomas, who would arrive two weeks later) with what appeared to be a problem. And so, Ott was given his walking papers and Watson was left feeling as if he were an orphan:

> So there I was on the second day of my new career and the person who had hired me had just been fired. Stan only told me that the Company's personal director and management consultant wanted to meet with me as soon as Stan had given me the bad news.[5]

Watson's experience was heavy on dealing with private enterprise and developers, which appealed to the company personnel people, he said. Watson also talked with William Mason, who oversaw engineering. Mason told Watson that he needed a partner and Watson could fill that role. Mason was also concerned that without an employee in charge of the planning function, outside consultants would end up with too much influence.

After again talking over the situation with his wife, Watson decided to stay.

While the Irvine Company had entered a transition period from agriculture to urbanization, farming and grazing would remain an important part of the business for years to come.

By the 1960s, the operating structure of farming had been well established on the ranch.

Crops were divided between citrus—mostly oranges but some lemons and grapefruit—and row crops: grains, beans, sugar beets, tomatoes, peppers, alfalfa. Walnut orchards, once the largest in Southern California, were on their way out largely due to weather and water issues.

There were dozens of tenant farmers on the Irvine Ranch, paying annual fees as well as a share of their profits. In 1960, most of the tenants had been leasing land for more than ten years, some for more than 20. Most tenants grew row crops.

There were also several citrus related joint ventures. The San Joaquin Fruit and Investment Company was capitalized in 1923 with 5,000 shares. The Irvine Company owned 2,367 shares, and Horace Stevens and his son each owned 1,309. And while San Joaquin Fruit and Investment showed growing crops as its principal business (it leased 1,000 acres of the Irvine Ranch), it also held around half a million dollars in bonds and collected interest on them. In 1970, the joint venture reported income of $246,000 from citrus sales—about $1.769 million in 2022 dollars.[6]

The Utt Development Company was another joint venture of sorts. It didn't develop anything—it raised lemons in Ventura County. Of the company's 5,000 shares, the San Joaquin Fruit and Development Company owned 2,548 shares. And Irvine Valencia Growers raised and packed citrus on Irvine Company property, with the Irvine Company owning all but five of its shares.[7]

It is only speculation that these vehicles may have been set up to minimize taxes, given JI's often stated hatred of taxation of all sorts. It could also be that joint venturing offered the Irvine Company some protection from crop losses due to weather.

By 1960, the company had decided to commit greater resources to citrus, especially the Valencia orange. Valencias were most often used for juice, but Ag marketers had discovered that the tasty fruit could be sold in Asian markets for direct human consumption. Thus, total acreage in citrus had risen from 3,890 acres to 4,130.

There were both sheep and cattle on the ranch in 1950, but by 1960 the sheep were gone. The cattle herd remained at around 1,300. The grand tradition of cattle ranching—Spring roundup—was held in Bommer Canyon, about a mile south of what would become the site of UC Irvine.

In an epilog to *The Irvine Ranch*, the book by Robert Glass Cleland that has become the touchstone of Irvine Ranch history, Robert V. Hine describes the scene of the 1961 event:

> The white-faced cattle were corralled and separated … the JI brand seared flesh just as it had for the first bearer of its initials. The scene was timeless, the job was immemorial. More than a thousand calves had been dropped off this year. Buyers watched. Cows bawled after missing offspring.
>
> Much was old, but much was also new. No longer were the irons heated in a wood fire, but by butane. Station wagons had brought over neighboring ranchers, the *rancheros visitadores*, and prosperity was in their every smile, in the suede jackets and neatly pressed slacks ranged atop the corral fence. And beside these new trappings lay an unexpressed but clear feeling that the whole spectacle—ropings and prizes and ensuing barbeque included—could soon not persist too much longer.[8]

As the company staffed up with planners and engineers, its new president, Charles Thomas, would grapple with the twin challenges of creating a team to build a new community of homes and businesses—which did not generate income—and sustaining the farming, orchard, and grazing businesses that generated sufficient income to pay salaries, dividends, and most important, property taxes.

Prior to the early 1960s, informal evidence indicates that Irvine Company agricultural properties enjoyed what might be referred to as friendly assessed values. Orange County was, after all, largely rural, and county and city government staffing and sophistication largely reflected it.

County Assessor Hugh Plumb, along with his deputy, Edward Jones, had hewed to the standard that land should not be reassessed until the actual usage of it changed. Thus, thousands of acres of Irvine Company farmland lying near and, in some cases, adjacent to new tracts of homes and businesses remained taxed for what it was used for—growing crops and citrus.

Plumb unexpectedly resigned in late 1964, leading the Board of Supervisors to create a competition for the post, and after considering 50 applicants, appointed Andrew Hinshaw to the post.

Within weeks, Hinshaw's announced plans for revising and updating assessment practices set off alarm bells at the Irvine Company. Company president

Thomas fired off a series of statements and press releases predicting that if Hinshaw's policies were enacted, it would mean the end of farming, grazing, and citrus in the county and the potential demise of the mighty ranch.

But help was on the way for the Irvine Company and many of the state's other landowners with properties in the path of development.

Assemblyman Fred Williamson drew up legislation in 1965 that would create a tax relief valve for farmers and ranchers. The Williamson Act allowed cities and counties to enter into agreements with landowners who farmed or grazed to lower property taxes for a rolling ten-year period. The reduced taxes would be based on the value of crops or livestock the acreage produced.

Farmers liked the plan because it gave them immediate financial relief. Local communities saw a tool that could slow or, for a decade, halt rampant and unplanned growth. And environmentalists endorsed it because it could create, perhaps for a lifetime, open spaces.

But the new law was not applied the same way in the state's 58 counties, so in 1966 agricultural interests promoted and passed an amendment to the state constitution that mandated assessors to value open space land based on actual use, not market value.

In 1968, the Irvine Company started the process of identifying company land that could qualify for the new tax break. Late that year, after asking for 60,000 acres to be included in the new zone, the company and the Orange County Board of Supervisors agreed that 48,660 acres would be included.

In February 1969, the Board of Supervisors approved the Williamson Act contract with the Irvine Company on a 3–2 vote. It was a close call for the company, as the board majority would change dramatically in 1970, with all three supervisors who supported the company in 1969 either being swept from office or declining to seek re-election.

The company's property tax bill in 1968–1969 was $5,560,000. By placing acreage into the Williamson Act preserves, the company expected its property tax bill to be reduced between $750,000 and $1,350,000.

The Williamson Act also provided the company with a peripheral benefit that would manifest itself later, when a young legislative staffer named William Geyer went into business as a lobbyist and was retained by the company. Geyer, a brilliant Stanford graduate, had done much of the research and drafting of the Williamson Act. Geyer's deep understanding of the legislation, plus his agile mind, would ultimately save the company millions of dollars, especially after passage of Proposition 13 in 1978 upended traditional public financing methods developers relied on.

The company was never in any danger of going out of business due to high property taxes. Lanny Eberling, who would later become chief financial officer, recalled that the company had a $5 million line of credit with the Bank of America that could be drawn on to pay taxes if necessary. But the company wanted to avoid debt, he said, and was very careful with its spending during the long transition from farming to urbanizing.

In one of his written recollections, Watson described how Thomas became the president of the Irvine Company:

> Ever since the death of Myford Irvine, there had been speculation as to who would lead the company. Would it be a member of the Irvine family, or an outsider? The vision of a new town, while exciting, was just that—a vision. Transforming the vision into form and substance was not a skill that existed with the current management of the company.
>
> While it had dabbled with real estate development on the coastal fringes of the property, the company's board, the family, and the foundation recognized the complexities and risks inherent to such an ambitious undertaking. First on their agenda was to find the right person to lead the company.
>
> For several months prior to the approval of the gift of land to the university, a headhunter had been trolling for engineering and planning professionals that might join the company. But the most important decision to be made was the selection of the president. By mid-summer, a huge step had been made in finding a person acceptable to all factions; the foundation and family shareholders agreed to offer the job to Charles Thomas, former Secretary of the Navy under President Dwight Eisenhower, and former president of Trans World Airlines (TWA).
>
> Only a few months earlier, during a trip to Pebble Beach, Thomas and his wife entered the Del Monte Lodge dining room for lunch and saw a familiar figure waving to him—a friend from World War II days, Loyall McLaren.[9]

In a memoir Thomas gave to researchers at Claremont Graduate University, he described the encounter:

> Loyall motioned me to come across the room, and he didn't say, 'hello Charlie, I'm glad to see you.' He said, 'can I talk to you confidentially?' (He was) very tense, and I said, 'sure.' So, we go back in the hall in a room. He closes the door and says, 'will you keep this absolutely confidential?' I said I would. He said, 'would you consider being president of the Irvine Company?' And I said, 'If I won't, my wife will.' And that's the way it came about.[10]

McLaren's timing was fortunate. Thomas had just turned down an offer from TWA to continue as president for another two years and his wife was fed up with the weather and urban life in New York City. In fact, according to Thomas' oral history, the morning of the lunch meeting with McLaren, "… she looks out the window over the Carmel Bay and says, 'Charlie, why do you make me live in New York when you don't have to?'"[11]

Thomas was no stranger to the Irvine Ranch. As a young Navy pilot he had flown over it during World War I. He was acquainted with James Irvine Jr., and in an uncanny bit of coincidence, had lived next door to Athalie Irvine Clarke in Pasadena when Joan was a toddler.

Figure 3.3 Charles S. Thomas in 1964.

(UC Irvine Special Collections and Archives)

Thomas was well aware of the conflict between Joan, her mother, and the foundation. He told McLaren he had to have the support of the entire family and all the foundation directors if he was to become president.

Thomas was attractive enough to family and foundation that the decision to bring him on was made without objection. On September 10, 1960, he signed a five-year contract at $60,000 per year plus deferred compensation of $10,000 per year for nine years after leaving the company. In 2022 dollars, his salary equated to about $565,000.[12]

Charles Thomas was the ideal man to take on the challenge. He came as a seasoned executive to a company that had suffered through the years with contentious leadership. He brought immediate political experience and stature to a company that spent little time caring about what "outsiders" thought. Then suddenly, everything the company needed to do would come under extensive scrutiny of agencies at virtually all levels of government.

Thomas was an experienced executive who knew how to work within the limitations of a regulatory system. The fact he had little direct real estate development experience was of no concern to the company or the foundation, and many public officials were probably pleased he didn't come with the built-in mindset of a subdivision home builder eager to carve up the ranch.

Watson's memories of Thomas parallel Thomas' memoirs on the subject:

> You go into the Navy, or TWA, whatever it is, and the job is to give them a good organizational structure, first of all, and then you get the best people

to fill those blocks. And then, another thing, you have got to keep the politics from getting in. Now I didn't know anything about air transportation when I went to TWA, but I sure selected some wonderful people to work with.[13]

Watson noted that one of the first hurdles Thomas faced was making good on the company's commitment to the University of California that it would provide all necessary infrastructure to the boundaries of the new campus by mid-September 1965. "And", he added, "… the infrastructure work needed to be coordinated with planning for the new town."[14,15]

Charles Thomas may have felt like Casey Stengel showing up the first day to consider the pool of talent he'd been handed at the New York Mets; the university, by contrast, was something akin to the 1938 New York Yankees. Watson explained:

> For the university, the five-year target was daunting but manageable—all their work was internally confined to the 1,000-acre campus site. They had an entire internal staff of engineers and architects experienced in planning and building campuses. Furthermore, as an independent state institution, the university didn't require local government approvals with their endless and time-consuming public hearings.[16]

By contrast, Thomas had inherited an organization almost completely devoid of anyone experienced in large scale land and real estate development, let alone new town development. "The company had a small engineering department (with) five or six employees. William Mason had been hired as vice president of engineering just six months earlier. And, as previously described, the vice president of planning had been fired."[17]

Employees who worked for Thomas remember him as formal and old school. "He was there to mold us into managers," recalled Lanny Eberling.[18] Thomas sent the young executives out to make speeches and join service clubs. He made it a point to invite VIPs to the remote Irvine Company headquarters, including then-vice president and presidential candidate Richard Nixon, who did a stop-by at the ranch on his way to a rally in Laguna Beach.

Watson got the assignment to brief Nixon the day he visited. He remembers Nixon as asking very astute questions.

Thomas, in Watson's recollection, was very genial and strait laced, and willing to give praise if it was deserved. Watson also gave Thomas high marks for leaving someone alone, once convinced that person was performing well. Thomas had no experience with land development but had a track record of managing and motivating people. Watson was also pleased that all the major departments of the company, including planning, where he worked, reported directly to Thomas.

Thomas kept a firm hand on finances. Warren Fix recalled that any expenditure for more than $5,000 required approval from Thomas.[19]

Thomas also brought in a heavyweight legal team from Gibson, Dunn and Crutcher in Los Angeles. The lead attorney was Guy Claire, who would remain a trusted Irvine Company advisor for years to come.

By all accounts, Thomas was confident he could handle the assignment. His demeanor and reputation had united the fractious family and foundation board; Joan Irvine had staged a large and lavish welcoming party for him in Newport Beach, replete with the who's who of local business and society; the man who held the real power behind the company—McLaren—was an old friend and peer. And Charles Thomas had worked successfully for the mercurial and increasingly eccentric Howard Hughes at TWA. Could the Irvine Company be any worse?

Notes

1. G. William Domhoff, *The Bohemian Grove and Other Retreats: A Study in Ruling-Class Cohesiveness* (New York: Harper & Row, 1974).
2. A PDF of what Mr. Domhoff describes as a re-working of his 1974 book is available at: https://whorulesamerica.ucsc.edu/power/bohemian_grove.html. Published online in 2021; accessed January 27, 2022.
3. Raymond L. Watson and Ann Lage, *Planning and Developing the New Town of Irvine California, 1960–2003: Irvine Company President, 1973–1977, Walt Disney Company Chairman, 1983–1984* (Regional Oral History Office, the Bancroft Library, University of California, Berkeley, 2005) 150.
4. Watson and Lage, *Planning and Developing*, 89.
5. Raymond L. Watson, "1960: A New Era," in *Raymond L. Watson Papers* (MS.R.120) (Special Collections and Archives of the UC Irvine Libraries, 2006) 4.
6. *Files of the San Joaquin Fruit and Investment Company and Frances Mutual Water Company* (Santa Ana, CA: Orange County Archives, 1970).
7. Robert Glass Cleland and Robert V. Hine, "Chapter 11 – Orchards and Water," in *The Irvine Ranch* (San Marino, CA: Huntington Library, 1984) 115–127.
8. Cleland and Hine, *The Irvine Ranch*, 139.
9. Watson, "1960: A New Era," 2.
10. C.S. Benson, *Charles S. Thomas Memoir* (Claremont, CA: Claremont Graduate School, 1976) 48.
11. Benson, *Charles S. Thomas Memoir*, 48.
12. Charles S. Thomas, *Personal and Business Files* (MS.R.003) (Special Collection and Archives of the UC Irvine Libraries, 1946–1966).
13. Benson, *Charles S. Thomas Memoir*, 100.
14. Watson, "1960: A New Era," 3.
15. During his first year as a planner at the Irvine Company, Ray Watson kept a diary, a chronicle of the activities he and his young colleagues were undertaking in their monumental effort to shape a new city out of the massive agricultural empire.

    The diary offers a fascinating glimpse into the balance between preparing the information, tools, and standards necessary for the ranch's long-term future against the day-to-day demands of builders and others clamoring to actually build a new home or shopping center.

    Watson's descriptions underscore the influence of William Pereira and his firm on the process—a senior Pereira employee is often mentioned in the diary; there are also dozens of instances of meetings with people representing a variety of interests requesting a chance to locate schools, businesses, or other uses (including a poultry farm and a chemical research campus) on the ranch.

Among the entries that reflected Watson's perspective from October 1960 to October 1961:

- "There is a serious sewage problem in the Tustin area as there are no public sewers in the vicinity. . . "
- "Southern California Edison wants to purchase all the electrical facilities owned and operated by the Irvine Company. . . "
- (On a trip to Signal Peak overlooking the ranch) ".. . we stopped on the way up, each time observing an increasingly magnificent view."

Watson's observations also touch on issues directly related to planning. For instance, in a meeting discussing a new golf course community, Watson and his planning peers recommended ".. . that no one developer or architect do all the housing units. . . a better product will result if there is a sense of competition."

16. Watson, "1960: A New Era," 3.
17. Watson, "1960: A New Era," 4.
18. Lanny Eberling, video interview by H.P. Oliver and C.M. Stockstill, July 20, 2020.
19. Warren Fix, telephone interview by H.P. Oliver and C.M. Stockstill, June 29, 2020.

4 "We are not Gods"

It is surprising that while William Pereira worked as an art director for Paramount Pictures, Central Casting never plucked him from his design desk and cast him as a judge, senator, or prominent businessman. Ayn Rand's "The Fountainhead" was filmed at the studio in 1949, with Gregory Peck as the willful and ultra-principled Howard Roark, but it was a part that Pereira—perhaps a few years and a few gray hairs later—could have credibly auditioned for.

Pereira, though not tall (just over six feet), projected authority and gravitas. A full head of wavy gray hair crowned a noble visage. Men with a face like Pereira's are often described as hawk-like. He had the leading man profile, but his eyes were warm and searching.

Ray Watson, who spent a great deal of time with him, recalled the Pereira mystique:

> Very handsome. Dressed meticulously. Had a presence, he could walk into a room and take command. He got a lot of commissions because he was a great salesman. You couldn't sit in a room with him without saying, 'if we do it his way, we'll be better off.'[1]

San Francisco Chronicle architecture critic Allen Temko once described Pereira as, "Hollywood's idea of an architect,"[2] a reference, according to Scott Johnson (who worked for Pereira shortly before his death), exemplified by Pereira's "… statuesque figure, his penchant for Bentleys and Lear Jet travel, his preferential dress in black and white, the perennial blonds and British that seemed to surround him." Johnson went on to say:

> We are reminded of how the storyline of an architect's life is inevitably merged with the history of his contribution. There is little question that Bill tapped into the romanticized zeitgeist of his time with work on tropical islands, desert landscapes, rugged coastlines and the exhilaration of aerospace, media, and world travel. (He had) a unique and triangular marriage of personal style, highly narrative programs and (a) penchant for archiving an iconic and idealistic moment with his architecture.[3]

DOI: 10.1201/9781003226291-5

Pereira's fame was international, but in Orange County, his name would always be synonymous with the Irvine Ranch, and the University of California Irvine.

Born in Illinois and raised in Chicago, he graduated into the face of the Depression in 1930, landing a job with a local architectural firm. He went on to start his own firm and was having success in Illinois designing theaters for Balaban and Katz as well as with other projects, including assisting with the creation of a few of the buildings at the 1939 World's Fair in San Francisco.

Pereira and his brother Hal moved to Los Angeles in 1939 and began a decade-long career in the movie business, an important part of his creative life that today is overshadowed and largely overlooked because of his subsequent fame as an architect and planner.

In an April 2020 post on *The Daily Mirror* blog, author Mary Mallory recounts that the:

> … ambitious and driven Pereira found success combining architecture with film work, be it designing buildings or sets … Pereira designed plans in 1939 for a $12 million studio for Paramount … while also serving as a member of the Advisory Board of the Modern Theater Planning Institute.
>
> Prolific as well as organized, Pereira also served as art director and contributor for special effects for Paramount films *Beyond the Blue Horizon*, *This Gun for Hire* and *Reap the Wild Wind*, for which he earned an Academy Award for special effects in 1943.[4]

Most Pereira biographies leave the impression the Academy Award was his alone. In fact, he shared it with Farciat Edourart and Gordon Jennings for photography and Louis Mesencop for sound. The winning sequence is a thrilling underwater battle between John Wayne and a giant squid, which realistically twists its slinky arms around divers as well as a sunken ship before the Duke sends it to an inky grave with his crowbar.

Pereira had become an established and sought-after creative force in Hollywood. He worked for Cecil B. DeMille and David O. Selznick, as well as on films with stars like Orson Welles and Joan Fontaine.

Mallory continues:

> In 1944 Pereira moved to RKO as an associate producer, shepherding films through design, shooting and editing. Pereira once again created an atmospheric production, helping it stand out from traditional melodrama. Box Office Daily called the George Raft starrer *Johnny Angel* 'a credit to Pereira'.[5]

Pereira's Hollywood credentials were also enhanced by his charity work. He helped to design the Motion Pictures Relief Fund facilities, Mallory, wrote. He also designed, pro bono, a hospital for the Motion Picture Home.

Pereira had long separated from motion pictures as well as from his profitable partnership with Charles Luckman when, in the last months of the 1950s, his connection to the University of California and the Irvine Ranch began to take shape.

Pereira and Luckman had parted shortly after their firm received a commission from the University of California to evaluate locations for a new campus in Southern California; Luckman would present the final report that led to the selection of the Irvine Ranch property for the new campus.

In the meantime, Pereira had formed his own firm and landed the contract from the university and the Irvine Company to evaluate how the campus and the land surrounding it should be developed.

Pereira is widely credited with the overarching vision of a UC Irvine campus built in a giant circle. It turns out the true author of the concept was UC president Clark Kerr.

In an oral history by UCI professor Sam McCulloch, Kerr describes a meeting with Pereira and Daniel Aldrich, the first chancellor of the UCI campus, when Kerr recalled a book by German economist named Von Thunan, *The Isolated City*. The book envisioned a new community built in concentric circles, alternating gardens, homes, parks, and business.

Kerr said he pulled out a green pen and yellow note pad and began sketching, with buildings for different academic disciplines forming a large circle, and more circles beyond labeled for parks, dormitories, and other uses. In the center of the circle, "… we talked about things like a Greek theater."[6] The concept appealed to Pereira, Kerr reported. Aldrich, in his oral history, confirms Kerr's description.

The campus would be highly walkable, with interlinking pedestrian pathways connecting like spokes of a wheel to the buildings. If the campus was the face of a clock, the library and administration buildings would be at 6, with classrooms arrayed from 8 to 12 to 4 above them. Major parking lots would be relegated to the bottom of the campus below the library and administration buildings, smaller ones adjacent to the buildings as necessary. Pereira expressed disdain for the automobile as a necessary and somewhat repugnant evil. Of the new town he would plan to connect to the university, he declared that, "… these communities will not be dominated by the auto … they will be communities where women can stroll to shops.[7]. . "

Watson recalled having some fun with Pereira's views on transportation:

> He'd talk about the need for rapid transit and trains … and how terrible the automobile was. Now, Bill Pereira lived on a golf course, in a single-family house, and had a chauffeur who drove him around in a Bentley. And I said to Bill, do you write those speeches while you are sitting in the back seat of your Bentley with your chauffeur taking you to your single-family home?[8]

His views of the auto aside, Pereira had a clear image in his mind of what the style of the Irvine campus would be, and it was modern and brutal.

Brutalism is an architectural style that is stark and massive, but that can also achieve a look of primitive elegance.

At UC Irvine, the library and administration building, as well as the first class-room buildings, were stunning examples of Brutalism. Massive concrete columns formed the sides, topped with high walled edges beneath flat roofs. The buildings were painted bright white.

Architecture writer and critic Alan Hess elaborated on the Pereira approach for UCI in a 2014 article in *Places Journal*:

> The buildings responded to the sunny climate with a passive solar facade of precast concrete sunscreens that gave a sculpted appearance; to avoid monotony, each building's screens had their own distinctive design. Though large, the buildings appeared to float above the rolling landscape (which had been grazing land) with their broad cantilevered terraces and inset ground floors, countering the heavy, raw look of Brutalist concrete architecture.
>
> Windows, railings, and parapets were used as opportunities to introduce forms that caught sunlight and shadows. At a crucial time when the flat, hard-edged lines of the International Style were being attacked as dated and sterile ... Pereira offered an alternative Modernism ...[9]

As the campus site had been cleared of vegetation to enable construction, land-scaping adjacent to the buildings was minimal at best. On days when the winds cleared the air and the weather warmed, the look of the campus left visitors either in awe or aghast, depending on their appreciation for design.

Brutalism aside, the Irvine Company leaders had seen enough. They wanted Pereira to create a plan for the new community of Irvine, and he was pleased to oblige.

Pereira assembled a group of his staff at the site of an old animal petting zoo on MacArthur Blvd., about halfway between the campus site and what would become Newport Center, where Irvine Company headquarters was relocated in 1966. What had once been known as the Buffalo Ranch was given a new title more fitting Pereira's lofty planning goals: Urbanus Square.

(Until Newport Center was built, most of the company staff worked in temporary buildings next to the Irvine family mansion in the northern section of the ranch. The mansion also housed some company staff but caught fire and was nearly destroyed in 1965. Donald Cameron, who was part of Pereira's initial planning team and later director of planning at the Irvine Company, mused to an associate one day that the fire may have been a blessing in disguise, as a lot of things the company probably would rather have never been made public were consumed in the blaze. Razed in 1968, a facsimile of the building was rebuilt as a branch of the Orange County Library system in 2013.)

The Pereira team took the plan for the university and essentially expanded it to the east and northeast to what would become the San Diego Freeway and to points west and south to form the boundaries of what became known as the Southern Sector of the ranch.

The Southern Sector plan would encompass 10,000 acres and accommodate about 100,000 residents. In her book comparing Irvine to two other New Towns built in the same era, author Ann Forsyth interprets the plan as based on other college communities like Oxford, Palo Alto, and Princeton.

Watson's recollections of the transition from the university plan to the larger plan are vivid; he had only been working at the Irvine Company for a few months. Pereira, Watson observed, was not involved in the details of land planning, and did not work directly with him. "Pereira was sort of above all that ... he had his people."[10]

However, a June 1996 profile of Pereira in *Orange Coast* magazine describes a more engaged Pereira. The days he visited Urbanus Square, "... were devoted to criticism sessions. Planners and architects would lay out proposals (and) Pereira's comments would establish the identity of the new village."[11]

Sometimes the sessions were more informal: "On Friday afternoons at the ranch, he would sit on a rocking chair by the fire ... and lecture the young staff on design, land use and modernism."[12]

The Southern Sector plan, in Watson's view, was cursory. He called it a very ordinary plan, showing where the essential things needed to go—roads, flood control, where utilities would come from and where the commercial centers were to be located.

While the Southern Sector plan may well have been cursory in Watson's view, a rare glimpse at an original Pereira plan for the entire Irvine Ranch reveals substantial detail for the company's Newport Beach landholdings.

Bound in a stitched leather portfolio and dated August 1961, the Irvine Ranch Master Plan (Revised Draft) shows both the bold vision of much of what was to eventually be built on Irvine Company lands, as well as a few predictions that were destined never to occur.

The 108-page document, published on oversized paper, is a combination of planning text, tables, photos, and maps for areas of the ranch that would become Newport Center, Eastbluff, University Town Center, University Park, and the Irvine Industrial Complex adjacent to Orange County Airport.

Pereira's team did not foresee development in what was called the Mountain Sector of the ranch—defined from the Santa Ana Freeway to Irvine Lake and beyond in the rugged mountains. At the time the area was planted almost entirely in citrus groves.

Pereira mistakenly predicted that the vast center of the ranch would remain in agriculture for the foreseeable future, a notion supported by three assumptions—two semi-valid, one completely invalid: the presence of noisy Marine Corps Air Station El Toro and limited land absorption were given as reasons to wait for development in the center, plus the erroneous expectation that state and federal law would soon encourage preservation of open space.

Looking back 60 years, it is understandable why Pereira's team felt this way. At the time the San Diego Freeway was only a line on a map, UC Irvine the same. Concentrating development around the soon to be built university made much more sense, economically and socially. It also reflected the Pereira vision of the new community tied closely to the university.

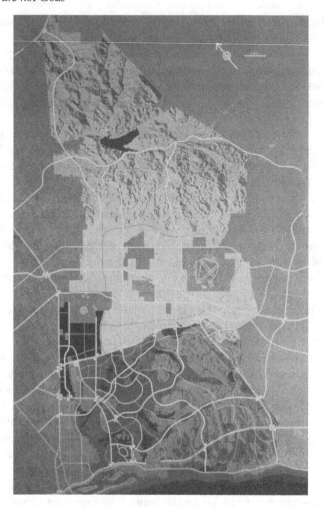

Figure 4.1 Land use plan for the Southern Sector of the Irvine Ranch prepared by William
L. Pereira and Associates (1961).

But in Newport Beach, the master plan document was quite specific when describing the potential for the residential neighborhoods of Eastbluff and Promontory Point, as well as the locus of commercial activity at what would become Newport Center (called Irvine Center in the plan).

The master plan schematics for Eastbluff describe with great precision the land layout that would be built three years later—a map of modern Eastbluff mirrors the key elements of the Pereira master plan almost to perfection.

The concepts for Promontory Point included both commercial and residential uses, especially hotels, something Pereira apparently believed would be economically feasible, but never materialized on that location. On nearby Linda Island, Pereira scooped out the center of the island to provide more waterfront for more housing, and envisioned public uses of a marine center there. Linda Island, however, became a private development, and unlike the Pereira plan calling for apartments, townhomes, and single-family dwellings, only the latter were built, and in far fewer numbers than the master plan envisioned.

The section of the master plan that describes Newport Center—written in 1961—proved amazingly prophetic. It begins: "the Irvine Center project has every reason to become the major focus point in the Coastal Sector, with influences reaching from San Clemente to Huntington Beach."[13]

> The initial development proposed here is to have many of the best characteristics of the best contemporary shopping centers, such as architectural integration and control, separation of auto and pedestrian traffic ... but it will differ in several fundamental ways. It is planned to include closely related office buildings, entertainment facilities such as theaters, galleries, restaurants, and financial and residential areas. It will be from the beginning an integrated part of the growing community with features and attractions destined to maintain an interesting and colorful activity throughout the day and evening.
>
> Irvine Center will grow to include additional commercial areas and three important satellite areas. These areas will include civic, office, medical and financial facilities ... they will be joined by short pedestrian malls within a four-minute walking distance of each other.[14]

All these uses now exist at Newport Center, but Pereira's vision for a garden recreation area was unfulfilled.

Also missing in today's Newport Center is a large complex of hotels, which in the Pereira plan was to be located where the Big Canyon gated community and golf course now exists. Pereira saw this element of the plan to reinforce the status of the new center and proposed upwards of 1,500 hotel rooms in varying degrees of luxury. There are two large hotels today close to the core of Newport Center, but nothing in terms of scale as the original Pereira vision. Nor is there any residential use along Pacific Coast Highway, another aspect of the original plan.

The hotels and center were to be accessed by the Pacific Coast Freeway, with a major interchange at Irvine Center. The plan for the freeway, which in concept would have run parallel to Pacific Coast Highway about half a mile above it, provoked a bitter and lengthy battle between the city of Newport Beach and state highway planners, culminating in the state withdrawing the entire freeway plan. Interestingly, planning documents written by the Irvine Company staff at the time didn't appear too concerned with the freeway's potential impacts. Company plans that anticipated the alignment and uses were moved around, added, or eliminated as the Department of Highways made more definitive alignments. When the freeway was killed, company developments were still far enough in the future that the decision wasn't critical.

In addition to maps and text, Pereira's team created a series of actual models of buildings for Irvine Center. A few were multi-storied, many low-rise. The retail center that became Fashion Island is near the center of the complex but is not the eye of a circle—that concept would come later, not from Pereira, but from Irvine Company planners like Al Treviño and Ray Watson.

Across the street from Irvine Center, Pereira drew a map that again, 60 years later, is remarkably like what has been built, this time in the Big Canyon community. Homes clustered along the ridges overlooking the 18-hole golf course are today located almost precisely as shown in the Pereira plan.

(The master plan document also devoted several pages to University Town Center and the inclusion areas of UC Irvine—the predictions and outcomes of both are described in Chapters 8 and 23.)

****

Examining the massive Master Plan document 60 years after its creation, one can only imagine the level of intellect and expertise that Pereira summoned forth from his small team of planners and engineers at Urbanus Square. And while Pereira didn't produce the details (Watson observed, "… he was not somebody who really had much experience in planning neighborhoods or communities"), Watson credits Pereira with the critical inspiration for what would become the City of Irvine and the urban transformation of the Irvine Ranch: "He did the most important thing of all. He's the one who came up with the vision, and he's the one that convinced a company and a university to launch the vision that is alive today."[15]

Pereira was never accused of having a small ego, but in 1983, two years before his death, he downplayed the acclaim, telling the Los Angeles Times: "We are not gods, never were. We could only try to predict trends and wants that would affect the future. We did a fair job if I can say so."[16]

Notes

1. Raymond L. Watson and Ann Lage, Planning and Developing the New Town of Irvine California, 1960–2003: Irvine Company President, 1973–1977, Walt Disney Company Chairman, 1983–1984 (Regional Oral History Office, the Bancroft Library, University of California, Berkeley, 2005) 114.
2. Scott Johnson, "William Pereira," L.A. Forum for Architecture and Urban Design no. 7 (October 27, 2015), http://laforum.org/article/william-pereira/.
3. Johnson, "William Pereira," L. A. Forum, no. 7.
4. Mary Mallory, "Hollywood Heights: William Pereira, Entertainment Architect," The Daily Mirror (blog), April 13, 2020. https://ladailymirror.com/2020/04/13/mary-mallory-hollywood-heights-william-pereira-entertainment-architect/
5. Mallory, "Hollywood Heights: William Pereira, Entertainment Architect.
6. Samuel C. McCulloch, "Interview with Clark Kerr," in Samuel C. McCulloch Oral Histories (AS-033) (Special Collections and Archives of the UC Irvine Libraries, 1969).
7. "The Man with a Plan," TIME 82, no. 10, September 6, 1963, 69.
8. Watson and Lage, Planning and Developing, 117.
9. Alan Hess, "Discovering Irvine," Places Journal, October 2014. https://doi.org/https://placesjournal.org/article/discovering-irvine/?cn-reloaded=1.

10. Watson and Lage, *Planning and Developing*, 115.
11. Thomas Curwen, "Wizard of Irvine," *Orange Coast Magazine*, June 1996, 58.
12. Curwen, "Wizard of Irvine," 58.
13. The name "Irvine Center" was used at the time to refer to the area in the City of Newport Beach, CA, that later became Newport Center and Fashion Island.
14. William L. Pereira, *The Irvine Ranch Master Plan (Revised Draft)* (Los Angeles, CA: Pereira and Associates, August 21, 1961) 65.
15. Watson and Lage, *Planning and Developing*, 116.
16. "William Pereira Obituary," *Los Angeles Times*, November 14, 1985.

5   Athalie

As the meeting of the Irvine Ranch Water District droned on, a visitor noticed an older woman sitting at the rear of the room.

Her gray hair was neatly styled with small curls at the back of her neck. She wore a dress fashionably appropriate for a woman in her seventh decade of life. A strand of pearls circled her neck.

While the subject matter centered on pipes, engineering, and measurements of water flow in cubic feet per second, her interest did not seem to waver; her eyes were clear, and occasionally a comment from the dais would engender a slight smile.

The visitor asked his companion:

"Who is that?"

"Athalie Clarke, Joan Irvine Smith's mother."

"What is she doing here?"

"Joan sends her to the IRWD meetings when she can't be here. Joan has an obsession with water supply. If she can't be at the meeting, she wants the directors to know she's watching them."

Athalie Clarke had hosted United States presidents in her home; they had welcomed her at the White House. Governors of California greeted her by her first name and had appointed her to prestigious boards. She had raised hundreds of thousands of dollars for Republican causes in California and the nation.

But tonight, she was at a local water district meeting because her daughter had asked her to be there.

****

Athalie Richardson was in her early 20s when she accompanied a friend on a business visit to the Irvine Ranch.

She was working as an illustrator for department stores and other commercial enterprises in Los Angeles.

She had likely never heard of the Irvine Ranch or its owners, including the young son of the fearsome Irvine family patriarch, James Irvine II. But she met

DOI: 10.1201/9781003226291-6

James Irvine Jr. that afternoon, and in 1929 would marry him. Four years later, she bore him a daughter, Athalie Anita Irvine, best known as Joan.

James Irvine Jr. died just six years after his marriage to Athalie Richardson. His death forged a lifetime bond between the two Athalies, mother and daughter; a bond that strengthened through adversity and conflict. Though the mother would remarry twice, the daughter four times, they were rarely apart, physically or emotionally.

In the book she published in memory of her mother—*Reflections of California*—Joan Irvine Smith made clear the depth of their affinity:

> She wasn't just a mother; she was my best friend and staunchest supporter and ally. We were partners in everything. Now that she is no longer here to counsel us directly, I feel her presence ever more intimately. She is a guardian angel for all of us.[1]

The book Joan published contains a detailed memoir her mother had written, intended only for her family. But Joan believed her mother's story deserved to be told, and long excerpts in sometimes vivid detail are included.

Clarke's memories of the relationship between her husband—the scion of the Irvine dynasty—and his father, James Irvine II, are of conflict, remorse, and rivalry.

Her first impression of the man she would come to call Father Irvine was less than positive. "He looked like a very stern, austere man. When he removed his hat, he was bald. I had never seen anyone like this before; it seemed to add to his stern, rigid appearance."[2]

(James Irvine II had insisted that his daughter Kathryn give birth at the family home. She died soon thereafter, sending him into a raging, guilt-induced depression. A few weeks later, JI lost not only the hair on his head, but all his body hair. According to Stephen Birmingham's *California Rich*, "... it gave him an odd, waxy appearance ...", for the rest of his life.[3])

Clarke describes a Shakespearean relationship between father and son, destined for tragedy. Jase—as he was known to family, and "Mr. Jim" to the ranch employees—was responsible for the day-to-day operations of the ranch, which, according to Clarke, he enjoyed. But he was limited by the after effects of tuberculosis, which he had contracted during military service in World War I.

The senior Irvine by most historical accounts was a driven autocrat whose word was absolute law on the ranch he had poured his life into. Father and son clashed over authority and judgment. Clarke described Jase returning from a visit to Washington D.C. bearing news of success in a tax case that saved the ranch thousands of dollars, only to be met with silence from his father. "Just one word of appreciation would have meant so much," he confided to his wife.[4]

There was also tension with JI's second wife, Katherine White Irvine, known in every history of the Irvine family as "Big Kate."

Accompanied by her retinue of Pekinese dogs and often outfitted with a large hat, Big Kate was reportedly as imperious as her husband; Clarke described verbal altercations between father, son, and stepmother.

As his health declined, Jase and Clarke moved around California with their new daughter seeking a mild, dry climate that would allow him to breathe better and diminish bleeding from his lungs. A final effort to improve his health with surgery failed (according to Clarke it was botched by the surgeon); James Irvine Jr. died on June 23, 1935.

On the advice of Jase's attorney, Clarke went to court two days after his funeral to claim guardianship of her daughter, as well as responsibility for her late husband's estate, which included shares in the Irvine Company. Clarke's memoir reports that JI called her soon thereafter demanding that he take charge of Joan's estate. She held her ground and said no, she would be both guardian of her child and manager of what she inherited.

Clarke also defied JI's wish to have Jase buried in the Irvine family crypt near San Francisco. Instead, at Clarke's instruction, his body was cremated, and the remains placed in a mausoleum at Forest Lawn in Glendale, California. (His remains were later removed to Fairhaven Cemetery in Santa Ana, California.)

A widow at 32, Athalie Clarke began her journey through grief and young motherhood by assuming responsibility for a Spanish language movie fan magazine that her husband had owned. *Cinelandia* was distributed in Spain, Cuba, and South America. While the magazine provided Clarke and her daughter photo opportunities with Hollywood stars like Bette Davis, when she took over management it was losing money. Her father-in-law had bankrolled it with loans during the final three years of her late husband's life. To settle the debt, she deeded a property in the Eagle Rock neighborhood of Los Angeles to JI, which he accepted. Clarke was ultimately able to sell the magazine.

Based on interest in farming she had absorbed at the Irvine Ranch, in 1937 Clarke purchased a farm in the Central Valley of California. Joan identified it as the Simms Ranch and said her mother held it until 1977. Clarke also bought property in the San Fernando Valley in 1942 and sold it off in parcels for decades thereafter—one section was developed into a shopping center; another was traded for a farm in Virginia.

Clarke also bought homes in the Coachella Valley communities of La Quinta and Palm Desert. She had remarried in 1938 to an entertainment executive, Thomas H. Mitchell, but the marriage ended in divorce in 1944. That same year, Clarke married the man whose name she would bear until the end of her life, Thurmond Clarke. He was a superior court judge at the time and would be appointed to the federal bench in 1955.

Whatever tensions there were between Athalie Clarke and JI dissolved in the years following the death of Jase. Both Clarke and Joan Irvine Smith reported frequent and cordial visits to the ranch, the beach, and other locales, with JI paying close attention to Joan's upbringing.

After World War II, with her future looking more certain, Clarke began what became a defining element in her life—active support of the Republican Party and candidates for public office.

Clarke attended her first national convention in 1952, one of a handful of women present. She had developed an interest in Richard Nixon while he served in the US Senate from California, and was no doubt pleased to see him move up to become Dwight Eisenhower's vice president.

The connection to Nixon would remain strong for his entire career. He reportedly wrote his 1968 nomination acceptance speech in Clarke's home in Corona del Mar and spent time relaxing at the house she owned on Kauai in Hawaii. He wrote a letter to her with the warm comment that, "Mrs. Nixon and I always agreed that Athalie was our First Lady." Clarke would also develop a lasting relationship with another California Republican destined for the White House, Ronald Reagan.

The most valuable skill anyone desiring real influence in politics is fundraising, and Clarke became very adept at it.

Jean Wood Fuller, who was president of the Federated Women's Clubs of California, describes her relationship with Clarke: "She was a tremendously wealthy woman. Any time I needed to have a special reception; she would open her house. She was extremely generous, she'd put on these big fundraising affairs, asking friends to sell not tickets but tables."[5]

Patricia Hitt, who served in Nixon's administration as an assistant secretary in the Health, Education and Welfare department, had a long history of involvement in California politics as a Republican activist. She had this to say about Clarke:

> Two women in ... California have been excellent fundraisers—Clarke and Margaret Martin Brock. I'm sure in the last twenty years there hasn't been a single fundraising dinner given for anyone or anything that they haven't bought at least a ticket and maybe a table.[6]

Joan Irvine's 18th birthday brought her inherited Irvine Company stock into her possession as an adult. With it, she made a generous decision: she placed half of it in a trust for her mother, with herself as its beneficiary.

The decision underscored the extraordinary emotional link between the two women. Clearly, Athalie Clarke didn't have to rely on the relatively modest income from Irvine Company dividends; since being widowed 16 years earlier, she had rescued a failing publication and sold it; she had purchased property and received income from it sufficient to maintain an upper-class lifestyle.

Joan's gift to her mother was an acknowledgment of love and devotion, and in many ways marked the initiation of the second great watershed in their journey together. The first had come in the aftermath of her father's death; Joan's first memories of him wrapped up in heavy blankets to protect his failing lungs, and thereafter trips with her mother to his gravesite.

The second watershed was Joan's entry into adulthood and an early marriage, followed by her mother's generous decision to give up her seat on the Irvine Company board of directors to her daughter.

From that point forward the mother and daughter merged into a single familial partnership that would mature, endure, and prosper for decades, each of them complementing the other.

Notes

1. Jean Stern, *Reflections of California: The Athalie Richardson Irvine Clarke Memorial Exhibition* (Irvine, CA: Irvine Museum, 1994) 15.
2. Stern, *Reflections of California*, 15.
3. Stephen Birmingham, *California Rich: The Lives, the Times, the Scandals and the Fortunes of the Men & Women Who Made & Kept California's Wealth* (Guilford, CT: Lyons Press, 2016) 204.
4. Joan Irvine Smith, *A California Woman's Story* (Irvine, CA: The Irvine Museum, 2006) 18.
5. Patricia Reilly Hitt, *From Precinct Worker to Assistant Secretary of the Department of Health, Education and Welfare: Oral History Transcript / and Related Material, 1977–1980* (Berkeley, CA: Bancroft Library, Regional Oral History Office) 79.
6. Hitt, *From Precinct Worker to Assistant Secretary of the Department of Health, Education and Welfare*, 79.

6 Joan

Joan Irvine was born into a life defined by wealth, tragedy, and ambition.

Fate was responsible for the wealth and tragedy, but the ambition and resulting conflict were hers alone.

Joan was 14 when she inherited 20 per cent of the shares of the Irvine Company from her grandfather.

It was a generous gift; other family members received a total of 27 per cent of the company stock, the James Irvine Foundation 53 per cent.

No doubt sentimentality was at work when James Irvine II set out the terms of his will. Self-named Joan—born Athalie Anita Irvine—was the only child of his son James Irvine Jr.

The inheritance was valued after taxes at $2,377,770. It would produce a generous annual income that allowed Joan to attend private schools, learn to ride, and own sporting horses and live in some of Southern California's most affluent neighborhoods.

Just 2 years old when her father died, Joan and her mother moved from Orange County to Pasadena and lived for a while with her mother's parents. Soon thereafter, they moved to Beverly Hills.[1]

In her autobiography, she describes carefree days along the shoreline of Irvine Cove, where the family built a modest two-story home on one of the most spectacular beaches in Southern California. Joan learned to bodysurf and combed the shoreline for shells and starfish.

Photos of Joan as a child show off her golden hair, resplendent in long curls flowing down the sides of her neck, held in place with a bow. She is dressed in an impeccable white jumper or dress, which she says her mother had to struggle to make her wear. "I was of course the proverbial tomboy," she recalled.[2]

When not splashing in the Pacific during summers at the ranch, Joan was a regular companion to her grandfather. She recounts trips around the huge landholding in JI's Packard automobile, combining instruction from him on the workings of the agricultural empire with elements of fun a young girl would enjoy—fishing, sightseeing, and riding.

Joan traces what would become her lifelong passion for horses—riding, competing, and ultimately breeding—to ranch hand Ray Serrano, whose family tree was planted in the early days of the Spanish land grant rancheros that the

DOI: 10.1201/9781003226291-7

Irvine Ranch ultimately subsumed. After learning the basics on a stock horse, Joan moved up to English-style riding lessons at the Riviera Country Club in Los Angeles at age 6. By the time she was in her teens, she was training at the Flintridge Country Club, riding some of the many horses she would own.

It was an Arcadian life for this privileged young woman, dividing her time between Pasadena, San Marino, and Laguna Beach.

She studied at the Westridge School in Pasadena, a girls' school on a small campus nestled beneath camphor trees that featured at least one building designed by Arts and Crafts builders Greene and Greene. Students wore long white dresses, skirts reaching their ankles as they strolled from class to class. Details on Joan's time there are scarce, but she apparently liked it enough to later make a donation to the school that resulted in her name being placed on the campus library.[3]

After school it was home to San Marino, a staid, conservative community of 11,200 people in 1950.

The city's spiritual center is the 500-acre Huntington Library and Gardens. Built by an heir of one of California's original railroad financers, the lushly landscaped grounds surround a massive Mediterranean Revival style building that houses priceless artworks and a research library notable for California, Western and Pacific Rim collections.

Figure 6.1 Joan Irvine Smith (left) and her mother, Athalie Clarke, standing in front of the Irvine family home on the Irvine Ranch in the mid-1960s.

(Orange County Archives)

Joan and her mother lived in the Lacy Park neighborhood, surrounded by majestic oaks and sycamores towering over well-manicured lawns and gardens. Most of the houses there in the 1950s were Spanish style, white stucco with red tile roofs, but there was a scattering of single-story modern homes as well.

San Marino was quiet and conservative, and residents liked it that way. San Marino's retail district was (and still is) barely two blocks long. The city's political outlook is reflected in the vote tally in 1966 gubernatorial election, where Democrat Edmund G. Brown received 778 votes to Ronald Reagan's 6,783. And in 1959, when the John Birch Society established a western headquarters, San Marino was the chosen location.

Perhaps the only flaw in San Marino's otherwise comfortable setting was the heat and smog of the era in the San Gabriel Valley. Southern California didn't begin to attack auto-produced smog until the late 1950s, almost too late to save cities like San Marino, Pasadena, Monrovia, and Sierra Madre, all built just below the foothills. In winter, as regular viewers of the Tournament of Roses Parade knew, the skies above Colorado Boulevard were clear and cold. However, on some days in summer, the San Gabriel Mountain range could literally be hidden by the layer of smog.

Joan's family had the option of driving to Orange County for summer and smog free days on the beach. In her youth that meant the modest but well located home on the Irvine Coast. But in later years—it is unclear precisely when—it meant a visit to another enclave of wealth in the community of Emerald Bay at the northern end of the city of Laguna Beach.

Emerald Bay is one community, but two separate living experiences.

Built around a large cove sheltered at either end by rocky outcroppings, the community is split in two by Pacific Coast Highway. The upper neighborhood holds about 70 per cent of the homes. While many of the homes have spectacular views, in the 1950s they were relatively modest in size. Below the highway the homes were built in a semicircle facing the beach, either at sea level for the ones on the southern end, or along the cliffside for those curling atop the northern ledge that overlooked the blue-green waters of the bay.

Joan Irvine's home was at 51 Emerald Bay. Built in 1936, in the 1950s it was one of just 64 homes in all of Emerald Bay. Joan's house faced north, with an unimpeded view of the Pacific. She couldn't see Catalina Island from her patio, but the sun disappeared below the northern ridge above the bay an hour or so before setting, bathing the bay, the sand, and the air in a golden afternoon glow. It was the perfect time for a final swim of the day, just steps away in the calm waters, or for a leisurely stroll on the sand.

On May 29, 1951, Joan turned 18 and by law, was able to take control of her inheritance. By the terms of JI's will, she received $2 million in a lump sum, and thereafter dividends from the earnings of the 200 shares of the Irvine Company he gave her. According to her autobiography, she studied briefly at Marymount College in Los Angeles and then at UC Berkeley but found neither college appealing.

But lifeguard Charles L. Swinden, a former track star, lean and good-looking, was appealing, and he and Joan were married in October of 1952. A wedding day photo taken with uncle Myford, aunt Thelma, and cousin Linda shows a blond, beaming Joan—who at a glance could almost be mistaken for a young Marilyn Monroe—clasping her new husband around the waist, wearing a summery white and polka-dot dress. Swinden is wearing a suit, a rep tie, and boutonniere. Apparently, it was a small, informal wedding.

Details of the Irvine–Swinden marriage are scarce, but on July 31, 1953, the union produced the first of the three sons Joan would bear in her lifetime: James Irvine Swinden. His godfather was Glenn Martin, an aviation pioneer who in 1913 had flown JI over his vast landholdings in one of the planes Martin parked on a portion of the ranch for a training airport. (JI was reportedly impressed by what he saw, but according to Joan never flew again.)

The marriage to Swinden lasted about two years, and in 1955, in addition to her usual activities in San Marino and Orange County, she was taking flying lessons. (Historian Jim Sleeper's files contain a 1974 letter from aviator Eddie Martin (no relation to Glenn) recalling that his brother Johnnie had rented a plane to Joan that was damaged, and he was very unhappy over the end results. This is consistent with a story Joan told a reporter decades later about losing an engine on a plane flight, forcing a hard landing.)

It was a flyer who became her next husband, Russell S. Penniman III, four years her senior. Penniman had flown fighter jets in the Korean War for the US Navy. In her autobiography, Joan described him as a "longtime friend."[4]

Although records indicate they obtained a marriage license in nearby San Bernardino County, other records, as well as a citation in a magazine article about them, list their wedding as taking place in Phoenix, Arizona.

Their honeymoon, which stretched for seven months, made news in the July 22, 1957, issue of *Sports Illustrated*. Under the headline "Sporting Start for a Marriage," a lengthy story chronicled their flying adventure in South America.

Planning for the honeymoon, Joan told the magazine, "I wanted to do things that other people would never think about, I wanted to live it up." Responding to his new bride's desires, Penniman created a plan for them to fly his Cessna 180 to South America and back:

> Altogether, *Sports Illustrated* reported, they logged 30,000 flying miles and made hundreds more by canoe, on horseback and by foot. Along the way they danced in Mexican nightclubs, collected three monkeys, hunted on the plains of Argentina, fished for marlin in Cabo Blanco and stuffed themselves on exotic food like grilled armadillo and roast ostrich.
>
> On the trip the Pennimans landed at no more than 75 places, setting down on any paved airport or muddy landing strip that promised adventure. At Acapulco Joan tried her first water skis, and in the Chilean Andes she floundered like any novice on snow skis. But flying was the biggest thrill for Joan, who got her license just before the trip and split the flying chores with Russ.[5]

After a brief chronicle of extensive fishing in the ocean and in fresh water that resulted in trophy trout and marlin shipped off to the taxidermist, the magazine continued its saga of the newlyweds:

> Through Central America and down the west coast of South America, the Pennimans water skied, explored old ruins, hunted futilely in canoes for wild pig … off the beaten path they found sporting life among the Latins is give and take. They were overcharged by merchants, charged by a surly cow, and bedeviled by red tape. They were contrastingly treated well by many sportsmen. In Argentina rich ranchers—as Joan put it, 'ten goal polo players and eleven goal drinkers'—led them on hunts to shoot antelope, deer and ostrich and black buck.
>
> The seven months ended up with more hunting up the Amazon and more fishing in the Caribbean. Now back in California, the Pennimans are wondering what continent would be good for a second honeymoon.[6]

(Joan's son Jim Swinden, in a 2012 oral history interview, recounts another story from the trip: Joan had grown tired of hunting—when her new husband and guides left for the day to track down a water buffalo they had wounded, Joan grabbed all the ammunition in the camp and dumped it in a stream.)

Whether or not there was a second honeymoon is not documented, but on August 16, 1957, their son Russell S. Penniman IV was born. Shortly after, she and Penniman divorced.

The divorce attracted press attention, as by now Joan was routinely described—rightly or wrongly—as one of the richest women in the world. *The San Francisco Examiner* covered the story by noting the Irvine family connection to the city, then explaining that "Joan was granted a divorce from … Penniman on the grounds that he slept until noon instead of getting up and off to his present job as an airplane broker."[7]

In 1958, Joan was a young mother with two sons, one an infant, the other age 5. She had joined the board of the Irvine Company, initiating what would become an epic series of clashes with the company's board of directors and the trustees of the James Irvine Foundation.

Her third husband was Richard D. Burt, a Laguna Beach contractor. Extrapolating from articles about the effort to promote a new university on the Irvine Ranch, it appears that Joan and Burt were married in the Spring of 1959. Walter Burroughs recounts in an oral history that it was then that he phoned Joan at her home in Emerald Bay to recruit her into a campaign to promote the university. She was willing, she told him, but it had to wait until she went to Las Vegas the next day to get married.[8]

Joan notes in a single sentence in her autobiography that she and Burt divorced in 1963. They had no children.

Eleven years, three marriages, two children. The first two marriages lasting about two years each, the third perhaps a year longer. On one side a lifeguard, a military officer, a contractor. On the other, a wealthy young woman raised in luxury, widely acknowledged as intelligent and headstrong.

Joan would marry a fourth and final time, this time to someone unlike her previous husbands, and much like her: a man who loved horses and was rich.

Morton Wistar Smith traced his family roots to the American Revolution.

The listing for his parents in the 1908 *New York City Blue Book of Influential Individuals* indicated that the Smith family had homes both in New York City and Smithport, Connecticut, and that Mr. Smith enjoyed memberships at various yacht clubs, as well as at the Lamb's Club. Mr. Smith was listed as a partner in the wine importing firm of Roosevelt and Schuyler, names that also traced to the earliest days of New York. (Other records of the time show Smith in the automobile business.)

Morton, known by his nickname of "Cappy," largely defined his adult life as much with horses as with humans. After service in the US Cavalry in World War II, Smith moved to the horse country of Middleburg, Virginia, and never looked back.

Starting in the early 1930s, Smith would, according to his obituary, "... dominate the (horse) show scene for three decades," winning national competitions in 1937, 1939, and 1954. From his home in Middleburg, Smith bred, raced, and showed horses. He was Master of the Orange County Hunt for years, promoting and protecting the sport of fox hunting.

Friends recalling Smith in his youth describe him as movie star handsome and larger than life. As a rider, he was equated as a near-God. William Steinkraus, the first American to win a gold medal in Olympic equestrian competition, simply said that, "Cappy was my idol, and I think in the view of many people the best Hunter/Jumper rider in America."[9]

Joan met Cappy for the first time when she was 14. She and her mother were sizing up the Foxcroft School in Middleburg as a possible location for Joan to attend. On the trip they met Smith; Joan became enamored with a young gelding he owned. She convinced her mother to purchase the horse and ship it to California.

It was at a horse show 16 years later in Del Mar, California, that Joan and Cappy met again. Cappy was judging; he recalled the earlier meeting with Joan. He invited her to a party and extended his visit to California by another three weeks. When he left, he promised to return and claim her hand, which he did in September 1963, in Nevada. According to her autobiography, Joan and her two sons moved to Middleburg. She was 30, Cappy was 48. Two years later, on August 12, 1965, their son Morton Smith III was born.

If Cappy Smith worked for a living, it isn't documented in any of the accounts of his life. More likely, given his blue-blooded lineage, there were resources from family trust funds or business holdings as a base, supplemented with the money he made breeding and selling horses. It can only be speculated how his wealth compared to Joan's.[10]

And Joan was wealthy.

Joan had received regular dividends from the profits of the Irvine Company since she was 14. Those funds were likely significant through the latter years of her teens, but not extraordinary. Moreover, everyday living expenses were most likely covered by her mother, who was wealthy in her own right due to her inheritance and subsequent investments. This allowed Joan's income to be invested and to grow. By the early 1960s, her dividend income was creeping up to around $100,000 per year, or roughly the equivalent of $942,000 a year in 2022 dollars.

In 1964, Joan and her mother each received about $2.5 million from a sale of various Irvine Company properties in Long Beach, Huntington Beach, and Santa Ana. Again, extrapolating to today's values, about a $22.5 million payday. And by 1969, annual income for her Irvine Company dividend was touching $240,000, which would equate to about $1.8 million in 2022.

If she had good investment advice, an estimate of Joan's net worth five years after her marriage to Morton Smith was about $10 million, or close to $90 million in 2022 dollars.

Joan's wealth allowed her to fit comfortably into the exclusive world of Middleburg, where people with names like Mellon, Whitney, and DuPont owned some of the 100- to 500-acre farms, and where the crops had four legs and were bred for speed.

Middleburg is one of several small settlements in the area. In 2020, the population was just over 700 people, not hard to understand given that most of the farms were protected by conservation easements that restricted the possibility of growth.

Middleburg's expansive, rolling green hills may have reminded Joan of the ranchlands owned by her grandfather, but the lifestyle there was built upon decades of gentility, history, and tradition.

In Middleburg, "… it is about style, not stylish …", writes Vicky Moon in her book *The Middleburg Mystique*: "The handsome dry-stone walls … classic hand painted signs … hood ornaments of foxes, favorite dogs. The fine art that graces the paneled or faux painted walls and the china on the table on the dining room makes a statement."[11]

And while daily attire for tramping in the mud at the horse barn argued for most of the women to wear jeans and boots (English style Wellingtons were a favorite), for the rest of an ensemble, a local women's store in Middleburg noted strong sales of, "… lines of cashmere and tweed from Barry Bricklin, as well as high end jackets from Belvest that are made in Italy."[12]

And of course, there was the fox hunt, a tradition imported by the English squires who moved to the Colonies to establish plantations.

Contemporary photos of the Middleburg Hunt likely mirror the natural and human landscape that Joan and Cappy viewed as they mounted their hunting horses for the chase. The masters of the hunt are resplendent in scarlet coat, offset with "apple green collars and buttons of brass with the initials MH," according to the official website of the hunt in 2020[13]. Other riders are in less formal attire, but all wear the distinctive peaked helmet, and some carry a small whip.

While Cappy and Joan lived together in his home on Landmark Road, at some point Joan bought her own place, also on Landmark Road, and named it the

Oaks. (Her mother also acquired a farm in nearby Byrnely.) Joan was living there in 1979 when a visitor described the experience of Joan's hospitality:

> The house was beautiful, warm, and cozy, fireplaces everywhere. Four poster beds were so comfortable you didn't want to get out of them.
>
> There was a fox hunt every morning. Before dinner the cooks served sherry, and there were several choices of wines, then after dinner drinks, then sinking into bed covered with a down comforter.[14]

Tennis anyone? The courts were reportedly heated to dispense with the snow or wet from rain. And if country life became too dull, a driver was summoned to take the guest to Washington, D.C.

Her luxurious bi-coastal lifestyle no doubt made Joan's daily comforts immensely satisfying, but they did not deter her from continuing her legal campaigns against the James Irvine Foundation. And her new home, just an hour's drive from Washington, D.C., had become the perfect location from which to launch a new and much more powerful war, this time in the nation's Capital.

Notes

1. Joan Irvine Smith's autobiography, *A California Woman's Story* (Irvine, CA: Irvine Museum, 2006), identifies a home on Landor Lane in Pasadena where she lived with her mother and Judge Clarke. Son Jim Swinden said in his oral history they lived in Pasadena, then in a home she purchased in San Marino, and in Emerald Bay.
2. Smith, *A California Woman's Story*, 74.
3. "Westridge School for Girls: Lives of Impact Begin Here," Westridge School for Girls | Lives of Impact Begin Here, accessed November 8, 2021. www.westridge.org/.
4. Smith, *A California Woman's Story*, 101.
5. "Sporting Start for a Marriage," *Sports Illustrated*, Sports Illustrated Vault, July 22, 1957, https://vault.si.com/vault/1957/07/22/sporting-start-for-a-marriage.
6. "Sporting Start for a Marriage."
7. *San Francisco Examiner*, February 9, 1958, 88.
8. Samuel C. McCulloch, "Walter Burroughs Oral History," in *Samuel C. McCulloch Oral Histories* (AS-033) (University Archives, UC Irvine Libraries, 1974) 12.
9. "The Legendary 'Cappy' Smith Dies," *Equisearch*, July 17, 2002. www.equisearch.com/new/eqsmith2499.
10. *The American Broker and Business Man: A Distinct Cyclopedia of 1921* (Chicago, IL: American Blue Book Publishers, 1921) 482.
11. Vicky Moon, *Middleburg Mystique: A Peek Inside the Gates of Middleburg, Virginia* (Sterling, VA: Capital Books, Inc., 2001) 50.
12. Moon, *Middleburg Mystique*, 52.
13. "The Middleburg Hunt," Middleburg Hunt, accessed February 8, 2022, www.middleburghunt.com/history.html.
14. Anonymous Source, interview by C.M. Stockstill, July 15, 2020.

7 The Birth of UC Irvine

Whenever Edmund G. "Pat" Brown would visit Orange County, both during his governorship and after, he would invariably tell the story of why a new branch of the University of California was built there: "You know," he'd smile, "... when I was elected governor in 1958, I won just about every county in the state except Orange County. I figured the folks there needed some more education, so I got the regents to build UC Irvine and improve the intelligence of future voters."[1]

Brown was a genuine proponent of the University of California, and his leadership in education at both the university and state college levels paid enormous economic and social benefits for the state.

But the decision to create a new branch of the UC system pre-dated his election as governor. And according to the recollections of an Orange County newspaper publisher at the time, Brown was promoting other places for the new university in Los Angeles County during the evaluation process to select the site.

At the close of World War II, there were two major campuses of the university at Berkeley and Los Angeles, smaller campuses at Davis and Santa Barbara. The state's rapid population growth made clear the need for additional higher education opportunities.

Led by President Clark Kerr, the university system drafted an internal report that called for building three new university campuses, one in the Santa Clara Valley, the other two in Southern California. In 1957, the regents hired the Los Angeles architectural and planning partnership of Pereira and Luckman to scour the southern region of the state to locate sites for new campuses. They drew up a list of 21 possibilities in southeast Los Angeles County and Orange County including one inside the Irvine Ranch. Kerr liked the Irvine site, believing that its vast expanse of empty land all held by a single owner would reduce the complexity of creating a large campus.

In his personal history of the UC Irvine location process, Ray Watson described a heretofore little-known element of the effort; a January 1958 report from the university's site selection committee titled *New Campus Location Criteria*:

> The importance of this report cannot be underestimated because in addition to declaring the need for 1,000 acres to accommodate an ultimate enrollment

DOI: 10.1201/9781003226291-8

of 25,000 students ... the report put on the table the importance of also considering the development immediately surrounding the future campus. By doing so they expanded the concept of university community by including concern for the quality and character of development outside campus boundaries.[2]

Thus, the first seed was planted which ultimately would sprout into the vision of a greater University Community; however, most of their concern was defensive. It warned the faculty and students must not be exposed to deteriorating conditions such as developed near the universities of Chicago, Columbia, and MIT, nor should they be priced out of the neighborhoods as they were at UCLA.

The report went on to describe strategies to achieve these goals, which Watson observed were:

> ... easier said than done unless they could find a site where one owner owned both the prospective campus site and the surrounding land. Ultimately it was the relative importance the different factions gave to this point that weighted the scales in favor of the Irvine Ranch.[3]

The decision making that led to the Irvine Ranch selection involved four factions that operated largely in parallel for months, occasionally overlapping one another:

- The first, of course, was the university system—academic and political leaders, bureaucrats, and consultants
- The second was a grassroots booster committee masterminded by Walter Burroughs, the publisher of the small but growing Costa Mesa/Newport Beach newspaper the *Globe Herald* (later the *Daily Pilot*)
- Third was the James Irvine Foundation, which by virtue of majority ownership of Irvine Company stock controlled the management of the company
- The fourth was Joan Irvine, granddaughter of James Irvine II, who descended like a raging tornado as the newest member of the Irvine Company board of directors in 1957, just as the university selection process was ripening.

Shortly after being hired by the university, Pereira and Luckman broke apart, with Charles Luckman and Associates assuming the UC contract. Pereira formed his own company—his subsequent efforts in the matter would far overshadow Luckman's.

Luckman's team did their due diligence, visiting 20 sites in southern California that eventually were narrowed down to eight—one in Yorba Linda, in northern Orange County not far from recently located California State University Fullerton, and seven on the Irvine Ranch.

"The fact that early in the process sites on the Irvine Ranch were among those identified should have come as a surprise to no one," Watson wrote. He went on to observe:

The Ranch sat in the geographical middle of the county and occupied one fifth of it. And two current university Regents and a loyal and well-known alumnus were associated with the Irvine Company. Edward Carter, CEO of the Broadway department store chain, and A.J. McFadden were members of the Board of Regents, and trustees of the James Irvine Foundation.

McFadden was also a member of the board of directors of the Irvine Company. In addition, foundation trustee and company director N. Loyall McLaren was both a graduate of and held an honorary degree from the university.[4]

While it may have appeared that this cast of inside players would make the selection a sure thing, just the opposite was the case.

Arthur McFadden, according to Burroughs' memory, was adamant in his opposition to donating Irvine Company land for a new campus.

Burroughs had been in touch with Clark Kerr early in the process through a mutual friend. Years earlier, Burroughs had observed the success of UCLA and the Westwood community that grew around it and was firmly committed to the Irvine site for the new campus. Burroughs knew the university was seeking a land donation and asked Kerr if he could lobby the Irvine Company for it. Kerr concurred and suggested that he first contact Pereira.

Burroughs visited Pereira at his new offices in the Union Oil building in downtown Los Angeles. Pereira shared some of the work he had done for the university and confirmed that of the seven possible sites in the running, two or three were on the Irvine Ranch

Burroughs decided to recruit local State Senator John Murdy to join him for a meeting with McFadden, who stopped them in their tracks with the comment, "I won't give a five-cent piece to the richest university in the world."[5]

McFadden's response was indicative not only of his own opinion but reflected the views of the Irvine Foundation. Minutes of the Foundation meetings from the time show that its members were carefully observing the Luckman work. Moreover, the Foundation had inside information: McFadden, as chairman of the state Board of Agriculture, was an ex-officio member of the Board of Regents, and a member of the site selection committee (he resigned in 1959).

(In an oral history interview taken in his 90th year, McFadden's recollection of his position on the UC Irvine land gift had changed: "I was strongly for it.")[6]

Spurned by McFadden, Burroughs tried his hand at development matchmaking. "I rallied some people in the area, specifically Paul Palmer (developer of Lido Isle in Newport Beach and a local banker), and Howard Lawson, the man who developed the Miracle Mile on Wilshire Boulevard in Los Angeles."[7]

Lawson and Palmer pitched McFadden on a land deal; they would buy 11,000 acres of land, donate a thousand of it to the university, and develop the rest. McFadden, according to Burroughs, said no.

Burroughs found another path to the Foundation, however, and it would pay off handsomely.

It turned out that Burroughs had made a connection years before with an attorney from the Los Angeles law firm of Loeb and Loeb. He happened to have lunch with his attorney friend, who brought along another Loeb and Loeb lawyer named Howard Friedman. Discussing the university siting effort, Friedman said he might be able to assist. A few days later Friedman called Burroughs to inform him that he represented Joan Irvine—she wanted to get together. Burroughs met Joan for lunch a few days later. She was adamant that the land gift be made, "but those damned old fools (the Foundation board) don't realize that it's the greatest thing that could happen to the Irvine Company to have the university." Burroughs' descriptions of Joan Irvine's advocacy for the land gift are consistent with dozens of news media and personal reports from the timeframe, including Joan's own recollection in her autobiography.[8]

Burroughs and Joan agreed that a public demonstration of support for locating the university was needed to bolster chances of success. Burroughs covertly obtained a list of a group of local heavy hitters and influence leaders in Newport Beach and, with Joan, scheduled a lunch at the Villa Marina restaurant (now the site of the Shark Island Yacht Club) on Newport Bay. The pair was assisted by a Cal alumnus named Brick Power, whose organizing abilities produced an overflow crowd at the event, where the formation of Friends of the University of California in Orange County was announced. Support cards were signed, lists were formed, and the organization began to spread. Eventually, Burroughs said, more than 40,000 individuals joined.

Meanwhile at the headquarters of the University of California, according to Watson:

The apparent debate between the two sites narrowed down to two issues:

> The Yorba Linda site was centrally located with the south part of Los Angeles and the north Orange County area the campus was expected to serve. The Irvine Ranch site was clearly beyond the southern edge of development and thus required greater commuting times to reach the campus. Furthermore, some regents argued that to build a new campus on land surrounded by property owned by one company potentially would unfairly enrich an already rich landowner, namely the Irvine Company.
>
> On the other hand, although William Pereira no longer was officially connected with the planning firm charged with analyzing the various sites, he made his views available to both university and (Irvine) company officials by arguing that by the time the campus matured the rapid growth of Orange County would spill onto the Ranch and further south, thus placing the school in a more central location.

But his most persuasive argument was that of all the sites that had been identified, it was only on the Irvine Ranch, with its single ownership, that the vision of creating a unique version of 'town and gown' was possible.[9]

Watson continued:

However, by now the interest of Irvine (Company) in securing the university for its land must have been obvious to the regents, so they weren't about to commit to either site until they had secured from the Irvine Company firm conditions on both the acquisition of the thousand acres and the development of the surrounding land.

So, by Oct.23, 1958, Pereira's vision was the subject of much discussion during the Company's regular board meeting. At the conclusion of that meeting, the directors passed a resolution, which stated that it was the consensus of the full board that the Company would 'cooperate with the university if they (the University) decided to locate on property of this Company submitted as Site No. 9 (the board's preference)'.

At that meeting President Myford Irvine was authorized to...hire Pereira and Luckman or other competent land planners to recommend a plan for development of a one-mile radius from the perimeter of the university site ... as for the thousand acres, the board agreed to set a price of fair market value.[10]

Watson underscored the enormity of the decision:

In retrospect a huge step had been taken by the Irvine Company; it was now preparing to not only aggressively attempt to attract the university, but to plan an orderly transition from ranching to urban development. Agreeing, however, to plan the land around the campus site in coordination with University plans clearly signaled to the University that the company wanted the university on its land and was prepared to negotiate terms acceptable to both parties. It also tipped the scale in favor of those who considered surrounding development as important as the precise location of the campus itself.[11]

And while momentum was gathering for the sale, looming in the background was a legal issue that could scuttle the deal. As Watson put it:

When James Irvine II gifted 54 per cent of his stock in the Irvine Company to the charitable foundation he created, he concurrently made specific prohibitions against the Foundation making gifts to any tax supported institutions. Although the Irvine Company (emphasis added) itself had no such restriction, the unresolved question was whether the Foundation directors could support such a gift.[12]

Soon, the legal issue would pale in the wake of one of the most tragic and lurid episodes in the history of the Irvine Company and Irvine family: the death of Myford Irvine.

****

Speculation surrounding Myford Irvine's demise is debated to this day. But for this history, it is not the circumstances of the death of the last Irvine to serve as president of the Irvine Company that matters most, but the consequences.

Myford Irvine was found dead in the basement of the Irvine family mansion on the afternoon of January 11, 1959. He had been shot three times, twice in the stomach with a shotgun, once in the head with a .22 caliber pistol.

As the impact of his apparent suicide began to sink in, details of the days and weeks prior to his death began to circulate.

Joan Irvine reported that she had spoken to her uncle just days prior to his death about his urgent need to raise $5.6 million, $400,000 in cash. Sale of a portion of his company stock was being arranged, and it appeared to Joan that he was satisfied the transaction would provide what he needed.

Then details of the death were provided to family members and questions arose. How does someone shoot oneself with a shotgun, and live to crawl across the basement floor, load a pistol, and place it to his head for the fatal shot?

After Myford Irvine was buried, additional details from the official investigation of his death were revealed, including the stunning news that the fatal bullet recovered from the scene was thrown away 30 days later—standard procedure for disposal of evidence by the Orange County Sheriff's Department at the time.

Ten months after it was interred, the body of Myford Irvine was exhumed and a second autopsy performed, paid for by Joan Irvine. The verdict remained the same as the original: suicide.

A 2012 book about notorious Los Angeles mobster Mickey Cohen claims that Myford was involved in gambling in Orange County.[13] Cohen died in prison a few years into his sentence; Joan and others repeated suspicion of foul play in Myford's death for decades that followed.

And a new history of Orange County by author Stanley Oftelie contains a detailed and compelling recitation of findings from Myford's FBI file that link him to years of gambling activity in Orange County, as well as strong connections to mob-influenced gambling business deals in Las Vegas.[14]

****

Watson picks up the story in the wake of Myford's death:

Who was to run the Irvine Company? No one other than an Irvine had ever exercised that role. Joan Irvine, Myford's niece and JI's granddaughter, immediately let it be known to the Foundation trustees that that the company should be run by an Irvine, and she should be the one. At that time, she was 25 years old, but together with her mother held 22 per cent of the stock in the company. But despite vigorous lobbying (according to Foundation members), the Foundation thought her to be too young and inexperienced.[15]

The Foundation recommended that the new president of the Irvine Company should be A.J. McFadden and N. Loyall McLaren should be vice president.

McFadden, 82 at the time, was the son of Orange County pioneer James McFadden, credited as the founder of the city of Newport Beach, and a prominent figure in the formation of Orange County in 1889. A.J. McFadden, Watson noted, was a graduate of Pomona College and Harvard Law School. "He was a leading agriculturalist in Orange County and had served with distinction as president of many grower organizations, including the National Council of Farmer Cooperatives, Agricultural Council of California and the California State Board of Agriculture."[16]

McLaren had known James Irvine II since early in the century. A UC Berkeley graduate, he had developed an astute understanding of tax law and had a knack for business development that propelled him into the upper echelons of California business at a relatively young age. Now in his early 70s, he had served as a director on state and national companies, and had been a director of the Federal Reserve Bank of San Francisco.

Joan Irvine asserted her claim to company leadership without success. The men she had been contending with for years swept her aside. A week after Myford's death they made it official at a special meeting of the shareholders, a majority of whom voted to elect McFadden president and McLaren to the board; the foundation had taken firm control.

Foundation or no, the potential location of the new university was still under evaluation, and according to a chapter in Stephen Birmingham's book *California Rich* on the Irvine family, Joan ramped up her efforts to bring the campus to the Irvine Ranch:

> She made speeches and gave newspaper, radio, and television interviews. She proved remarkably skillful at manipulating the media, gathering them for formal press conferences as well as chatty meetings, with drinks, at her house on Emerald Bay in Laguna Beach. She succeeded in getting press coverage of normally closed board meetings through the whimsical device of issuing temporary proxy votes to reporters, infuriating the board, of course, in the process.[17]

Joan's attacks on the board weren't limited to the campus issue. She called the aging board members "old bozos" and accused them of making

> ... cozy deals with each other that benefited themselves more than the shareholders. She made the Irvine Company's directors sound like miserly

curmudgeons, narrow-minded enemies of higher education and the public weal. Her pretty but unsmiling face was soon familiar to readers and viewers throughout southern California.[18]

Whether Joan had ground down the foundation board or circumstances of the ongoing selection process caused a shift in their attitude, their "fair market value" position began to erode, with McFadden—acting as president of the Irvine Company—altering the offer to a gift of 650 acres of land and an option for the university to purchase 350 acres adjacent at full price.

In mid-July, following a tour of the Irvine Company site by several regents, the university and Irvine Company agreed to jointly retain and fund a study of the proposed site by William Pereira and Associates. The study was to be bifurcated with the initial part analyzing the economic feasibility, the second part to outline how a master plan for the university-oriented community surrounding the campus should be developed.

What led to the company's change of heart? No one knows for certain. In the end, the attractiveness of building a university and community simultaneously became so appealing to all factions that any individual agendas were eventually forgotten.

Watson's history continued:

> Before the foundation trustees could vote their shares in approval of the gift, they had to find a way to reconcile the apparent conflict between the Irvine Company's offer and JI's explicit instructions ... to make no gifts to tax supported institutions.[19]

Not for nothing had McFadden been educated at Harvard Law School and McLaren served on a branch of the preeminent financial arm of the United States.

Watson recounts that:

> ... they had figured out a way around the no gift dilemma. They hired a real estate consultant to analyze the economic consequences to the Irvine Company's surrounding land should the university locate there. The consultant's conclusion: the increase in value of the remaining land...would exceed the value of a thousand-acre gift. Thus, to the Irvine Company, since it wasn't a gift, JI's admonition had no bearing.[20]

On June 20, 1960, the board of directors of the Irvine Company—Joan Irvine included—voted unanimously to sell the land for the new campus to the University of California for one dollar.[21] It must have been a sweet, but fleeting moment for Joan—her attacks on the foundation trustees would resume soon thereafter.

The university system filed a friendly lawsuit to assure that the foundation board's approval of the sale was legal. Upon satisfactory adjudication, in December

Figure 7.1 UC Irvine under development in the early 1960s

(Orange County Archives)

1960, the university accepted the gift.[22] The sale of 990 acres for one dollar was recorded the following month.

Three years later, the Irvine Company agreed to sell the university an additional 510 acres of 660 acres designated as the Inclusion Areas in the university community master plan prepared by the Pereira firm[23]: "... In exchange for the university agreeing that the land would be restricted to university related uses the Irvine Company sold the land for a reduced price of $6,147 per acre."[24]

Notes

1. Author's recollection.
2. Raymond L. Watson, "The University of California's and the Irvine Company's Historic Agreement," in *Raymond L. Watson Papers* (MS.R.120) (Special Collections and Archives of the UC Irvine Libraries, 2006) 7.
3. Watson, "The University of California's and the Irvine Company's Historic Agreement," 4.
4. Watson, "The University of California's and the Irvine Company's Historic Agreement," 4.
5. Samuel C. McCulloch, "Walter Burroughs Oral History," in *Samuel C. McCulloch Oral Histories* (AS-033) (University Archives, UC Irvine Libraries, 1974) 10.
6. Stephen Gould, *Arthur J. McFadden Oral History* (LAWRENCE DE GRAFF CENTER FOR ORAL AND PUBLIC HISTORY, CALIFORNIA STATE UNIVERSITY, FULLERTON, 154b 1970).

7. McCulloch, "Walter Burroughs Oral History," 10.
8. McCulloch, "Walter Burroughs Oral History," 13.
9. Watson, "The University of California's and the Irvine Company's Historic Agreement," 6.
10. Watson, "The University of California's and the Irvine Company's Historic Agreement," 6.
11. Watson, "The University of California's and the Irvine Company's Historic Agreement," 7.
12. Watson, "The University of California's and the Irvine Company's Historic Agreement," 7.
13. Tere Tereba, *Mickey Cohen: The Life and Crimes of L.A.'s Notorious Mobster* (Chicago, IL: Independent Pub Group, 2012).
14. Stanley Oftelie, *Shaping Orange County* (Fullerton, CA: Tesoro Publishing, 2020) 226–233.
15. Watson, "The University of California's and the Irvine Company's Historic Agreement," 7.
16. Watson, "The University of California's and the Irvine Company's Historic Agreement," 7.
17. Stephen Birmingham, *California Rich: The Lives, the Times, the Scandals and the Fortunes of the Men & Women Who Made & Kept California's Wealth* (Guilford, CT: Lyons Press, 2016) 219.
18. Birmingham, *California Rich*, 219.
19. Watson, "The University of California's and the Irvine Company's Historic Agreement," 9.
20. Watson, "The University of California's and the Irvine Company's Historic Agreement," 9.
21. Watson, "The University of California's and the Irvine Company's Historic Agreement," 9.
22. Watson, "The University of California's and the Irvine Company's Historic Agreement," 10.
23. William L. Pereira & Associate: A University Campus and Community Study (May 1960).
24. Inclusion Area purchase agreement made and entered into on January 3, 1964, by and between THE IRVINE COMMPANY, a West Virginia corporation and THE REGENTS OF THE UNIVERSITY OF CALIFORNIA and recorded by the County of Orange on February 17, 1964.

8 Inclusions, Exclusions, and the Campus that Never Was

In the 62 years since the agreement was consummated between the Irvine Company and the University of California to create UC Irvine, the story has been told so often in print and oral history that the rough edges of personality, petty rivalries, and business interests have been worn down, with some of the most compelling aspects of the process lost or overlooked.

Additionally, key details of the transaction—identification of what became known as the Inclusion Area—has faded into relative obscurity.

The behind the scenes and public drama of Joan Irvine and her hostile compatriots on the board of the Irvine Company was grounded in easily identifiable facts and figures—how many acres of land to change hands for a new university? What would be the price, if any? Just where would the campus be located on the vast Irvine Ranch acreage?

But another issue that would seep into the negotiations was based largely on anecdotes, misunderstanding, and what today would be called urban legend: that the Irvine Company would not sell homes or land to Blacks or Jews.

Both inside and outside the Irvine Company during the 1970s and 1980s, vague references to discriminatory covenants on the land would find their way into conversations.

Ray Watson, in his oral history, recalled just such an experience shortly after joining the company. "I learned, after I was here for a while, that the county had an old reputation for discrimination against two groups, Blacks and Jews."[1]

The first Jews in the county came to the central cities of Santa Ana and Anaheim in the late 1880s. Anaheim, settled initially by immigrants of German extraction, became the center of Ku Klux Klan activity in the county in the 1920s, when well-known business and community leaders joined the Klan.

The first organized Jewish community formed for worship was in Tustin in 1919; in 1945, the county's first temple was built in Santa Ana, Temple Beth Sholom. The next, Temple Beth Emet, was formed in 1956 in Anaheim as a conservative congregation.[2]

So, did the original owner of the Irvine Ranch, James Irvine I, or his son, JI, ever insert language into land deeds or documents for Irvine Ranch property that would prohibit subsequent sale to Blacks, Jews, or other people deemed non-desirable?

DOI: 10.1201/9781003226291-9

Orange County had a population of just over 30,000 in 1920, when the Irvine Ranch was maturing, under JI's guidance, into a prospering agricultural operation with multiple crops, irrigation systems, and a workforce of dozens of men to oversee it. Of those 30,000 people, might 1 or 2 per cent of them have been Jewish? Or Black?

At the end of a day of labor in the fields and citrus groves, as JI looked out over his empire, did it occur to him that he needed to restrict it from Jews?

If he chose to take that action, it would not have been unusual. Throughout California at the time, restrictive covenants on property were common. Indeed, just a few miles away in Westminster, one of the first landmark judicial decisions striking down a similar restriction was made in 1947, removing a prohibition that forbade children of Mexican descent from attending schools with other children.

That state decision was followed in 1948 when the US Supreme Court issued a ruling that ended governmental enforcement of restrictive covenants.[3]

But assuming at the turn of the century JI did seek to discriminate, the first hurdle to creating the legal restrictions would have been to write language into his property deeds—covenants—spelling out who was to be excluded.

If the deed to the Irvine Ranch was a single document, it would have been a relatively easy transaction, but likely, by that time, the ranch had been divided into dozens or perhaps hundreds of parcels. Would the notoriously frugal JI have paid an attorney to accomplish this task?

(The earliest Irvine Company land deed in the records of the Orange County Archives is dated 1905 and signed by James Irvine and his wife. It contains no racial covenants.)

According to both an oral history with Samuel McCulloch at UC Irvine, as well as his autobiography, Clark Kerr said the issue of alleged discrimination came up during the land sale negotiations. He said matter of factly that, "... Irvine (Company) had a practice of not letting Jewish people in ... they had been exclusionary about Jewish people."[4]

Apparently, Kerr's view had been reinforced by Norton Simon, a UC regent. Simon claimed that he had attempted to purchase a home in Emerald Bay—an exclusive community that was once part of the Irvine Ranch—and was unable to do so because he was Jewish. Simon laid the blame on the Irvine Company and made it clear to Kerr that it bothered him to the point that he might not support any deal with the Irvine Company.

Kerr could have found a similar situation had he researched *Janss v. Walden*, a 1925 California Supreme Court case.[5] The Janss family were the sellers (at a very generous discount) of 325 acres of their land that would become the University of California at Los Angeles (UCLA). Subsequently they developed residential neighborhoods nearby and Westwood Village as a commercial center immediately adjacent to the new university. In doing so, they placed covenants on the land preventing the sale or lease of their property to anyone who was not white. The Supreme Court upheld the discrimination, citing a contemporary appeals court finding.

Discrimination against Jews was also an issue at UC San Diego, which was being birthed by the university system at almost the same time as UC Irvine.

In a 1985 interview Dr. Roger Revelle, who as head of the Scripps Institute was intimately involved in organizing and staffing the San Diego campus, recalled a conflict over an anti-Semitic restrictive real estate covenant in La Jolla, the area where the campus is located. Much as Kerr said he had done at UC Irvine, Revelle laid down the law for the real estate community. "I said ... you can't have a university without having Jewish professors. The real estate brokers association and their supporters in La Jolla had to make up their mind whether they wanted a university or an anti-Semitic covenant. You couldn't have both."[6]

Simon's Emerald Bay story likely explains what really happened in Orange County and on properties owned, then sold by the Irvine Company. And as it turns out, there are several conflicting histories relating to the creation of Emerald Bay.

One has JI selling off the land around the beautiful cove in what is now the northern edge of Laguna Beach in 1906, allegedly to raise $26,000 to pay off gambling debts. In and of itself this seems questionable, as JI's reputation as a notorious skinflint is at odds with gaming.

A similar story alleges sale of the property in 1928 to one W.T. Gray, and then from Gray to a pair of investors known only as Miles and Callendar in the 1940s. Yet another report has the land passing from the Irvine Company to George Hart, then to Charles Jonas, and finally from Jonas to Henry Harriman in 1932, whereupon, Harriman sold out to his lawyers and others.

Emerald Bay was one of the few properties sold while JI was alive, most likely to raise funds for improvements to the ranch. After his death in 1947, more sections of the ranch were sold to developers. It is logical to conclude that whoever bought Emerald Bay subsequently added a racial and religious covenant to the deed, a reflection of prevailing attitudes at the time, as did future developers and homebuilders.

Neither Norton Simon nor Clark Kerr knew the history of the Emerald Bay land transactions. In their minds, by virtue of its proximity to the Irvine coastal property, the Irvine Company was guilty of discrimination, and Kerr would put a stop to it.

> One of the toughest things I had to tell them (Irvine Company/Foundation) was there had to be an absolute understanding—we didn't want it in writing, or anything else—that they would drop their exclusionist principles, drop them completely—there could not be a vestige left.[7]

Kerr was good to his word regarding the deed that conveyed the land to the University of California in September 1960 (and accepted officially a month later and recorded in January 1961); there was no mention of discrimination, past or future. However, three years later, for another land deal, it was a different matter.

****

The UCLA campus has become one of the most valued jewels in the UC system crown, competing with Berkeley for academic excellence and prestige. It has attracted billions of dollars in endowments for scholarship, as well as for research. And in the golden years of John Wooden, its basketball prowess was undisputed. Today, competition for admission to UCLA is on par with some of the best Ivy League schools.

But shortly after it was founded, UCLA developed a problem, one that Kerr and the regents wanted to avoid with the new campus on the Irvine Ranch.

Neighborhoods around UCLA became wildly expensive, partly the result of market forces, but also because the Janss family positioned the communities they planned and built around the campus as upscale and exclusive. In nearby Holmby Hills, the lot sizes were generous; homes were built in Spanish Revival splendor that attracted the well to do and the occasional movie star. (The Playboy Mansion was in Holmby Hills.) Bel Air, developed by Alphonzo Bell, was immediately next to the campus and decidedly swank.

A few fraternities and sororities managed to snag houses on the periphery in the early years, and within blocks of campus some apartment designed to rent to students popped up. But few, if any, professors, let alone support staff, could afford to live within a mile of UCLA.

Westwood commercial properties were expensive as well, although some student-serving businesses did well, and a luxurious Fox theater screened first run films well into the 1990s.

All these factors were top of mind for Kerr, the university officials, and regents as they homed in on the Irvine Ranch. As the details of the transaction to create the campus reached a conclusion, it was with the understanding of both sides that another deal would follow for what came to be known as the Inclusion Area.

Donald Cameron, former director of planning at the Irvine Company, described the Inclusion Area as a major planning concept, an interpenetration of campus and community, especially providing economic protection for low-cost housing. As noted in the 2007 update to UCI's Long Range Development Plan, initial planning for the campus that took place during 1959 and 1960 identified the Inclusion Area as a place, "... to be reserved primarily for the development of economical housing for University students, faculty, and staff, and for the services necessary to create complete university-oriented neighborhoods in close proximity to the campus."[8]

The boundaries of the campus form a rough trapezoid. Place a clock face on it, with 6 at the bottom (along Campus Drive) and 12 at the top, the three Inclusion Areas were like bites taken out roughly at 9, 12, and 2. Labeled A, B, and C, the three sections of land totaled about 510 acres. The Irvine Company reserved a section of land between A and B for future use (see Figure 8.1).

Negotiations for the location and purchase of the Inclusion lands began in 1962. Initially, the university was represented by Bob Underhill, a senior administrator who had experience in real estate transactions. Kerr lost faith in Underhill and took over the negotiations himself.

"I felt that Underhill, who had a reputation as being a real tough negotiator, had been giving the place away," Kerr said in his oral history taken by UCI professor Sam McCulloch, adding, with language one might consider surprising from the president of one of the most prestigious universities in the United States, "... he was a lot tougher bargainer taking away a store from some Armenian rug merchant in Berkeley for a student union than he was with the Irvine Company with all its power in the State of California."[9]

Later in the oral history, Kerr made no secret that he viewed his duty to ensure there would be no windfall profits because of the university's location decision:

> But certainly, a consideration in my mind was that I didn't want to see the Irvine Company benefit the way the Janss brothers did, and by God if they did, they were certainly going to give something in return, and they gave the 1,000 acres, they gave us this low price on the (Inclusion Area) ... they gave quite a lot.[10]

Kerr and Watson have different recollections of specifics of the discussions, but both agreed that they were intense. Elaborating on his earlier description of the negotiations in his interview with McCulloch, Kerr described the bargaining as very tough. Watson's view was similar, recalling years of contentious meetings.

The decision to sell the Inclusion Area to the university instead of keeping it and allowing the Irvine Company to develop it, according to the "university related" criteria, was based on research Watson did. He recommended to the Irvine Company board of directors that it would be more productive to sell the land and let the university be the developer. After all, Watson concluded, the university would have more access to development funds at minimal interest rates, and as a public institution would not be paying property taxes on what was built.

Kerr's memoir described the Irvine Company negotiators, including McLaren, McFadden, and company president Charles Thomas, as determined to get a "commercial price for the 510 acres, around $25,000 to $35,000 an acre," or upwards of $15 million in total.[11]

"The negotiations were really heavy going," said Kerr. At one especially contentious point, Daniel Aldrich—who was to become the chancellor of the new campus—stepped into the hall and called Kerr out of the meeting. "His face was white, and he said to me, 'you are losing my campus.' I said Danny, I am winning your campus," and returned to the negotiating table.[12]

Here, Kerr and Watson's memories on specifics of the negotiations diverge. Kerr writes that as was the case with the original deed of sale (or more properly, gift) for the campus property, there needed to be language to prevent discrimination due to race or religion.

Watson begged to differ.

Kerr's book came out in 2001, Watson's oral history was taken in 2003.

The tone of Watson's comments in the oral history was familiar to both the authors and others at the Irvine Company who either innocently or—God help them—purposely raised the subject with him. Watson was adamant that racial and religious discrimination didn't happen at the Irvine Company. The genial smile that was almost always present would fade to a thin line, and his tone became curt as he lectured the fact in a pointed manner.

The depth of his opinion is evident in his oral history.

> I wanted to have a restriction on the (Inclusion Area) property that they (the university) could only use the land with the same restrictions we (the Irvine Company) would have been bound to ... and Kerr didn't want any restrictions on the property.[13]

Watson vigorously rejected Kerr's assertion that the restrictions at issue were related to discrimination. The Irvine Company had already decided to address the issue, he said, "... because I am the guy who insisted on the restrictions, and I can pull out the minutes of the (Irvine Company) board meetings to prove it."[14]

After reading Kerr's oral history, Watson said, "I sent a copy of the minutes to the person who did the oral history."[15] No doubt, he wanted to reinforce his version of what transpired.

Eventually, compromise in terms of price and conditions was achieved. The price for the 510 acres of Inclusion Area dropped to $6,500 per acre, $826,750 payable upon completion of the deed, the remainder payable over ten years in payments of $248,625 at a 2¾ per cent interest rate.

Additional elements of the agreement gave the university the flexibility to adjust the borders of the Inclusion Areas by exchanging parcels with the Irvine Company, so long as the total acreage for university campus use did not exceed 990.8 acres. Three years later, an exchange was made.

In his oral history with McCulloch, Kerr modestly gives himself credit for achieving the final deal after deciding that UCI staff negotiator Robert Underwood, "... was being too soft with Irvine, (so) I took over the negotiations personally and saw them through."[16]

Finally, Section 8 of the agreement reads:

> So long as any of the land within the Inclusion Area or within the 10,000 acres of the university community remain within the (Irvine) company's direct or indirect control, the sale, lease, or other disposition of such land shall be made without discrimination based upon race, religion, or national origin ...[17]

****

Evolution of the UCI Campus Land Holding in the Early 1960s

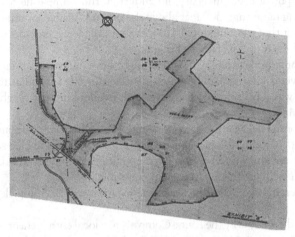

January 1961 - The approximately 990 acres that the University of California acquired for $1.00 to serve as the campus for UC Irvine as reflected in Exhibit B to the deed signed on September 30, 1960, accepted by the Regents on January 19, 1961, and recorded on January 20, 1961.

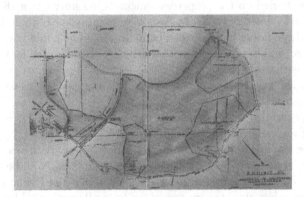

February1964 - The UC Irvine campus land holding as reflected in Exhibit A to the deed as adjusted on December 30, 1963, accepted on January 13, 1964, and recorded on February 17, 1964. This deed implemented modifications in the original boundaries and the addition of approximately 510 acres of Inclusion Area land acquired by the Regents at a discounted price of $3.315 million and brought the UC Irvine campus land area to total of approximately 1,500 acres.

Figure 8.1 Evolution of the UC Irvine campus land holdings in the early 1960s.

(Orange County Recorder. Exhibits annotated by H.P. Oliver.)

(a) January 1961 The approximately 990 acres that the University of California acquired for $1.00 to serve as the campus for UC Irvine as reflected in Exhibit B to the deed signed on September 30, 1960, accepted by the Regents on January 19, 1961, and recorded on January 20, 1961.

(b) February 1964 The UC Irvine campus land holding as reflected in Exhibit A to the deed as adjusted on December 30, 1963, accepted on January 13, 1964, and recorded on February 17, 1964. This deed implemented modifications in the original boundaries and the addition of approximately 510 acres of Inclusion Area land acquired by the Regents at a discounted price of $3.315 million and brought the UC Irvine campus land area to total of approximately 1,500 acres.

A familiar sight on the San Francisco Bay is the gleaming white tower on the Berkeley campus of the University of California, the Campanile tower, built in 1914 and rising more than 300 feet above the ground. Visible for miles, the tower reflects the fact that the campus, at 170 feet above sea level, provides a commanding view of the bay and its famous bridges.

And but for a quirk of fate, UC Irvine might have enjoyed a similar setting.

One of several Orange County sites identified by the Luckman team for the new campus was a hillside in Newport Beach overlooking the neighborhood of Corona del Mar.

Beyond Corona del Mar lies a magnificent vista of the Pacific Ocean and, on its horizon, Santa Catalina Island. During the summer, the placid blue sea is dotted with sailboats; in the winter, atmospheric conditions create breathtaking sunsets streaked with brilliant yellows, reds, and magentas.

William Pereira liked what he saw—the location was his top pick. But it had a fatal flaw.

The site had been sold by the Irvine Company to a local entrepreneur who planned to develop it into a cemetery. In her autobiography, Joan Irvine Smith says she tried to find another location for the new cemetery owner, but he declined the offer.[18]

And to make sure the land would remain as he planned, he arranged for six corpses to be buried on the property—quickly. One story has it that remains from a pauper's cemetery in Santa Ana were obtained. Another recounts an individual whose father had just died being informed he could have his father buried for free, and his deceased mother disinterred and buried for free as well, if he moved with dispatch.

No matter the specifics, the burials were apparently sufficient to vest the property as a cemetery.

Clark Kerr recalled in his oral history that, "... we wanted it, and then we decided that we couldn't fight the dead."[19]

Today, the remains of many prominent Orange County residents—including John Wayne—rest in peace at Pacific View Memorial Park. And the views from UC Irvine—built on a gentle hillside—encompass not the Pacific Ocean, but perhaps more fitting, almost every acre of the Irvine Ranch spread before it.

Notes

1. Raymond L. Watson and Ann Lage, *Planning and Developing the New Town of Irvine California, 1960–2003: Irvine Company President, 1973–1977, Walt Disney Company Chairman, 1983–1984* (Regional Oral History Office, the Bancroft Library, University of California, Berkeley, 2005) 267.
2. "Jewish Orange County Timeline," Orange County Jewish Historical Society, 2016.
3. Shelley v. Kramer. 334 U.S. 1. 68 (May 3, 1948).
4. Samuel C. McCulloch, "Interview with Clark Kerr," in *Samuel C. McCulloch Oral Histories* (AS-033) (University Archives, UC Irvine Libraries, 1969), 7.
5. Janss Investment Co. v. Walden, 196 Cal. 753 (1925).
6. Kathryn Ringrose, "Roger Revelle Interview," in *UC San Diego Oral History Project* (San Diego, CA: University of California, 1985) 17.

7. McCulloch, "Interview with Clark Kerr," 8.

8. *2007 Long Range Development Plan* (UC Irvine Campus Physical and Environmental Planning, 2007) 7.

9. McCulloch, "Interview with Clark Kerr," 34.

10. McCulloch, "Interview with Clark Kerr," 35.

11. Clark Kerr, *The Gold and the Blue: A Personal Memoir of the University of California, 1949–1967* (Berkeley, CA: University of California Press, 2003) 234.

12. Kerr, *The Gold and the Blue*, 244.

13. Watson and Lage, *Planning and Developing*, 336.

14. Watson and Lage. *Planning and Developing*, 336.

15. Watson and Lage. *Planning and Developing*, 336.

16. McCulloch, "Interview with Clark Kerr," 6.

17. "Inclusion Area Sales Agreement," *Land Agreements between the University of California and the Irvine Company* (AS-090) (Special Collections and Archives. The UC Irvine Libraries, 1964) Section 8.

18. Joan Irvine Smith, *A California Woman's Story* (Irvine, CA: The Irvine Museum, 2006).

19. McCulloch, "Interview with Clark Kerr," 34.

9 Pipes and Plans

Scattered development was underway on sections of the Irvine Ranch in the 1950s, nearly all of it in areas where mainline infrastructure had already been installed or was close by.

But to build UC Irvine—and the community it would spawn—millions of dollars in water and sewer systems would have to be identified, designed, financed, and built.

Water issues were an integral part of Irvine Company business, dating to the turn of the previous century when James Irvine II assumed ownership of the Irvine Ranch.[1]

Orange County's principal natural water source—the Santa Ana River—was well west of the ranch. Until tamed by the US Army Corps of Engineers in 1941 the river had regularly flooded the southwestern communities of Costa Mesa and Fountain Valley, as well as parts of Santa Ana. The devastating flood in 1825 sent so much soil into the Pacific Ocean that it formed the Balboa Peninsula. (The northern boundary of the ranch touched the Santa Ana River, but the hills of the Lomas de Santiago created an uncrossable barrier from the river to the agricultural flatlands.)

Two natural drainages crossed the ranch. The largest was San Diego Creek, which bisected the ranch on its path to the Upper Newport Bay and the Pacific Ocean.

As a result of the geology on the ranch, there was water beneath the ground. Before the advent of electric pumps, wells were drilled, and water was hauled up by hand. By the 1920s, more than 1,200 water wells with electric pumps had been drilled on the Irvine Ranch.

James Irvine II also built several dams on his property, the largest on Santiago Creek, located behind the Lomas de Santiago ridgeline. Irvine built an underground pipeline and a gravity flow canal to move the water from Irvine Lake to his croplands. The High Line Canal was constructed of concrete and remained in active use into the 1970s.

In 1934, water users in the west, central, and northern areas of Orange County—including nearly every acre of the Irvine Ranch—formed the Orange County Water District (OCWD) to manage groundwater resources. Two years

DOI: 10.1201/9781003226291-10

later, to protect his water rights, Irvine sued the OCWD, one of several water-related legal actions he would be involved in throughout his life.

In the case of the OCWD lawsuit, Irvine agreed to arbitration to stave off prolonged litigation. "I know of nothing more indefinite, intangible, with definite undiscernible excessive costs than a nice, juicy water lawsuit," Irvine wrote to the OCWD in 1940. "In my opinion no opportunity should be lost at any time to come to a reasonable compromise settlement in any water issue."[2]

In that case, settlement was achieved in 1942, limiting groundwater replenishment in the upper water basins of the Santa Ana River, to the benefit of OCWD and its members, including the Irvine Ranch.[3]

By 1960, while wells and runoff were sufficient to irrigate a great deal of Irvine Company farmland; the output would not come close to adequately supplying the new university and city. Statewide water sources would have to be tapped. To meet the need, the company turned to its chief engineer, William R. Mason.

Mason had joined the company in 1959 as an administrative engineer. He had strong academic credentials, including an undergraduate degree in civil engineering from the University of Washington, and a master's degree from one of the nation's most prestigious universities, the Massachusetts Institute of Technology (MIT). He started his career as an assistant professor of civil engineering at the University of Washington.

Mason was a big man, six foot three and weighing 230 pounds. He was described by many who worked for and with him as dedicated, formal, serious, and honest. In an earlier era, he might have been called a "straight arrow" or a "Boy Scout."

Figure 9.1 William R. Mason in 1970

Indeed, one of Mason's private passions in community involvement was the Boy Scouts of America. He was also a senior advisor to Chapman College and helped to establish the Orange County chapter of Junior Achievement.

Mason's attitude and performance won him the confidence of company president Charles Thomas, who named him vice president of engineering, and then in 1965 vice president of land development. A year later, upon Thomas' retirement, he became president of the company. Thomas described him in a memo to the board of directors as, "... well qualified, imaginative and inquisitive ... he works well with people and is well regarded by his associates. He also has a good working rapport with public officials."[4]

(Thomas also let Mason know what he was getting in for with the company board of directors that included Joan Irvine Smith. In his letter congratulating Mason on his appointment, he felt compelled to point out that, "... only 180 of the 396 shares held by the minority stockholders (the Irvine family)" had not joined with the majority shareholders [the James Irvine Foundation] to extend "their sincere wishes of congratulations." Thomas put the best spin on it he could conjure up, pointing out that Mason was, "... starting your administration not only with the support of the majority stockholders, but with a majority of the minority stockholders").[5]

Ray Watson described his relationship with Mason as a partnership of mutual respect. Each man listened to the other and deferred to one another on key subjects. Lanny Eberling remembers Mason as clean cut and very punctual. Being on time was so important to Mason, Eberling recalled, he and other executives would make it a point to arrive 10 or 15 minutes early to Mason's home for social events. Mason was a Christian Scientist and a teetotaler, so such gatherings were usually on the staid side. Philip Bettencourt remarked that, "Bill Mason's idea of informality was to unbutton his sport coat."[6] But other employees described Mason as approachable, and despite his sometimes-reserved demeanor, he was known universally as Bill.

All the company's toughest issues, many of them that had stirred up public controversy, landed on Mason's desk to tackle. Asked on one occasion to explain how he coped with the rigor of company leadership, he noted that, "... running a candy shop would be easier, but it (the pressure) comes with the job." He went on:

> Other businesses aren't involved in a business that touches people's lives as directly as our does. If we owned a candy business, we would survive based on the quality of the product. Our product—land and the way we plan its use—it's different.
>
> People look at our hills, our orange groves, our bayfront ... with a special proprietary interest. I appreciate and understand that interest.... I think we are proving that man can make a better living environment for himself. Planning on a broad scale can work ... the most important aspect of it all (is) the people; not the houses, the greenbelts, the parks ... it is how they work together ... the environment, in other words, has motivated the people.[7]

And Mason was a man of faith, both privately and in his work. Richard Reese remembers reviewing a copy of the company's prospective budget that Mason wrote an introduction to, with words to the effect that the budget supported the company's responsibility to both its owners and the communities it operated in. In a speech he made during the campaign to incorporate Irvine, he emphasized that all those involved needed to, "... have faith in the system, with each of us understanding each other's role in it."[8]

Perhaps one of the most telling examples of Mason's ideals is the 1970 letter he sent to Irvine Company employees, which reads, in part:

> I wish to pause this Yule Season to sincerely thank each of you for support of, and dedication to, the principles on which your Company is founded.
> The quality of our work ... will provide an example which can stand for all to judge. I am confident that our day-to-day performance toward our goals ... will help in people's understanding of our high ideals.
> And who is the Irvine Company? It is you, the employees ... who can by expressing positive ideas and constructive action, forge ahead to make better, finer contributions (which) stem not only from dedication, but also from inspired hearts and minds. In this holiday season, let us all pause to renew our faith in a power greater than any of us and reach towards a better understanding of what constitutes good and pursue that path during 1971.[9]

Recollections of Mason's management abilities and style from former colleagues were almost universally positive, bordering on reverent. "He was my best friend at the Irvine Company," said Richard Reese.[10] Lanny Eberling was more direct: "I loved him."[11]

(Mason's untimely death in July of 1973 at age 54 prompted an outpouring of grief, as well as tributes from business, government, and community leaders. His obituary in *Irvine World News* ran for pages. Watson, who would succeed Mason as president, was especially hard hit. Writing in the newspaper, he said he considered Mason, "almost as a brother ... he was more than our president, he was our rock of Gibraltar, our guiding light, our friend."[12])

To solve the urban water challenge the company faced, Mason devised a solution centered squarely in water law written for agriculture. Among the dozens of water management and governance agencies defined in the California Water Code, a provision is found for a California Water District.

Unlike districts where power is vested either in registered voters, or holders of defined water rights, the California Water District is governed by the value of the land within it. One dollar's worth of assessed value equals one vote in determining who is elected to the district board of directors.

The structure made sense for agricultural holdings, especially in the state's Central Valley. Larger landowners typically used more water, and when it came time to raise funds for water improvements, those with the most valuable land would arguably receive the greatest benefit. And there were already six California Water Districts in Orange County.

It was obvious to Mason that drawing a new water district's boundary entirely or nearly entirely coincident with the Irvine Company property would give the company control of how the district was operated. (In his oral history, Ray Watson said that there was debate within the company as to whether the water district should be owned by the Irvine Company or as a public entity. After considering factors such as contending with hundreds and then thousands of customers when water rates were raised, the company opted for the public option.)

Not that the new district could operate in a unilateral manner. State law proscribed that the district would be a public agency, with its deliberations governed by the Brown Act, the bedrock of California's law on open meetings. The district's documents would be public as well, and public notice would be required for major actions.

While Mason was privately moving forward with plans to form what would become the Irvine Ranch Water District (IRWD), others were on a similar mission.

L.E. Cox had been named vice chancellor for business and finance at the newly formed University of California Irvine as its administrators began to organize plans for building the campus.

Cox, according to an oral history, had initiated conversations with the giant Metropolitan Water District, the master distributor of water from northern California and the Colorado River, when he "woke up one day to an announcement that the Irvine Company had formed a new water district."[13]

With a map of the proposed new 39,489-acre water district in hand, Mason and the Irvine Company moved swiftly to start the legal process for its inauguration.

The formation petition was filed with the Orange County Board of Supervisors in November 1960 and adopted on December 20 of that same year. The formation election of the new district's board of directors was held on January 10, 1961, the polling place conveniently located at 13042 Myford Road—Irvine Company headquarters.

Five directors were elected: W.F. Graves, Max C. Hoeptner, Willis Mitchell, Walter Pollard, and A.J. McFadden. The top vote getter was Graves with 5,365,780 votes, and Pollard fifth with 5,289,130.

McFadden was president of the Irvine Company; the others were local farmers. Also elected was an assessor-tax collector, one George Rasmussen, with 5,342,590 votes (apparently California Water Districts had their own assessor-tax collector, as Mr. Rasmussen was not the Orange County assessor or tax collector).

After retaining a small staff and attending to bylaws and procedures, the IRWD set out to raise money. In June 1961, the board authorized issuance of $9 million in bonds with a 15-year maturity at an interest rate not to exceed 6 per cent. Five months later, $5.2 million of the bonds were sold.[14]

(In 2022 dollars, the $9 million would be worth about $83.9 million, the $5.2 million about $48.5 million.)

As preparations for the bond sale were underway, the IRWD made a deal with the Municipal Water District of Orange County (MWDOC), the local subsidiary of the giant Metropolitan Water District, which served virtually all of Southern

California. MWDOC would build a feeder line from its regional water plant near Yorba Linda, through the cities of Anaheim, Orange, and Santa Ana, connecting to the future site of a reservoir to be built in the hills of Corona del Mar (part of Newport Beach). The estimated cost was $21.5 million.

Apparently, to spread the benefit and the cost, a separate transaction was concluded between the IRWD and the Tri Cities Water District serving communities at the southernmost area of the county to connect the new MWDOC line to a feeder line south of the IRWD that would serve Tri-Cities.

To sweeten the deal, the Irvine Company agreed to provide water from some of its wells to MWDOC.

The water supply was just part of Mason's problem; sewage had to be dealt with as well. According to a history of the IRWD, Irvine Company executive Lanny Eberling, who served on the IRWD board in later years, recalled that until Mason got the law changed, California Water Districts could not provide sewer service. The change made the IRWD one of the first dual service districts in California.

Mason is also credited by Eberling and others as the creator of the IRWD's water recycling program.

Nowhere in Orange County, or the state, for that matter, were water districts using recycled water on the scale that the IRWD would. "Going with recycling was a tough decision to make because of limited funds," Eberling recalled.[15] But Mason's vision would pay off in an astounding fashion as the district grew to serve the new city. First used for landscaping, the ubiquitous purple pipes that snaked into every greenbelt, park, and schoolyard would eventually find their way into the toilets of office and industrial buildings. Millions of gallons of recycled water took the place of fresh water, keeping water bills relatively low and creating an environmental benefit for which the Irvine Company, the IRWD, and William Mason would never be fully recognized.

UC Irvine opened in 1965. The first homes in the vicinity soon followed. Now there were real voters within the IRWD, and although the assessed value of their homes was growing, it would be decades until it would equal the millions attributable to the value of the Irvine Company's land.

The IRWD and the company decided to select a local resident to sit on the board, as well as some of its own executives. The first was E. Ray Quigley, an airline pilot active in local community and Republican Party affairs. His service began in late 1969 and concluded in October 1971, when he ran for (and won) a term on the council of the newly incorporated City of Irvine.

Local politics in Irvine from 1971 to 1977 were largely focused on the new city council and school district, but rumblings about control of the IRWD prompted the board in 1977 to expand from five to seven members, creating two seats largely populated by residents. In the first election thereafter, Wayne Clark and William Eppinger won the resident seats.

In 1978, the district was sued in Orange County Superior Court by James A. O'Toole and Robert Mitchell, alleging that the California Water District law was unconstitutional. On October 4, 1979, the court agreed and ordered that IRWD elections be conducted on a residential voter basis starting in June 1980.

Assemblywoman Marian Bergeson and State Senator John Schmitz each introduced legislation to enable the elections, ensuring that control of the district would pass to residents.

In 2020, 23 per cent of the IRWD's total water supply was from recycled water, a legacy from William Mason.

Notes

1. Carl Nelson, *A History of Water Resource Development on the Irvine Ranch, Orange County, California* (Irvine, CA: Self-published, 2009).
2. Shawn Dewane, "A History of the Orange County Water District," Orange County Water District, 2014, 17. https://www.ocwd.com/about/history.
3. In the early 1960s, Leonard Moffitt, a UC Irvine planner, was assigned by UC Irvine Chancellor Daniel Aldrich to analyze the social, political, and business atmosphere of Orange County to help the new campus leaders better understand their new home. Moffitt wrote *Community and Urbanization in Orange County* (Langson Library, UCI Special Collections and Archives, 1964). It is a densely researched 1,100-page report that went far beyond its assigned parameters, delving deep into the county's history. Among his findings are pages of interviews and research about water supply and flooding. Underlying his findings is a theme of distrust of the Irvine Ranch and James Irvine II on these topics. Moffett noted that at least three times Orange County residents unsuccessfully attempted to pass flood control bonds. It was only when the federal government stepped in that the Santa Ana River was finally dammed near the Riverside border, ending the regular flooding of the county.
4. Charles S. Thomas, *Personal and Business Files* (MS.R.003) (Special Collections and Archives of the UC Irvine Libraries, 1946–1966) Folders 18–21.
5. Thomas, *Personal and Business Files*
6. Philip Bettencourt, interview with C.M. Stockstill, May 6, 2020.
7. William R. Mason, *William R. Mason Papers* (Corona del Mar, CA: Sherman Library and Gardens).
8. William R. Mason to Irvine Company employees, December 18, 1970.
9. Mason, *William R. Mason Papers.*
10. Richard Reese, interview by C.M. Stockstill and H.P. Oliver, August 26, 2020.
11. Lanny Eberling, video interview by H.P. Oliver and C.M. Stockstill, July 20, 2020.
12. *Irvine World News* (July 19, 1973) 1.
13. Spencer Olin, *Oral History of UC Irvine Faculty and Staff* (AS-145) (Special Collections and Archives of the UC Irvine Libraries, 2006) 14.
14. Irvine Ranch Water District. *District records.*
15. Lanny Eberling, telephone interview by C. Michael Stockstill and H.P. Oliver, July 20, 2020.

10 Defending the Borders

Under jurisdiction of the County of Orange, the Irvine Company had in 1963 begun building its first residential village in what would become the City of Irvine. But University Park began life not as a part of the more comprehensive vision that Pereira had outlined in what Watson described as, more a vision than a plan.

The Southern Sector General Plan that would more clearly define the 10,000 acres adjacent to the university was winding its way through the county planning department when Watson and his colleagues received some ominous news: the City of Santa Ana was preparing to launch an annexation that would have blocked any possibility of expanding the 10,000-acre new town into the central valley of the Irvine Ranch.

"Strip" Annexation Attempt by the City of Santa Ana

The City of Santa Ana had reached an accommodation with retirement community developer Ross Cortese, who was seeking to develop property on the opposite side of Irvine Company lands. To satisfy a requirement that land annexed to an existing city had to be contiguous, Santa Ana created a 300-foot wide, 8.5-mile strip of land roughly along the alignment of the yet to be built San Diego Freeway, connecting Santa Ana and Cortese's planned community of Leisure World.

Not only did the city's plan surprise the Irvine Company, but it also came barely two years after Santa Ana had signed a pledge not to annex any of the company's land that was within the 10,000 acres designated for the university community.

Many of the county's surrounding cities took the City of Santa Ana plan as a joke, because if approved, it would result in creating a city shaped like a dumbbell, with a huge existing city at one end of the strip and a new retirement city nearly nine miles apart. But Watson and the company soon learned that for Santa Ana, the proposal was no joke.

Watson spent the following three months trying to block or slow down Santa Ana's maneuver. He sought unsuccessfully to meet with councilmembers and city manager Carl Thornton. He even attempted some personal diplomacy with city planning director Jim Teffer, a neighbor. "Some weekends I would wander over to his house with benefit of a beer in hand to attempt to debate the planning

DOI: 10.1201/9781003226291-11

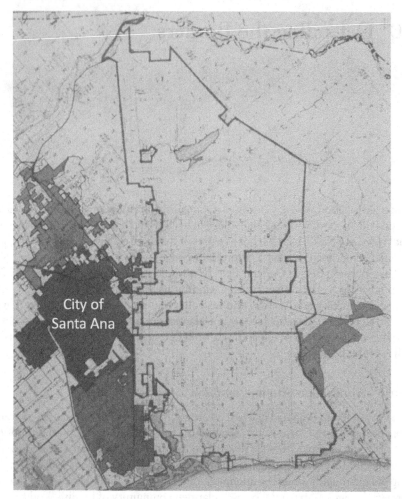

Figure 10.1 The narrow "strip" annexation across the Irvine Ranch attempted by the City of Santa Ana in 1963.

merits of the proposed annexation." Like the city manager, Teffer stonewalled.[1] Thornton was correct when he repeatedly said the annexation was legal. State law at the time allowed the Local Agency Formation Commission (LAFCO) to review annexation requests but had no authority to approve or reject them and "finger" or "strip" annexations had yet to be outlawed.

Thornton laid out the city's reasoning for the unusual approach to a local breakfast club that sponsored a debate on the plan. He acknowledged the annexation would block the expansion of the future university town, but argued that in competition with Los Angeles, Orange County needed a major city, which should logically be the City of Santa Ana. Watson reluctantly concluded that public debate and logic were going nowhere; Thornton and the Santa Ana city council also had a vision for the future, and they were going to pursue it.

A public hearing at the City of Santa Ana planning commission gave Watson and other opponents a forum to expand on the absurdity of the proposed expansion, but the fix was in, and the commission approved it on a unanimous vote.

Running out of time, Watson and company lawyers, engineers, and planners scrambled for a strategy to throw a roadblock in the way of the county's largest and most powerful city.

Finally, it was an overlooked parcel of land that proved to be the fatal weapon.

A company civil engineer had reviewed the entire length of the strip and discovered that within it there was a 20-acre parcel that the company had sold to the state for an interchange on the future route of what would become the San Diego Freeway. Apparently, the parcel had not been shown on the maps Santa Ana used to draw the annexation boundaries. And the city had carefully crafted the size of the strip to assure that the cumulative assessed value of the company's land was less than Cortese's, giving him more votes for the annexation tally.

State law made clear the potential power of the discovery: a public agency owning land within a proposed annexation could object to it as part of the LAFCO process and void the annexation. Watson and UC Irvine officials prevailed upon the State Division of Highways (now Caltrans) to file an objection, which was done. The annexation was dead, leaving the city with, "... the only choice ... to remap the strip to avoid any other public lands. Why they didn't was never revealed." Watson believed that the furor over the issue left both Santa Ana leaders and Cortese without the will to continue the fight.[2]

In September 1965, just a couple of years after the strip annexation battle, UC Irvine welcomed its first freshman class. And early in 1966, the first families moved into the new town that by then the Irvine Company had named Irvine. Students and families made their respective decisions to buy into the Irvine dream based mostly on what they hoped the community and campus would become. There were just a few buildings on the university campus and only the initial phase of the very first residential village in the new town of Irvine had been constructed.

The opening of University Park prompted the Irvine Company to look beyond the Southern Sector plan that had been approved by the county, expanding planning into the giant central sector of the ranch, and requiring a decision: either create a second new town or expand Irvine.

The central section of the ranch was shaped like a saucer. The western slope of the San Joaquin Hills and the eastern slope of the Lomas de Santiago both drained into the flat plains of the central valley. Extending the city's boundaries to the rims of the hills provided a strong visual edge while also containing the natural drainage within one city. Fortunately, the case for one city was strengthened because the existing elementary school district encompassed the entire central sector. The company was advocating creation of a single, K-12 unified school district, sealing the decision that William Pereira's plan for a 10,000-acre, 100,000-population town would be expanded to a city of more than 50,000 acres.

Imbedded in William Pereira's 1959 University/Town study was the recommendation that the future town become self-governing. Pereira also understood the critical role schools played in the family's identification of community. And to demonstrate that, he also secured a promise from the Orange County Committee on School District Organization that they would attempt to hold future school district boundaries coterminous with those of the proposed new city.

There were four school districts adjacent to the ranch and within it. A boundary study was underway at the same time that the Irvine Company was coming to terms with the outlines of the new city. Watson convinced the school planners to hold off on a final report until the company could finish a study that would:

> ... attempt to determine the future economic soundness of the university city, which will include estimates of future costs for all urban services, not just schools.
>
> If a particular city or district finds itself with an inadequate tax base, there will be pressures within the district or city to shift industrial lands to such a location as to create a more adequate tax base. The Irvine Company wants to see a division of industrial areas so that each of the districts can be economically healthy.[3]

It would be seven and a half years before Irvine incorporated, and nearly eight years before the Irvine Unified School District was formed, but the promise made in 1964 was honored, and as a result the city and school district each share, in large part, the same boundaries.

With the decision made to substantially expand the Pereira plan, Watson sought support from UC Irvine. Chancellor Daniel Aldrich expressed no objections, but wanted the UC Regents to be briefed, especially Norton Simon, who had opposed locating the new campus on the Irvine Ranch.

Watson briefed Simon and Aldrich at a meeting on campus. It did not go well:

> Simon paid little heed to any of my planning points. He asked no questions nor offered any specific objections. He ended the meeting, however, by inferring that the Irvine Company must have some ulterior self-interest in proposing the changes and he was opposed to enlarging the city.[4]

Taking the role of contrarian, either with the regents or in business, was nothing new to Simon. A self-made billionaire who amassed an art collection sizeable enough to require his own museum, Simon challenged financial cutbacks at the UC system, sympathized with student activists, and opposed the firing of UCLA lecturer and admitted communist Angela Davis, who had been tried and acquitted in a sensational murder trial involving a prison breakout.

Fellow regents, in a pair of oral histories, painted an unflattering portrait of Simon.

Elinor Raas Heller came from a family with deep roots in San Francisco and had a long career in public service. Recalling the significant time commitment to serving as a regent, she found Simon petty and selfish because he would not serve on committees. Like any other large and complex enterprise, the UC Board of Regents broke out issues and assigned them first to committees for consideration, then to the full board. Simon, according to Heller, would have none of it: "Norton Simon, for example refused to serve on any committees. Didn't believe in it. You can assign him forever: he wouldn't come." She went on to say, "Norton made things very difficult, I assure you, by refusing to go through the committee process."[5]

William Coblentz, a well-connected lawyer and political activist from San Francisco (the Grateful Dead was among his clients), said that Simon enjoyed stirring the pot, taking glee in irritating others. He cited, in particular, Simon antagonizing fellow regents Ed Pauley, Edward Carter, and Dorothy Chandler in a dispute about the Los Angeles County Museum of Art.

Simon pressed his views on the UC Irvine campus selection process inside regents' meetings. Accusing Carter of promoting the campus so his Broadway department stores in Orange County would be boosted by the presence of the new university, he also took on regent William French Smith because he represented the James Irvine Foundation as an attorney.

Coblentz served on a regents' committee dealing with UC Irvine issues and told Simon there were no conflicts for the two other regents. "Norton said, 'You sold out.'" Coblentz laughed it off and said, "I don't know what I sold out for."[6]

Why did a liberal-minded billionaire find fault with another company for potentially making money? *The New York Times* described Simon as a "... brooding, driving man ... who, despite his success, was perennially dissatisfied." "I believe in a paradoxical view of life...," he once told an interviewer. "I don't believe anything is wholly right, but both right and wrong. There is a thin line between. There is a Chinese proverb that life is a search for truth, and there is no truth."[7]

(And Simon was willing to talk to just about anyone about his negative view of the Irvine Company. In an oral history, L.E. Cox, UC Irvine's first vice chancellor for business affairs, recalled that "Simon shook his finger in my face and warned me not to do anything to make the Irvine Company' richer than it already was."[8])

Simon's opposition notwithstanding, the company moved forward with a plan for the center section of the ranch in the anticipation that, eventually, a new city would incorporate in the area. And it was at this point that the company, with a statement from its president, William Mason, made clear it would encourage and support such a move.

County planners were reviewing the Irvine Company submittal, but weeks and then months passed without action. Watson laid the delay to the new makeup of the board of supervisors.

> Relations between the company and the newly elected county supervisors progressively had become strained. These were the anti-war years and years of new environmental sensitivity. Big was beginning to mean bad, and right or wrong, the Irvine Company and other large institutions were feeling the brunt of that sentiment.[9]

Riding this wave were freshmen county supervisors Robert Battin, who represented Santa Ana, and Ron Caspers, representing the southern end of the county. Battin, an attorney, had boxed as a young man and as such was known as "Battling Bob Battin." Caspers was a wealthy savings and loan executive who ushered in a new era on the board with the help of local political consultant Fred Harber. The two new supervisors joined north county supervisor Ralph Clark, who had been mayor of Anaheim. Two year later Ralph Diedrich, a rough-hewn bully who enjoyed being called "Super D," was elected.

(Battin was removed from office in 1975 for misuse of campaign funds. Caspers and Harber were lost at sea, along with two of Caspers' sons, in a boating accident off Baja California the week after he was re-elected in 1974. Diedrich was convicted in 1977 of taking a $75,000 bribe from a home developer and served 20 months in jail.)

What Watson viewed as the increasing polarization of the county planning process came home after a planning commission meeting when again, no progress was forthcoming on the company's plans:

> At the conclusion of the meeting the commissioner representing the first district invited me into his office. He opened the meeting by asking, 'Do you want to know how to have the commission begin the process of reviewing your submittal?' He then informed me how: the company needed to get the Santa Ana (now Orange County) *Register* off his supervisor's back. I told the commissioner we had no ability to influence the *Register*. I left not knowing when, if ever, the planning commission would bring up our plans.[10]

Watson discussed the encounter with William Mason. The two concluded:

> ... we had been speculating when the new residents (of Irvine) might be ready to seek their independence. Until then, there had been no spontaneous stirring within Irvine to make that move. Although incorporation was an idea that was a decade old, the longest any resident had lived in the community was less than five years.
>
> Families were furnishing their homes, sending their kids off to school and having any local conflicts resolved by their own community associations. They were busy organizing their new lives into their new neighborhoods and saw no compelling reason to take on cityhood.[11]

Irvine Company management decided the residents needed a push, and they had just the tools to do so.

Notes

1. Raymond L. Watson, "Irvine's Road to Cityhood," in *Raymond L. Watson Papers* (MS.R.120) (Special Collections and Archives of the UC Irvine Libraries, 2006) 4.
2. Watson, "Irvine's Road to Cityhood," 5.

3. Watson, "Irvine's Road to Cityhood," 7.
4. Watson, "Irvine's Road to Cityhood," 7.
5. Elinor Raas Heller, *A Volunteer Career in Politics, in Higher Education, and on Governing Boards*, oral history conducted 1974–1980 by Malca Chall (Regional Oral History Office, the Bancroft Library, University of California, Berkeley, 1984) 519.
6. William Coblentz, *San Francisco Lawyer, California Higher Education, and Democratic Politics: 1947–1998*, oral history conducted in 1997–1998 by Leah McGarrigle (Regional Oral History Office, the Bancroft Library, University of California, Berkeley, 2002) 301.
7. Eric Pace, "Norton Simon, Businessman and Collector Dies at 86," *The New York Times*, June 4, 1993, 22.
8. Spencer Olin, *Oral Histories of UC Irvine Faculty and Staff, Interview with L.E. Cox* (AS-145) (Special Collections and Archives of the UC Irvine Libraries, March 15, 2006),4.
9. Watson, "Irvine's Road to Cityhood," 8.
10. Watson, "Irvine's Road to Cityhood," 8.
11. Watson, "Irvine's Road to Cityhood," 9.

11 The Campaign for Cityhood

Having decided to cast its fate to a future city council instead of an increasingly hostile Orange County Board of Supervisors, the Irvine Company took the first step to introduce, explain, and advocate the subject of incorporation to the citizens.

The company owned two powerful communications vehicles, a weekly newspaper (*Irvine World News*) and a cable television company, that served developments built on the Irvine Ranch. Community Cablevision produced occasional informational programs about Irvine on its public access channel. The June 1970 broadcast provided just the forum to lay out the issue. Watson invited leaders from the seven Irvine community associations to discuss creating a new city.

During the live broadcast, Watson pointed to a 177-acre industrial site that had been leased to Collins Radio that was designated to be in the future Irvine city. But Collins Radio had other ideas: annex the property to the City of Newport Beach, change the zoning to office and hotels, and reap a windfall of profits. The company warned the Irvine residents the Collins Radio ploy could be the start of annexation raids by surrounding cities, potentially the beginning of the end to Irvine as a separate city. Now, Watson emphasized, was the time to act.

After the broadcast, viewers were invited to call in. One of the first calls came from Alan Snodgrass, president of a community association in the village of Turtle Rock. He urged formation of a mutual effort to protect the new city's master plan and economic base.

The seven community leaders in the studio voted unanimously to set up a steering committee to study incorporation. Three weeks later the Council of Communities of Irvine (CCI) was created. Snodgrass became president, and John Burton, the president of the Village Park Community Association in University Park, was elected chairman.

Burton was just 34 at the time, and by his own admission, "... didn't have a clue about knowing what it took to lead a grassroots citizen group." But after the energy of the effort began to build, he was caught up in it. Recalling the feeling in an interview 50 years later, Burton said that, "... while it may sound corny, I felt it was my patriotic duty to get this thing done. People (in Irvine) wanted it; they saw that other cities were trying to take what was ours."[1]

DOI: 10.1201/9781003226291-12

At the CCI meeting, the original seven were joined by a broad mixture of homeowners, merchants, and industrialists. Soon thereafter, UCI administration, faculty, and student representatives joined. The mood of those present was a mixture of enthusiastic support for cityhood, measured by a sense of urgency.

Two months later, CCI held its first open public meeting, and the reaction was the same: get moving.

The Irvine Company's position was that if the citizens of Irvine wanted to take control of their own destiny, the status quo was not an option. The immediate job before them was to understand the economic, social, and political consequences of both annexation and incorporation.

The audience impatience became contagious, with first one then another speaker urging CCI to not wait until it had completed its study of the feasibility of incorporation, but to file for it immediately. Sensing the mood of those present, Burton and Snodgrass said it could take as long as 13 months before they were ready to officially file.

The audience's immediate concern was the threat of additional annexations in the Irvine Industrial Complex, the company's development area adjacent to the Orange County Airport (now John Wayne Airport) reserved for manufacturing companies and support businesses.

"We must act fast," one attendee said. "I've lived in a bedroom community that had no tax base, and I know the kind of taxes I had to pay." Another reminded the CCI leaders the Irvine Company had a master plan, and, "... if that's not the homework of ten years, I don't know what homework is."[2]

Watson's account of the meeting came just after the Collins Radio annexation proposal had been approved by the Local Agency Formation Commission (LAFCO), a fact that had likely fueled the urgency of those present. Watson left the meeting convinced that the next step was to engage UC Irvine's leadership on behalf of incorporation.

It was late summer, 1970, when Watson reconnected with Chancellor Daniel Aldrich, seeking support. Aldrich placed the issue on the agenda for the November meeting of the University of California Board of Regents.

Watson wrote:

> Not having heard from Regent Simon since my earlier meeting, I wondered what his position would be. I was soon to find out. In early October I was informed by the LA Times that Regent Simon had called a press conference on the subject of the Irvine's proposed incorporation.[3]

At the press conference, it was clear that Simon's opposition had intensified. According to Watson, "On Oct. 5th (1970) Simon began his remarks by stating '... he believes he is raising questions which properly should be asked about the relationship between the Irvine Company and the University.'"[4]

Watson recalled that at this press conference Simon went on to claim, "... that the proposed fivefold enlargement of Irvine from that originally proposed would result in 'unjust enrichment' of the Company," which he estimated at $450 million and stated that at their next Regents meeting he would ask his fellow regents to "… begin a suit for compensatory and punitive damages against the Irvine Company for proceeding with the development of the City of Irvine in a manner which violates the agreement with the university."[5]

Simon further stated that, "… the public will be shocked when the full story is told at the Oct. 15th and 16th Regent's meeting." He concluded by describing the matter as, "… the largest cookie jar that can be recalled without going back to the Teapot Dome scandal' but did not disclose the details of his accusation."[6]

The showdown vote on the issue took place at the November meeting of the regents.

UC Assistant Vice President Robert Evans reviewed events of the past months which compelled, he said, CCI to act swiftly when the city of Newport Beach moved to embrace a sizeable portion of the Irvine Industrial Complex. The regents, he went on to say, were now faced with three choices: to move forward and support incorporation, which could create a viable new city; oppose incorporation, and thus kill the hopes for a new city; or take no position, which would be irresponsible.

Simon didn't deliver any of the bombshells he had promised in his press conference. Instead, he sought to delay consideration, stating paternalistically that he was not against incorporation, but wanted to be sure it was in the best interests of everyone. His motion lost on a 7–12 vote.

The final vote was to approve in principle the incorporation of an appropriate and viable city of not less than 10,000 acres, including the UC Irvine campus. The vote to approve was 18–2. The regents also voted to authorize further studies on the issue at a cost not to exceed $25,000. Simon grumbled that the Irvine Company spent $1 million on the plan, the county was spending $500,000 and the university was spending $25,000.

The lopsided vote must have stung Simon. Perhaps if he had attended committee meetings and displayed a more cordial attitude toward fellow regents, it might have been different.

Was there discreet or outright lobbying on the matter? It seems highly likely, given the intertwining relationships between the UC and the James Irvine Foundation, where N. Loyall McLaren had strong ties to the UC system and individual regents like Ed Pauley (who he had traveled to Russia with after World War II on a presidential commission); where regent Ed Carter had once served on the foundation board; and where William French Smith was foundation legal counsel. And after all, Governor Ronald Reagan made his first speech as a political candidate in Anaheim, and by 1970 had plenty of friends in the county, some of whom might have wanted to see a new city succeed. Acting in his constitutional role as a regent that day, Reagan voted yes.

The CCI leadership was active in the lead-up to the regents' meeting, releasing a summary of studies that had been prepared on incorporation issues. CCI had also recruited the retired county planning director, Harry Bergh, who lived in Irvine, to help argue their cause. He told the residents:

Only an informed electorate can continue to make the General Plan work. The plan will not take care of itself. If we have only one government to address ourselves to, informed voters can elect city officials who will be in sympathy with the objectives of the plan. If our communities are split among several cities and the county, we will have to address our interests and arguments to all these jurisdictions.[7]

Linking the preservation of the Irvine General Plan to self-governance resonated with the community. The theme of Irvine as a planned community of villages had dominated the company's messages from the day the concept was introduced, and by 1970 the residents had bought into it.

CCI filed an incorporation petition with LAFCO, which held its first public hearing on the matter on January 6, 1971. Speaking in favor were representatives from CCI and the Greater Irvine Industrial League, as well as chancellor Daniel Aldrich and the godfather of the master plan, William Pereira.

At the second hearing a week later, it was the opposition's turn. Other than a few Irvine citizens who asked for more time, the only opposition came from Santa Ana, where city manager Carl Thornton and Mayor Loren Griset testified against the petition.

Supervisors Battin and Caspers had tried to deter incorporation by a last-minute maneuver to replace a pro-incorporation LAFCO member with an opponent. CCI attorney Tim Strader learned of the ploy and on the weekend before the Monday meeting filed an emergency lawsuit, seeking a restraining order.

"I got the approval from Judge J.E.T. Rutter on Saturday," Strader recalled. "But the judge said it wouldn't be official until he put his seal on it, and his seal was in his courtroom." Accompanied by a process server, Strader arrived at the courtroom at 8 am, then raced into the stairway of county offices to surprise Battin and Caspers on their way down to the LAFCO meeting: "My process server threw the papers at them and told them they had been served."[8]

For good measure, Strader staged the same service as Caspers and Battin came into the LAFCO meeting and tried to ram through the new changes. Strader recounts how he had to threaten the LAFCO staff attorney with a contempt of court hearing to persuade the two supervisors to back down. Strader believes that the resulting publicity for the supervisors was so bad that their willingness to expend political capital on incorporation evaporated.

LAFCO approved the incorporation on a 3–2 vote, allowing an incorporation election; the boundaries of the new city would have to be approved by the Orange County Board of Supervisors. But Santa Ana wasn't finished. Within days, the city sought a temporary restraining order against allowing the incorporation election.

Now the Irvine Company had to decide how much of its property would be included within the boundaries of the new city. Watson and company president William Mason briefed company board members at their April 13, 1971, meeting, and presented a resolution authorizing company management to act for the company in all matters relating to the proceedings for the incorporation of the city of Irvine.

Joan Irvine Smith objected. She argued that Irvine's tax base was not sufficient to support the services it needed, and its population was too small. Watson cited CCI studies to the contrary. The board voted 6–2 to approve incorporation support, with Joan Irvine Smith and Keith Gaede (Myford and Thelma Irvine's son-in-law) voting no. Six months later, Smith would go public with her objections.

The citizen group wanted only university land and a portion of the future city that included existing developments and areas projected to be developed in the next five years—a total of 18,145 acres—included in the petition for the new city. John Burton's recollection of the map creation was that "I drew it on my coffee table and then we took it over to Newport Center." The company agreed and signed the petition to reflect that number.[9]

The next step was to have the board of supervisors approve the map. But the City of Santa Ana had filed suit in the Superior Court seeking an injunction against holding the incorporation election, claiming that CCI had included in the application a 938-acre industrial park owned by the Irvine Company that the company had previously agreed Santa Ana could annex.

The industrial park, established in the mid-1960s, had becoming the fastest growing in the county. Located between Orange County Airport and the Marine Corps Lighter Than Air Base (MCLTA) about a mile northeast, it was indeed the subject of an Irvine Company/Santa Ana agreement. In 1963, following the rejection of the attempted strip annexation, the company had agreed that it would not oppose a Santa Ana annexation of the park after May 20, 1971. (The MCLTA housed blimps during World War II. By the early 1950s, the blimps had departed, and Marine Corps helicopters used the two giant hangars that remained on site.)

To resolve the conflict, CCI offered to withdraw the industrial park from the incorporation filing, but the olive branch was not accepted by Santa Ana. In 2020, Burton recalled that Santa Ana feared that, "… the city of Irvine was a threat to Santa Ana's domination of Orange County. They felt they must at least acquire the central portion of the Irvine Ranch."[10]

Santa Ana lost its lawsuit when Judge Raymond Thompson ruled the 1963 agreement invalid. Now it was up to the county supervisors.

Burton did not expect any opposition to the incorporation map proposal at the scheduled September 21 hearing; the law required an initial public hearing to consider any protests from landowners. With the company and university on board with the residents, the likelihood of objection was remote.

What Burton didn't know, but was soon to learn, was that Joan Irvine Smith had lunched with Supervisor Battin the day before, asking him for a lengthy postponement of the cityhood proceedings. Battin did so at the meeting, gaining a vote from Supervisor Caspers, but short of a majority. Battin's motivation was easy to understand as he represented Santa Ana, but Caspers seemed to be out of step with his constituents, who lived in Newport Beach and Irvine. He told reporters he was concerned about Smith's request because she owned 20% of Irvine Company stock.

Never one to pull punches, Joan unloaded on the whole process, telling the *Daily Pilot*, "City of Irvine incorporation would be premature and lead to the creation of slums."[11] A stinging retort came from Andrew May of the pro-incorporation City of Irvine Now (COIN) group:

> Since when is self-government premature? Mrs. Smith is not a resident, not a landowner, not a voter. She should stay in Virginia where she evidently prefers. Her fight is with the Irvine Company. She should keep it in the board room where it belongs.[12]

Following Smith's interview, seven Irvine family members, who together owned 23 per cent of the company stock, sent a letter to the board of supervisors supporting incorporation.

The Board of Supervisors hearing in late September was anti-climactic. After arguments from Santa Ana, Joan Irvine's lawyer, Lyndol Young, and counter missives from Burton and CCI attorney Strader, it was a 4–1 vote (Battin opposed) to set the incorporation election for December 21, 1971.

A total of 35 candidates filed for the five council seats in the new city. Watson described them as:

> most(ly) college graduates, some with advanced degrees. They covered the spectrum of professions, including lawyers, pilots, teacher, economists, financial managers, designers, and housewives.
>
> ... Most were running as individuals, some ran as teams, either by their own choice, or as slates from their community associations. All but one candidate supported incorporation. The issues they espoused were open space, taxes, local control, master planning, and provision of schools to meet future growth, addition of low-income housing and protection of the environment. Neither of the two organizations most active in the election, CCI and COIN, endorsed any of the candidates.[13]

Joan Irvine Smith kept up her opposition. Just two weeks before the election she spoke to 500 students and a smattering of Irvine residents at the UC Irvine Science Lecture Hall.

The *Daily Pilot* headlined its story on her speech as "Heiress Rips Cityhood, Fires Salvos in UCI Talk," going on to describe her speech: "... the tangled web of Irvine family fortunes and tragedies was unraveled before a capacity audience as Joan Irvine Smith spoke out against what she termed the premature incorporation of the City of Irvine."[14]

Watson noted that she went on to say,

> The move to bulldoze premature incorporation of the new city is nothing more than a power play on the part of the corporation to usurp control over lands from the Orange County Board of Supervisors that would be done by

installing a company-controlled city administration which would carry out the required plans for development.[15]

She continued, "Premature development would damage my investment as a stockholder, reduce your property values and destroy the university environment for the students."[16] Smith allowed that she would support incorporation once she took control of the Irvine Company away from the James Irvine Foundation and the new city had grown to a sufficient population that in her view would not require "confiscatory taxes" to sustain it.

Watson concluded that,

> In my view, Mrs. Smith's attempts to intervene merely strengthened the resolve of the residents and the candidates to take control of their city. They ran the two-year process and felt empowered by it. Neither Mrs. Smith nor any other non-resident, nor the Irvine Company or other politicians were going to take that choice away from them.[17]

A council candidate put it more bluntly, telling the *Daily Pilot*, "Mrs. Smith is really saying hold up incorporation until I have time to gain control of the Irvine Company."[18]

It was probably true. The Tax Reform Act of 1969 had passed two years earlier, and the time allocated for foundations to divest themselves of control of companies like the Irvine Company was running out. Joan Irvine Smith, for whatever reason, apparently thought incorporation could interfere with her desire to wrest the company out of the clutches of the foundation.

(There is also a school of thought among Burton and others that Joan was secretly funding the Irvine Tomorrow anti-incorporation campaign, using the services of Irvine resident Arnold Forde, at the time a budding Orange County political consultant. As there were almost no requirements for campaign disclosures at the time, it is impossible to document the allegations. Burton also believes that Joan and her public relations agent, Frederick "Chip" Cleary, had a hand in the decision of North American Rockwell—where he was working—to thwart his efforts by placing him on an unpaid leave of absence shortly before the incorporation.[19])

Another ploy to influence the election came from State Senator Dennis Carpenter, who sent a letter to the city's voters endorsing a five-person slate for council. It didn't work. As a result, even the candidates Carpenter endorsed sought to distance themselves from him, and as a result only two of the candidates he endorsed were elected.

Carpenter sent the letter at the suggestion of CCI attorney Strader, who was hoping to become the new city attorney for Irvine after incorporation. Recalling the effort 50 years later, Strader allowed that his career as a corporate attorney and developer turned out to be far more satisfying than had he become city attorney.

As the first returns were counted on December 21, the scope of the incorporation victory became clear, with 3,214 votes in favor, 1,560 against. Just over 72 per cent of the city's voters turned out.

Five candidates were elected to the council: William M. Fischbach, John Burton, Henry Quigley, Gabrielle Pryor, and E. Ray Quigley. Watson noted that,

> … the organization that backed three of the winners, interestingly enough, was Irvine Tomorrow, which campaigned against incorporation, taking the position it was premature. Nevertheless, they backed the three apparently believing that if incorporation passed, they would act independent from any company or organization.[20]

(Irvine Tomorrow would remain a force in city affairs until the city's voting population grew to the point that its liberal views were diluted. Basil "Bill" Vardoulis, who five years later ran successfully for a council seat, recalled that the small communities in the northern-central area of the new city—places like The Ranch, California Homes, and College Park—considered the Irvine Tomorrow members intellectual highbrows who looked down on those communities, with their more blue-collar, non-university viewpoints. Burton felt the same way, noting in an interview in late 2020 that he fought for the expanded city boundaries to ensure the "elitists" at the university didn't dominate the new city.)

Daily Pilot reporter George Leidal had covered Irvine for months. Days after the election, he wrote of the,

> … infectious spirit and hope the residents have for their new city (which) unlike any other in history, may become something other than a pretty, suburbia-perfect New Town. It may indeed set the standard for a new city.
>
> The difference between Irvine and any other new town is that while others are truly company towns, dominated by the master planning of the developers, Irvine is the lone experiment in residential land use now controlled by a citizen-selected city government.[21]

The Irvine Company had placed nearly all its chips on a new city; now it would find out if the bet was a good one.[22]

Notes

1. John Burton, telephone interview by C.M. Stockstill, November 15, 2020.
2. Raymond L. Watson, "Irvine's Road to Cityhood," in *Raymond L. Watson Papers* (MS.R.120) (Special Collections and Archives of the UC Irvine Libraries, 2006) 10.
3. Watson, "Irvine's Road to Cityhood," 11
4. Watson, "Irvine's Road to Cityhood," 11
5. Watson, "Irvine's Road to Cityhood," 11.
6. Watson, "Irvine's Road to Cityhood," 11.
7. Watson, "Irvine's Road to Cityhood," 13.
8. Timothy Strader, telephone interview by C.M. Stockstill, July 10, 2020.
9. Burton, telephone interview, November 15, 2020.
10. Burton, telephone interview, November 15, 2020.
11. Watson, "Irvine's Road to Cityhood," 17.
12. Watson, "Irvine's Road to Cityhood," 17.

13. Watson, "Irvine's Road to Cityhood," 19.
14. Watson, "Irvine's Road to Cityhood," 20.
15. Watson, "Irvine's Road to Cityhood," 20.
16. Watson, "Irvine's Road to Cityhood," 20.
17. Watson, "Irvine's Road to Cityhood," 20.
18. Watson, "Irvine's Road to Cityhood," 20.
19. Burton, telephone interview, November 15, 2020.
20. Watson, "Irvine's Road to Cityhood," 21.
21. Watson, "Irvine's Road to Cityhood," 22.
22. A little more than a year after the City of Irvine was incorporated, a citizen group from the northern communities of the city organized and began to make noises about separating from the city, perhaps to form a new city in the unincorporated county area of Lemon and Cowan Heights. The movement fizzled out shortly thereafter.

12 The New City

Partners or Antagonists, or a Little of Both?

COMPANY TOWN: A community that is dependent on one firm for all or most of necessary services or functions of town life (as employment, housing, and stores).

Webster's New Collegiate Dictionary

The five newly elected members of the new City of Irvine were ready to be sworn in. More than 350 people had crowded into the Science Lecture Hall at UC Irvine to witness the historic occasion.[1]

The deputy city clerk leaned into the microphone. "May I call this first official meeting of the city council of the city of the Irvine ... Company ... to order please?

The council and the audience burst into laughter of "uproarious delight" at the Freudian slip. In a single sentence, the future political and social dynamic of the new town of just 18,000 people was unintentionally—but accurately—defined.

Who were these five individuals elected to govern the new City of Irvine, and how would they organize, manage, and operate a community that was geographically one of the largest in Orange County as well as one of the smallest in terms of population?

In his oral history, Ray Watson looked back 31 years and remembered his personal attitude that working with decision makers closest to the issues at hand was preferable to those distant, whether at the county or in the state capitol: "Other community developers said by supporting incorporation you're going to lose control. I said well, that's one of the yokes of democracy. You've got to learn to deal with it. I know how to deal with the local folks."[2]

(Watson's attitude reflected a trait he demonstrated throughout his Irvine Company career; that the force of the winning Watson personality, which was both friendly and firm, could almost always moderate the objections of opponents. His comment also underscored how comfortable he felt in his role as the "outside man" for the company, even though he was not its president at the time.)

Optimism about democracy aside, Watson and the Irvine Company were not starry-eyed about handing over the future of the company to a group of citizens. Deciding just how much company land would become part of the new city was a carefully calculated decision. The company was supportive of incorporation but did

DOI: 10.1201/9781003226291-13

not know how the newly elected council would view company development proposals. Watson and Mason deliberately kept some company land within the county so
that the company had the ability to play one jurisdiction against the other.

Whether the new city council had figured this out or not, they acted decisively
at their first meeting, enacting a 90-day freeze on new building permits, and elect-
ing the person who received the most votes in the election as the new mayor.

William Fischbach was an attorney who lived in University Park. He was
on the legal staff of a large oil company. Carol Flynn, who became Irvine's first
city clerk, remembers Fischbach as, "… brilliant, with an extraordinary brain."
Fischbach, Flynn said, was heavily involved in the creation of policies and even
ordinances for the new city. He also presided over the council meetings with
extreme fairness, she recalled. John Burton recalls meeting Fischbach through
their wives and having a couple of dinners where the incorporation was discussed.
Burton was surprised when Fischbach informed him he was running for council
on the Irvine Tomorrow ticket.[3]

Burton finished second; he had been the leader of the incorporation movement and arguably the most prominent figure associated with it. Burton had connections to the county's Republican political community, which at the time was
transitioning from extreme conservativism to a greater degree of moderation. The
John Birch Society was still prominent in nearby Tustin, the hometown of former
Congressman James Utt, one of the most reactionary elected figures the county
ever produced. Utt had been succeeded by John Schmitz, an equally polarizing
figure who tempered his hard-right conservatism with a quick wit and genial
manner. (One of Schmitz's most famous bon mots was his reaction to President
Richard Nixon's groundbreaking trip to China. "I didn't mind that he went, I just
objected that he came back."[4])

Burton was no firebrand; he had a young family and aspired to leadership, having joined his community association and been elected its president. Burton had
a quick wit that could turn cutting and sarcastic. He combed his blond hair over
his forehead, prompting opponents to liken him to a young Julius Caesar.

Two Quigleys (what were the odds?) were elected: Henry Quigley and E. Ray
Quigley.

Henry Quigley listed his occupation on the ballot as a finance expert. Just 32
when elected, Quigley was tall, with an angular face framed with black horn-
rimmed glasses. Articulate and agile on his feet in debate, Quigley was a quick
study on complex issues. However, once on the council, Quigley habitually equiv-
ocated on the matters before the new governing body. He sensed, often correctly,
that he would be the swing vote on many issues. Quigley was also highly sensitive
to be labeled one way or the other because of a vote. More than once, he called
reporters covering the city to give elaborate, sometimes excruciating, explanations of the way he voted and what it *really* meant.

Quigley had a good sense of humor, and like Burton was quick-witted. Seeking
to draw a distinction between himself and the other Quigley, his campaign materials referred to him as "Just Plain" Henry Quigley. Burton thereafter in conversation often addressed him as "Just Plain."

Henry Quigley was ambitious. He ran unsuccessfully for the Republican nomination for the local assembly district, and then in an amazingly audacious move, for the party nomination for state treasurer. An early user of a mobile phone, Quigley drove up and down the state, running a shoestring campaign and finishing second to the winning candidate, John Kehoe, who got 553,751 votes to Quigley's 446,763 (two other candidates ran as well).

E. Ray Quigley was an airline pilot and, like Burton, had been active in local Republican politics. He had been appointed to a seat on the Irvine Company-controlled Irvine Ranch Water District when the company tried to assuage residents about the company's monopoly not only on all residential, commercial, and retail land in the city, but the water district as well.

E. Ray Quigley was a reliable Burton ally on the council. He had a rich baritone voice and an authoritative presence on the dais, a reflection of his career as a commercial airline pilot. For his own pleasure, Ray Quigley loved to sing, and with his square jaw and winning smile, would have been the perfect Billy Bigelow for a production of *Carousel*.

Gabrielle Pryor, like Fischbach and Henry Quigley, had been endorsed by Irvine Tomorrow. Small and slight, she had a mischievous smile and a pixie-cut hairstyle. Pryor was probably the most intelligent person on the council, educated at Stanford and with sophistication reflecting the fact she moved around the country as the child of a Navy submariner, and had studied voice at the prestigious Guildhall School of Music in London. Pryor weighed in on every issue and regularly sparred with Burton. It was often evident to council meeting attendees what she was thinking, as she would roll her eyes or assume a face of mock horror at comments from others.

At one council meeting, a member of the local Rotary Club appeared before the council seeking an endorsement for an event. Pryor scolded the hapless representative, pointing out that as Rotary did not allow women to join, she wondered how it could meet its own "Four Way Test," which included "Is It Fair?" as one of its tenets. She voted no, to the amusement of the other council members.

The initial meetings of the council were freewheeling; debate often went on for long periods without the customary procedural requests to speak. The council met every week, sometimes well into the evening. City Hall was a small assemblage of rooms in the two-story office building directly across from UC Irvine that housed the campus bookstore and a bar.

Just a month after incorporating, the council hired its first city manager. He would stay for 17 years, helping to oversee many of the formative decisions that would shape the city for decades.

William Woollett Jr., called Bill by nearly everyone who knew him, was 43 in 1972, a veteran of local government primarily in the Los Angeles County region of the San Gabriel Valley. Woollett had run two cities there, Monterey Park and Temple City, where his pugnacious attitude in dealing with labor issues earned him the sobriquet "Wild Bill."

Woollett was a compact man, solidly built naturally, and reinforced by regular visits to the gym. One eye was missing, the result of his military service in the Korean War, where he was nearly killed at the Battle of Pork Chop Hill. Woollett was also an extremely shrewd judge of character, both in the employees he recruited and in sizing up the small army of supplicants who descended on the new city seeking contracts or access.

Before joining Irvine, Woollett had been the general manager of the Hollister Ranch in Santa Barbara. Adjacent to the growing UC Santa Barbara campus, Hollister's owner, the Macco Corporation, had visions of urbanization and had hired Woollett to manage the planning. Macco, however, had financial ties to the Penn Central, and went down when the massive railroad conglomerate filed for bankruptcy.

Woollett left Hollister with his reputation as an efficient city manager intact, and shortly after taking the Irvine post recruited a young protégé he had known in the San Gabriel Valley, Paul Brady.

Brady, serving as assistant city manager, and Brent Muchow, hired as director of public works, along with city clerk Carol Flynn and director of administrative services James Harrington, formed the nucleus of the day-to-day management for the new city. Woollett explained through the course of his long career that the key to success was to hire people "smarter than me and let them do their job."[5]

Woollett adopted a Groucho Marx-like conviviality with nearly everyone he dealt with, be they titans of industry or the local press corps. A *very* firm handshake and smile would usually be followed with a joking insult at the expense of the guest's wardrobe, occupation, or political outlook. "You're a lot smarter than you look," was a typical Woollett response to an entreaty from a serious-minded guest to his office.[6]

Was Bill Woollett just a bit irreverent? Behind his desk was a beautiful model of a tall-masted sailing ship; it appeared to be a gift or honorific until visitors looked carefully and read the tiny etched words on the brass plate attached to it: "You Miserable Bastard."[7]

Matching Woollett for colorful personality was the city attorney, James E. Erickson.

Erickson was a veteran at municipal law who worked at Orange County's most venerable law firm, Rutan and Tucker (several Rutan attorneys served as contract city attorneys).

Tall, broad shouldered, and with a large head, Erickson had a presence. He also had a resonate voice, the result of both genetics and the fact that as a young man he had trained to sing opera. But Erickson's most memorable trait was his deep love for the English language. His vocabulary was extensive and his ability to declaim was unmatched.

And Erickson loved to declaim.

At one council meeting, Pryor asked if the council had the legal power to accomplish some mission. Most city attorneys would have given a simple "yes" or "no," perhaps with a brief citation of law.

Not Jim Erickson. He drew himself up in his chair an inch or two, and looked out at the audience:

"Madame, whatever the mind of man can conceive, or the tongue of man can describe is available to this council."[8] Pryor stared at him for a moment, then gave a slight smirk as the meeting continued.

It would not be the last time Erickson's mellifluous baritone vocalized lengthy, logical, and often entertaining observations regarding the law or, on occasion, policy matters at the council. Reporters covering the meetings were especially happy to repeat his words in print to enliven their stories.

Because California cities typically elect a five-member city council to staggered four-year terms, alternating two, then three candidates every two years to assure a degree of continuity on the governing board, the March 1974 election would determine which of the five seats before the voters would have a four-year term and which would get a two-year term.

Pryor, Burton, and Henry Quigley won a four-year term, and newcomers Art Anthony and Robert West took the two-year terms.

By the time the second election had rolled around, the city was deep into planning and implementing policies and programs to guide future operations and land development.

Donald Cameron, who would become Irvine Company director of planning four years later, was involved in much of the day-to-day interaction with city staff. He summarized many of the activities in a planning book called "Innovations for Future Cities."

Cameron wrote that:

> untrained, inexperienced citizens were elected to positions of the Irvine City Council and appointed to the city commissions that comprise the governmental structure. The Irvine Company has had to respond to new political pressures as a result ... the company and the public recently have begun to work toward a common end and are trying to grow away from the suspicion and antagonism that too often exist between developers and the jurisdictions that control them.[9]

The size of the Irvine Company holdings and its single ownership, Cameron continued,

> ... have provided an exciting opportunity for the city and the company to participate in the community building process. Mutual goals, policies and guidelines for development can be established; detailed long-range planning that reflects both public and private interests can be undertaken.... Since the city was incorporated, it has attempted innovation and mutual action. Although this has not always been absolutely successful, each attempt has led the way to the next step, in what has been for all parties involved a somewhat painful, step by step learning process.
>
> Night after night at Irvine, at the meetings of the city council, the planning commission, the community services commission, the transportation commission, the community associations, the water district board, the unified school district and countless special-purpose citizen committees, an unusually large number of people who live in, work in or work for the city are involved in the concerns of building this particular new community.[10]

The most pressing and critical regulatory requirement for the new city was a general plan.

In Cameron's view, the city selected the firm of Wilsey and Ham for the job, "... because of the obvious enthusiasm of its young planners and because of their detailed outline of techniques for citizen involvement."

> The planning process took one year and eventually involved most of the city staff, all elected and appointed officials, hundreds of citizens, many special consultants, and a great number of members of the professional staff of the Irvine Company. The process was lengthy, embattled, and passionate, but the final product did have some worthwhile, innovative features, the most obvious of which—the land use and circulation plan—had been the subject of the greatest disagreement.[11]

Three plan options came out of the effort, each with a similar foundation but with varying degrees of intensity for future growth and population.

The first was what Cameron called the,

> ... base line (which) reflected the moderate position toward urban growth and is the most realistic." Option 1 was similar to the Irvine Company general plan but did not allow housing along the southeastern edge of the city adjacent to the El Toro Marines Corps Air Station.
>
> Option 2 assumed that El Toro would someday be closed (as it was in 1999) and development would proceed both on the closed base and around it.
>
> Option 3 is the minimum urbanization plan and illustrates what would happen if a large proportion of land presently in agriculture were to be permanently retained in that use. This is a very popular idea with a large number of citizens ... some are seriously concerned about the destruction of agriculture on prime land in California; there are others who are romantically attached to the beauty of open space as a visual amenity.
>
> There are also those opposed to growth of any kind, no matter what the economic realities. In Irvine ... many of the people drawn there to live are interested in a new community in the 'garden city' sense only.[12] They are anti-urban; they are not 'city builders.' This group is extremely hostile to any hint that the Irvine Company really has planned to build a complete new city, with urban as well as suburban parts. These people use the agricultural issue, in part, as a screen behind which this no-growth and no-city bias can be hidden.[13]

Cameron concluded that the Irvine Company was not threatened by the three-option general plan the city adopted, as its most

> ... important feature is the similarity ... for the development of the area presently within the city boundaries and programmed for development in the next five years by (the company) and other major landowners ... with the exception of one major area and a few much smaller, scattered pieces,

the phasing plans of the city and the company coincide to 1980. Beyond that date there is considerable disagreement.[14]

The company and the city would collaborate on four other major planning efforts after the adoption of the general plan: a zoning ordinance, a capital improvements plan, a transportation study, and an urban design implementation plan.

Cameron's description of the intensive interaction between Irvine citizens, staff, and company employees and consultants reflects the reality of those first years. Irvine was a small town, just 18,000 people, which meant that the core of citizens involved in civic matters was relatively modest. Moreover, while top Irvine Company executives lived in Newport Beach, some mid-level employees resided in Irvine; they intermingled with city elected officials and staff at PTA meetings, at church, or on the soccer field.

David Kuhn, who was a project manager at the company, lived in Turtle Rock, the hillside neighborhood above University Park. Several of his neighbors were appointees to the planning commission or other city commissions, so lobbying or information sessions could be conducted informally on a sidewalk or in the park.

Watson, who was overseeing most of the day-to-day interactions with the city on the planning and development front, viewed the evolving process through the lens of his populist upbringing and personal philosophy. Martin Brower, the company's director of public relations at that time, describes an incident that embodied the Watson outlook:

> Watson stood in the crowded multi-purpose room at University High School and applauded along with the citizens of Irvine. A citizen spokesman named Art Anthony had just completed an attack on the Irvine Company plan for a new project. 'You're not supposed to applaud,' Brower chided. 'Sure, I am (Watson replied), this is real democracy in action, with each of us respecting the other's view'.[15]

Watson's idealistic outlook would be tested two years after incorporation when the company moved forward with a plan for a new development in the center of the city.

The village of Valley View represented the company's first attempt to respond to an issue that had been simmering before and throughout the incorporation process: creating housing for a broad spectrum of the economic market, especially for people at the low end.

The company proposed a new community of 1,791 homes on 400 acres, enough housing for some 11,000 people. Prices would be designed to accommodate families making from $8,000 to $12,000 per year in three segments of housing: 375 apartments, 504 detached homes, and 912 townhouses.

The city planning commission, which included members who had been affiliated with Irvine Tomorrow during the incorporation campaign, signed off on the plan and sent it to the city council.

Martin Schiesl, writing in *Postsuburban California: The Transformation of Orange County Since World War II*, picks up the story: "Homeowners living near the proposed (village) were not happy with the commission's decision."[16]

Schiesl goes on to quote urban planners who advise that, "... in order for integration policies to be implemented successfully, resident support is vital ... it is important that residents are aware of the integration goals and, if possible, involved in the decisions regarding integration."[17]

According to Schiesl, neither of these procedures were followed by Irvine Company leaders and city planning officials and,

> ... as a result, planned development in this case was not the same thing to them as it was to the homeowners in the affected area. These residents and many other Irvine homeowners believed that one of the basic purposes of planning was to minimize the threat that unknown changes would present to their social status and monetary investment.[18]

The change most feared by the nearby homeowners was the construction of markedly less expensive housing nearby. Their concerns were voiced in several heated hearings held by the council on the proposed project. Some residents argued the densities were too high (the planning commission had reduced the proposed unit total from 1,791 to 1,358). Others charged that the project would adversely affect traffic and surrounding property values and incur huge costs for flood control.

Still others expressed opposition to class and racial integration. One resident worried that most of his new neighbors would be on food stamps. Another strongly objected to making room in the new city for minority groups, families on welfare rolls, and transient young adults. In the face of all this prejudice and protest, the council voted unanimously against the Valley View project.

The Valley View experience, followed by a council debate about accepting federal rent subsidy funding, were the prolog for a future series of debates that ultimately led to lawsuits and Irvine Company policy changes that would satisfy few urban planners and idealistic residents, but tamped down the issue as one that would define candidacies in the city.

The combination of the thousands of hours of citizen involvement in the general planning process, as well as the initial months of city planning commission and city council debate, was both exhausting and exhilarating. But it also built a foundation that—years later—would prove to be the most potent weapon the company could wield in anti-growth battles in the city; the almost unshakeable belief citizens held in the general plan and the promise of a planned community.

Notes

1. Raymond L. Watson, "Irvine's Road to Cityhood," in *Raymond L. Watson Papers* (MS.R.120) (Special Collections and Archives of the UC Irvine Libraries, 2006) 21.
2. Raymond L. Watson and Ann Lage. *Planning and Developing the New Town of Irvine California, 1960–2003: Irvine Company President, 1973–1977, Walt Disney Company Chairman, 1983–1984* (Regional Oral History Office, the Bancroft Library, University of California, Berkeley, 2005) 198.

3. Carol Flynn, telephone interview by C.M. Stockstill, April 3, 2021.
4. David Haldane and Jean O. Pasco, "John Schmitz; Former Right-Wing Congressman from Orange County," *Los Angeles Times*, January 11, 2001.
5. Author's recollection.
6. Author's recollection.
7. Author's recollection.
8. Author's recollection.
9. Gideon Golany, *Innovations for Future Cities* (Westport, CT: Praeger, 1976) 85.
10. Golany, *Innovations for Future Cities*, 91.
11. Golany, *Innovations for Future Cities*, 92.
12. Cameron was likely suggesting that those opposed to growth were misinterpreting Ebenezer Howard's concept of a "garden city."
13. Golany, *Innovations for Future Cities*, 92.
14. Golany, *Innovations for Future Cities*, 96.
15. Martin A. Brower, *The Irvine Ranch: A Time for People* (Bloomington, IN: Authorhouse, 1994) 41.
16. Rob Kling, Spencer Olin, and Mark Poster, eds., *Postsuburban California: The Transformation of Orange County Since World War II* (Berkeley, CA: University of California Press, 1991) 74.
17. Kling et al., *Postsuburban California*, 74.
18. Kling et al., *Postsuburban California*, 74.

13 The Magic of Planning

Planning had a magical aura in the early 1960s at the Irvine Ranch.

The dominant figure was William Pereira, architect and planner, creator of museums, airports, skyscrapers, and television studios.

Pereira had completed two defining planning assignments in Orange County; the master plans for UC Irvine, and for a new community conjoined to it on the empty slopes of a section of the Irvine Ranch.

Those two finished products were largely inspirational and conceptual. Translating them into the details of building neighborhoods of homes, schools, parks, and shopping centers would fall to a small cadre of people gathered in makeshift offices adjacent to the former home of the Irvine family.

Ray Watson, whose oral history and writings form the heart of this book, had much to say about planning in the years after he left the Irvine Company. In his written words, his thoughts were less than uniform. In his oral history, by its very nature, the subject of planning is interwoven with a variety of other recollections and anecdotes. Some of his most focused observations are drawn from his critiques of the works of others, usually academics, who were writing books or a thesis on the Irvine experience.

A recurring theme in Watson's memories was the extraordinary opportunity before him and his colleagues to transform 93,000 acres of fields, farms, and orchards into an urban environment. It was something that had never happened before, at least not in his experience.

Coupled with the challenge was the realization that the planners and engineers were faced with a blank canvas, and a very, very large one at that. Watson admits that, "… everybody was lost. I found that exhilarating, to be able to afford to spend the time to find out, what is a city?"

He continued:

> The reality was, there was little experience to call upon. We had to plan the city from scratch. We had to sort through all the theories and adopt the one we considered most appropriate. And we had to remember that we would be operating with the constraints of the economic system; we would be limited by what the prospective homeowner or new business wanted more than planning theories.

DOI: 10.1201/9781003226291-14

(This was) a limitation I welcomed because it was the ultimate test against which all city planning theories would be measured. We recognized while the ultimate reputation of the Irvine developments would be measured by the strength and sense of community they grew into, their crucial initial success depended on our ability to provide developments the public was willing to buy into.[1]

Planner Al Treviño arrived at the rural company offices the same day as Watson. Harvard trained, he would work on some of the company's signature residential and commercial developments over the next six years. He recalls his initial days there vividly: "It was chaos."[2]

Which is not to say that Watson, Treviño, and others were not prepared—they were. All were well educated and although relatively young, schooled in the philosophical tenants of city planning that Pereira had considered in completing his initial proposals.

Often cited was the English planner Ebenezer Howard, founder of the Garden City movement as an alternative to the grime, crime, and filth of the crowded streets of dense cities like London or Manchester. His idea was to build a new, self-contained community of 32,000 people on 9,000 acres of land. The design would incorporate houses, industry, and agriculture arrayed in a spiral, with large green spaces separating urban uses. An early community built to reflect this thinking was Letchworth, located outside London.

(While Watson mentions Howard in his oral history, according to Ted Dienstfrey, who worked closely with Watson from 1966 to 1970, using the Garden City model in Irvine was never seriously considered.)

Another academic who Watson cites as influencing his thinking on planning was Kevin Lynch, author of *The Image of the City*.[3]

Lynch proposed five key elements of what he labeled "humanistic design" in a city:

- Paths—the streets and sidewalks residents use every day
- Edges—linear elements not used or seen as such by the observer, such as walls, railroad tracks, or even large barriers like a river
- Districts—areas with architectural or design character that creates a separate visual identity. Lynch cited Beacon Hill in Boston as one example
- Nodes—strategic points identifiable to the area's residents, perhaps a street corner or busy intersection
- Landmarks—usually seen but not often entered, like mountains, domes, or large buildings.

Watson also mentions planner Deyan Sudjic's thoughts. His book *The 100 Mile City* reflected his view that the automobile had expanded the traditional definitions of an urban city, leading him to a conclusion that the home had become:

... the center of life ... from it the city radiates outward as a star shaped pattern of overlapping routes to and from the workplace, the shopping center and the school … each destination caters to a certain range of the needs of urban life, but they have no physical or spatial connection to each other in the way that we have been conditioned to expect of the city.[4]

Watson and his compatriots were also familiar with contemporary examples of new city development, such as Radburn, New Jersey, a small assemblage of homes and businesses that featured early use of greenbelts and cul de sac streets.

Preceding the planners on the mission were the engineers, responsible for out-lining and identifying the physical framework of improvements needed to serve whatever form of new community that was ultimately devised.

The engineers examined the two major natural drainages that crossed the ranch—San Diego Creek and Peters Canyon Channel—and saw the potential for flooding. It didn't rain much in this part of Southern California—about 12 to 14 inches a year—but on occasion, rain fell in abundance. A few miles west of the Irvine Ranch the Santa Ana River had inundated huge sectors of adjacent low-lying communities within living memory of many county residents. The US Army Corps of Engineers had stemmed that threat by building a large dam upstream of the flood zone, as well as lining channels with concrete.

But there were only three tiny dams in the Lomas de Santiago above the vast central plain where the new community would be built, and the San Diego Creek and Peters Canyon channels remained largely in their natural states. The engineers put flood control on the list.

The engineers looked at the Santa Ana Freeway, already in place, and the route for the San Diego Freeway, a line on a map, the two major northwest/south-east transportation corridors through the ranch. For east/west transportation, there wasn't much other than a couple of farm roads. The engineers put streets and highways on the list.

Water and sewer? None. Those went on the list. Power lines? Southern California Edison had a route in mind for the big 100KV lines and a substation or two, but nothing beyond. Telephone lines? The planners had already convinced company management to try an innovation—undergrounding all phone and electric utilities. Why not? It was a blank canvas, and unlike an existing city where undergrounding meant tearing up streets and sidewalks while obtaining permission from hundreds of property owners, here there was just one property owner. Bring in an army of backhoes and start trenching. Oh, and while we're at it, lay down miles of television cable lines, so there won't be a forest of TV anten-nas above the new homes and businesses.

The engineers prepared their maps and budgets. The outlines of the playing—or should we say, planning—field, were established. Turn the dreamers loose and let's see what they come up with.

Watson often said that he authored his presentations about planning a new community by describing not what was *going* to be built, but what was *not*.

He'd fill his slide carousel with images of existing Los Angeles and Orange County cities, describing oozing suburbia, cookie cutter homes with little or no architectural detail. Streets laid out in straight lines that vanished over the horizon, strewn with parked cars where there was a wild array of signs on buildings and little in the way of greenery, trees, or shrubs to soften the landscape. Watson thought it was a depressing sight.[5]

To counter it, the new vision of Irvine would be built, in Watson's view, on a series of principles. Each one would complement the other, directly or indirectly. They were:

1 The Irvine Company is a master developer that builds communities, not subdivisions, all in accordance with a master plan
2 Irvine Company properties will remain in single ownership
3 Irvine will be a city of villages. Each village will have an identity
4 The physical nature of the area will be reflected in the siting and development of villages
5 Innovative designs will be incorporated in communities.
6 The villages will have a range of housing types, at different prices, to encourage diversity
7 Architects will oversee the plans for homes in each village
8 Homeowner associations will be established in every village
9 Market forces and economics must be considered in the overall equation of creating a new city; the Irvine Company was a business that had to turn a profit
10 Continue the tradition of land stewardship by reinvestment that will contribute to the long-term quality of the communities the company builds.

As the planners pondered concepts like these, they often returned to what might seem an unlikely model for the vision of a new city. It was Balboa Island, on the eastern shore of Newport Bay, miles from the new university and the new city.

Created in the early 1900s by an accumulation of dredge spoils from the underwater excavations in Newport Bay, the 40-acre island was subdivided into a grid of streets and alleys; small lots designed for summer homes were sold off, many to people from Pasadena (from the 1950s to 1980s many engagement or wedding notices reported the bride's parents lived in Pasadena and Newport Beach).

Life on Balboa Island was largely defined by the seasons; winter was quiet, but during summer vacation months it was alive with crowds of families seeking cool breezes and a spot on the few sandy fringes of beach below the concrete retaining wall that surrounded the island. The Fun Zone was a short ferry ride away on the Balboa Peninsula. In the 1930s and 1940s, the Rendezvous Ballroom on the peninsula was a date night hotspot where famous Big Bands performed.

But it wasn't the lifestyle of Balboa Island that enchanted the planners, it was the nature of the place itself. Watson explains: "On Balboa Island you have apartments, houses, attached houses, a commercial area, recreational facilities. And because it is an island surrounded by water, one can visualize the distinct place it is."[6]

The island, Watson went on,

> ... was a local and very visual example to explain to the public what we were proposing. The term 'planning' has an aura about it—it's something you ought to do—but it is difficult to visualize what's going to come out of it. So, I would refer to Balboa Island or areas like Sausalito in the Bay Area, which is a distinctive place close to San Francisco.
>
> I also talked about the negatives of where I grew up in Oakland, which was indistinguishable from the adjacent towns of Berkeley or San Leandro or Hayward; you didn't know when you'd gone from one to the other. The vision I said we were seeking was that every place, every village we built, was to be as distinguishable as Balboa Island if we could.[7]

Creating this sense of place, Watson said, was a critical factor in making a village or a neighborhood into a community:

> I didn't want the neighborhoods to be just single-family subdivisions with shingled roofs all looking alike. So that our villages, like Balboa Island, would be places they would identify with, and that was the most important thing for them to identify with.
>   Villages
>   Community design
>   Sense of community.[8]

These themes formed the physical and philosophical definitions that transformed the Irvine Ranch. At the heart, was the village.

Watson called a village a development that was smaller than a city but larger than a neighborhood. Eventually there would be more than a dozen villages built on the Irvine Ranch. They varied in size, from modest ones like Deerfield, to the mega-village of Woodbridge.

And candidly, not all villages were created equal. National economic conditions, local political atmospherics, business needs, and ownership vision all played a role in the ultimate manifestation of the villages of Irvine, Tustin, and Newport Beach.

Critical to Watson and the planners, as evidenced by the reference to Balboa Island, was that the village had to be distinguishable, first physically. It had to be somewhere that created a place in the minds of the residents. Watson referenced Cambridge, where Harvard University is located, as another example. People, he said, would say they lived in Cambridge and in doing so had a mental picture of what was there that defined Cambridge.

Diversity of housing and architecture was another theme that, in Watson's mind, was embodied in a village. Single-family homes would be blended into neighborhoods with condominiums and apartments. A commercial center and school would be thoughtfully located, elements that created the whole. "All of this had to be worked out, which we (did) in detail ... we had different densities

... we had different setbacks. We could do all those kinds of things with the objective of creating this neighborhood."[9]

And it was precise:

> We didn't just want to have a little blob of green showing (on the plan). We wanted to know where the exact road was going to be, where the churches were going to be, where the high school was going to be.[10]

Another important aspect of village creation was the concept of a physical edge that defined its boundaries. As planners, Watson and his colleagues had read about the great walled cities of the world, where the barrier built to ward off attackers also set the limits of that city.

Elsewhere in Orange County that medieval concept not only lingered, but it was also embraced. To drive through sections of nearby Huntington Beach in the mid-1960s was to experience a streetscape of mile after mile of pink backyard fences made of concrete building blocks on either side of arterials like Gothard, Warner, or Ellis. The fences were bare of vegetation and most often bordered the street with a sidewalk.

In Irvine, where the Irvine Company was blessed with a canvas of more than 90,000 acres to draw upon, building a landscaped setback along major streets was a relatively modest tradeoff between land lost to development versus enacting the planner's vision of an edge for a village. So too could entry streets into a village be broadened and softened with trees, plants, and lawns.

There were walls in Irvine, but unlike those in other communities built mindlessly mile upon mile, the fencing in Irvine was designed and sculpted, amended at the base with carefully selected planting to reflect the architectural style of the village. In Woodbridge, river stone and timbers formed the monuments at the entrances to the village, a theme that recurred throughout the entire community. In Westpark, Spanish-style arches covered with bougainvillea and flecked with colorful tiles reinforced the Mediterranean feel the planners created.

There were edges of another sort in Irvine, long rows of towering eucalyptus trees planted around the turn of the century as windbreaks. When the hot Santa Ana wind swept across the open fields, the windrows, as they were known, slowed the winds to protect the thousands of delicate orange blossoms in JI's orchards.

The windrows sometimes gave the planners a natural edge to a village, at other times they were viewed as impediments. But the city leaders in Irvine had embraced the village concept, and had learned to appreciate the value of edges, setbacks, and landscaping. When the plan for the largely non-Irvine Company village of Northwood was presented to the council by its collection of landowners, most of the dozens of windrows in the village were shown as destined for the woodpile.

That was not to be, the city council ruled. The windrows were both an historical and design element the city wanted preserved. And most were—today Northwood's parks and walkways are largely built along the windrows.

Interwoven into the individual villages were design elements that created varying degrees of identity within the urban fabric. Over the years, there were likely dozens of innovations, but two are offered here as prime examples.

The initial Irvine Company villages of University Park in (what was to become) Irvine and Eastbluff in Newport Beach were defined in large part by greenbelts, wide swaths of grass, trees and plants that meandered through the neighborhoods.

Greenbelts were owned in common by the homeowner association in each neighborhood. The result was that for most homes, the private backyard was quite small, and the fencing at the edge was low, promoting a view onto the soft, undulating ribbons of greenery. And it stayed green year-round, thanks to recycled water piped into the neighborhoods as they were built.

A greenbelt could have a walking and biking path, or it might be an open vista, designed as much for tossing a football as for a visual break in an urban landscape. In Eastbluff, some greenbelts tumbled toward the edge of the community, affording a view of Upper Newport Bay. In University Park, residents could walk from one end of the neighborhood to the other almost entirely on a greenbelt. Mothers turned their children loose on a greenbelt and never worried about an errant ball finding its way onto a street. In the evening, the sun cast the verdant scene in dancing hues of green, then faded to nightfall, when lights sparkled from the homes on the borders.

Some homes in villages were separated using a zero-lot line. Instead of a traditional lot with a ten-foot strip of land forming a border on both sides, one side had no border—the side of the house was built directly upon the lot line. (Owners agreed upon purchase to allow their neighbors access for maintenance.) The result was a home that had a more usable yard.

As company planners began proposing unorthodox approaches like zero-lot lines and setbacks, they discovered that cities were not equipped to deal with them. Watson explains:

> Because of what we wanted to do—mixing densities of housing supported by schools, parks and shopping—the city's type of zoning didn't work. So, what emerged were called planned community planning ordinances, which required you to submit a much more detailed plan for the entire development before we could create a single piece. So, our first job was to write an enabling document which they accepted.[11]
>
> Such new regulations became known as Planned Unit Developments (PUDs).

****

Midway in his oral history, Watson was asked by his interviewer to "recreate some of the planning process." What follows, with minor edits, is his answer:

> By 1966 ... I became vice president of land development, which means I had all the real estate, engineering, and planning reporting to me. Dick Reese became vice president of planning.
>
> I created what I called in-house joint ventures, which included all the disciplines. So, for each village we formed a group of representatives

including commercial, real estate, engineering, financing, and planning. I would appoint one person to manage the whole process, which created a planning and development democracy to keep the process moving. That's where the ideas got thrown around. I would, in the early stages, sit in on those meetings—they became the fulcrum from which people started building ideas.[12]

To promote creativity and responsibility, Watson laid down:

> ... several rules. First, that everybody is equal—no one person or discipline has a monopoly on any part of the process—everyone is on equal footing. So, when we argue or discuss or challenge each other on ideas and check them out to see if they are feasible or not (we are equals).
>
> Finally, however, their question was: what about implementation? The representative of each discipline wanted to know if they could be overruled in the planning (of the project), how could I hold them responsible?
>
> (I told them) Out of these committees, (your discipline) will come up with a concept and design for (your proposal) and where it fits into the plan that the committee has decided upon. Then when you come to me (for approval) you have to demonstrate how it contributes to the community we want to create.[13]

If Watson found the proposed project compatible with the overall village plan,

> I will put my business hat on, and it has to show me that it is going to be profitable, if it fits our criteria of what returns we expect to get. It created an attitude that community building and business are not exclusive—we are a community development company. And we had to constantly remember that as we got larger. I said, it is easy for us to pull off into disciplines and start building apartments and shopping centers as fast as we can, and just have our own way about it. But that isn't the way we are going to do it here.[14]

Watson's explanation reflects three important elements. First, who he was.

Watson was in the best sense of the word, a democrat—he believed in people. Having grown up in a boardinghouse among decent, honest men and women who, in his words, were hard of luck, he had experienced their disappointment and suffering first hand. He saw them as equals, people whose economic fate didn't make them bad or whose opinions should be ignored.

His own success was in large part the result of native intelligence combined with labor—a lot of it. Thus, his willingness to structure a decision-making process where equality among business disciplines was encouraged.

Watson was also amiable and accessible. In interviews with individuals who worked with him at the time, every recollection of Watson the leader and manager was one of a man who was open, curious, fair, and encouraging. Watson promoted discourse and debate—he believed it stimulated creativity.

Second, Watson respected the bottom line. The Irvine Company was a business, and even though more than half its annual profits at the time were turned over to a foundation to be given away, projects had to generate revenues. Under William Mason and Watson, the company created five-year business plans with specific spending plans and profit goals.

Third, every action the company undertook was built on a foundation called community development. Projects, villages, commitments to major infrastructure, plans—all led to a goal of a new community built in a new way, where places were distinct in the eyes of their residents, as well as elements in a larger, comprehensive world of home, work, study, and play.

Richard Reese, who inherited the mantle of vice president of planning from Watson, gave a summation of the processes underway in the mid-1960s in a simple, yet compelling, description of what he and dozens of others experienced at the time: "Everything was sequential, we took it one step at a time. As time went on, everything became clearer and clearer. It was an incremental establishment of a tactical and strategic approach to planning the property."[15]

Notes

1. Raymond L. Watson, "Post University Agreement," in *Raymond L. Watson Papers* (MS-R120) (Special Collections and Archives of the UC Irvine Libraries, 1992–2005) 7.
2. Alvaro Treviño, interview by H.P. Oliver, July 20, 2020.
3. Kevin Lynch, *The Image of the City* (Cambridge, MA: MIT Press – Joint Center for Urban Studies, 1960).
4. Deyan Sudjic, *The 100 Mile City* (San Diego, CA: Harcourt, Brace, 1993) 337.
5. Raymond L. Watson, "Irvine's Road to Cityhood," in *Raymond L. Watson Papers* (MS.R.120) (Special Collections and Archives of the UC Irvine Libraries, 2006) 108.
6. Raymond L. Watson and Ann Lage, *Planning and Developing the New Town of Irvine California, 1960–2003: Irvine Company President, 1973–1977, Walt Disney Company Chairman, 1983–1984* (Regional Oral History Office, the Bancroft Library, University of California, Berkeley, 2005) 228.
7. Watson and Lage, *Planning and Developing*, 238.
8. Watson and Lage, *Planning and Developing*, 228–229.
9. Watson and Lage, *Planning and Developing*, 121.
10. Watson and Lage, *Planning and Developing*, 121.
11. Watson and Lage, *Planning and Developing*, 118
12. Watson and Lage, *Planning and Developing*, 275.
13. Watson and Lage, *Planning and Developing*, 276.
14. Watson and Lage, *Planning and Developing*, 276.
15. Richard Reese, telephone interview by H.P. Oliver and C.M. Stockstill, August 26, 2020.

14 From Plans to Reality

Eastbluff and Newport Center

Three years after the planners immersed themselves in theory, the first major village the Irvine Company would develop began to take shape in Newport Beach, followed closely by a large commercial and retail center.

The name of the residential village reflected the location: Eastbluff.

Situated along a shelf of land bordering the Upper Newport Bay, Eastbluff was a rough square of property about 300 acres. It was relatively flat, so much so it had been used by early aviators in the area, later given the formal name Palisades Navy Landing Field.

Substantial development in the remainder of Newport Beach had taken place sporadically since the turn of the century, when the city began to evolve from a small coastal village into a mix of beach bungalows and typical suburban tracts.

In 1904, James Irvine II sold a parcel of his land adjacent to Newport Beach to land developer George Hart. The 700 acres went for $150 an acre and was branded by Hart as Corona del Mar, Spanish for "Crown of the Sea." The land overlooked the Pacific Ocean at the southern boundary of the community but had little to no access to water. No water meant no crops, so JI disposed of it, likely to raise funds for improvements to the ranch further inland.

Hart divided the land into 2,300 small lots and offered them for sale at $750 with a view, $100 without. Sales were slow, then slower, forcing Hart to return 305 acres to the Irvine Company. In 1916, he traded what was left for 5,000 acres in Riverside County. Construction of Pacific Coast Highway through the community in 1926 helped sales, but it wasn't until the late 1940s that the community began to fill in significantly and was subsequently annexed by the city.

At the edge of the sea on Balboa Peninsula, a small colony of homes had been built, one by one, starting in the years prior to World War I. By the 1930s there were more, including a mansion for safety razor mogul King Gillette, and smaller but elegant homes designed by famous architects like Paul Revere Williams. Early photos of Newport Bay also show that by the 1930s, Balboa Island was quite dense.

On the flatlands on the northern side of Upper Newport Bay, the Irvine Company had been selling off land incrementally to individual builders and developers, where the communities of Westcliff and Dover Shores were built.

DOI: 10.1201/9781003226291-15

Eastbluff, however, would be unique, the first master planned community designed and executed to reflect the company's commitment to villages as defined by its planners, led by Ray Watson.

Eastbluff is a single village divided in two sections by the type of homes built there. The dividing edge for the sections was, and is, Alta Vista Drive. The homes above Alta Vista, nearest Jamboree Road, were laid out in a typical tract array; a series of long, straight streets where the houses faced each other. The homes there were typical single story, ranch style, but on a smaller lot that might be found further inland.

The original layout for Eastbluff, according to company planner Al Treviño, placed the single-family homes in the lower two-thirds of the site, with the attached homes at the top—a concept championed by Jack Bevash, an employee of William Pereira. Treviño, tasked with developing a grading plan for the entire community, flipped the Bevash vision in part so he could use grading to break up compacted soil in the area.

Below Alta Vista, the remainder of the village was given the name of The Bluffs, where the planners made a radical bet, using a concept from Radburn, New Jersey: greenbelts.

In his oral history, Watson explained:

> The design of Radburn has a park/greenbelt with the houses facing onto it. And on the back side of the house, where the garage is, there is a public street. What we did in Eastbluff is the reverse of that—we put the front door on the street and the back door on the park. What we learned from Radburn is ... when you have guests or anybody else driving home or visiting, they entered through the backdoor.[1]

It was not just the layout of The Bluffs that made it unique, it was the type of housing—condominiums—which as Watson said, "... was a relatively new phenomena at the time." And, he noted, "... it was a real market risk in 1964."

The Eastbluff design decision reflected the desire of Watson and the other planners to create a community that was diverse and multi-generational:

> We had a vision that we wanted our villages to have a diversification of housing types. The Bluffs would be smaller units, probably for those who no longer had children, although a family could still buy the units. Therefore, we'd build townhouses and have a greenbelt with it. On the hill (above Alta Vista), there would be traditional single-family houses, but they would be in the same village.
>
> The idea was that when we are all together at the shopping center, and our kids are in the same school, (we would) recognize that those who live in the townhouses probably were older or younger, but they were still part of the same community. So, the cross-section of family life from early marriage to senior citizen status could remain in the same community, shop at the same stores, kids go to the same schools. That was the image we had of what a diversified village should be.[2]

Having created a non-traditional community, the company now had to find homebuilders and buyers. To lessen the risk, "... we made the terms under which the builders

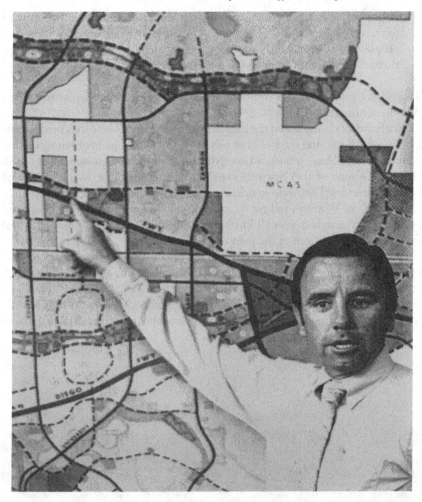

Figure 14.1 Ray Watson discusses plans for future development in 1973, the year he became president of the Irvine Company.

started very advantageous for them to do it." The company also made the watershed decision to build the units on leased lots. Paying an annual lease payment made the home more affordable but violated the almost Biblical norm that homeownership in Southern California meant just that—owning the land and the dwelling on it.

The Irvine Company promoted the new development by accentuating the positives: a scenic and temperate location adjacent to the Upper Newport Bay (many of the condos in The Bluffs enjoyed a view of the bay), and the cutting-edge community design concept of homes nestled along greenbelts. Watson recalled that:

> … our ads said, 'come visit a new community on a greenbelt.' We never mentioned it was leasehold, because we knew that fifty percent of potential

buyers would not even come and look at the project because they wanted to own their own land ... We were fortunate—we had a great location that people wanted to come to, and the price was right. The job was not to scare them off before they came to see it for themselves.[3]

The buyers came, and the resistance to leasing proved to be a weak barrier. Watson continued:

"With the lots being leased the overall price seemed less when compared to buying both the house and the lot. That was successful. If that hadn't been successful, it probably would have influenced everything from then on. Remember," he added, "Eastbluff is (one of the) first projects that did influence (the Irvine Company) board of directors. They were wondering, well, we'll give these guys a chance."

Eastbluff, in Watson's telling, "... turned out to be an incredibly successful project ... ultimately it won all kinds of architectural and planning awards and exceeded our projections of the sales rate and prices."[4]

A visit to Eastbluff today confirms the wisdom of the concept and its execution. At the far southwestern corner of the village, an elementary and high school share acreage adjacent to a large church and shopping center. The landscaping has grown and matured in both neighborhoods above and below Alta Vista. Stately sycamores spread out along the greenbelts, and the attached homes

Figure 14.2 Eastbluff under development in the mid-1960s.

(Alvaro Treviño)

are full of families. Nearly all the original homes above Alta Vista have been remodeled and expanded, although a few of the original homes have the same curbside look from 1964.

Ray and Elsa Watson were among the first homeowners in Eastbluff. They remained there the rest of their lives.

****

The large plateau that would become the site of Newport Center and Fashion Island sat roughly equidistant between the Upper Newport Bay to the north and the San Joaquin Hills to the south in Newport Beach.

Until the late 1950s, the land was the exclusive domain of cattle raised by the Irvine Company. The sole exception of human habitation was temporary, but memorable: in July 1953, the Boy Scouts of America held their annual jamboree on the site. Irvine Company vice president William Spurgeon was a Scouting advocate, as was ranch general manager Brad Hellis. They lobbied for the event, winning the support of company president Myford Irvine.

More than 50,000 Scouts and Scouters descended on Orange County, most arriving by rail, to attend the first (and last) national jamboree ever held on the west coast. The late Orange County historian Phil Brigandi described some of the highlights:

> The Jamboree campsite was nothing less than a temporary city ... there were commissaries, trading posts, a hospital and fire crews, and about 30,000 tents.
>
> At the opening ceremony ... after the American flag was raised, the flags of 54 nations around the world that had Scouting organizations were raised together. Comedian Bob Hope would later dub the Jamboree 'the United Nations in short pants.'
>
> Entertainment started with a grand pageant, 'The Building of the Nation', (tracing) the history of the country through various eras and areas ... each scene was played out on a grand scale, with covered wagons, mock Indian battles and two genuine steam locomotives on specially laid rails.
>
> (The next night's) show was Hollywood's Salute to Scouting, with a parade of stars, (including) Danny Kaye, Debbie Reynolds, Jane Powell, Lash La Rue, June Allyson, Rory Calhoun, Dick Powell, and Will Rogers Jr.[5]

There was also a rodeo featuring roping star Monty Montana, songs from Roy Rogers, and visits to nearby Huntington Beach for swimming. President Eisenhower sent a filmed message and California Lt. Governor Goodwin Knight and Vice President Richard Nixon visited in person. Myford Irvine welcomed the Scouts, calling the event the greatest moment of his life. Even a very pregnant Joan Irvine made it to the opening ceremonies on July 17; she gave birth to her first son two weeks later.

Nat Read came to the jamboree from Dallas, Texas. "When the train arrived at Union Station in Los Angeles, the passenger tunnel was crammed with Scouts singing 'The Eyes of Texas' at the top of their lungs." Read remembers the jamboree site

> ... stretched over a massive area, the unpaved roads full of Scouts walking to the various facilities. We were constantly being loaded onto buses to sites such as the La Brea Tar Pits, Knott's Berry Farm and Catalina. We were constantly being offered free oranges from an industry that wanted us to keep the habit once we returned home.[6]

The jamboree lasted one week; cleanup took another four days. Today there are two reminders of what happened there—a small plaque at the Fashion Island, and a wide, modern highway, the successor to the trail that was first scraped out of the dirt to provide access to the site: Jamboree Road.

For the next ten years, the large, square plateau remained undisturbed as scattered pieces of residential and commercial development began to crop up within sight of it.

It would become Newport Center, with the shopping center Fashion Island in the middle of it, defined by Pacific Coast Highway at the western foot of the

Figure 14.3 Entrance to the Boy Scouts of America Jamboree at the future site of Newport Center in 1953.

(Orange County Archives)

property, Jamboree Road to the north, MacArthur Boulevard to the south, and a natural, twisted runoff channel called Big Canyon to the east.

The concept for a regional shopping center at the corner of MacArthur Blvd. and Pacific Coast Highway was being discussed when Ray Watson arrived at the Irvine Company in 1960.

The original thinking included single-family homes behind the center, but that image was scrapped, Watson recalled, and evolved, "… the area becoming a regional shopping, business, hotel and civic center …"

> I wanted it to be the center of many regional and local uses within visually defined edges. Using the major roads as edges we put Fashion Island right in the middle, and we put a road around it we called Newport Center Drive. The process of siting the various uses took considerable time, but the vision of identify and diversity bound together in a strongly identifiable place was the model that has become identified with what the company does.[7]

Watson's oral history recounts working on the overall Newport Center concept plan for two years, using clay models. Watson is credited by several sources for the design of Fashion Island's interior, where the stores are a series of staggered buildings offset from one another.

Building Newport Center as a giant circle, with Fashion Island "floating" in the middle—hence the name—is credited by Al Treviño to Al Auer, the company executive in charge of retail.[8]

Figure 14.4 First Newport Center office building and Fashion Island retail mall just prior to opening in 1967.

(Orange County Archives)

(Probably because of the famous circular plan for UC Irvine, and the fact that his firm designed the initial office buildings at Newport Center, William Pereira is sometimes—erroneously—given credit for the Newport Center layout.)

Treviño also identified Auer, along with marketing consultant John Parker, as responsible for making Fashion Island an outdoor mall rather than a traditional enclosed one.

Treviño recalled being asked by company president Charles Thomas to join him and Auer on a tour of southern Orange County with some New York City financiers. As the tour concluded, Thomas swung by the Newport Center site and enthused about the planned retail center there. Auer, Treviño recalled, remarked that, "I don't think an enclosed mall is the right approach for Orange County." Flustered, Thomas, "... stepped on the gas and when he got back to the office said that Auer had queered the deal with the New York people."[9]

Parker had returned from a trip to Chicago about the same time, where he had visited a new outdoor mall near Northwestern University. It would be perfect for Newport Beach, he said, easier to lease and with much lower operating and maintenance costs. Parker's views prevailed and the retail center was constructed in the open air.

But the plateau presented another challenge: it was not level.

The Los Angeles architectural firm of Welton Becket was hired to create the land plan for the center and the retail mall, but there were complications; each of the major department stores had their own architects designing their buildings—coordination was a challenge. William Watt, who had recently joined the company, was assigned by Watson to coordinate the overall project.

Watt recalled that Al Auer once again came up with a creative approach to allow construction of the retail center on a single level behind a massive retaining wall at the western boundary of the center. Shoppers entering Fashion Island there would park below it and ascend more than 50 feet onto the upper level on an escalator. Shoppers entering from the opposite side would find the stores at the same level as the parking spots. (Robinsons added a door at its basement level so customers could do their bargain shopping there and then ascend to the main floors on *their* escalator.)

Treviño was given the tricky task of creating a grading plan to contour not only the Fashion Island site, but also the pads for offices surrounding it and Newport Center Drive.

Treviño's credibility had been called into question before the grading assignment. He had proposed a series of bridges from the retail area over Newport Center Drive to the offices. The Welton Becket architects vetoed the idea, concerned that they would block signage on the department stores.

Treviño mapped out the grading approach, but Frank Hughes, in charge of engineering for the company, didn't think it would work. After further refinement, it turned out that Treviño's calculations for moving millions of cubic yards of earth came within 100,000 yards of his estimate. Interviewed 53 years later, Treviño was modest: "I got lucky," he said.[10]

While a medical office building had already been built at Newport Center in July 1967, Irvine Company executives chose the 21st of that month to celebrate the groundbreaking of the new office complex, positioning it as, "... a new era in Orange County financial and professional circles." [11]

The company selected an historical theme for the event, according to the description in *Orange County Business*:

> An oxcart, preceded by Spanish Dons riding spirited horses, provided a dramatic opening for the ceremonies.... With beautifully costumed senoritas standing by ground was not only broken, but a replica of an old Spanish sea chest containing significant documents, photos, and resolutions ... was lowered and buried in a time capsule vault.[12]

More than 300 business leaders and public officials attended the ceremonies, which focused on the first of two nine-story office buildings that would be built with an aim to serve the financial industry. The company promised that Newport Center would be the largest center of its kind catering to financial interests without a stock exchange as its nucleus.

Just two months later, it was Fashion Island celebrating its grand opening with style, flair, and extravagance, inviting 15,000 people to a giant reception on the evening of September 9, 1967.

The weekly *Newport Ensign* called it the biggest social event in Newport Beach history, an assessment agreed to by the *Daily Pilot*'s coverage of the event.

The theme was "Flight to Fashion Island," reflected by the presence of 15 Air California stewardesses on hand to help pass out food and drink. The visitors strolled by some of the 52 shops scattered through the outdoor mall, which was anchored by major department stores including Buffum's, JC Penney, and the Broadway. (The event benefited the Assistance League of Santa Ana which had an odd connection to the company; JI had bequeathed a single share of company stock to the league in his will, presumably a nod to his second wife, Katherine, who was active in the group.)

The evening's entertainment included the Stan Kenton Orchestra, Les Brown and His Band of Renown, the Mariachi Brass, and the Ink Spots. Kenton and Brown would become regulars in the future at the free summer concerts at the center. The following morning, California Lt. Governor Robert Finch presided at the dedication, then stepped aside to let eager shoppers into the stores.

Fashion Island and Newport Center were multimillion dollar investments for the Irvine Company and were undertaken after the company's owners and executives made the fundamental decision that the properties would be owned and operated as company assets. Watson explained the dynamics of how the conclusion was reached three years earlier when planning began for the first shopping center the company developed: Westcliff Plaza, a ten-acre property on the border of Newport Beach and Costa Mesa:

> At first, we weren't going to own it because we hadn't built anything, the company didn't own any commercial real estate. We started talking to different developers about them leasing land and building and owning the center.

As we went through the process, commercial real estate broker John Parker ... convinced us we ought to own it.

First, we did an economic pro forma to see whether it would be an acceptable return for the risk.... that set the stage for saying, as we build a company, the negative to ... just selling or leasing land is, you don't own anything at the end, you're just doing a liquidation of your property over the years.[13]

The Westcliff decision underscored the momentum for what would follow at Newport Center. And while the initial office building there was constructed and owned by another developer, everything that would follow would become part of the company's portfolio, starting with a nine-story building at 550 Newport Center Drive that would become the company's headquarters.

In his oral history, Watson painted a confident portrait of the office development that followed in Newport Center, where a second nine-story building adjacent to 500 was built when 550 was fully leased. But Al Treviño remembers the situation with a twist; the nine-story buildings were originally planned to be four stories higher. Watson, he said, wasn't sure they could be fully leased, so the size was reduced. (Ten years later, some of the new managers of the company scoffed at the low rents paid by a law firm leasing the top two floors of 550 Newport Center. Veteran company executives who remembered the relatively limited market for such office space in Newport Beach in 1968 tried to put the lease rates in context, with little success.)

Notes

1. Raymond L. Watson and Ann Lage, *Planning and Developing the New Town of Irvine California, 1960–2003: Irvine Company President, 1973–1977, Walt Disney Company Chairman, 1983–1984* (Regional Oral History Office, the Bancroft Library, University of California, Berkeley, 2005) 239.
2. Watson and Lage, *Planning and Developing*, 241.
3. Watson and Lage, *Planning and Developing*, 242.
4. Watson and Lage, *Planning and Developing*, 242.
5. Phil Brigandi, "1953 Boy Scout Jamboree," OC Historyland, accessed August 10, 2020. www.ochistoryland.com/jamboree.
6. Nat Read, telephone interview by C.M. Stockstill, March 15, 2021.
7. Watson and Lage, *Planning and Developing*, 229.
8. Alvaro Treviño, interview by H. Pike Oliver, July 20, 2020.
9. Treviño, interview, July 20, 2020.
10. Treviño, interview July 20, 2020.
11. Orange County Business Magazine (July 1976), 1.
12. Orange County Business Magazine (July 1976), 1.
13. Watson and Lage. *Planning and Developing*, 232.

15 The Tax Reform Act of 1969

The Tax Reform Act of 1969 was like a mighty legislative freight train, driven by the Democratic congressional leadership in the engine, carrying a long line of boxcars, tenders, and flatcars loaded up with every imaginable tax code amendment, revision, redefinition, exemption, and realignment.

Joan Irvine Smith wanted desperately to climb aboard that train and ensure the adoption of a single element—limiting foundation ownership of private companies. Doing so would diminish the power of her hated adversary, the James Irvine Foundation. If she succeeded, it would clear a path to her control of the Irvine Company.

Federal examination of private foundations had been brewing since the 1950s. House and Senate staff, as well as Treasury Department officials, developed several reports and analyses questioning the tax status of both non-profit entities and foundations.

By the mid-1960s, interest in the power and influence of these institutions, which in some cases held hundreds of millions of dollars in assets, was increasing. What also drew congressional attention was the fact that some foundations held controlling interests in multiple private companies.

How foundation money was disbursed also generated scrutiny from both political parties. Republicans and conservatives noted that the Ford Foundation, whose president McGeorge Bundy was a prominent New Frontiersman with President John F. Kennedy, had funneled grants to individuals linked to the campaign of Robert F. Kennedy. Other grants to the Congress of Racial Equality (CORE) supposedly for community organizing seemed to some more likely to result in voter registration funding. Even a long New York City teachers' strike was blamed in part on a Ford Foundation grant for experimental schools in the city.

Wright Patman, a Democrat from Texas, was chairman of the House Financial Services Committee, where he convened hearings to examine foundation taxation and power issues. First elected in 1928, Patman had a reputation as a populist who championed small business interests.

And Patman minced no words regarding his opinion on how private foundations had lost their way. Testifying to his colleagues at the Ways and Means Committee hearings in 1969, he laid out his views in stark terms:

DOI: 10.1201/9781003226291-16

Philanthropy, one of mankind's more noble instincts, has been perverted into a vehicle for institutional and deliberate evasion of fiscal and moral responsibility to the nation ... the use of the tax-free status ... reveals the continuing devotion of some of our millionaires to greed, rather than conversion to graciousness.[1]

That an old New Dealer like Patman would form an alliance with an Adolfo-clad heiress residing in the heart of the Virginia's snooty horse country is just one of the oddities in the panorama of lawyers, accountants, trust funders, and tax reformers who convened in Washington, D.C. for the contentious process that would redefine the influence of foundations on the nation's commonweal.

As the battle lines had formed, Joan and her advisors focused on a key provision of the legislation being formulated by Treasury and congressional staff: prohibiting any charitable foundation from owning more than 20 per cent of a single business entity. The Irvine Foundation controlled the Irvine Company with its bare majority of total company stock; reduce it, and the 20 per cent controlled by Joan and her mother alone might be enough—if the shares went public—to cobble together a majority stake and control. Other Irvine family members owned the remaining 27 per cent. If Joan could bring them along, taking control would be that much easier.

Joan framed the argument in good government terms in her testimony to the House Ways and Means Committee in 1969. She pointed out that if the Irvine Foundation would have to sell 282 shares to meet the 20 per cent level, and at $1 million a share, it would realize $282 million. Selling those shares to the public would mean hundreds of new owners receiving dividends and paying taxes on them, while with "proper development" of the ranch, its value would rise to $2 billion, generating even more income tax for the government.

Her testimony omitted any speculation about who might ultimately end up controlling the Irvine Company.

In her autobiography, Joan devotes a single paragraph to the issue, noting with pride that she spent six years lobbying for the issue in Washington, D.C. Testimony and documents from congressional hearings tell a far more extensive story of all that transpired.[2]

****

Joining the battle for the Tax Reform Act of 1969 was the culmination of a 12-year campaign Joan began upon joining the board of directors of the Irvine Company, replacing her mother at the table with seven men old enough to be her father or grandfather.

Her principal adversary was N. Loyall McLaren, who years before had been fondly known to her as "Uncle Blackie"—a trusted advisor to her grandfather who had also counseled her mother on financial matters. In her testimony to the US Congress before the House Ways and Means Committee on February 21, 1969, Joan presented a long litany of her conflicts with the foundation, first focusing on McLaren, who had been her grandfather's accountant. In Joan's view he had, "... inveigled himself into the confidence of my grandfather to the extent ..." that JI created the foundation that would, upon his death, hold a majority share in the Irvine Company.[3]

Joan had started fighting soon after the first board meeting she attended, exposing what she described as self-dealing on a land transaction between the Irvine Company and its general manager, Brad Hellis. (Joan also made a thinly veiled accusation that Hellis had been responsible for the death of JI in Montana.) After making the charges she followed up with a lawsuit against the company and foundation, the first of many that would follow. Hellis decided to resign and retired from the job he had held for decades.

Joan went on to describe—in words some of the committee members must have found either shocking or amusing coming from this elegant and attractive Virginia horsewoman—a conversation with McLaren involving the foundation's plans to have the company form a partnership with a New York developer named Roger Stevens. Joan and McLaren squared off on the subject at an Irvine Company board meeting, with Joan complaining that the structure of the proposed deal would not benefit her and other family stockholders because they would receive no gains. McLaren countered that the Montana ranch and Imperial Valley holdings could be sold. No way, Joan retorted, their value hasn't gone up much, the real money would come from Orange County land. "Well, that's where we've got the stockholders where the hair is short," Joan quoted McLaren as saying, ". . . you are not going to get any capital gains here."[4]

Furious, Joan turned her lawyers loose and found a loophole in the company's incorporation documents, discovering that as the Irvine Company was a West Virginia corporation, her and her mother's 20 per cent stock holdings were enough to block the transaction. McLaren and the foundation retreated.

And so, the conflicts continued, the foundation with absolute control of the Irvine Company, Joan with millions of dollars to retain a small army of lawyers and public relations advisors.

Threatening litigation became Joan's principal weapon against the foundation and the company. Sometimes the mere threat of months of lengthy (and expensive) legal wrangling was enough to convince both that whatever Joan objected to wasn't worth the time or energy. But when Joan tried to strike at the heart of the legal integrity of the foundation, it fought back. Such was the circumstance in the action she took in August 1966 in federal court.

Her lawsuit challenged the very underpinnings of the James Irvine Foundation, listing five different arguments why the legal documents that established it were, in her view, invalid. The accusations ranged from complex legal minutia to the practical—that the stock certificates of the Irvine Company were never physically transferred to the foundation until after JI's death.

By the time the case reached the court of appeals (Joan lost at trial), more than 17 attorneys were representing plaintiffs and defendants. The record of the appellate court proceedings, according to later testimony by foundation attorney Howard Privett, ran to 4,000 pages and 297 documents. Privett noted, likely with a small smile, that the ruling against Joan by the court of appeals was 56 pages long. With her legal options shrinking, it was another motivation for Joan to look to Congress for relief.

In the 1960s, there were few records kept on campaign contributions or lobbying activity, so it is difficult to estimate with any accuracy just what Joan Irvine Smith's self-described "six years of lobbying" in the nation's capital consisted of. She certainly had the advantage in access: Middleburg Virginia, where she lived, was no more than a two-hour drive from Washington D.C. If principals from either the foundation or the company wanted to lobby members of Congress in person, it was an all-day flight from the west coast.

The foundation did hire the D.C. law firm of Covington and Burling in 1965, but were their pinstriped attorneys a match for a glamourous, blond Joan Irvine Smith? Joan had demonstrated in her public relations advocacy in California that she knew how to court the press and influence leaders. And in his oral history, Loyall McLaren said that Joan,

> ... spent a great deal of money entertaining, lobbying and so on, and some-how or another ... she got very close to Patman. Then the minute she gets close to (him), Patman really starts after the James Irvine Foundation, and it only ends with his death.[5]

Whether it was her personal advocacy or energetic policy direction, or both, Patman's Select Committee on Small Business did indeed place the James Irvine Foundation at the top of its list to investigate regarding potential changes to tax law for it and similar institutions. The opening paragraphs of the committee's report on its investigation were blunt:

> In short, our investigation focus, in part upon the legal proprietorship of one of the most important realty kingdoms in the country ... taxpayer associations say the Irvine Company is under assessed ... small businessmen complain they are unable to do business with the Irvine Company because they are not part of the 'inner circle'.[6]

Its mission clear, the committee staff and members executed a deep and probing dissection of the James Irvine Foundation and the Irvine Company's policies, personnel, and records.

Irvine Company and James Irvine Foundation tax returns, balance sheets, and meeting minutes from decades in the past were demanded. Compensation records and even specifics of health benefit plans were deemed relevant to the investigation. (Details of the Irvine Company health plan showed line-item maximum payments for everything from appendectomy [$150] to cataracts [$225]. Not covered: pregnancy.)

Dozens of individuals in both organizations were required to fill out lengthy questionnaires asking about any loans from, or deals with, the company or foundation. Not only were employees and trustees queried, but the committee demanded to know if spouses or children were involved.

Joan cheered on the process with her formal testimony, echoing themes she no doubt expressed in private meetings with members and staff, excoriating McLaren and the other foundation trustees as double dealing, hostile curmudgeons. Similarly, she complained of the "niggardly" rate of return—and thus dividends—paid by the company to stockholders like her and her mother.[7]

So deep was the research into the foundation and company, it reached all the way back to 1931 and the prenuptial contract between JI and his second wife, Katherine Brown White. The staff and members of Congress learned that in return for eschewing any claim to the Irvine Company or any other landholdings of JI's, the soon-to-be new Mrs. Irvine would receive $1,500 a month for clothes, spending money, as well as the assurance of a house to live in, staffed with servants. JI further agreed to set up a trust for her that would provide an income should he die before her.

Also included in the committee reports were copies of JI's will, probate reports, inheritance tax records, and even the receipt for his funeral expenses. (Oddly, for a man whose entire adult life was dedicated to the Orange County ranch property, he was buried in the huge Cypress Lawn Cemetery in Colma, south of San Francisco. But JI was notoriously thrifty, and the family plot had already been purchased.)

Records of the Ways and Means Committee hearings show that hundreds of people representing foundations large and small gave testimony or submitted written commentary on the issue. From the mammoths of American charity, with names like Kellogg, Rockefeller, Ford, and Mott, to tiny institutions established in rural communities, often by a single benefactor, thousands of pages of deliberations remain in the files of Congress.

The focus on foundations was best summed up by Wilber Mills, chairman of the Ways and Means committee. Speaking specifically about the James Irvine Foundation during testimony by foundation officials, Mills questioned if a foundation should be allowed to control a business like the Irvine Company. He also wondered whether it was in the public interest for such a circumstance to continue, either in Orange County or anywhere else in the nation.

The mighty freight train reached its destination, signed into law by President Richard Nixon on December 30, 1969. It made several sweeping changes to the tax code, including creation of the Alternative Minimum Tax (AMT).

But there was no concern about the AMT at the James Irvine Foundation. Along with hundreds of other charitable institutions, it had ten years to divest itself of the majority shares of companies it owned.

But the James Irvine Foundation would not go quietly. Like Joan, the foundation had its own intelligent, creative, and dedicated attorneys and advisors, and the foundation trustees were prepared to use them.

Notes

1. U.S. Congress, House, Committee on Ways and Means, *Subject of Tax Reform: Hearings before the Committee on Ways and Means*, 91st Congress, 1st sess., February 21, 1969, 4673.

2. Joan Irvine Smith, *A California Woman's Story* (Irvine, CA: The Irvine Museum, 2006).
3. U.S. Congress, House, Committee on Ways and Means, *Subject of Tax Reform*, 473–504.
4. U.S. Congress, House, Committee on Ways and Means, *Subject of Tax Reform: Hearings before the Committee on Ways and Means*, 91st Cong., 1st sess., February 21, 1969, 483.
5. Gabrielle Morris and Ruth Teiser, *Business and Club Life [of N. Loyall McLaren] in San Francisco: Recollections of a California Pioneer Scion* (Berkeley, CA: Regional Oral History Office, the Bancroft Library, University of California, 1969) 138. https://digitalassets.lib.berkeley.edu/roho/ucb/text/mclaren_norman_loyall.pdf
6. U.S. Congress, House, Select Committee on Small Business, Subcommittee Chairman's Report to Subcommittee No. 1. "Letter of Transmittal," *Tax-Exempt Foundations and Charitable Trusts: Their Impact on Our Economy*, 90th Cong., 1st sess., April 28, 1967, iii. www.tinyurl.com/2p89878n
7. U.S. Congress, House, Committee on Ways and Means, *Subject of Tax Reform*, 487.

16 Acceleration

During the decade between 1961 and 1971, the Irvine Ranch passed a series of milestones as it transformed from a giant agricultural empire to a community developer. Among them:

- The gift of nearly 1,000 acres of land for the University of California Irvine
- William Pereira's creation of the master plans for UC Irvine and the Irvine Ranch
- Establishment of the Irvine Ranch Water District
- Two transitions of company executive management
- Passage of the Tax Reform Act of 1969, which set the stage for the sale of the Irvine Company
- Incorporation of the City of Irvine.

During this time there was also a tremendous surge of activity underway, on the ground, if you will. It was an acceleration that turned ideas into reality with impressive speed and execution. Planning would continue to rank at the top of the business hierarchy of the company, but it would soon be equaled by actions of builders, financers, and managers.

The following is an examination of the highlights, beginning with a reminder that as urban development was getting underway, agricultural operations remained a critical source of income and profits.

****

Miles from Newport Center, Eastbluff, and the emerging campus at UC Irvine, rhythms of labor on large parts of the Irvine Ranch remained unchanged.

A person walking into orange groves in the Spring could melt into blissful intoxication from the fragrance of hundreds of thousands of blossoms. Or riding a horse into the foothills, hearing not a car, or an airplane, only the wind and the low moaning of a newborn calf. Or standing in the middle of a field, surrounded by endless rows of tiny green sprouts that in a few weeks would bear the sweet, red fruit of the strawberry.

DOI: 10.1201/9781003226291-17

Agriculture dominated the ranch's business from the day Ray Watson arrived, transformed, and consolidated during his time as Irvine Company president, then slowly diminished as the new century approached. (In 2022, the authors estimate that around 1,500 acres of avocado groves and 30 to 40 acres of strawberry fields remain as the only legacies of the once dominant farming empire created by James Irvine II.)

Urbanization in this period was taking place on a piecemeal basis, leaving vast tracts of the company's acreage in crop production or grazing.

The citrus orchards clung to the gentle foothills of the Lomas de Santiago, then spread into the flat acreage below, past Irvine Blvd. and down to Interstate 5. Most of the citrus crop was Valencia oranges, with a smattering of lemons and grapefruit.

In his oral history, Watson noted that the company was one of the first large citrus growers in the state to experiment with drip irrigation: "... (we were) so early that the plastic pipe that we used had not been perfected and was eaten up by the rodents."[1]

On the flatlands, corn, peppers, and tomatoes were still growing in 1967 when a new vice president for agriculture instituted a radical change in crop production.

Watson described Bill Williams as a big man with a big voice, a lot like the company president at the time, William Mason. Williams' strength was marketing, "... he understood how to make deals for the crops, where to sell them, who to go through, what market to go through."[2]

Williams advocated a shift to high-risk, high-profit crops like strawberries and asparagus as mainstays, while rotating other crops through Southern California's lengthy growing season, a reflection of the mild climate and relatively predictable rainfall cycles (which also meant that freezes were rare).

Asparagus and strawberries were labor intensive—both had to be picked by hand. Asparagus was particularly unusual; after seeding, the plant first grew into what appeared to be a wildly maned weed. The weed was then chopped off at ground level by hand, and a few days later the familiar spear of an asparagus would pop through the soil. Watching the asparagus harvest was akin to seeing a group of archers—without their bows—strolling through the fields, bending down with a blade, then tossing their asparagus arrows into the quiver strapped to their back.

Strawberries were similarly harvested by hand, except in a backbreaking fashion.

Farm laborers descended on the long rows of berry plants that grew in bunches just a few inches above the ground. The fruit hung over the sides and ripened in a matter of days, which meant that it had to be picked by numerous pickers in a relatively short time. Workers carried wood or cardboard flats and filled them to capacity, then hurried over to the crew chief to have it recorded—most strawberry picking was calculated piece rate.

In photos of the Irvine Ranch taken in the 1920s and 1930s, the faces of all the laborers were white, including the men behind the reins of mule teams that pulled threshers for harvesting wheat. (The authors attended a company retire-ment reception in the early 1980s; one retiree was feted for more than 45 years of service. His first job title: muleskinner.)

In the 1940s, with many men away at war, the federal government instituted the Bracero program, allowing Mexican farmworkers to travel to the United States to harvest crops. The program was discontinued in 1964.

A 1981 paper by UC Irvine historian Lisbeth Haas documents both Bracero labor in Orange County agriculture, as well as the employment of local farmwork-ers of Hispanic descent, likely immigrants who came to the county from Mexico and were never naturalized.

In the late 1960s and into the 1970s and 1980s, the Irvine Company employed and housed farm workers on a full-time basis. Some of them lived in a modest but comfortable trailer park at the base of the Lomas de Santiago.

While there had never been any labor unrest in Irvine Company fields, Williams kept a close watch on Cesar Chavez and the United Farmworkers of California (UFWC). Williams joined other state agriculture interests in funding an unflattering documentary film about Chavez and screened it for some com-pany employees, including Ted Dienstfrey. Dienstfrey's politics were as far to the left as Williams' were to the right, so when he raised his hand after the film and asked Williams why he was so afraid of Chavez, Williams reported Dienstfrey to company President William Mason as a communist.

Watson, who had hired Dienstfrey (and likely privately shared his views), met with Mason and dismissed the entire situation as comical. And while there are indications that UFWC operatives visited Orange County fields on occasion, no organizing on the Irvine Ranch was ever reported.

Documenting revenues and profits from Irvine Company agricultural opera-tions is difficult. The last public revelation came during congressional hearings in 1973, following up on the pace of implementation by foundations in response to the Tax Reform Act of 1969.

In 1971, according to the Irvine Company, revenue from agricultural operations totaled $5,104,363 against operating costs of $5,130,190, for a loss that year of $25,827. The following year was much better, with revenues of $7,827,116 against operating costs of $5,203,086, a profit of $2,624,030. Company management noted in the report that it was the best fiscal performance by the Ag division in the history of the company.[3]

Alas, the numbers remain cloudy, as there is no indication if revenues included Imperial Valley or the Montana cattle ranch operations. Nor were property taxes apportioned farm versus urban. What was known—due to various published reports elsewhere—was that citrus acreage was expanding.

Nevertheless, with the knowledge that their fields were destined to diminish, the company farm managers waged an aggressive and sophisticated campaign to squeeze every dollar possible from the land until it was converted to homes and businesses.

The managers kept a close eye on crop production and weather in other parts of the state and nation, and if an unexpected freeze or windstorm wiped out a crop that could be duplicated in Orange County, the fields would be cleared of whatever was growing there and quickly planted and harvested to replace what had been lost elsewhere.

Agriculture also created an employee fringe benefit that was widely appreciated—the opportunity to glean the fields after harvest. Usually on a weekend morning, secretaries, planners, and vice presidents all mingled in a field of corn, asparagus, or strawberries to gather the leftovers. Corn and asparagus could be blanched and frozen as could strawberries, but the sweet red fruit was at its flavor peak the moment it was picked.

****

The first non-company apartment community in the decade of acceleration was built and operated by San Francisco developer Gerson Bakar.

Bakar, like Ray Watson, came from humble beginnings—his parents were chicken farmers. He attended UC Berkeley (Business, 1948) and like Watson displayed a lifelong sympathy for the economic underdog.[4] It is not surprising, then, shortly after the two met, Watson recruited Bakar to create a large apartment complex near Newport Center.

Watson had seen the thousand-unit Woodlake apartment complex Bakar's company built in San Mateo, a growing suburb located on the southern San Francisco Bay peninsula that would ultimately turn into the Silicon Valley.

Woodlake was a combination of apartments and condominiums built in five pods, each with a pool. The design of the community-oriented living spaces was inward, away from nearby streets. There was heavy landscaping to shield residents from noise, and in its earliest years, sculptures decorating the pools. Woodlake appealed to Watson's desire to see apartments that were more than just units—he envisioned a mixed-use complex.

The company offered to lease Bakar 55 acres of land at the corner of Jamboree Road and San Joaquin Road that overlooked Upper Newport Bay and Bakar was eager to accept it.

A sticking point arose immediately—the company had designated each corner of the intersection for a service station. Bakar objected to the one on his corner, and Watson overruled the commercial executives so the project could proceed. Bakar brought in a trusted architect and obtained financing from Traveler's Insurance, which would also participate in ownership.

The project had its problems, starting with a $23 million budget that ballooned to $31 million as he and his contractors contended with permitting issues, as well as the unexpected expense of adding fire retardant to the underground garage, a condition of occupancy.

In the end, Park Newport achieved the mixed-use vision Watson wanted, with swank apartments, pools, playground, salons, conference rooms, on-site conveniences like a dry cleaner, exercise room, and an array of other services. It also developed a reputation as the hottest spot for young singles in Newport Beach to find each other and … socialize.

Bakar would eventually purchase the land lease from the Irvine Company for $11 million.

****

Two other apartment projects would soon follow Park Newport, but these would be owned and managed by the Irvine Company, assets in the company investment portfolio. One proceeded in relative tranquility, while the second would prove politically contentious as well as a planning and construction challenge.

Views were important to the citizens of Newport Beach, and by the late 1960s they were diminishing.

One of the first disputes over public vistas of Newport Bay and the Pacific Ocean came in 1948 with the development of the Balboa Bay Club along Pacific Coast Highway.

A long, narrow strip of land and its even narrower beach had been donated to the city in 1928 by James Irvine II, who stipulated that it could be used for docks but not for "industrial purposes." Twenty years later a group of local investors convinced the city that a private club would improve both the site and the city's image, and the Balboa Bay Club was born. The club attracted Hollywood stars like Humphrey Bogart and John Wayne, as well as political figures and members of the Rat Pack, lending an air of swinging sophistication to the city.

But the buildings blocked the view of the Lido Channel, and there was no public access to the beach. For a small but vocal group of Newport Beach residents concerned more about the natural environment than the artificial one at the club's bar, the city's decision to allow the club to be built rankled them for decades.

Just a mile south of the Bay Club, also on the ocean side of Pacific Coast Highway, was a similar piece of property, dubbed by Irvine Company planners as Promontory Point. It was about half a mile long and relatively flat on top. What would normally have been the only buildable portion was narrow, and it sloped off quickly on the side facing the Balboa yacht basin and Balboa Island.

Watson assigned William Watt as project manager in charge of both design and construction.

Watt had come to the company three years earlier and had immediately been thrown into the Newport Center and Fashion Island projects to help with construction management. Watt had a degree in civil engineering from Stanford, followed by two years in the Navy handling projects that required engineering expertise. He had been hired after sending Watson a query letter and drawings.

After finishing up at Newport Center, Watt had started work on two other large apartment projects, including one in Irvine called Park West, where he hired an upcoming Los Angeles architect named Frank Gehry as the designer. He retained several project managers to oversee construction, then turned his attention to Promontory Point.

Promontory Point was proposed to be big—536 units on 30 narrow acres. It was directly across a saltwater channel from Balboa Island, and when residents there saw what it would do to their view, they got angry, then organized.

Between 300 and 400 Balboa residents and some from nearby Irvine Terrace jammed the city planning commission's first hearing on the project on December 3, 1970. According to the *Daily Pilot* reporter covering the meeting, the "… audience was hostile … spectators repeatedly heckled Irvine Company officials trying to explain their plans." There were so many people present, the paper added, some were standing outside the hearing room, peering through windows.[5]

The hearing lasted five hours. If anyone dared to support the project, it wasn't reported either in the *Pilot* or the local weekly, the *Ensign*. The commissioners could see what was coming. A month later they rejected the company's plan on a 4–2 vote and suggested making changes to accommodate resident concerns, which also included potential traffic impacts on local neighborhoods.

The City Council did the same a month later.

After spending the next five months making revisions, including dropping the total number of apartments, the company received planning commission approval in June, followed by a surprisingly positive 6–1 vote of approval by the city council two months later.

The council placed more than two dozen conditions on the project, including one that required creation of a large gap between buildings to provide what the council called a "window to the bay." Watt wanted to fight it, he recalled, but was told by Watson to let it go.[6]

Another condition that bothered Watt was the requirement that the company build a public walkway on the top of the bluff opposite the project along Pacific Coast Highway. Again, Watt went to Watson, and again Watson overruled him, pointing out that, "… no one would use it and it's not the end of the world." Thinking back on the decision nearly 50 years later, Watt allowed that as usual, "Ray was absolutely right."[7]

Watt believed he needed a creative architect to tackle the narrow bluff top site, where the zoning allowed 520 units. He selected Joe Escherick, who had designed hundreds of private residences in the San Francisco Bay Area, as well as an initial series of homes at Sea Ranch on the rugged Sonoma County coast of northern California. Sea Ranch became famous in planning and architecture circles for the requirement that homes blend into the windswept landscape with minimal profiles and natural materials for outer wall coverings and roofs.

Promontory Point was just the opposite of Sea Ranch. Snaking along the long, narrow bluff, it would dominate views from Pacific Coast Highway on one side and Balboa Island on the other.

Escherick developed the concept of building the apartments so they stairstepped down the slope of the bluff facing Balboa Island. The company had determined that the project would be wood frame, which limited construction to three stories in height. Additionally, there was no allowance for elevators, requiring the architect to design a plan where tenants didn't have to walk up more than a single flight from carport to their front door.

After Escherick had been at work for three months, Watt was getting nervous. Recalling the situation in a 2020 interview, Watt complained to an associate that, "… this wasn't working." The associate counseled, "Don't worry, this is the way Escherick works. We just deal with all the aspects of the project and then a solution just presents itself."[8]

Watt didn't agree. He compared trying to ascertain Escherick's approach to, "… going into the woods and touching and feeling around in the dark."

While his architect pondered, Watt grappled with another design challenge—the large, flat area at the base of the bluff on the Balboa Island side. The parcel ran the length of the project boundary, with tiny Bayside Drive 100 feet or so in front of it, hugging the shoreline of the seawater channel across from Balboa Island.

It was Jack Raub, the consulting civil engineer on the project, who came up with a solution that was practical and profitable, Watt recalled. "Raub proposed to re-route Bayside Drive to the base of the bluff, then cut a deep-water channel and bay, resulting in property where we could build houses with boat slips." After the company's engineers developed drawings for the concept and received city approval, Promontory Point had a new property line at the base of the bluff. Watt used the new project geography as an excuse to part ways with Escherick and brought on Fisher Friedman Architects to come up with a new approach.[9]

Two months later, Watt recalled, Fisher Friedman proposed building a series of large buildings on seven levels but constructed in a manner that showed only three levels. This was achieved by constructing the buildings with the façade shaved off at a 45-degree angle. The design softened the appearance of the buildings and created the visual impression that the apartments were cascading down the slopes.

With working drawings in hand, construction began. After a few minor problems were resolved (the framing company went bust and the Irvine Company had to pick up the work), the project was finished just over the $20 million budget.

With bright, whitewashed stucco walls and equally bold red tile roofs, the apartments presented drivers along Pacific Coast Highway and residents on the edge of Balboa Island with a bold, stark profile. Some people found the look objectionable and were not reluctant to say so.

The final flaw in the project presented itself as the rainy season arrived, and runoff began accumulating on the decks of many of the apartments. Watt and his construction team figured out the problem and constructed a fix. In the end, from a business standpoint, Promontory Point was a winner, and even with some of the highest rents in the city, filled up. And as the generous landscaping on the site grew and flourished, complaints about its appearance waned.

Figure 16.1 Promontory Point in Newport Beach in 1974, shortly after construction and prior to maturation of landscaping.

(Orange County Archives)

Watt spent his final five years at the company overseeing the design and construction of every subsequent Irvine Company apartment project.

****

The success of Eastbluff, with its radical inclusion of greenbelts as a key design element, gave company planners the incentive to duplicate the concept in the first major village they would build in Irvine.

Al Treviño claims the honor for naming University Park, located at the edge of Culver Drive and the planned alignment of the San Diego Freeway.

(Culver Drive, which would eventually become Irvine's "main street," was named for Fred "Humpy" Culver, who owned a farm at the intersection of Culver and what would become Interstate 5. His nickname reflected the fact that he had a hunchback.[10])

Treviño was sketching out the boundaries of University Park when William Mason stopped at his desk to show him the newly approved alignment of the freeway. Treviño was aghast—it went through the middle of the new village. Mason went back to the state highway planners to seek an adjustment but was met with resistance. Treviño and Mason then learned the highway planners needed a large amount of fill dirt to elevate the freeway alignment elsewhere, so Mason offered a borrow pit a few miles south in Laguna Canyon. That sealed the deal, and Treviño hired a planner from William Pereira's firm to design the final alignment, convincing the state to lower the freeway a few feet along the village edge.[11]

Location of Initial Villages—Eastbluff and University Park

Treviño also turned to Pereira to gain internal approval for his University Park plan. Ray Watson, Treviño said, kept asking him if he could make the plan work. Treviño, who believed Watson was a better talker than designer, called Pereira and asked him to review the plans Treviño had drawn up with

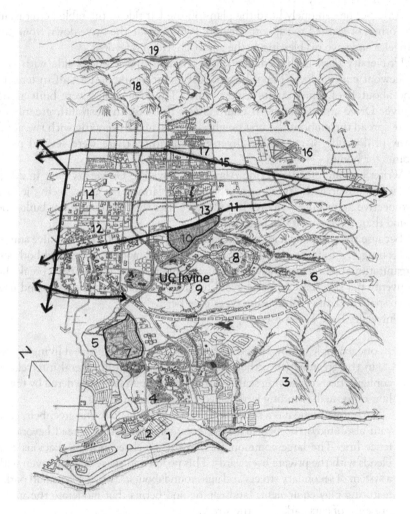

Figure 16.2 The areas highlighted in this bird's eye view of the Irvine Ranch that shows development by 1977 identify the first two master-planned residential neighborhoods developed by the Irvine Company—Eastbluff in Newport Beach (#7—opened in 1964) and University Park in Irvine (#10—opened in 1966) are highlighted (a duplicate of this map appears at the end of Chapter 31 and identifies all other numbered locations).

Map hand drawn by Robert Dannenbrink, Jr, FAICP in June 2021 and digitally edited by Jason Baesel and H. Pike Oliver in July 2021.

Watson. Treviño was careful to let Pereira know that he would present two sets of plans, and that he considered the plan on the *left* side of the table the best one.

Treviño had the advantage; months earlier, Pereira had learned of Treviño's reputation as a planner at the Victor Gruen firm and had tried to hire him. When Treviño turned him down, Pereira recommended him for a position at the Irvine Company.

Whether he genuinely liked the plans on the left side of the table better than the other, or wanted to support Treviño, Pereira made the drive down from Los Angeles and gave his blessing to the approach Treviño favored.

University Park is shaped like a tall triangle tipped on its side with two somewhat curvy edges. The village is just about a mile and a half in length, and about ¾ of a mile at its widest point. The first homes were built along Culver Drive at the northern end. As was the case in Eastbluff, greenbelts were spread throughout the first neighborhoods, and in keeping with the company philosophy of creating a diverse community, there were several price points for homes.

Writer and architectural critic Alan Hess moved to University Park in 2004. He was familiar with Irvine as a professional planner, but upon seeing it as a prospective home buyer—more than 40 years after the community was built—he found that, "... the visit was a revelation."[12]

Because the company had convinced county planning officials to waive standard zoning, "... in favor of a superblock that allowed more creative neighborhood organizational patterns, (it gave company planners) more flexibility to break the conventional suburban grid and avoid homogenous densities and uses, and mix open space and different housing types together ..."[13]

University Park, Hess observed, is:

> ... one example of how they translated abstract theory into real living spaces ... in the greenbelt(s).... the open space is designed in several interrelated configurations of varying scales—from broad, open lawns bordered by townhouses to small, winding landscaped paths between homes.
>
> Each townhome has a small yard, but by backing up to the greenbelt, each yard also enjoys the benefit of the common spaces that spread beyond its fence line. The large common area, in turn, feels even more spacious as it blends with the private back yards. This pedestrian space is interwoven with a system of secondary streets and auto roundabouts...(which) are small parks, featuring play equipment, landscaping and berms that moderate the visual presence of cars parked on the street.[14]

Planners eschewed the traditional grid pattern of streets in University Park, arraying arterials as well as neighborhood lanes in gentle curves of asphalt and concrete. There were large, landscaped medians, and generous setbacks along each side of major streets, planted with a mix of deciduous trees and conifers.

But University Park was isolated. There was no grocery store or pharmacy for miles. Nor were there dry cleaners, a bakery, or liquor store. For some new buyers, especially those with ties to nearby UC Irvine, the novelty of University Park was appealing, but for others it was not. Sales were slow, and one of the first builders went out of business. To keep the project going, television personality Art Linkletter, who had diversified into development, stepped in to complete the homes.

Just up the hill from University Park, what would be for decades the most afflu-ent village in Irvine got underway three years later.

Turtle Rock was named for a local landmark, a large outcropping of rock that resembled a turtle poking its head out of its shell.

The village was a little more than 1,800 acres, forming a rough square two miles on either side. It was also unique in that near the center there was a 70-acre par-cel of land that had been sold to a branch of the Lutheran Church for a planned university.

But it was the geography of Turtle Rock that presented the most significant opportunities and difficulties for Irvine Company planners.

The western and northern edges of the village were well defined. Culver Drive would be extended from its termination at Campus Drive to form the boundary with UC Irvine property. Separating Turtle Rock from University Park was both University Drive and the meandering regional park (much of it wetlands) the company had donated to the county. The southern and eastern sides of the village

Figure 16.3 A 1970 view of attached homes on either side of a wide greenbelt in University Park, the first master-planned residential village that became part of the City of Irvine the following year.

blended into grazing lands—it would be years before development of homes and open space took place there.

To provide access to the village, the company pioneered what would become a long loop road called, appropriately, Turtle Rock Drive. But in the early years of development only half of the road would be built.

From an economic standpoint, it was clear that the gentle hillsides that rose less than 300 feet from Campus Drive at the northwestern base of the village could be graded into home sites with spectacular views of the county. Views meant price premiums, and company planners wasted no time in recruiting a builder to construct single-story homes in the area. Below the hills, in keeping with the company's desire for diversity, smaller homes in a denser array were planned.

It was three large hills in the village that proved limiting in terms of development. Lots could be carved out near their bases, but as the slope increased, grading and shoring would prove more costly. In the end, three hillside areas were set aside as open space, but the top of the highest hill at the center of the village was reserved for what would eventually become Turtle Rock Summit, a mixture of homes and lots where the city's first custom houses would be located.

Turtle Rock expanded in its initial years on a north/south axis on either side of Turtle Rock Drive. Many of the homes were single story and built with an atrium. A long tract of homes was located on streets that all started with the word Sierra (Mia, Soto, Raton, etc.), and the area was lumped together among residents and Realtors as simply "the Sierra streets."

Like their compatriots in University Park, the first residents of Turtle Rock had to make a long drive for the daily essentials. A retail center was never built within the Turtle Rock village boundaries; Richard Reese, who was vice president of planning at the company at the time, recalled the people there rejected the company's plan to locate a center at the intersection of Culver and Campus Drives, preferring instead a site for a new high school.

****

One of the philosophical foundations of Irvine Company master planning was the establishment of a commercial/industrial zone that would provide an employment base close to the new communities.

Prior to 1960, there had been individual land sales and leases to large business enterprises toward this goal. One of the first was the 1956 lease of 99 acres by Ford Aeroneutronics on a parcel that bordered Jamboree Road at Ford Road (Pereira designed the facility where high-tech armaments were produced).

Three years later, the Newporter Inn, the first large hotel on company land, opened for business on Jamboree Road below Newport Center.

Next came a 178-acre lease to Collins Radio, followed by 20 acres to Douglas Aircraft for Astropower Science Laboratories.

Commercial and industrial development was moving toward the Orange County Airport, which had been expanded after the county bought 166 acres adjacent to it in 1963 from the Irvine Company. The airport had originally been part of the Irvine Ranch, acquired by the county from the company in a land trade in 1939. The airport expanded following World War II, and by the early 1960s two regional airlines were providing service to San Francisco, San Diego, Sacramento, and Las Vegas.

The company decided to go into the industrial development business itself, and in 1964 created a wholly owned subsidiary company, the Irvine Industrial Complex (IIC) to develop a 2,600-acre industrial park in the area around and above the airport. Its board of directors mirrored company and James Irvine Foundation ownership, including Joan Irvine Smith and her mother.

In his oral history, Ray Watson explained that at first, the company wanted to lease industrial properties. But it soon became apparent, he said, that there was too much land for sale in other parts of the county potential buyers would select because they wanted to own it. Once the change was made, sales began to take off. The first users, Watson said, were distribution outlets for businesses in the Los Angeles area that were selling more products in growing Orange County. "Little did we know," he said, "that high tech industries and other industries related to it were coming on at the embryonic stage of forming new companies and they were coming to places like ours."[15]

Like the Irvine Company's communities of homes, the IIC would be planned.

The streets were extra broad and spaced out to accommodate the large trucks that would deliver raw materials and export the finished products. For industrial users who needed rail access, a spur line of the Atchison, Topeka, and Santa Fe Railroad had been installed.

Setbacks from the street were configured into the lots that would be sold or leased to users. There were clear rules governing landscaping for the buildings that would be built. Someone driving on a main road of the IIC in its early years may have mistakenly believed they had happened upon a series of grassy parks with a few buildings scattered in between. IIC promoters described the area as like a college campus.

Rules were established governing allowable colors for buildings, and there were requirements for screening trash and storage areas. Barbed wire fencing was not allowed.

One of the first headquarters purchases in the IIC came in 1968 when Allergan Pharmaceuticals built a ten-story brick edifice adjacent to a production facility that preceded it.

Allergan was one of the few users in the area when Richard Cannon found a job as a junior salesman at the IIC in 1969.

Cannon had left a family real estate business in La Canada-Flintridge for Newport Beach on the theory "… find a place you like to live and then find a job." He ran into a former fraternity brother while knocking on doors, who sent him to another fraternity brother at the Irvine Company. Cannon was hired by the IIC, where then-president John Murphy was hustling to ramp up sales.[16]

(Richard Reese worked with Murphy and considered him "a genius." He said that Murphy believed industrial users were as choosy as home buyers and advocated that, "… you pretend you are in the shoe business, and order shoes of each type and size for everyone, put them on the shelf so they can look at them and pick out what they want." Lot size, Reese recalled, became the key selling factor in Murphy's strategy.[17])

Cannon found that Murphy's straightforward approach to selling began to pay off as more companies became aware of the project. "Industrial companies wanted to look at the price sheets—they wanted it simple." The IIC kept it simple as well, Cannon recalled, as for the land price, "there was no negotiating."[18]

Along with a standard land sale, the IIC offered a lease/purchase plan as well—four-year lease, then purchase. A condition of sale was that the buyer had to build a facility within two years, Cannon said, either by hiring their own contractor or having the Irvine Company do the construction.

As the IIC continued to expand around the airport, leaders of the companies that were locating there recognized an opportunity to harness the energy of new business leadership into an advocacy organization. The Greater Irvine Industrial League (GIIL) was formed in 1970, with Irvine community leader E. Ray Quigley tapped as its first executive director (Quigley resigned when he ran successfully for the Irvine City Council).

In 1972, Cannon said, Murphy apparently experienced a life-changing event and departed for India. His replacement was Thomas Wolff Jr., recruited to lead the industrial group from a similar position in Maryland at the Rouse Company.[19]

Wolff was barely five and half feet tall but had the energy and presence of someone twice that size. Todd Nicholson, who joined GIIL as its executive director after Quigley left, said that Wolff was, "… in perpetual motion, he never stopped. He could synthesize in a single sentence or a word why a company should relocate to the IIC."[20]

Wolff was always "upbeat and enthusiastic," Nicholson said, and had extraordinary sales skills.

Initially, Nicholson said, GIIL was largely involved in relatively mundane issues such as, "… freight rates, postal zones, and new zip codes." But it wasn't long before other more substantial matters drew its attention, including Orange County Airport. There were only two airlines flying there in the early 1970s, and the planes they operated were loud. Newport Beach residents took notice and objected to the increasing number of flights. Nicholson said the issue gradually diminished as new planes that were much quieter were put into service. (The controversy would never go away—lawsuits and lobbying to restrict capacity at the airport—now John Wayne Airport—continued for decades.[21])

Perhaps the most significant addition to the IIC came in 1974 when Fluor Corporation built a huge glass and steel headquarters building adjacent to the San Diego Freeway. Cannon recalls visiting Fluor executives at their offices in El

Segundo to pitch the Irvine parcel. As was the case with other land sales, he said, the IIC set the price and stuck to it.

Wolff appeared at an Irvine City Council meeting where the Fluor zoning was being considered. He described the opportunity for the city to have the firm locate there as one that could not be turned down. Fluor, he said, would become a great corporate citizen.

According to Nicholson, Wolff was right. "Fluor jumped right into our issues," he said, with top executive Jay Reed bringing experience and enthusiasm to the table, along with monetary support.

The Fluor executive offices were unlike anything ever seen in Orange County, where even the most substantial firms did business in surroundings that reflected the casual vibe of Southern California, usually with modern, low-key décor and plenty of plants in the hallways. Fluor, by contrast, featured a reception area that was almost three stories high, where an imposing chandelier hung in the middle. The offices of the top executives were similarly high-ceiling and were finished with dark wood paneling. One executive explained to an awe-struck visitor that a company dealing with Saudi princes required a formidable image to instill confidence (Fluor constructed oil and gas infrastructure throughout the Middle East and around the world).

In 1974, Wolff was promoted to oversee all land development for the Irvine Company, and Richard Cannon became president of the IIC, five years after joining the organization.

****

The final eight miles of the San Diego Freeway from the Orange County Airport to its connection at Interstate 5 had just been completed when the Irvine Company received an unusual proposal for a land lease just south of the junction.

The acreage was largely grassy, with a few specks of low sagebrush and scrub. In the heat of the summer, it could have been mistaken for the savannah of Africa.

Enter entrepreneur Harry Shuster, a group of his fellow South African investors, and a creative concept: build an open-air wild animal park. (Ironically, the location had been shown on the original 1961 Pereira Irvine Ranch master plan as a site for a zoo.)

Shuster convinced the company to lease him 500 acres of land for the project, and in June 1970 autos filled with curious visitors found themselves windshield to animal face with a variety of African wildlife including giraffe, zebra, ostrich, camels, and, of course, lions, the namesake of Lion Country Safari. Shuster spent $12 million ($86.2 million in 2022 dollars) for the project. "No expense has been spared in the effort to assure authenticity," he told *Irvine World News* in January 1970.[22]

For the company, it was a good deal—sit back and collect a regular payment from Shuster and watch, with amusement, how he and his talented vice president

Figure 16.4 Frasier the Lion, AKA "Frasier the Sensuous Lion" at Lion Country Safari.
(Orange County Archives)

of marketing, Jerry Kobrin, dished up enough publicity to drive attendance into the millions in the first years of operation.

Kobrin's crowning public relations achievement was Frasier the Lion, aka, Frasier the Sensuous Lion.

When he arrived at Lion Country, Frasier hadn't yet acquired his name, and he was old—he'd been purchased from a circus. But he still had his bulk and his mane, and from a distance, a passing resemblance to the King of the Jungle.

And it turned out, the aging lion had retained something else: his virility.

Within a few months of being turned loose among the lady lions at the park, Frasier had sired a dozen cubs. Kobrin, an ex-newspaperman and publicist, knew a story when he saw one, and brilliantly exploited it. He named the aging lion Frasier, added "Sensuous," and kept the story alive for years until the happy but exhausted lion died. Kobrin recruited bagpipers from Clan Fraser for the funeral and followed up by writing and producing a G-rated movie based on the legend of Frasier.

Showcasing Frasier's libido (36 cubs in all) turned out to be the high point for Lion Country Safari. After a few years attendance began to fall off, forcing Shuster to turn back 200 acres of land to the Irvine Company. By the time the Irvine Company was sold to new owners in 1977, Shuster had branched off into a partnership with Elizabeth Taylor and her jewelry company, Elizabeth Taylor Diamonds.

Shuster had a few other ideas for the property he was leasing, which would eventually lead to a contentious legal battle with the Irvine Company. And Frasier the Lion would prove to be the only—and most famous—four-legged business partner the company ever had.

Promise and Progress During the 1960s

Figure 16.5 A summary of progress in transforming the Irvine Ranch during the decade of the 1960s. *(Continued)*

(Midge Mason Browning)

Figure 16.5 (Continued)

Notes

1. Raymond L. Watson and Ann Lage, *Planning and Developing the New Town of Irvine California, 1960–2003: Irvine Company President, 1973–1977, Walt Disney Company Chairman, 1983–1984* (Regional Oral History Office, the Bancroft Library, University of California, Berkeley, 2005) 129.
2. Watson and Lage, *Planning and Developing*, 137.
3. U.S. Congress. House. Committee on Ways and Means, *General Tax Reform (Testimony from Administration and Public Witnesses): Public Hearings Before the Committee on Ways and Means, House of Representatives, 93rd Congress, First Session, March, April and May 1973* (Washington, D.C.: U.S. Government Printing Office, 1973) 5915.
4. Lisa Rubens and Elizabeth Castle, *Gerson Bakar, Real Estate Developer and Philanthropist* (Regional Oral History Office, Bancroft Library, University of California, 2007).

5. *Daily Pilot*, December 3, 1970, 1.
6. William Watt, video interview by H. Pike Oliver and C.M. Stockstill, July 8, 2020.
7. Watt, interview, July 8, 2020.
8. Watt, interview, July 8, 2020.
9. Watt, interview, July 8, 2020.
10. Chris Jepsen, "O.C. Answer Man: Who was Irvine's Culver Drive Named for?" *Orange Coast Magazine*, November 9, 2016.
11. Alvaro Treviño, interview by H.P. Oliver, July 20, 2020.
12. Alan Hess, "Discovering Irvine," *Places Journal*, October 2014. https://doi.org/ https://placesjournal.org/article/discovering-irvine/?cn-reloaded=1.
13. Hess, "Discovering Irvine," *Places Journal*, October 2014.
14. Hess, "Discovering Irvine."
15. Watson and Lage, *Planning and Developing*, 281.
16. Richard Cannon, interview by C.M. Stockstill and H.P. Oliver, August 28, 2020.
17. Richard Reese, interview by C.M. Stockstill and H.P. Oliver, August 26, 2020.
18. Watson and Lage, *Planning and Developing*, 281.
19. Richard Cannon, interview, August 28, 2020.
20. Richard Cannon, interview, August 28, 2020.
21. Todd Nicholson, interview by H.P. Oliver and C.M. Stockstill, November 18, 2020.
22. *Irvine World News*, January 8, 1970, 6.

17 Conflicting Visions of the Upper Newport Bay

If ever there was a conflict between the Irvine Company and an opponent worthy of the label David versus Goliath, it was the one resulting in the preservation of the Upper Newport Bay.

The mighty Irvine Company along with the County of Orange, each with a score of lawyers, engineers, and virtually unlimited funds, versus a modest husband and wife who just wanted to save the shoreline their children used as a playground.

But the contest was much larger than the Upper Newport Bay; it became the harbinger of an environmental movement in Orange County that flourished for decades. As a result, in addition to the Upper Bay, thousands of acres of land would be preserved by dedication and purchase, powerful organizations would be formed that would alter or halt major developments, and attitudes about the environment held by business and real estate leaders would be reconsidered.

Frank and Frances Robinson would become local folk heroes, rightfully remembered as "the grandparents of environmental activism" in Orange County.[1]

This chapter is taken almost exclusively from Ray Watson's memoir on the Upper Bay and as such reflects how the controversy was viewed from his, and the Irvine Company's, perspective. Interspersed in his narrative and identified as such is greater detail on the Robinson's and their allies.

First, a description of Upper Newport Bay:

The bay resembles a giant upside-down letter L, beginning where Pacific Coast Highway crosses the lower bay.

The long side of the L is almost three miles in length, the short side about a mile.

The bay was formed by repeated ancient flooding of the Santa Ana River, a few miles to the west. Today it is fed largely from San Diego Creek.

There are cliffs on both sides of the lower length of the bay; on the west, the communities of Dover Shores, the Castaways, and Westcliff expand back from the edge of the cliffs. On the other side of the bay is Eastbluff, the first major village in Newport Beach developed by the Irvine Company. At the top of the bay there are fewer than a dozen large homes on multi-acre lots that overlook it, as well as a denser, newer community of homes, a hotel, and a county environmental center devoted to the bay.

DOI: 10.1201/9781003226291-18

Back Bay Drive curls along the edge of the bay below Eastbluff; on nearly every day of the year it is filled with walkers, runners, and bicyclists.

The interior of the bay is a tidal marsh, with wide, shallow channels meandering throughout. As the tides rise and fall, the borders of the large islands within the bay expand and contract, covering and uncovering the grasses and reeds that provide food and shelter to birds from land and sea.

Visitors to the bay invariably find themselves enveloped in an atmosphere of beauty and quietude. The only interruption that mars the experience is noise from airplanes departing from John Wayne Airport.

****

(Watson's story begins):

Upper Newport Bay is located at the head of better-known Newport Bay.

The transformation of lower Newport Bay from its early 20th century reputation as one of the "... greatest natural habitats for wildlife and game birds in the world," to its current reputation as one of the finest yachting and recreational harbors on the California coast began in 1935.

For years, city fathers had visualized dredging the bay's remaining mud flats and repairing and extending the entrance jetties with the objective of turning it into a world class boating harbor. A countywide bond issue was approved in the early 1930s to fund the improvements, and in 1935 dredging began. Directed by the US Army Corps of Engineers and overseen by city engineer Richard Patterson, 8.5 million tons of sand and 50,000 tons of rocks were removed from the bay.

With the lower bay work accomplished, Patterson turned his attention to the Upper Bay. In 1936 he submitted a plan for extending the newly dredged Newport Harbor into the Upper Bay.

But the nation was still in the depths of the Depression, followed by World War II. So, Patterson's plan lay dormant until the late 1950s, when the Orange County Harbor District published a tentative plan for the Upper Bay incorporating his vision of dredging it for water recreational uses.

William Pereira was preparing his plan for the University of California Irvine and became aware of the county plan for the Upper Bay. He advocated for a connection to the bay, proposing that "... the Irvine Company offer to give the university a five-acre site on Upper Newport Bay, to be connected to the campus proper by a 100-foot corridor."

The upper bay ... is in the process of becoming an outstanding recreation area. A 56-acre county park exists at the south end and a second aquatic park is proposed on the west shore. The county plans to develop yet another aquatic park on some 130 acres at the extreme north end of the bay ... the site given to the university would be at the upper turning basin of a proposed 2,000-meter rowing course, which will extend from the bay into the proposed county aquatic park.

Company and university officials approved the overall Pereira plan for the campus, and implementation efforts began in earnest. One of those tasks was to move forward on the county plan for the Upper Bay. Harbor District executive Ken Sampson and Irvine Company chief engineer William Mason joined together to make it happen.

As a starter the county made it clear it had no funds to acquire the company's islands in the Upper Bay and suggested a trade of county lands for the islands. The county's plan had included the concept of utilizing the dredged material from the islands to fill the area behind the new bulkheads, thus converting a portion of the natural tidelands into uplands. Sampson and Mason agreed that for the trade to be politically acceptable the economic value of the islands had to exceed the value of the new uplands.

By early 1962, Mason and Sampson had arrived at a tentative agreement on the trade. However, both knew there were serious legal and political hurdles to be overcome. During this two-year period there was little public awareness of what the county and company were contemplating. After all, most of the plan that the company and Harbor District were attempting to implement had been contemplated for more than 30 years.[2]

For the Robinsons, it began with a bike ride.

They had moved to Newport Beach from La Canada in 1962. Frank worked at North American Rockwell as an engineer, Frances was a housewife, thinking about returning to college.

In early 1963, their son Jay biked to North Star beach on the Upper Bay and found No Trespassing signs posted by the Irvine Company. The signs were new. Jay biked home to tell his parents and the decade long battle commenced.

From a newspaper article she had saved, Frances discovered the extent of the proposed development. It discussed in detail the channelization and development of a new private waterfront community. But first, a land exchange between the county and the Irvine Company would take place...Frances thought that public access to the bay would be cut off. But she noted a potential hitch in the plan: the State Lands Commission and California Supreme Court had to approve the plan.

(Frank Robinson) began to probe the details of the land exchange, including the historical facts and legal opinions on which it was based. Frank became a tidelands expert through countless hours of work over the ensuing two years. 'As we got into it,' he recalled, 'it became a little bigger than a bellyache about not having a beach for our kids."[3]

(Watson's version of what transpired resumes):

> Their (the Robinsons') vision of the bay was in sharp contrast to the Harbor Commission's plan. To them, the Upper Bay was one of the last remaining natural estuaries in highly urbanized Southern California. By the mid-1960s, a growing segment of the community was expressing interest in the preservation of our fast-disappearing existing environment.

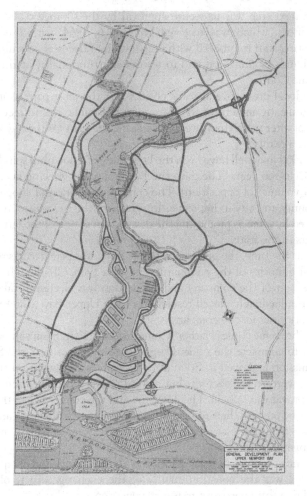

Figure 17.1 Early plan for marina and residential development in and around Upper
Newport Bay prepared for the Orange County Harbors Department in 1950.

(Orange County Archives)

The growing opposition came as a surprise to both the company and the
county. After all, they were attempting to open the Upper Bay to the public
in accordance with a plan that had existed for decades. With the company's
commitment to UCI there was an incentive for the company to make con-
cessions that it had not offered before. But now there was a group not only
opposing the trades but also the actual dredging of the islands, regardless of
who owned them.

Frustrated by the growing opposition, Mason sought to enhance the deal
by offering additional land, which he believed could hasten the trade and
improve public relations.

The next step was to secure approval by the Orange County Board of Supervisors, which was received on May 6, 1964, with the supervisors instructing staff to proceed with preparation of necessary documents to the State Lands Commission and to test its constitutionality at the California Supreme Court.

The local press coverage was positive, for the most part, as it recounted the significant amount of water frontage the public was to receive and the fact that after more than twenty-five years, the plan for the bay was soon to become a reality.

But 1964 may well have been the beginning of a downhill spiral that lasted more than ten years. The Save the Bay group was growing fast, in number and in volume (of opposition). The company's position of cooperating with the county and city in implementing plans for the bay was soon being characterized by some as promoting the destruction of one of the last natural bay habitats in the state.

But at the time, the opposition to the trade was perceived as representing a vocal minority of the community. In June 1966, Charles Thomas retired as president of the company and Bill Mason was elected to take his place. Mason immediately placed resolution of the Upper Bay (issue) high on his list of priorities for the company.

At the same time Harbor Commissioner Ken Sampson joined with Mason to complete the trade. Despite growing opposition, the State Lands Commission approved it. Soon after, pressure was brought on the commission to overturn the decision, but in 1967 after a second hearing, their previous approval was upheld. The company and the county began the exchange process by putting their respective parcels—county tidelands and company islands—in a joint escrow account where they were to remain until all legal challenges were resolved.

The most important legal question both the county and company wanted answered was the constitutionality of the exchange. To resolve it, both agreed to a third-party suit to test the question.

That process took six years, during which time the county political climate changed substantially. In the summer of 1970, Earth Day was celebrated throughout the nation and in Orange County. New county supervisors were elected who had either questioned the trade or opposed it. Soon the company found itself in the bizarre position of awaiting court approval of a trade that the other party no longer appeared to support.

Then the process split into two tracks. The constitutional lawsuit continued while the county was attempting to rescind the exchange; the company attempted to hold it together at least long enough to find out if it was legal. Then the county brought a separate lawsuit against the company to establish public prescriptive rights around the Upper Bay, which prompted the company to file a cross-complaint charging inverse condemnation (the Robinsons and two other couples filed as intervenors in the second county lawsuit).

With the county now doing everything it could to abort the trade, it became obvious it was doomed. But the company still wanted the constitutional question answered as it could potentially impact the company's and the public's ability to make future trades involving uplands and tidelands. Finally, after three years, the lower court ruled the transaction constitutional. That decision was immediately appealed, leading to three more years of uncertainty and growing turmoil. In 1973, the appeals court overturned the lower court and ruled that the concept of exchanging tidelands for uplands was unconstitutional because in this case the magnitude of tidelands involved was excessive.

Mason took the rejection hard. He believed he had crafted an agreement with the county that would have created a public recreation area that had been dreamed of for years. Instead, while coming within striking distance of reality, the community had changed its mind and all his hard work had come to naught. While Mason acknowledged that the comprehensive plan for the Upper Bay was dead, there was no clear vision of what the company would do next. The company still owned the islands, and the county owned the surrounding tidelands. Over the previous year Mason had made several informal inquiries to local, state, and federal agencies seeking any interest they might have in purchasing the islands, but there was none.

Further complicating the future for the company was that as part of the pending trade process both the islands and uplands had been placed in a single escrow account. With the county and company's properties comingled, the county assessor, Andrew Hinshaw, had designated both properties as owned by "Irvine Company, et al," and assessed their value as $50 million, sending a property tax bill to the company.

And there the issue stood on July 14, 1973, when the phone rang in my home. It was Bill Mason's 17-year-old daughter. Her first words were, "my father has had a heart attack and he is dead." At the time I was executive vice president and as I soon discovered, had become the interim chief executive of the Irvine Company. Two months later I was elected president. I had lost a friend; the company had lost a wonderful and dedicated leader; resolution of the Upper Bay quagmire was now my responsibility.

The Upper Bay was one of many issues I discussed with the company's board of directors. My position was that for the better part of 12 years the company had acted responsibly and in good faith ... in attempting to implement the development of the Upper Bay, but that vision was no longer viable, either practically or politically. I informed the board my objective was to find a buyer for the islands and put the issue behind us.

Over the next year, with the help of Robert Shelton, we did just that. Shelton had been city manager of Newport Beach when I joined the company in 1960. Although he no longer worked for the city, there was no better respected individual in local government than Bob Shelton. The two remaining substantive issues we needed to resolve were an agreeable price and the resolution of the unpaid property taxes.

After months of give and take negotiations, we arrived at what I believed was an acceptable resolution to both issues: the California Department of Fish and Game would buy the company's islands for $3.4 million, with the company taking a note in that amount with full payment in five years. As the accrued unpaid property taxes exceeded by a considerable amount the sales price, the next step was to resolve that issue with the county.[4]

(The company had started the negotiations by valuing the islands at $27.5 million.)

The county settled the property tax dispute for a company payment of $1.65 million. Soon thereafter the company authorized the sale of "approximately 527 acres in Upper Newport Bay." Thus, the net to the company was $1.75 million that by any calculation was significantly less than had been expended in the aborted four-year saga. But from my point of view the issue was now behind us.

But before the rejoicing could begin, a segment of the Save Our Bay group, led by the Robinsons, objected to the agreement. Frank Robinson claimed he had discovered a long-lost map that proved the islands were tidelands and thus owned by the public, not the company. His position, however, was that since he knew the company would dispute his claim, he suggested we reduce the price by $1 million and if we did, he would support the sale.

I told him the authenticity of the islands and uplands had been ruled on by both the courts and the State Lands Commission and the company had been paying property taxes on them for decades. Thus, I had no interest in conceding his point and I proceeded with the sale.

Because all the issues resulting from the years of litigation, the actual conveyance of the lands was "pursuant to a settlement" which the county and company signed in 1975, fifteen years after Pereira first referred to the Upper Bay, and forty years since Newport Beach's engineer, Richard Patterson, first proposed turning it into a marina.

What the company conveyed to the state was: all its rights, title and interest in and to the three islands plus the land beneath Back Bay Drive, over 200 acres of acknowledged tidelands at the head of Upper Newport Bay held by the company pursuant to Tidelands Patent 204, the surrounding uplands contiguous to Upper Newport Bay to the ten foot contour line, thereby guaranteeing perpetual public access to the entire Upper Bay, and certain other valuable property intended for use by the public as a scenic viewpoint of the Bay.

I felt very good on that summer day in 1975 when representatives from the county, city and state joined me on a bluff overlooking the magnificent bay as we signed the settlement. The vision of an ecological preserve had prevailed. At the company, we could put the controversy behind us and get on with the business of building out the Irvine Ranch.[5]

****

Watson had been gone from the Irvine Company for two years when in 1979, another lawsuit challenging the sale of the Upper Bay was filed by the Robinsons. They repeated their earlier arguments that the islands were public tidelands, and the company should pay back what the state paid them. The process to adjudicate it was torturous and lengthy, with the Irvine Company prevailing in the end over the objections of Sierra Club attorney Phillip Berry, who groused years later in his oral history that his clients had been "hometowned" by Orange County Appellate Court Judge Judith Ryan, who ruled against the Robinsons, the Sierra Club, and in favor of the Irvine Company.[6]

The depth of Watson's personal feelings about the Upper Bay are not entirely revealed until the closing pages of his written record of the issue. Called back to defend the company's actions, Watson—ever willing to intellectually challenge a company opponent—describes a conversation with Berry:

> As Phillip Berry, Sierra Club attorney, and I entered the courtroom on the first day of the trial, I turned to him and said, at the conclusion of the trial I had a personal request of him; would he have dinner with me, and my four children (to) explain the public benefit he is seeking in this trial. We (the company) had, after all, conveyed all the islands and surrounding lands in the Upper Bay to the state. The compensation received was far less than had been paid in property taxes through the years. And the title company had provided the state with title insurance assuring them that the company did own the uplands and the issue of ownership had been settled in court sixty years ago. He had no response. We went to trial.[7]

One former company employee described the loss of the Upper Bay plan as "... a very bitter pill for Watson to swallow."[8] And it seems possible that in addition to whatever personal pain he experienced, Watson was conflicted during the months that Mason managed the issue. Mason is quoted in various sources as describing the Robinsons and their motives in a demeaning manner. Frances Robinson's obituary in the *Los Angeles Times* reported that Mason once called her a "birdbrained housewife."[9]

Watson's instincts, which at times could be combative on a philosophical basis, rarely translated into personal attacks. On the contrary, Watson believed his approachability and empathy could sometimes create an atmosphere where the most contentious disputes could be mediated to a favorable settlement for all involved.

But Watson was a good corporate solider. There is no record of a break between he and Mason on this issue or any other.[10]

****

Today the Upper Newport Bay is a natural sanctuary, owned and managed by the California Department of Fish and Wildlife, and watched over by hundreds of volunteers from the Newport Bay Conservancy, founded in 1968. Each year the organization gives out an award named in honor of Frank and Frances Robinson.

The County of Orange owns a large parcel on the northwestern corner of the uplands that overlook the bay, and operates an interpretive center there, where the theater inside is named in honor of Ray Watson and his wife, Elsa. The handouts at the center were prepared by the Newport Bay Conservancy, whose history of the bay omits any mention of the Irvine Company.[11]

No plaques, inscriptions, or signs are found anywhere around the Upper Newport Bay recognizing the role of the Irvine Company in its preservation.

Notes

1. Martin Feldman, "Beating Goliath," *Orange Coast Magazine*, December 1996, 106–109.
2. Raymond L. Watson, "Upper Newport Bay: Conflicting Visions," in *Raymond L. Watson Papers* (MS.R.120) (Special Collections and Archives of the UC Irvine Libraries, April 5, 2005), 1–3.
3. *Los Angeles Times*, February 26, 1990.
4. Watson, "Upper Newport Bay: Conflicting Visions," 3–7.
5. Watson, "Upper Newport Bay: Conflicting Visions," 7–8.
6. Ann Lage, *Phillip Berry Oral History: A Broadened Agenda, A Bold Approach* (Regional Oral History Office, the Bancroft Library, University of California, Berkeley, 1984).
7. Watson, "Upper Newport Bay: Conflicting Visions," 8.
8. Philip Bettencourt, interview with C.M. Stockstill, May 6, 2020.
9. *Los Angeles Times*, July 1, 2001.
10. Watson, "Upper Newport Bay: Conflicting Visions."
11. "About Us," Newport Bay Conservancy, accessed November 11, 2021, https://newportbay.org/about-us/.

18 Politics and Media

Politics in Orange County until the early 1960s reflected its largely agricultural, small town, and Republican atmosphere.

Apart from a few thousand acres in the city of Newport Beach, the Irvine Ranch was in unincorporated territory; land use decisions, law enforcement, and most other government services were under the jurisdiction of the Orange County Board of Supervisors.

Some supervisors in those times measured their careers in office by decades—there were no term limits, no political contribution restrictions. Cecil M. "Cye" Featherly, for example, logged 21 years as a supervisor; Willis Warner, 24. In his oral history, Ray Watson said that during this time, supervisorial races were tame, low-cost affairs, with a $100 check an unusually large donation, and where total spending might touch $1,500.

Just how close JI may have been to individual politicians isn't well documented, but it is a fair assumption that the owner of one-sixth of the entire county was both listened to and involved. Athalie Clarke's memoir reports that on one of her visits to the ranch, JI and his wife were hosting Supervisor George Jeffrey for lunch. Jeffrey was a familiar face at the ranch—he had been a tenant farmer there for years before election to the board of supervisors. And a reference to Supervisor Heinz Kaiser identified him as Jimmie's friend, as in James Irvine Jr., from whom he reportedly won the right to a land lease for a restaurant in a poker game.

After JI's death in 1947, most political decisions were probably left in the hands of Brad Hellis, general manager of the ranch. Hellis was a member of the Lincoln Club, the county Republican business community fundraising arm, as well as a director of local banks and the largest hospital in the area. He was also experienced in the governance of all important local water companies and agencies.

The baton passed to the new president of the company, Charles Thomas, in 1960. His political career was one of the reasons Thomas got the job. He had been Secretary of the Navy and was on a first name basis with President Dwight Eisenhower, who appointed him.

When he was hired in 1967, former US Marine Corps Colonel Gilbert (Gil) W. Ferguson was the first staff person at the Irvine Company in a senior position with direct responsibilities for government relations, media relations, and community relations.

DOI: 10.1201/9781003226291-19

Ferguson enlisted in the Marines at age 18 and saw action in the South Pacific, including at Tarawa, where he was awarded a Purple Heart. He remained in the reserves after the war and studied at the University of Southern California. During the Korean War he was called up, then ended his service with a stint in Viet Nam, where he commanded a battalion and worked as a combat correspondent. Ferguson had also directed a community relations program for the Marine Corps.[1]

Ferguson's military history and bearing, along with his solid Republican outlook, must have appealed to William Mason, who had become company president in 1966. Ferguson certainly would have found common ideological ground with the county's state and national representatives, who included two conservative Republicans whose districts encompassed the Irvine Ranch: Representative James Utt, and State Senator John Schmitz.

Utt's family had farmed land on and adjacent to the Irvine Ranch—his father was well known to JI. Schmitz arrived as a Marine Corps pilot at Marine Corps Air Station El Toro and stayed in the county after his service ended. He rode a wave of rising conservatism into the state senate in 1964, beating a well-known and well-liked former assemblyman, Bruce Sumner. Schmitz succeeded Utt in Congress when Utt died in office in 1970.

Other local state representatives presented themselves as solid Republicans, but with a softer edge than Schmitz and Utt. Assemblyman Robert Badham's family owned a hardware store in Newport Beach—he was a traditional, small business, mainstream representative. The other state senator was Dennis Carpenter, an attorney and former FBI agent. Avuncular and blessed with a sense of humor, Carpenter maintained his conservative credentials but was rarely averse to a compromise if he could obtain something beneficial for his district.

Irvine Company lobbying in Sacramento was the domain of Hunt Conrad, who also represented landowners like Tenneco, which had huge agricultural and oil holdings in the state's Central Valley.

Conrad is remembered by Philip Bettencourt, who joined the company in 1973, as "... definitely old school," someone whose advocacy approach was founded largely on relationships. Bettencourt recalled flying to the state capitol with an armload of briefing papers to use for persuasion purposes, only to be told by Conrad to set them aside and join him and the targeted elected officials for lunch at Frank Fat's, a famous capitol watering hole and restaurant.[2]

But times were changing in Sacramento. The one man one vote decision by the United State Supreme Court transformed the California State Senate from rural domination to urban, as senators from then forward represented districts drawn to reflect actual population. And the entire legislature went from meeting on a part-time basis to full time, a reflection of the myriad of issues facing a state soon to be the nation's most populous.

Joining Conrad representing the company was William Geyer (see chapter 3), a former legislative staffer at the capitol with a cerebral style and policy expertise. While the relationship-based model Conrad exemplified would survive for a while, it was a dying breed; Geyer and those with skills like his would increasingly dominate lobbying.

One of the most critical political issues facing the company during this period was the California Coastal Act, passed as an initiative in 1972.

The Coastal Act was a largely grassroots reaction to the perception that the state's beautiful beaches in the south and coastal bluffs in the north were under attack by development and access restrictions. At the time, the Irvine Company's coastal holdings were closed to the public and plans for development were in the early stages of formulation. The prospect of state regulation by a panel of unelected decision makers was ominous.

Moreover, the company had other assets operating within what would likely become part of the new coastal zone, including retail centers, restaurants, and hundreds of boat slips. Based on some of the campaign rhetoric that accompanied the issue, it seemed possible that the new commission would leverage permits to encourage—or force—public access to beaches (California law made all state beaches public below the mean high tide line, but property owners could block access to the beach, rendering the high tide line demarcation essentially meaningless).

The initiative set out broad parameters of protection for the coast but required that legislation be passed by a date certain to fill in the details as to precisely how it would be administered and interpreted.

The initiative created a coastal zone, proscribed by a line from Crescent City in the north to Imperial Beach in the south, generally set at 1,000 yards inland from the shoreline. All development within the zone would be subject to the new rules created by the legislation, and overseen by a series of six 12-member regional commissions, and a single statewide commission, also with 12 members.

The Irvine Company had opposed the initiative on philosophical and practical grounds and contributed funds to the campaign against it. But once it passed, Ray Watson—who was soon to become company president—acknowledged that it was law and the company would have to find a way to live with it.

Then the map showing the proposed coastal zone boundary came out, and Watson's position changed.

The line bisected Newport Center, the company's flagship commercial and retail development; it included the company's headquarters, several medical office buildings, a theater complex, and, most important, the Fashion Island Shopping Center.

Had the line remained as drawn, it would have literally cut through the heart of the outdoor mall, placing a shoe store within the coastal zone and the JC Penney store adjacent to it outside the zone. Expanding the mall or making any improvements would have meant a separate application and consideration by the new commission.

No one knew what standards the commission would establish. Environmental forces emboldened by the passage of the initiative were lobbying for aggressive enforcement. (Because the Coastal Act contained a provision citing watersheds connected to the coast as potentially eligible for protection, developers joked that left unchecked, the coastal zone would reach into the Sierra Nevada mountain range hundreds of miles inland, where rivers that eventually reached the sea originated. Passage of time would prove the fear of overreach not entirely unjustified.)

Watson was invited by then-Speaker of the Assembly Leo T. McCarthy to join negotiations in Sacramento to hammer out the enabling legislation.

Watson spent his airplane trip to Sacramento trying to persuade a local assemblyman (he didn't name him in his oral history, but it was probably Robert Badham) to vote the legislation out of committee. As the plane landed, Watson said, the assemblyman reluctantly agreed to do so.

> We get up there, and while they are having the public meeting, where people are coming in and arguing pro and con on the new bill—McCarthy puts me in a room with the Sierra Club and other environmentalists who are debating about the location of the coastal line. They wanted me to support the bill, which (I was willing to) on the basic premise of the bill, but I said not unless the line was changed.[3]

According to Watson, the Sierra Club representative would not agree to a change. He described how McCarthy broke the impasse.

McCarthy returned to the anteroom and reminded the environmentalists that he considered them friends, then turned up the heat:

> We want this bill supported by the industry as well as the environmental world. We don't want to just have a bill that is supported by one faction against another. I have brought up to you the person from the company that has the most respect in the field of the environment and planning, and if you can't get along with him, you can't get along with anybody and I won't support the bill.
>
> "They then agreed," Watson said. "Then I go into the next room, and I watch the process, and (McCarthy) is going to each assemblyman saying, 'the Irvine Company has come aboard,' and the bill passed."[4]

The Irvine Company did not employ a lobbyist in Washington, D.C. until 1980. The man who recruited the federal lobbyist had recently joined the company as an employee after serving it for years as a consultant. His name was Robert H. Shelton.

Shelton was studying at Pomona College when World War II broke out. He joined the US Navy V12 program and saw service in the South Pacific and occupied Japan at the close of the war. Young Ensign Shelton then found his way to Washington, D.C. (A few months before his death in 2016, Shelton confided to two former company employees that he had been recruited into the CIA at the conclusion of the war and stayed for several months.)

Returning to California, Shelton finished his undergraduate degree at Pomona College, earning a Phi Betta Kappa key, then took a graduate degree at UC Berkeley. At age 32 he was the city administrator for the City of Santa Barbara, and four years later was selected to be city manager of Newport Beach. Shelton's five-year tenure at Newport Beach ended when he was hired away by developers and New York financiers planning to build a new city in the Santa Monica

Mountains adjacent to Los Angeles. The plan was that Shelton would help obtain government permission to build the new city and then become its city manager.

The city in the mountains was never built, but the work Shelton did on its behalf took him to Los Angeles City Hall and to Sacramento, where his low-key style and solid credibility won him relationships on both sides of the political aisle. By the late 1960s, Shelton's principal consulting client was the Irvine Company.

Bob Shelton got along with everyone—that, along with intelligence, integrity, and good looks, were his gifts. Moving quietly behind the scenes, leveraging relationships forged at city halls and county administrative buildings, Shelton was a master at creating an atmosphere of openness, trust, and confidence. Shelton once schooled a young associate on the art of dealing with elected officials and staff, advising not to get too dressed up, to wear a suit that came off the rack—and a modest priced one at that—so as not to intimidate the low paid county or city employee whose decision could make or break a project.

Shelton was also sensitive as to how to converse with others, and how best to make a request. "May I invite you to consider this" was a favorite Shelton phrase, along with "... can we find a way for both of us to agree on how to approach this?" And while Shelton could teach others, it was his presence and persona that, as years progressed, became one of his most valuable assets. He remarked to an associate that, "... in some ways, I'm like a priest; if I am in the meeting, it brings a degree of credibility or comfort that wouldn't otherwise be present."[5]

One of Shelton's signature pieces of negotiating advice—offered only half-jokingly—was, "... when in doubt, be generous."[6]

****

The media landscape in Orange County in the late 1960s and into the 1970s was dominated by two major newspapers whose circulation overlapped the Irvine Ranch: the *Santa Ana Register* and the *Daily Pilot*.

The *Register* reached every community in the county, as well as a few readers across the county line. Owned by the Hoiles family, the *Register's* philosophy was ultra-right, a view that also colored its news coverage. Public education, for example, was a frequent target of the *Register* editorial page, and reporters were required to refer to schools as "tax-supported schools" in any story about education.

Reporters who wanted to maintain their jobs soon learned that stories attacking or debasing government in any form would tend to find their way onto the front pages. Reporters and editors were notoriously low paid, and turnover was frequent, but there were a handful of dedicated, fair-minded journalists who found ways to report with credibility.

The *Daily Pilot* had started as a weekly paper in Costa Mesa, then went to seven days a week. The *Pilot* focused coverage on the coastline of the county, with small news bureaus in San Clemente and Laguna Beach to the south. Laguna Beach and Newport Beach received special attention from *Pilot* editors—both communities were affluent and well-educated, a rich target both for circulation and advertising.

Pilot owner and publisher Walter Burroughs actively supported and promoted the University of California's plans to establish a new campus in Irvine, and when the new community there began to grow, the *Pilot* aggressively covered the incorporation campaign and when it passed, the new city council.

One of the *Pilot's* most talented reporters had been hired away by Gil Ferguson to become the Irvine Company's director of public relations.

Jerry Collins was an outstanding writer. He was also something of a newsroom character. Tall and lanky, Collins had an irreverent sense of humor combined with the usual cynicism reporters acquire after years of covering politicians and dueling with PR agents. Collins was a smoker, which made him an oddity at the Irvine Company, and he was also diabetic, which could occasionally lead to aberrant behavior when his blood sugar ran low in long meetings. Collins was rarely seen in his office or in the halls without a soft drink in his hand.

And while company executives were careful about their appearance, Collins got away with varying degrees of dress that could charitably be described as informal. (Bettencourt recalls being mildly admonished by a superior for showing up on casual Friday wearing a silk turtleneck).

Collins perfected a public relations strategy the Irvine Company would employ for years when issues reached a critical moment: the full-page ad.

There was a certain mystique to the Irvine Company—it owned one-sixth of the county. Its headquarters were in a stunning, tall (for Newport Beach) office building overlooking the Pacific Ocean. The people who worked for the company were well-educated and well spoken. And it was powerful, at least in the minds of many people.

So, when the Irvine Company spoke, people paid attention.

Using primarily the *Daily Pilot*, and later when it established an Orange County presence, the *Los Angeles Times*, Collins persuaded company managers to advertise when a press release or an argument in print wasn't effective. At those times, he counseled, it was wise to go over the heads of reporters, editors, and publishers and speak directly to residents (and voters).

A full-page ad made an impact—readers literally couldn't miss it. And because it was expensive and required little effort by the newspaper to mockup (the company made sure of that by creating it with in-house graphics talent), the company demanded and received favorable placement in the paper, often on the back page of the main news section.

Thoughtfully conceived and written in the kind of clear, compelling prose that Collins was adept at composing, a full-page ad from the Irvine Company could set a tone, recast an issue, or stimulate positive dialog where just yesterday there had been division.

The full-page ad was a great success, but it came at a price. After executing the ad, it was not unusual for Collins to disappear from the office for a day or two. Sometimes he'd go to a movie, other times take a drive in his newest sports car (Collins went through a lot of cars, often neglecting to change the oil until an engine overheated or burned out).

"Jerry is like a great baseball pitcher who goes nine innings and throws a one-hitter," one of his fellow employees observed. "And like a great starter, after a win he needs a few days off until his next game."[7]

The Hardy to Collins' Laurel was a jovial, rotund former *Register* reporter, Ed Portmann.

While Collins was often aloof and brusque with reporters and colleagues alike, Portmann was the epitome of the glad-handing public relations operative. Portmann got along with everyone and was universally liked by the reporters in the county press corps—he created a human face for the company. Portmann took the lead organizing the grand openings and receptions that were often staged to celebrate a new product or development. No reporter ever left an Irvine Company event unsatisfied in food or drink if it had been put on by Ed Portmann.

While Collins was churning out full-page ads and Portmann was schmoozing reporters, Ferguson turned his attention to the small but growing community in Irvine.

Ferguson sensed, correctly, that Irvine residents would find it helpful to receive a regular communication that listed community events and other information. He sold company management on creating a monthly newsletter sponsored by the Irvine Company to send to the new communities. It was well-received, leading Ferguson and Collins to take the next step: turn it into a weekly newspaper.

Ray Watson found Ferguson's theory a good one. "He cited the issue of a newspaper, if it had advertising in it, it's more legitimate in the customer's minds. It seems more real than if it is just the Irvine Company telling you everything."[8]

(Prior to Ferguson's arrival, the company had published a quarterly newsletter written by Jim Sleeper, who had worked there as "Irvine Company Historian." It disappeared when Sleeper resigned and returned to freelance writing.)

The first editor of *Irvine World News* was Jeanne Keevil, who had worked with Collins at the *Daily Pilot*. Joining Keevil was George McDonald, who had worked for daily papers in northern Orange County. Both were accomplished journalists and set out to cover the new community thoroughly and fairly, but with the daily knowledge their careers and paychecks were overseen by the Irvine Company.

Ferguson was torn: "...no one will believe a paper if you don't have both sides," he recalled. "It pained me to allow both sides. I had to explain to management why it was important to allow someone who didn't like us to go on at such lengths."[9]

But when it came to incorporating the new city, the incorporation proponents, *Irvine World News*, and Irvine Company management were all on the same page; they supported it wholeheartedly. (John Burton, who led the incorporation effort, recalled regular visits to Collins, who taught him the fine points of dealing with the press. Burton was grateful: "I didn't have a clue how to do that."[10])

The *Daily Pilot* didn't take sides in the incorporation battle in its news columns but covered it extensively. Reporter George Leidal's byline was ubiquitous during the months leading up to the election; thereafter he covered the new city for several years.

Ferguson's enthusiasm for incorporation led to the perception among some community leaders that the Irvine Company, both through *Irvine World News* and in other ways, was supporting candidates for the new city council while promoting incorporation. Whether that was the deciding factor, or there were others, not long after the new city was created, Ferguson and the Irvine Company parted ways, opening the door for his successor, Thomas Wilck.

(Years after leaving the Irvine Company, Ferguson—who won a seat representing Newport Beach and Irvine in the California Assembly—lamented the decision to create the paper. "It is amazing how quickly we lost control of (it)," he told Don Dennis, who edited the paper in the 1980s.[11])

In addition to managing political and media duties, Wilck inherited a robust community relations operation that had grown under Ferguson at the direction of Philip Bettencourt, who had come to the company after serving as assistant city manager in Newport Beach.

Bettencourt joined a half dozen other individuals who provided and promoted outreach primarily to Newport Beach, then to Irvine.

"I created the first systematic monitoring system of issues and people" for the company, Bettencourt recalled, starting with the basics—a calendar in the "… ready room" for planning communications and events, as well as a map of the county with identifying pins to locate the homes of elected officials and other VIPs. His department also installed one of the first fax machines at the company, "… which became a real curiosity."[12]

Bettencourt started a clipping service for the company, delivering to executives a daily compendium of newspaper and magazine articles about local issues.

In those years, Bettencourt said, systematic outreach and staging large community events was "… part of the company's DNA." Each summer at the outdoor mall, Fashion Island, free weekly concerts were held, with musical offerings in the vein of the famed Boston Pops. For years thereafter, company executives marveled at how the audience grew, observing with a mixture of amusement and cynicism how millionaires and multimillionaires from Newport Beach maneuvered for the best free seat on the lawn.[13]

Each spring, the annual cattle roundup became an excuse for a rodeo and lavish barbeque, attended by hundreds. (There was also a separate event just for the press.) Held in Bommer Canyon, a short distance away from the growing campus at UC Irvine, the roundup was a reminder of the ranch heritage that was quickly fading away.

(One rodeo, Bettencourt recalled, was attended by members of the Orange County Grand Jury. A juror happened to witness a calf being castrated. Horrified, she asked one of the company's agriculture executives, Dean Buchinger, how such a barbaric practice could take place. Buchinger replied that as for the calf, "I'm not saying it was the best day of his life, but he'll get over it."[14])

In addition to the roundup, smaller events focused on specific neighborhoods and influence groups took place with regularity. At the time, the company was constantly opening new homes and shopping centers, which were almost always celebrated with a reception or party. And as the Irvine Company's reputation grew, visitors from the nation and abroad would arrive for tours, which Bettencourt and his compatriots gladly provided.

Rounding out the array of community relations tools were, Bettencourt fondly recalled, "... four tickets in the second row for Lakers games, and two corporate apartments for special guests of the company." Docked at one of the marinas the company owned on Newport Bay was a 40-foot Grand Banks motor launch, the *Isla Bella*. Over the years, many an Orange County or Newport Beach staff person enjoyed a catered sunset cruise on the bay, as did aides to members of Congress, assemblymen, and senators.[15]

The company also gave generously to charities on the ranch and beyond. So much was given and so many events accompanied the donation, one executive recalled, it became an almost full-time job for a community relations secretary just to fill tables.

The face of company community relations at the time was a genial former insurance agent named Michael Manahan.

If Central Casting had been called seeking an actor to portray a community relations representative, Michael Manahan would have taken the role hands down. Dapper, immaculately dressed, and well-shod, Manahan navigated the world of chambers of commerce, service clubs, PTAs, Little Leagues, women's clubs, and the dozens of other community entities with a broad smile and friendly handshake.

Manahan was a team player who was occasionally put on the spot by someone with a gripe against the giant landowner. Manahan never crossed the company line in public, but he was sometimes vocal in staff meetings if he saw merit in a complaint. He was also a talented observer of human behavior, privately and accurately assessing the foibles and strengths of upper management with those he trusted.

Tom Wilck's professional pedigree included two high profile organizations— the Walt Disney Company and the administration of Richard Nixon.

Wilck handled a variety of public relations duties for Disney, even occasionally lugging a first run film for its premier if necessary. He assisted with the creation of Cal Arts, a private school in California, and with Disney World in Florida. During his consulting career for the company, he was often in Walt's private office, where he met and married Walt's secretary, Tommie.

His first position in the Nixon administration was relatively modest—congressional liaison for the Small Business Administration—but he moved up to the Republican National Committee and worked at the 1972 convention. Wilck left Washington untouched by Watergate and arrived at the Irvine Company in 1973 with solid credentials for a conservative company in the most conservative urban county in California.

Many of his colleagues found Wilck hard to read. He usually dressed in sport coat and slacks and had steel gray hair. Wilck also wore heavy, black horn-rimmed glasses, and in many settings his demeanor was close to somber. Wilck had a sense of humor, although he was careful to show it only with trusted associates. The serious demeanor faded into sometimes loud and raucous laughter in private after the second round of his favorite drink, a Rob Roy.

Wilck found himself with a large organization, and a hole to fill in public relations. Shortly after Ferguson's departure, Jerry Collins had been fired. Wilck quickly determined that however serious his infraction had been, Collins would do less damage inside the company than at the *Daily Pilot*. Collins returned to the public relations staff.

But Wilck knew that the company's growing profile with the national media would require more sophisticated skills and a person with a demeanor less problematic than Collins'.

Martin Brower was happy with his job at the Los Angeles architectural firm of Welton Becket when Wilck asked him to join the Irvine Company. He turned down Wilck's initial overtures, but after an offer of a substantial pay rise and outstanding benefits like a company car, unlimited gas, and membership at the Balboa Bay Club on the shores of Newport Bay, Brower convinced his wife that Orange County was worth a try.

Brower would become one of the most successful public relations executives in the county, but at the time, as he chronicled in his memoir, *Orange County Jew*, he was a pioneer at the Irvine Company:

> One of the first public relations professionals I met happened to be Jewish. Gloria Zigner ... could hardly conceal her joy that the Irvine Company had hired a Jew to head public relations. It had not occurred to me, but I soon realized I was the only obviously Jewish person in management at the time. I attributed that not to any anti-Jewish sentiment, but rather to the relatively few Jews in Orange County.[16]

(Brower's ethnicity was not his only Irvine Company oddity: he was a graduate of UCLA working in Newport Beach, fondly known at the time to some local wags as the "USC alumni ghetto.")

Wilck was also a UCLA graduate, but unlike the open and affable Brower, he rarely discussed any aspect of his early life with professional colleagues. No one, for example, knew that Wilck had grown up at Marine Corps bases, and then in tiny Farmville, Virginia, where his family settled after his father retired from the Marines. Wilck had served in the Marine Corps from 1950 to 1952, another part of his life that was rarely shared. As far as most people knew, Wilck's personal and professional history began in California.

Wilck found himself in the role of a media executive in addition to his political and community relations duties. The company's cable television unit, Community Cablevision, reported to him. The cable system occasionally aired public affairs programming and reserved time for events to fulfil its public access requirements, but most customers were too busy to watch—they were exploring the dozens of new cable channels available to them instead of the usual 13 on network television.

(The cable system programming during the City of Irvine incorporation battle was a key factor in that effort. But cable's potential as a political tool was never considered, according to Warren Fix, who along with company executive Frank Hughes, journeyed to the tiny town of Oroville in northern California to examine the cable operation there while evaluating its potential for Irvine Company properties. Fix also recalled that while the cost per resident for cable was a meager 50 cents per month, there was some pushback from homeowners.)

More problematic was the weekly newspaper and to a lesser degree, the bi-monthly magazine, *New Worlds*.

New Worlds, published every other month starting in 1969, was a coffee table publication—it went from the mailbox to the den or living room and was picked up again and again to be perused. One of the magazine's defining elements was photography, lots of it, in full color. Aerial views of the dramatic Newport Beach coastline, artistic abstracts of Irvine Company buildings, happy families gamboling in the parks and greenbelts of Irvine—*New Worlds* had them all.

New Worlds also served as a medium to explore in greater depth some of the social and political issues in Irvine Ranch communities. When company opinion surveys found a rising resistance to building new apartments in Irvine, *New Worlds* commissioned articles profiling the variety of individuals who lived in existing apartments in the city. Careful attention was paid to long-term residents, some of them older, who had lived in apartments for years. Young families were also featured, portraying their apartment experience as the first rung of the homeownership ladder that would lead to purchasing a single-family home in the city. The transient apartment dwellers that residents were wary of were nowhere to be seen.

Every year the new mayor of Irvine and Newport Beach was the subject of a *New Worlds* profile; what politician didn't like seeing a flattering photo montage of themselves delivered to every home in town, along with their life story? *New Worlds* was also a not-so-subtle vehicle to promote individuals who were allies or potential allies of the company. William Ficker, for example, had been the captain of an America's Cup sailing team, a natural subject of interest to nautical enthusiasts in Newport Beach. Ficker was also the leader of an organization promoting construction of a new bridge over the Newport Bay channel. Local anti-growth leaders opposed it. Guess who was profiled in *New Worlds*?

The magazine format allowed for the occasional thoughtful, in-depth article addressing issues like affordable housing or rate of growth, a perennial local issue. Such pieces were balanced out by regular offerings promoting new housing or commercial products from the company, as well as chronicles of the many building industry awards the company received. (In the years immediately following passage of the Tax Reform Act of 1969, *New Worlds* readers began to learn more about the James Irvine Foundation and its members through a series of articles, including a lengthy one listing the dozens of charities that received funding from the foundation. One article went so far as to portray the notoriously thrifty James Irvine II as a Scotch Santa Claus because he had created the foundation.)

While there were regular editorial meetings at Irvine Company headquarters to discuss stories for *New Worlds*, there were none for the staff of *Irvine World News*.

The weekly paper during the years of Wilck's tenure was treading the unseen line between robustly and honestly reporting on the vibrant and energetic young City of Irvine while considering how their choice of headlines or descriptions of issues would be received by their owners and executives at the Irvine Company.

Wilck did his best to protect the staff from company meddling. The paper carried a weekly column, The Irvine Company Report, under the byline of a company executive, ghostwritten by a public relations or marketing staff member. The editorials were rarely extreme, nor were there attacks on elected officials, but it was clear to most readers that the company's outlook on issues were reflected in editorials. The paper did not endorse candidates for office but accepted political ads.

Like Ferguson, Wilck understood that the paper was credible if Irvine residents believed it was fair, and for his tenure as publisher hewed a path that rarely gave in to pressure from the company to affect it. One of Wilck's toughest calls came when the paper created a poll to determine who were the most influential people in Irvine. City councilmembers were excluded from consideration, but everyone else was fair game. Wilck had to ask himself, what if a company opponent gets a high rating? What if Ray Watson gets a low rating or, worse, no rating at all? The paper shrewdly listed the ten winners not in order of finish, but alphabetically. The article made a strong impact, reinforcing the paper's independence and Wilck's willingness to give it a long leash.

During Wilck's tenure from 1973 until the sale of the company in 1977, there was continual political ferment in Newport Beach and Irvine, at the county board of supervisors, and among interest groups adept at stirring up public opinion.

Environmental advocacy, for example, had been growing ever since the *Friends of Mammoth* case led to the requirement that developments of almost any size had to prepare a report on how they would affect the physical landscape: the environmental impact report was born.[17]

On the southern border of the ranch in Laguna Beach, a movement to create a greenbelt of open space around the city had been waged for years by a local bookstore owner, James Dilley. The rumpled, soft-spoken Dilley cut an almost cartoonish figure in public meetings, but he was fiercely determined to see his dream come true. In doing so, he nourished a non-profit called the Laguna Greenbelt, which gathered funding and attracted intelligent, articulate volunteer leaders.

The Irvine Company had been badly stung by the battle to keep the Upper Newport Bay undeveloped, showing opponents of growth and development that a grassroots effort could have a genuine impact if managed in a sophisticated fashion. Out of that battle, the anti-growth group Stop Polluting Our Newport (SPON) was born. It would remain a burr under the company saddle for decades.

The four-mile-long company coastal property between Laguna Beach and Newport Beach was a cause waiting to happen, and in 1976 Friends of the Newport Coast was created. Eventually attracting a reported 2,000 members, Friends waged a determined, sophisticated campaign to limit development on the coastline.

There were business and commercial related issues smoldering as well. As the county had grown, airline service at Orange County Airport (now John Wayne Airport) had increased. Commercial jets were noisy, and their takeoff pattern went over some of the most expensive homes in Newport Beach. Residents there reached for their checkbooks instead of picket signs, hiring lawyers and noise consultants to wage a fight over the number of allowable flights and operating hours that continues to the present day. And while the company didn't have a direct interest in the airport, there was concern that the ability to build and rent commercial and industrial properties could be impacted if owners and managers were counting on unlimited ability to hop a jet.

Finally, as residential and commercial growth expanded, the county's road system didn't keep up.

There were several reasons. First, the county's conservative congressional representatives were blamed for refusing to seek federal road funding on philosophical grounds, as they had done for years. Millions of dollars that could have gone to Orange County projects found their way to other jurisdictions.

And just when state funding was needed most, Edmund G. "Jerry" Brown had been elected governor, ushering in the "era of limits" and an emphasis on funding for transit projects instead of freeways.

Transportation became one of the hottest issues in the county. Frustrations grew and elected officials held their fingers to the wind and swayed to the greener side of their respective parties.

Wilck's greatest strength was strategy. Behind the office door he habitually kept closed, he had the time and intelligence to think, sifting through the issue of transportation and how to deal with it. A few months after the new owners of the company brought in a new management team, Wilck proved his value to them with a single idea that led to a dramatic and effective shift in how the county approached transportation funding and construction.

Notes

1. Jocelyn Y. Stewart, "Gil Ferguson, 84; Conservative Served 10 Years in State Assembly," *Los Angeles Times*, May 9, 2007.
2. Philip Bettencourt, interview by C.M. Stockstill, May 4, 2020.
3. Raymond L. Watson and Ann Lage, *Planning and Developing the New Town of Irvine California, 1960–2003: Irvine Company President, 1973–1977, Walt Disney Company Chairman, 1983–1984* (Regional Oral History Office, the Bancroft Library, University of California, Berkeley, 2005) 182.
4. Watson and Lage, *Planning and Developing*, 184.
5. Author's recollection.
6. Author's recollection.
7. Author's recollection.
8. Watson and Lage, *Planning and Developing*, 368.
9. Mark Pinsky and George Frank, "Irvine Co. Weekly Performs a Delicate Balancing Act: Credibility, Power to Influence Are Goals of Irvine World News," *Los Angeles Times*, May 29, 1988.
10. John Burton, telephone interview by C.M. Stockstill, November 15, 2020.
11. *Orange County Register*, July 22, 2013,
12. Philip Bettencourt, interview, May 4, 2020.
13. Philip Bettencourt, interview, May 4, 2020.
14. Philip Bettencourt, interview, May 4, 2020.
15. Philip Bettencourt, interview, May 4, 2020.
16. Martin A. Brower, *Orange County Jew* (Bloomington, IN: Authorhouse, 2010) 20.
17. Friends of Mammoth v. Board of Supervisors. 1972, 8 Cal. 3d 247, 502 P.2d 1049 Cal. Rptr. 16 4 ERC 1593 (1972). Supreme Court of California.

    This landmark ruling altered California environmental law, determining that projects undertaken by private parties were subject to the California Environmental Quality Act (CEQA) that was enacted in 1970. Previously, only public agency projects were covered by CEQA.

19 Low-Cost Housing

"A Problem from Day One"

An undercurrent of skepticism and disappointment accompanied the Irvine Company's otherwise much heralded and celebrated transformation of the Irvine Ranch into a New Town.

The issue was housing. Specifically, housing for people who were not white and not affluent.

To put the issue in the perspective of the mid-1960s, it is helpful to explore an urban planning and development concept of the time: building New Towns.

As the label implies, the New Town movement was a reaction to how—after World War II—builders raced to build new homes for returning veterans. The resulting soulless sprawl of mass-produced tracts of houses, exemplified by Levittown on Long Island, caused urban planners and other academics to shudder at the sight. Surely, they argued, we can do better.

Doing better meant fleeing the urban core for the countryside and starting from a blank page, planning a completely new community that was utopian in vision and self-contained in execution. The idea had been tried in England to replace housing that was destroyed by the bombing of London and other areas and had resulted in several new communities built as New Towns. Why not try it in the United States?

Several New Towns sprang up around the same time as Irvine; the two best-known were Reston, Virginia, and Columbia, Maryland.

One of the hallmarks of planning for Reston and Columbia was a commitment to actively integrate the communities. As both were in states that had once either joined the Confederacy or were on its border, integration meant Black people. It also meant housing that was affordable to individuals and families on the lower end of the economic scale, many of whom were Black, but others who were not.

Fairly or not, when it came to housing policy, Irvine was compared to both communities.

Columbia was like Irvine in its approach to planning and community development. It had villages, a town center, and even a lake. And while it did not emanate from the Olympian mind of a planner like William Pereira, its creator was both an idealist and realistic businessman.

James Rouse had become financially successful as a commercial developer but yearned for success on a larger scale. He spent several years quietly piecing

DOI: 10.1201/9781003226291-20

together farmland outside of Baltimore until he and his partners obtained 14,000 acres. Rouse named the new community Columbia and set out to build it.

> Columbia was James Rouse's ideal vision of the country's future: a cultur-
> ally diverse, integrated city ... Rouse promised that every single person who
> works in Columbia could afford to live there ... Rouse and his compatriots
> fought to ensure that subsidized housing and apartments were built alongside
> larger single-family houses.[1]

Rouse's commitment to a diverse community reflected his personal values and experience in the development business. How many of his peers—then or now—would say something like this: "Profit is not the legitimate purpose of business, (it) is to provide a product or service that people need and do it so well that it is profitable."

Reston was built on a similar vision of equality by its founder, Robert Simon.

Simon was a New Yorker whose family was active in real estate development in the city. One of the family's holdings was Carnegie Hall. When it was sold, the proceeds provided Simon with enough money to purchase a 6,750-acre farm a few miles outside of Washington, D.C. where he created the new community. Reston's name was based on his initials, RES; the new city's humanitarian goals reflected his outlook on life.

Reston planning was founded on the Simon-authored Seven Principles, a document "that enshrined egalitarian values into Reston's soul and zoning code."[2]

Though much smaller in scale, Reston's physical planning was much like Columbia's, with a variety of housing types and densities. The town became a symbol of what progressive Virginians saw to overturn what one planner labeled the state's Jim Crow past. Speaking at Simon's 100th birthday celebration in 2014, Senator Tim Kaine said that "Bob took a state ... facing backward and turned it to face forward."[3]

Ray Watson's life and outlook on life left little doubt among those who worked with him that he cared deeply about injustice, discrimination, and opportunity. But Watson's role at the Irvine Company was nothing like Rouse's or Simon's at their respective communities; they were owners—their decisions were their own and were final. Watson was a manager, reporting to a board of directors controlled by a foundation and often riven by disputes with Irvine family members.

****

In California in the late 1950s and early 1960s, racial issues were a political and social fact of life. A contentious battle to eliminate racial bias in the rental or sale of housing began in 1963 with the passage of the Rumford Fair Housing Act. Its protections against discrimination in sale or rental of housing were overturned in a statewide referendum the following year, then reinstated into law in 1966 by the California Supreme Court. In August 1965, the Black community of Watts in southern Los Angeles erupted into rioting, quelled only when the National

Guard was summoned into the streets. The Black Panther Party was formed in Oakland in 1966, exacerbating racial tensions in the San Francisco Bay Area.

In contrast to urban woes elsewhere in the state, Orange County experienced almost no racial animosity or violence. A likely reason was that in 1960 Orange County's population was about 0.5 per cent Black.

During and after World War II, when Black people migrated to Southern California in larger numbers, the largest and most prosperous Black community took hold and expanded in the southern section of Los Angeles. Along Central Avenue, Black businesses thrived. Middle-class and upper-middle-class Blacks established homes in the Crenshaw-Adams area near the University of Southern California and later in a small enclave called Baldwin Hills (Ray Charles was among its residents). And while in 1948 the US Supreme Court had outlawed racial covenants on land sales, Southern California was still firmly, if unofficially, segregated.

In Orange County, the first notable concentration of Black residents arrived at the military bases at El Toro and in Tustin (there were Black Marines at Camp Pendleton, but off-base life there focused more to the south in Oceanside and San Diego). According to *A Different Shade of Orange*, a history of Black life in the county, a handful of Black individuals and families slowly began moving to Santa Ana and Fullerton in the same timeframe.[4] Santa Ana seemed to be the most accommodating community, while the City of Orange was known as a sundown town, meaning Blacks were unofficially banned from city streets after sunset.

The largest minority group in the county in the early 1960s were Hispanics, a little more than 10 per cent of the total population. Outside of a small legacy settlement of Hispanics in San Juan Capistrano, Santa Ana was the center of Mexican American social and commercial life in the county. Asians barely registered at 2 per cent of total county population. The people who made up both groups were largely poor and politically uninvolved. (In Santa Ana, which had the largest population of Hispanics, the seven-member city council would be all white until the late 1970s. A contributing factor: it is likely that a significant percentage of Hispanics living there at the time were not citizens.)

There were a few idealistic and liberal voices in the county arguing that measures should be taken to encourage or, if necessary, force integration and diversity in local communities. The Orange County Fair Housing Council had been founded by just such leaders in 1965, and there were branches of the American Civil Liberties Union (ACLU) and the National Association for the Advancement of Colored People (NAACP). But Orange County was better known as a stronghold of the John Birch Society, and with one or two exceptions, its political, social, and business leadership was not sympathetic to pleas for integration.

And so, in Irvine, while race was a minor factor in the housing issue, building homes that virtually everyone could afford translated into the political shorthand of "affordable housing."

In his oral history, Watson confirms that, "... the price of housing, it has always been a problem, from Day One. From lawsuits that were filed to make more affordable housing, to interest groups that said, 'why don't you build more affordable housing?'"[5]

The issue of affordable housing in Irvine received a probing analysis in *Postsuburban California: The Transformation of Orange County Since World War II.* Leading the charge was Martin Schiesl, a professor of history at California State University Los Angeles. Writing in 1991, Schiesl was less than charitable in his view of the Irvine Company's—and Watson's—commitment to achieving a diverse community:

> Least promising to (Watson) and other Irvine (Company) executives was low-income housing. They claimed to be committed to population diversity and repeatedly spoke about a reasonable range of building types and prices. . most of their homes, however, were luxury dwellings ... affordable only to upper-middle and upper-class people. The average selling price of a single-family house on the Irvine property was $35,000, more than twice the average for the county.[6]

(Professor Schiesl may have been guilty of selective or erroneous analysis of statistics: Irvine Company property would have included land in Newport Beach, where prices were naturally higher because of the coastal location and the city of Newport Beach had no commitment, legal or otherwise, to building low-cost housing. Also, in Irvine there were at least three communities within the city that had been constructed on land not owned by the company. The homes there were priced considerably lower than homes built on land owned by the company. Were they included in his calculation? We don't know.)

Citing work by other scholars, Schiesl attributed the outcome to the economics of development, which are, in the words of the scholars "... designed to escalate values as rapidly as possible. Not only may housing for lower income persons be seen as threatening necessary appreciation in land values but rising prices themselves make it exceedingly difficult to build moderately priced housing units.[7]"

Schiesl then made his own conclusion: "Acting on these considerations, the Irvine Company chose not to hold down the costs of new houses and continued to advertise its urban landscape as a high income, homogenous place to live.[8]"

Interviewed in 2003, Watson repeated his oft-stated, personal commitment to building diverse communities. "I was an advocate of (affordable housing), but the question is, how do you do it?"[9]

He harkened back to an example of housing market dynamics that is as valid today as it was in the 1960s, the timeframe of his example. "I became convinced early on that (with regard to housing prices) the market is the market."[10]

Watson described what happened then when the Irvine Company, feeling pressure to make homes affordable, hired two companies to build homes near Newport Center in a community called Harbor View Hills:

> The company made an agreement with two local developers to build it, with the requirement that in the end, they had to be able to sell the houses for $35,000 or less on leasehold. For Newport Beach, that was a very affordable

price in those times. They built the houses. The first weekend they sold out, and the following weekend the houses were resold by those who bought them for $10,000 more.[11]

The only way to assure that housing would be affordable to lower- or moderate-income residents, Watson argued, was to either subsidize the cost of the land and construction and/or restrict the price upon subsequent sale. He used the example of the Inclusion Area around UC Irvine, where the company had restricted development to housing, and where the university system had imposed its own resale restrictions on faculty and staff who bought there. Prices in the area were allowed to go up, but only as much as allowed by a special formula, keeping prices far below what the market was nearby.

Watson repeated his view that market prices would determine housing costs and only intervention either by the developer, the builder, or government to control the market dynamic would keep home prices affordable.

Implicit in Watson's ruminations on the subject was the unstated position the company took on the matter: it would not unilaterally reduce the price of land, nor would it impose its own restrictions on the price of a house built in a company community.

The Irvine Company was not alone in this attitude in Orange County—no one building or developing there was restricting prices on housing. It was true that in the older and less desirable parts of the county, land prices were lower and subsequently so was the price of a house. Irvine, however, for a variety of factors, was drawing more affluent, better educated, and more sophisticated buyers. They wanted and could afford homes with more amenities. Neighborhoods in Irvine also had community pools and playgrounds, amenities rarely found in older cities in the county.

And the new community of Irvine was better located than the similar planned communities of Mission Viejo, further south along Interstate 5—Irvine was closer to the employment centers in Anaheim and Fullerton, and even closer to the growing Irvine Industrial Complex adjacent to Orange County Airport. Not to mention near the coast and more temperate. To quote the trite but true phrase about real estate, it was all about location, location, location.

Debate about Irvine Company housing issues up until late 1971 took place in the realm of either the County of Orange or the city of Newport Beach. The county had approved the company's southern section master plan in 1964. There had been discussion about housing prices and diversity during the review of the plan, but there were no restrictions or goals placed in the zoning document by the board of supervisors. And in Newport Beach, where sprouts of anti-growth sentiment were peeking into view, no official actions had been taken on housing costs.

It would take the incorporation of Irvine and a small group of motivated individuals to bring the issue of housing cost out of theory and into the courtroom for a decisive confrontation.

****

Wesley Marx was a part-time academic and author who with his wife Judy were among the first residents of University Park.

Marx was a Stanford graduate (Political Science, 1956) who had worked as a journalist in Los Angeles, first on the Pasadena *Star News*, then on magazines. He had branched off into book writing with publication of *The Frail Ocean*, a dense, well-researched examination of environmental issues affecting the world's oceans. It was a natural subject for Marx, who enjoyed diving and body surfing.

Judy Marx was a teacher. Of the two, Wesley was more cerebral and softer spoken, and often displayed a more serious demeanor. Judy, by contrast, was a smiling dynamo. She taught public speaking at a local high school and was good at teaching it because she was good at doing it.

The couple, like a core of early residents of University Park, were politically active and liberal. They became members of Irvine Tomorrow, a small but vocal group committed to shaping the new community in the vision of William Pereira as a city of intellect, fairness, and opportunity for every sector of society.

Despite Irvine Tomorrow's opposition to Irvine cityhood, three of the winning council candidates had been endorsed by the group, and Wesley Marx was appointed by one of them to the city planning commission.

Their environmental views had brought the Marx's into the orbit of Frank and Frances Robinson and their crusade to prevent the Upper Newport Bay from being developed into a marina and water recreation area. They were plaintiffs with the Robinsons in the first lawsuit against the Irvine Company challenging the Upper Bay agreement with the County of Orange.

Wesley Marx learned of a recently formed Southern California public interest law firm; among its youthful founders was Carlyle Hall.

Hall got a job with the well-connected Los Angeles firm of O'Melveny and Myers after law school, but before starting to practice he went to Uganda for three years to help the new country build a law school.

When he returned, full of idealism, he and three friends founded the Center for Law in the Public Interest. O'Melveny was supportive, Hall recalled in a 2021 interview, and he and the other founders devoted a lot of their time raising funds for the new endeavor toward the goal of, "… bringing social and environmental change to Southern California."[12]

In 1972, the landmark *Friends of Mammoth*[13] ruling altered California environmental law, determining that private projects were subject to the California Environmental Quality Act (CEQA). Previously, only public projects were covered by CEQA.

The ruling spurred creation of detailed, lengthy analyses of private development projects, soon labeled as environmental impact reports (EIRs).

The invention of the EIR had an important benefit for individuals and organizations wanting to amend or stop developments; it made it possible to file a lawsuit not against the development itself, but against the now-required EIR that sought to justify it. And filing a lawsuit was relatively inexpensive, essentially just the time it took for an attorney to write it up and pay the modest court filing fee.

This was the method Marx, his wife, and a few other Irvine residents chose to make their stand on the issue of affordable housing in the new community. Their target was the EIR for the large industrial development the Irvine Company planned to build at the southeastern border of the city where the I-5 and I-405 Freeways met. The company called it Irvine Industrial Complex-East (IIC-East).

The Marxs and two other couples filed a lawsuit against the City of Irvine's consideration of the EIR for the IIC-East (the city was the target because it was the sponsor of the EIR; the Irvine Company joined the suit as a real party in interest and assisted the city with its legal strategy).

Acting as the spokesman for the six Irvine residents, Marx explained their reasoning in a lengthy article in the *Irvine World News*.

Their main motivation, he said, was,

> ... to have the city develop a plan that discloses how it will meet its stated obligation to meet the housing needs generated by the city's industrial complexes. This plan will disclose to the citizens what they can expect in terms of low- and moderate-income housing ... it should provide a mechanism showing how the housing proposals will be met and which steps will be taken ... for the city to proceed.[14]

Contrasting the planned, higher density University Town Center directly across from UC Irvine with Turtle Rock, decidedly less dense, Marx said "there is definitely a need for the city to give priority to projects with a diversity of housing opportunities."[15]

As a condition to achieving zoning approval for the massive Woodbridge project, the Irvine Company had reluctantly agreed to price 10 per cent of the units in the village to meet the standard for moderate incomes. When asked if the condition showed a willingness of the city and the company to address the housing issue, Marx said "... it is a dangerous illusion to say that Irvine has done more than other cities to meet housing needs when most of the workers in the existing Irvine Industrial Complex don't live here."[16]

Marx was critical of the city council:

> If the city cannot accept federal housing assistance—and other cities don't seem to have this hang-up—the city could use suggestions made in its own housing implementation plan (which included higher densities, easing of park dedication requirements, low interest loans, etc.).[17]

Marx was asked directly if the lawsuit was aimed at stopping growth. Not so, he said. "In general, we are after the kind of growth and development that will solve problems, not create them."[18]

As might be expected, city councilmembers queried for the article made comments ranging from mildly bombastic to hostile. Watson, representing the Irvine Company point of view, expressed frustration as he tried to put the issue into perspective: "Whenever issues like these are tied up in court, it can take years to finally resolve them," Watson commented:

> The courts are not a super zoning body. They cannot resolve the problems of housing, the economy, the environment, or other matters by using the statutes of the city ... Irvine is a new city with limited resources, and Irvine has done more in a democratic manner to address the problems of building a new city, and there are many of them besides housing ... than any other city.[19]
>
> All cities are struggling with housing. The city and the Irvine Company have worked to provide a cross mix of housing as best they can in view of the economy and environmental restraints. I get frustrated when people ignore what has been done here in terms of housing.[20]

Watson ended his comments on a conciliatory note: "I don't question the integrity of the petitioners. I understand their frustration. I also disagree with the means they are using to approach the problem."[21]

(Interviewed in 2021, Judy Marx recalled that Watson invited her and Wesley to lunch at the Irvine Company while the lawsuit was underway. "There were forty Irvine Company employees there, and we sat at Ray's table. He asked us to come, he told us, to show his compatriots that we didn't have horns."[22])

(Judy Marx also remembers looking around the lunch crowd and seeing a single woman, who was doing the serving. She asked Watson how the company's affirmative action program was working, and said Watson got a big laugh out of her inquiry.[23])

The lawsuit filed by the Marx's challenging the EIR for the Irvine Industrial Complex-East was the first to be heard in court and was dismissed a few months later. The Orange County Fair Housing Council and the Center for Law in the Public Interest filed a companion lawsuit, attacking the city's general plan and the failure to provide a solution to the imbalance between jobs and housing. This lawsuit survived, but as time passed it became increasingly evident that its fate was uncertain, leading its sponsors to float the idea of a settlement.

The settlement proposed an annual subsidy of $72,882 for 10 per cent of the 644 families earning less than $12,000 per year, a figure generated using expected employment in the IIC-East. They calculated the ten-year total for the subsidy at $4 million, plus a two-year transition period subsidy of $1.4 million. There would then be a series of credits for the city and the company based on federal funds received by the city and low-income rental units the company would build. It was unclear precisely where the money would be generated from absent those provisions.

The city and the company rejected the proposal but did find a nugget of positive news. As *Irvine World News* reported in its story on the rejection,

> ... one significant aspect of the proposed settlement is an acknowledgement that creation of for-sale low-income housing is next to impossible. To quote

the settlement proposal, 'because ownership of newly constructed homes for low-income families is unthinkable in the current housing market, the proposal assumes the housing needs of these families to be met by rental housing.[24]

The company and city countered a year later with a ten-year plan for 478 low-cost units that would be dependent on state and federal assistance. The company estimated the value of the offer at $5 million. The plan went nowhere.

As the settlement talks ran hot and cold, Hall was contacted by the company with an urgent request. A planned auto center adjacent to the IIC-East was running into problems—auto dealers were aware of the pending lawsuit and reluctant to invest money in a project that might get dragged into the litigation.

An auto center was a big deal for a city. Sales tax revenues were a critical part of city finances, and while the center was in a prime freeway location, if it stalled another city might lure it away. The city and the company, Hall said, pleaded with him to convince his clients to promise not to oppose the auto center. Hall believed doing so would increase the chances of a settlement, and the agreement was made.[25]

It turned out to be a wise decision. Hall said that subsequent private discussions with high level Irvine Company executives, including Watson, were cordial and increasingly positive. "They wanted to reach a settlement," he said. However, the company was consumed by the bidding war for shares of the James Irvine Foundation, and an agreement remained unattainable.[26]

It would fall to the new owners of the Irvine Company to bring the lawsuit to a conclusion.

A few months after Watson departed and new management was installed at the company, yet another settlement was proposed, with a 12-year term and provision of at least 700 units of low-cost rental units, and the possible use of some of the land at UC Irvine.

The new settlement gained traction and became the basis for the final agreement made in late September 1977, just a month after the new owners assumed control of the Irvine Company. The deciding factor was a provision that a new element of state law would be signed by Governor Jerry Brown guaranteeing that the company had the right to build the IIC-East in the event of future litigation. That was enough to convince the city council to accept the deal on a 4–1 vote.

The agreement mandated the Irvine Company to build at least 700 rental or for-sale units for low-income individuals, with half of the units to be aimed at persons with annual income of $8,400 or less. It also included a provision for new lower-cost units on the UC Irvine campus in the Inclusion Area (this never happened, and instead the company built an additional 700 low-cost units in apartment complexes in Woodbridge). The city made a modest contribution of $329,000 toward the deal from state and federal funds.

(Recalling these events in 2021, Hall mentioned a radical legal strategy he and others considered as they wrestled with the lawsuit: challenging the Irvine Company as a monopoly. The theory, Hall said, would be built on the argument

that by leasing land instead of selling it, the company was behaving in a monop-
olistic, and therefore illegal, manner. The idea evaporated when the company
stopped leasing land that homes were built upon and sold it instead).[27]

The agreement largely closed the door on the issue of low-cost housing in
Irvine. It was replaced as the years went forward with general unease about how
fast new homes were being constructed and the perceived lack of road capacity
throughout the county to handle traffic, both in Irvine as well as in other communities. As freeways became more clogged, drivers found that using the major
east/west roads in Irvine was better than waiting on the I-5 or I-405, especially
during peak hour, which increased local transportation concerns.

Pre-dating the lawsuit, the company had sponsored a HUD apartment project
in University Town Center across the street from UC Irvine. It attracted little
notice, pro or con. There was also a small amount of lower-cost housing built
on two non-company parcels in Irvine—the Meadows and the Groves mobile
home parks. The Meadows was built in 1970 with 360 units. The Groves was
built nine years later with 533 units. There were also senior living facilities built
in University Town Center, offering levels of care ranging from active to infirm,
but they were high priced. And after the settlement was reached, the company
sponsored another moderate cost project for seniors on a small parcel of land near
the Woodbridge Village Center.

One strategy that helped alleviate the issue was the Irvine Company's ability
to scatter the units set aside for low-income individuals throughout the hundreds
of apartment units it was building. Apart from the single Section 8 project in
University Town Center that was entirely low-income, the other 1,400 subsidized
apartments were intermingled with market rate units.

The for-sale moderate income units in Woodbridge were also virtually unde-
tectable to all but the experienced eye. The company made it a point to landscape
them to the same level of intensity as market rate homes, and to the degree possible add a few architectural details on the exterior. The units were built in small
clusters and like the apartments, sprinkled throughout the giant village, usually
(but not always) toward the interior.

Interviewed nine years after Ray Watson's death, his daughter Kathy Godwin
remarked that in terms of its ability to deliver a range of housing at every level—
including for people of moderate means—her father considered Woodbridge a
failure, despite all the accolades it received.[28]

No matter what his views were on housing prices, Watson was extremely
proud (and sometimes mentioned it in his speeches or writing) that unlike
Reston and Columbia—where founders Rouse and Simon had to sell their ownership stakes to keep the communities solvent—the Irvine Company never suffered the same fate.

Notes

1. J. Stamp, "James W. Rouse's Legacy of Living Through Better Design,"
   Smithsonian Magazine, April 23, 2014. www.smithsonianmag.com/history/james-
   w-rouses-legacy-better-living-through-design-180951187/.

2. "A Brief History of Reston, Virginia – Founding Principles," Reston Museum (Reston Historic Trust), accessed July 15, 2020. www.restonmuseum.org/restonhistory.
3. Karen Goff, "Virginia Senator Tim Kaine is Clinton's VP Candidate," *Reston Now*, July 22, 2016. www.restonnow.com/?s=Bob+took+a+state.
4. Robert A. Johnson and Charlene Riggins. *A Different Shade of Orange: Voices of Orange County, California, Black Pioneers* (Fullerton, CA: California State University, 2009).
5. Raymond L. Watson and Ann Lage, *Planning and Developing the New Town of Irvine California, 1960–2003: Irvine Company President, 1973–1977, Walt Disney Company Chairman, 1983–1984* (Regional Oral History Office, the Bancroft Library, University of California, Berkeley, 2005) 247.
6. Rob Kling, Spencer Olin, and Mark Poster, eds., *Postsuburban California: The Transformation of Orange County Since World War II* (Berkeley, CA: University of California Press, 1991) 65.
7. Kling et. al., eds., *Postsuburban California*, 65.
8. Kling et. al., eds., *Postsuburban California*, 65
9. Watson and Ann Lage, *Planning and Developing*, 247.
10. Watson and Ann Lage, *Planning and Developing*, 247.
11. Watson and Ann Lage, *Planning and Developing*, 247.
12. Carlyle Hall, telephone interview by H.P. Oliver and C.M. Stockstill, June 28, 2020.
13. Friends of Mammoth v. Board of Supervisors. 1972, 8 Cal. 3d 247, 502 P.2d 1049 Cal. Rptr. 16 4 ERC 1593 (1972). Supreme Court of California.
14. *Irvine World News*, October 9, 1975, 1.
15. *Irvine World News*, October 9, 1975, 1.
16. *Irvine World News*, October 9, 1975, 1.
17. Judy and Wesley Marx, telephone interview by C.M. Stockstill, June 3, 2021.
18. J. and W. Marx, interview, June 3, 2021.
19. *Irvine World News*, October 9, 1975, 1.
20. *Irvine World News*, October 9, 1975, 1.
21. *Irvine World News*, October 9, 1975, 1.
22. J. and W. Marx, interview, June 3, 2021.
23. J. and W. Marx, interview, June 3, 2021.
24. *Irvine World News*, December 9, 1976, 1.
25. Hall, telephone interview, June 28, 2020.
26. Hall, interview, June 28, 2020.
27. Hall, interview, June 28, 2020.
28. Kathy Watson Godwin, interview by H.P. Oliver and C.M. Stockstill, December 7, 2020.

20 The Jewel in the Crown

There were nearly 10,000 people gathered at the sales office; they had been shuttled in from an offsite parking area on the warm June day in 1976, past open fields along Culver Drive. For a few minutes, traffic on the San Diego and Santa Ana Freeways had backed up as drivers exited on the way to the big event. The anticipation was palpable, one former Irvine Company executive remembered 44 years later: "it felt like the Oklahoma Land Rush."[1]

Neighborhoods of new homes were opening all over Orange County and Southern California in 1976, but there had never been anything quite like this one.

Television crews from CBS, NBC, and ABC recorded the scene, including one from a helicopter hovering overhead. Irvine Company hostesses and hosts, who had carefully and methodically been recording names on the interest list for more than a year, organized the paperwork for the imminent lottery process. In just a few minutes, happy cries and shrieks would be heard as the first 200 homes were allocated to eager buyers.

Just a few yards away from the crush of humanity, employees who had been working around the clock were making last minute touchups on the home models, landscaping, and the swimming lagoon on the signature lake at the center of the new village. (The new manager of the homeowner association did his part as well, hiring college students to swim in the lagoon and canoe on the lake, living advertisements of the lifestyle to come.)

News stories on the real estate frenzy would be broadcast that night to millions of viewers on the evening news of the three networks. The next morning on NBC, the *Today Show* would air a segment. The Irvine Ranch was ready for its closeup, Mr. DeMille, and what a closeup it would turn out to be.

The attraction was the Village of Woodbridge, a sprawling new Irvine Company development in the heart of a city just five years old. At 2.7 square miles in size, it would eventually be home to 25,000 people.

Woodbridge represented perhaps the boldest effort to turn the city and company's visionary master plan into reality. In addition to being bold, it was risky, both financially and from a market standpoint. Millions of dollars had been spent on infrastructure to serve the new homes the seven builders on site would be offering for sale. Additionally, the first of two man-made lakes had been scooped

DOI: 10.1201/9781003226291-21

out, contoured, landscaped, and filled with water; at one end of the lake stood the signature symbol of the new community, a stylish wooden bridge.

Despite an economy that was still feeling the effects of an 18-month recession and a statewide unemployment rate of 9 per cent, Irvine Company executives were hopeful. Woodbridge, they believed, was the culmination of everything they had learned about what people wanted in their homes and their communities.

Ray Watson told Doug Gfeller, the project manager for the massive undertaking, that if land sales to builders cleared more than $100,000 an acre, all would be well. As it turned out, the prices were much, much better.[2]

Richard Reese had joined the company as director of planning in 1965. One of his first assignments, he recalled, was to look at the vast central valley of the ranch and begin to develop conceptual plans for it. There were dozens of projects and planning initiatives underway at the time, and Reese was involved with many of them. He found he had little time for serious examination of a part of the ranch which was little more than, "… asparagus fields fertilized with chicken manure."[3]

According to Watson, planning for Woodbridge (Village A, as it was known before it was officially christened) began in earnest in 1973. By then, he said in his oral history, "Irvine had been incorporated for two years. We had villages just west of the Santa Ana Freeway and west of the San Diego Freeway with a gap between each. Woodbridge was to be the bridge between the two areas."[4]

At first, Watson said, "we were concerned its 1,700 acres might be too large and that we could break it down into two villages." The flood control channel

Figure 20.1 The man-made north lake in Woodbridge and the wooden footpath bridge.

that ran through the middle of the acreage would have provided a natural sep-aration point,

> ... but we chose to make the portion on each side of the channel 'echo' each other with a lake in each sector, and with the entire area governed by one community association. Plus, we were entranced with the idea of a large village.[5]

Watson was also worried that, "Irvine was becoming two towns," another argu-ment for creating a single village. In the final analysis, the fact that, "... we were close to utilities in both areas and for practical reasons it was efficient to make Woodbridge into one large village."

> The other thing was, what is the theme going to be? Not that theme was a huge issue each time, because all (the villages) were supposed to be family communities, with some units for non-families, all mixed together, and a diversity of housing types and people.[6]

Watson reviewed how greenbelts were designed in Eastbluff and then University Park, as well as the placement of swimming pools within and adjacent to them. In University Park, he noted,

> ...the greenbelts became pathways to the community recreational facilities and schools, and therefore became much more usable. So, in Woodbridge, we kicked around the different experiences with the emphasis and theme of a recreational village with the internal paths connecting the lakes and the recreational facilities.[7]

With the vision of recreation and the lakes becoming clearer, Watson recalled, "... that began to dominate the visual aspect of what Woodbridge was going to look like, because now you're going to have these two lakes, sort of a mirror image of each other."[8]

(The idea of lakes and a bridge was inspired from a visit by company planners to Hilton Head, South Carolina, according to Gfeller. "We were fascinated by the role the lighthouse played in the image of the community," he said, which led to the bridge and lake.[9])

Gfeller had been at the company just six years. He started in finance, as a controller. It was a step down for him—he'd been the chief financial officer for another company in Santa Barbara before relocating to Newport Beach. Gfeller was happy to have the job; he'd sent resumes to a few companies and only the Irvine Company had replied. During his interview with Warren Fix, who would be his supervisor, "I couldn't tell him how much money I made in my last job because it was more than he made," Gfeller recalled.[10]

Gfeller was assigned to the residential and multi-family divisions as their finan-cial advisor. He remembered his first days in that role in a company that had,

"... great camaraderie but not a lot of structure." Within a few months Gfeller switched to operations and was soon heading project teams for developments. Watson liked what he saw in Gfeller and gave him the biggest job of his career at the company as head of Woodbridge.

Watson and his team happily discovered groundwater within 500 feet of the planned lakes, "so basically we were going to use our own water."[11]

Southern California was experiencing a drought during that time, Watson said,

> ... we were worried about that, (and) we got some criticism. But we had covered ourselves well, because we had an analysis made of the difference between water consumption for parks and a lake, and it turned out a lake consumes less water.[12]

Another planning issue in the creation of Woodbridge that Watson remembered was the question of public access alongside the two lakes:

> Our planners wanted to have a public sidewalk like Balboa Island, and a bridge to go across the lake giving access to the public on one side. On the other hand, the real estate people said, 'you are giving up value by putting that public sidewalk in because we receive much more for our land and can sell the houses at a higher price if they're right on the water and have their own dock for their own boats.'[13]

Watson's egalitarian outlook pushed him toward the total public path, but his business obligations led him to hire an appraiser to consider the value proposition. The outcome, he recalled, was inconclusive, and a compromise was reached—a public path was constructed around most, but not all, of the two lakes, leaving a few choice parcels completely private. The bridges were entirely public.

Another critical decision made early in the Woodbridge planning process related to auto access.

Traditional communities in Orange County and the rest of Southern California were built on parcels, large and small, that lined up along major arterial roadways. As the builders obtained land, they created internal streets to serve the dozens of homes being crafted there, tying them into the arterials. The result was a grid pattern ultimately stretching for miles, with multiple entry and exit points into neighborhoods.

Woodbridge would be different.

Of the four sides of the village, one was along the San Diego Freeway, which meant no entry points at all. Three regional roads—Culver Drive, Jeffrey Road, and Irvine Center Drive—formed the other boundaries, becoming one of the principal elements the planners considered in the design of the village—the edges. The edges created form as well as identity.

For Woodbridge, the edges would establish a physical barrier, forcing the focus and activities of the residents into the center of the village, and making the boundaries something like the moat around a castle or fortified town in the Middle Ages.

When motorists drive past Woodbridge on Culver Drive, they see what looks like a landscaped wall that obscures the view of the housing. Planners and landscape architects designed a berm that was heavily landscaped, forming what Watson called a moat that extends around the 1,710-acre village.

Inside the massive square that would eventually fill in to form the entire village, the planners placed a single circular road: Yale Loop.

Yale Loop served two purposes. First, it gave residents of the internal neighborhoods within Woodbridge a way to access other parts of the village without being forced to drive to one of the three major streets that formed the borders of Woodbridge. Second, it discouraged those just passing through the village from entering the neighborhoods in search of a quicker route.

It was hoped that Yale Loop's configuration would promote walking and biking, as the greenbelts and paths within each neighborhood would connect to destinations more quickly on a bike or on foot than getting in the car and making a long drive on the loop road. The planners wanted to limit traffic within neighborhoods to a reasonable degree. As a result, it was difficult at first for some residents to find their way to and from home because internal streets were full of curves and cul de sacs—a wrong turn might lead to a dead end. The challenge of giving accurate directions to friends for parties or just to stop by for coffee became a standing joke in the early years in Woodbridge.

But drivers just passing through Woodbridge had to get from one side to the other, and to accommodate those needs, two parallel arterial roads were constructed from west to east.

The two roads connected Culver Drive on the west to Jeffrey Road on the east. They were built on either side of the San Diego Creek flood control channel and were named Barranca and Alton. The two arterials formed the edges of a key concept for the Village of Woodbridge the planners called the Activity Corridor.

Viewed on a map, the Activity Corridor looked like a belt that stretched from one side of the development to the other.

The concept was simple: place the commercial, educational, and institutional uses common to any community directly in the middle of it, encouraging people nearest to them to eschew their automobiles and walk or bike to the grocery store, to school, or to church.

Philosophically, the Activity Corridor reflected the broad-brush planning strokes that William Pereira had envisioned in his plan for the Irvine community beyond the university. Indeed, when the first conceptual plans for Woodbridge were roughed out, Watson asked Richard Reese to have Pereira review them. Reese recalled that in the plan Pereira had done for the university community, because of geographic limitations he had concentrated all the commercial and other non-residential uses in a single area. Reese drew up a schematic reflecting the Pereira approach and tried it out. The Great Planner nodded in agreement and the Activity Corridor took form.

At the geographical center of the village and the Activity Corridor, the company located the Woodbridge Village Center, where the first grocery store and drugstore would be built. Also in the retail center was a bakery, stationary store, two restaurants, and a bookstore. To generate mixed use, there were a few small offices built on the second story of the center—the hope was that a dentist or doctor might rent them, adding to the retail draw. At the edge of the center a branch of the Bank of America was built, and a fast-food outlet. Four years later, the first movie theater in the city would open there.

Soon after the 1977 change of ownership, new employees recruited into company management reviewed the performance of the multiple retail centers and found Woodbridge Village Center wanting. One look at the map, they said, explained why: the center was in the wrong place. Why, they asked company executives who had remained after the sale, was such a basic mistake made? (Watson and many other senior company executives had departed soon after the 1977 sale.)

A variety of explanations were offered, but one stood out. The center was placed where it was because Irvine Company executives involved in the planning of the village—including Ray Watson—wanted it there.

In his oral history, Watson was never asked about this matter, nor did he choose to make any specific comments about it. But it is evident that he and the other planners were heavily invested in the concept of the Activity Corridor both as an homage to the original Pereira vision, as well as trust that their own instincts were correct.

Watson often alluded to this outlook in conversation with colleagues; research and facts can only take a person so far, he said, and then there is the leap of faith.

The other indicator that rings true decades later in his oral history is the admonition Watson made to those who followed him at the company: "I still remind all the executives that while they are building all their office buildings, shopping centers, apartments and homes, just remember: your main job is to build communities."[14]

The Activity Corridor concept went beyond Woodbridge. The company's plans for villages adjacent to Woodbridge and those above it, all the way into the Lomas de Santiago, showed the Activity Corridor snaking through the middle of each one. But as Woodbridge developed, the Activity Corridor never manifested the robustness of diverse activities the planners had imagined. Nor, interestingly, did the vision of the engineers who designed the flood control channel on San Diego Creek that was at the center of the Activity Corridor. Doug Gfeller mentioned that a concept of mirroring some of the walkable quays along the River Seine in Paris was considered, but never acted on.

Thus, the Activity Corridor began and ended in Woodbridge. As time passed and land values throughout the city began to climb, parcels in the Activity Corridor were discounted and marketed to churches that had been priced out of other neighborhoods of Irvine. Today, in addition to large athletic fields at either end of the corridor, there are seven churches, two synagogues as well as

Woodbridge High School, the headquarters of the Irvine Unified School District, medical offices, a nursing home, and a non-Irvine Company retail strip shopping center that was developed on land the company sold to the school district for educational purposes but neglected to restrict for re-use.

A key element in the realization of Woodbridge that worked with spectacular success was the variety of housing types and how well they sold. It was the result of a company marketing executive that his colleagues all remember with the same description: a genius.

Ken Agid came to the Irvine Company after serving in the US Air Force, where he achieved the rank of captain, followed by a time at the well-known marketing firm of Sanford Goodkin. (Goodkin was the source of the famous response to the question, how valuable is the Irvine Ranch? His answer: "God gave up his option to purchase the Irvine Ranch only after Heaven came along."[15])

Agid's timing was good. By the early 1970s, the company had been refining its relations with individual builders to create and promote different kinds of housing styles to appeal to customers. Watson mentions in his oral history that the company conducted surveys of new home buyers to determine levels of satisfaction with their purchase. Builders who scored low on the surveys could either react and correct on their next subdivision, or potentially be replaced by another.

According to Irvine Company executives who worked with him, Agid revolutionized the process of collecting and analyzing data about homebuyer desires, refining the concept of market segmentation into both a science and art.

In an interview with the *Los Angeles Times* about a year after Woodbridge opened, Agid described the detailed level of market research the company had conducted.

Woodbridge, Agid told *Times* reporter Art Siedenbaum, had 39 segments of potential buyers that were identified by intensive interviews. In addition to asking Irvine residents, the researchers went to nearby Mission Viejo, where Agid bragged "we interview more people in Mission Viejo than Mission Viejo (Company) itself."

The basic categorization comes from a matrix based on life cycles and lifestyles, he went on, including age, income, and family composition. A sampling:

- YM2B is a small family with both partners working
- FM2 means Family Move Up, a couple between 35 to 44 who want a better house
- Empty-Nester is a family whose children have grown up and moved out
- Never-Nester is a childless couple
- YS are young singles who may buy a house planning to live with a roommate.

After gathering all the information, the company came up with a variety of housing styles to recommend to its homebuilders, targeting each of the 39 categories with a specific home that would appeal to them. If the calculations were correct, supply would match demand and sales would result.

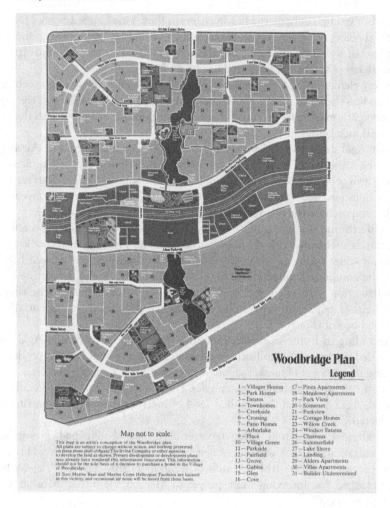

Figure 20.2 The land plan for the nearly three-square mile Village of Woodbridge as constructed by the early 1980s with the last of four quadrants remaining to be
developed.

(Courtesy Orange County Archives)

Then Agid made comments in a manner familiar to many who worked with him.

Community centers created to serve neighborhoods were, in his view, pretty
much useless, designed by architects who want them largely to illustrate their
talents. He expressed similar disdain for planners: "Planners look at drawings.
They don't look at life."

For those who admired Agid, the comments reflected his superior intelligence
and self-confidence. After all, with his insights, homes in Woodbridge and the
Irvine Ranch were selling well. For his detractors, it was just another example of
Agid's arrogance. One wonders as he trash talked architects and planners if he

remembered that the president of the company was an architect, and the foundation of the company's reputation as a community developer was built on excellence in planning—by planners.[16]

Agid had good reason to talk in such a self-assured style. He had played a critical role not only in positioning the product types that the seven hand-picked builders in Woodbridge would be selling, he also oversaw the strategy for the sales methodology, a sensitive element in the overall introduction of the new village to the public.

Agid was also responsible for designing one of the most talked about and creative home styles in Woodbridge, the Estates.

The Estates homes were duplexes and triplexes, unusual in and of themselves, as nowhere on the Irvine Ranch had duplexes been built, let alone a triplex (while connected to one another, each home had a separate owner).

Agid conceived the Estates as a façade, but one that would create the image of stability and affluence. The effect was created by building the duplex or triplex on Yale Loop, atop a small, gently sloping berm that would run the length of the street in the first quadrant of the village. To implement it, Agid turned to another man who would go on to enjoy a long, successful career in marketing and homebuilding, John Martin.

Martin had substantial experience in turning ideas into physical reality. Employed at the Irvine Company for several months, he had become frustrated with the committee-driven decision-making process that took up hours of time with little to show for it.

Martin had worked with builders in the past on a home design that he knew could be translated easily into the Agid scheme. He placed the front of each duplex or triplex facing directly onto Yale Loop—the garage at the rear, out of sight. The effect was just as Agid had planned; drivers cruising along the large arterial saw the duplexes and triplexes not as individual homes, but as a large, imposing near-mansion, something that might be expected in Beverly Hills or Pasadena.

The Estates were also a visual counterpoint to the relatively high density of the rest of Woodbridge, where, as Martin pointed out in an interview 44 years later, the average size of a lot was just 5,000 square feet instead of the standard 8,000.[17]

The Estates sold as well as any home in the village, the vision not of an architect, but a marketing genius.

****

The company had stimulated interest in the village as construction began, first by fencing off the entire initial quadrant, which created an air of mystery as to just what was going on behind it.

In an interview noting the 25th anniversary of the Woodbridge opening, Watson recalled that letters were sent to other parts of Irvine and surrounding communities hinting at what was coming. "We also sent a little tree seed on a card," he said, underscoring the company's plan to heavily landscape the new community.[18]

"We planned to start a massive advertising program in May of 1976, but by early May we had received 50,000 responses to our letters, so we cancelled the advertising."[19]

Until the Woodbridge auction, home sales in developments where demand was high were often conducted on a first come, first served basis, which meant being *physically in line* at the door of the sales office. And when the door opened on the day sales commenced, buyers counted off as they entered the office—the last home was sold to whoever held that spot in line. This policy led to campouts at sales offices, with eager buyers staking a tent days in advance of the start of sales, and sleeping on site.

Agid and the company wanted to avoid campouts, so as qualified interest cards arrived, they went into a single hopper to be pulled out like numbers at a bingo game.

To prevent speculators from unfairly gobbling up inventory, rules were established by Agid and his team. They were:

1　The buyer had to be present at the lottery and have a deposit in hand
2　Buyers could reserve only one home
3　Escrow would be opened and closed in the name of the person on the lottery ticket.

As demand for homes in Woodbridge (and later, elsewhere) soared, so did prices. Builders who had a tract of, say, 80 homes would typically build three or four models and then an initial phase of perhaps 20 homes. This limited financial exposure for the builder in case the market suddenly turned, and it also promoted the ability to see how the home design held up in real time, with new owners making their own changes to the interior or exterior of the new home or complaining to the builder about lack of linen closets or puny pantries.

As builders added a new phase, they increased prices, usually in a measured fashion, but sometimes dramatically if the market was especially hot. It was not unusual for the last homes built in a tract to be thousands—sometimes tens of thousands— of dollars higher in price than those built first.

As Woodbridge took off and prices skyrocketed, it became obvious that buying a home in the first phase of a new tract meant a virtually guaranteed windfall profit a few months or years later. It wasn't long before rumors began to circulate at City Hall that some sort of regulation might be necessary to insure fairness in the home sales process. However, nothing official was ever done.

In building a community that would eventually be home to 25,000 residents, the company had considered what kind of political clout would result, especially as the decision had been made to form a single, "master" homeowner association (HOA) for the village (smaller HOAs were created for individual neighborhoods—the master association maintained the lakes and recreation facilities and village-wide landscaping, in addition to sponsoring a variety of recreational classes and activities).

Homeowner associations were not new in Orange County—Emerald Bay formed one for its private community on the coast in 1929. The Irvine Company installed an HOA in Eastbluff, and in subsequent new villages throughout Irvine.

The HOA had two main responsibilities. First, to enforce the Conditions, Covenants and Restrictions (CC&Rs) that were part of the title to every home within the homeowner association (most HOAs in Irvine became known as community associations). The CC&Rs were a logical extension of the Irvine Company's desire—and insistence—that the design of the community, its look and feel, would be maintained, and protected. This translated into restrictions on paint color for homes and walls, landscaping appropriate to the scale of the neighborhood (and trimmed so as not to inhibit views), prohibition of CB antennas, and a host of other urban ills common to other suburbs that would not be allowed in an Irvine Company village.

The second HOA responsibility was to collect monthly dues from each homeowner and allocate them to the maintenance of commonly owned areas and facilities, usually a swimming pool and clubhouse, and (in areas that had them) greenbelts.

The HOA was governed by a board of directors of homeowners—eventually.

Elections for HOA boards were organized by the Irvine Company as soon as enough residents had moved into the first phase of a tract. To promote continuity and to ensure that nothing critical to the future of the village fell through the cracks, the company usually placed its employees on the board to represent its interests. It was legal—the company would own most of the lots for months while home construction was underway. As the residents neared a majority, company representatives would drop off, one by one, until the residents took complete control.

A small section of the company's community relations department did little else than shepherd HOA boards of directors into existence, coaching them on how to organize and operate.

Once firmly in the hands of residents, the HOAs became the first and most effective breeding ground for community leadership. Of the five people elected to the first Irvine City Council, three had been on the boards of their homeowner associations.

Establishing a single HOA that would govern Woodbridge seemed to some company executives a recipe for disaster, promoting the potential that a clever and sophisticated individual or group would use the platform of the giant organization to build a political juggernaut.

As it turned out, the fears were unjustified. In the 50 years Irvine has been incorporated, just one director of the Woodbridge Village Association won a seat on the city council.

It would be nearly a decade before the final homes in Woodbridge were constructed. In the interim, the look and feel of the village would be tested by a change in company ownership, a major economic downturn, and an array of other market and political forces in the region.

It takes a sophisticated eye, attentive to details of design and execution, to make a complete tour of Woodbridge and notice the reality versus the dream. Most obvious is the generosity of parks and greenspaces in the initial quadrant and the diminishment of the same in the last quarter that was built. There are fewer Estate homes on Yale Loop as one leaves the first quadrant, and the tree plantings seem sparser in the medians.

Woodbridge Village Center has seen regular turnover of retail tenants, and the once-first run movie theater is now bargain priced. In 2019, the company invested millions of dollars to redesign the center, opening it up with a large public open space that takes advantage of the lake view. Directly across the street from the center, in the first years the village was built there were two restaurants, one white tablecloth, the other a family style hamburger and pie emporium. Both had stunning views of the lake. Both are now gone.

What was once a neighborhood elementary school closed and was sold off to a homebuilder, who jammed it to the legal maximum with two-story homes, altering the architectural balance nearby.

In some neighborhoods, bright colors on stucco and trim have appeared, as the Woodbridge Village Association relaxed previous standards of what some locals dubbed the Suburban Rainbow of Allowable Colors: White, Off-White, Navajo White, Beige, Mock Beige, etc.

But these are just minor flaws in an otherwise dazzling jewel, one that has stood the test of time and remains a vibrant, beautiful community that works—people are drawn to its quiet neighborhoods where schools and parks are close enough to walk or bike to. Home values continue to increase, and there are plenty of apartments for those who choose to rent. Homeowner associations keep the pools clean, the hedges trimmed, and the lawns green. Ray Watson's commitment to diversity is alive in Woodbridge and all of Irvine, now with significant populations of men and women from almost every corner of the world.

Almost unanimously, when asked to name the greatest planning achievement of their era at the Irvine Company, former executives say it was, and is, Woodbridge.

Let Ken Agid have the last words, the ones he wrote in 1976:

"We know Woodbridge is well-planned, but that plan is only a paper dream until the people arrive and bring the promises to life."[20]

Notes

1. Donald Moe, interview by H.P. Oliver and C.M. Stockstill, August 8, 2020.
2. Douglas Gfeller, interview by H.P. Oliver and C.M. Stockstill, August 18, 2020.
3. Richard Reese, interview by H.P. Oliver and C.M. Stockstill, August 26, 2020.
4. Raymond L. Watson and Ann Lage, *Planning and Developing the New Town of Irvine California, 1960–2003: Irvine Company President, 1973–1977, Walt Disney Company Chairman, 1983–1984* (Regional Oral History Office, the Bancroft Library, University of California, Berkeley, 2005) 274.
5. Watson and Lage, *Planning and Developing*, 274.
6. Watson and Lage, *Planning and Developing*, 274.

7. Watson and Lage, *Planning and Developing*, 275.
8. Watson and Lage, *Planning and Developing*, 277.
9. Gfeller, interview, August 18, 2020.
10. Gfeller, interview, August 18, 2020.
11. Watson and Lage, *Planning and Developing*, 277.
12. Watson and Lage, *Planning and Developing*, 277.
13. Watson and Lage, *Planning and Developing*, 277.
14. Watson and Lage, *Planning and Developing*, 447.
15. Author's recollection.
16. Art Siedenbaum, *Los Angeles Times*, April 24, 1977, Part VIII, 1–7.
17. John Martin, interview with C.M. Stockstill and H.P. Oliver, September 16, 2020.
18. "Celebrating Woodbridge's 40th Anniversary," *Reflections*, Woodbridge Village Association, March 2016, 1 and 5.
19. "Celebrating Woodbridge's 40th Anniversary," 1 and 5.
20. *Irvine World News*, June 11, 1976, 6.

21 The Best of All Possible Coasts

Populated coastal communities in Orange County were sparse until the early 1900s. The arrival of Henry Huntington's Pacific Electric Railway in 1901 brought tourists for a day at the beach on the popular Red Cars, usually to the broad sands of western county beaches in Newport Beach and Pacific Beach (renamed Huntington in honor of the rail baron).

On the southern coast of the county, the beaches diminished, the coastline defined largely by steep cliffs and small coves. Homes there crowded together on rocky ledges or clung to the hillsides. Artists found inspiration in the views, and gathered with other free thinkers, writers, and iconoclasts in Laguna Beach. During and after World War II, San Clemente, the southernmost city in the county, shared its coastal vibe with Marines from Camp Pendleton, and in the early 1970s, with a president.

As beach cities grew and modernized over the decades, a four-mile section in the middle of the Orange County coast remained largely untouched, nearly as wild as it had been when its first inhabitants gathered mussels and abalone for food there and lived in simple shelters of brush and branches.

It was the Irvine Coast.

The westernmost border of the vast Irvine Ranch, the Irvine Coast was largely ignored by James Irvine II as he wrestled to shape the interior section of his property into productive fields and orchards. And the coastal beaches, while beautiful, were difficult to get to. Before the automobile, a day at the beach for the Irvine family meant rising early, hitching up a team of horses or mules, and plodding more than ten miles down Laguna Canyon and then an additional two miles to Morro Canyon.

The trip improved vastly in 1926 when Pacific Coast Highway opened between Newport Beach and Laguna Beach, but access to the shoreline remained a challenge.

The Irvine Coast was stunning, at once primitive, but molded by time and geology to the point that human access and the potential for habitation was possible.

From the four miles north to south, where the land meets the sea, the edge is almost entirely a cliff. From there, the land climbs gently inland for about a quarter of a mile, leaving a modest plateau that accommodated Pacific Coast Highway with minimal need for bridges or significant cut and fill. Above the highway the pitch of the land increases, rising for about a mile to a long, narrow ridgeline.

DOI: 10.1201/9781003226291-22

Figure 21.1 A view of the Irvine Coast looking southeast from Newport Beach, prior to development of the northernly portion as the Newport Coast.

At the top of the 1,000-foot-high ridge, an ambitious amateur archeologist could dig up fossilized marine shells a few inches beneath the surface of the ground, revealing how in ancient times the ridges rested on the floor of the Pacific Ocean.[1]

There were three large canyons that slashed through the land: at the middle, Los Trancos, then to the south Muddy Canyon, and at the far southern end at Irvine Cove, Morro Canyon.

It wasn't easy, but a sure-footed hiker climbing through the seasonal streambeds at the bottom of the canyons would find a lush, verdant canopy of sage, scrub oak, and sycamores. The thirsty sycamores were ubiquitous in the coastal canyons of California, sending long, twisting limbs in every direction, often just a few feet from the ground. Their bark presented a speckled pallet of the native hues of the coastal sage scrub environment—dusty whites, light tans and grays, small hints of tawny greens and yellows. Leaves were large, reflecting the Spring sunlight in a bright, lime green, then turning to dark greens and eventually crisping to brown within a few months of a growing season.

Higher in the canyon, coastal California oaks competed with scrub manzanita for space along the steep foothills.

At the turn of the 20th century, motion pictures were being made 50 miles north of the Irvine Coast, and location scouts had discovered the sunshine-soaked vistas there. The first movie crews made landfall where Los Trancos emptied into the sea—they planted palm trees for a South Seas movie set; when Pacific Coast Highway opened a few years later, movie production along the coast increased to the point the Irvine Company hired an employee to coordinate it.[2]

The Irvines enjoyed the beach, and they visited often. In her autobiography, Joan Irvine Smith recounts numerous days along the shore, and historic photos of the family show JI with camera in hand recording the activities; he was especially fond of July 4th and a seaside fireworks display.

Soon others were making regular treks to the beach at Los Trancos Canyon; a few visitors began pitching tents for shelter. Most of them were either employees of the Irvine Company or business associates. As they didn't cause trouble, JI initially took a benign view of the situation and allowed the tents to grow into shanties, and then with the help of whatever floated in on the tide, more substantial buildings.

Along with the friendlies, squatters found their way to the area that frequent visitor Elizabeth Woods had named Crystal Cove. Order was required, JI decided, and in the mid-1930s, he formalized residency with leases. A natural gas line was also installed about that time, making it possible for a few people to live there year-round.

At the same time, a small group of Japanese American farmers began tilling the coastal slopes and selling produce from stands alongside Pacific Coast Highway. (How the crops were sufficiently irrigated is never explained in various histories. Either water was stored from winter runoff in the small canyon streams, or it was trucked in, as no groundwater was available.)

World War II and the internment of people of Japanese heritage put an end to the Irvine Coast farms.

By the mid-1950s, in addition to a few dozen people residing either seasonally or permanently at Crystal Cove in 43 ramshackle (but habitable) cottages, what had been known as Tyron's Camp at the southern end of the coast was turned into a trailer park, with primitive single and doublewides placed on the sand and on a small slope just inland, which was connected to the beach by a tunnel under the highway.

Figure 21.2 A view of the Irvine Coast looking northwest from Morro Canyon beach, prior to development of the northernly potion as the Newport Coast.

(While geographically part of the original Irvine Coast, Irvine Cove—just to the south of the beach at El Morro—was impossible to reach at the shoreline because of the vertical, rocky cliffs that plunged directly into the sea. The intimate cove had a lovey beach and was relatively flat, which allowed the company to subdivide it and sell lots; a handful were reserved for members of the Irvine family.)

With the arrival of the planners and engineers at the company in the early 1960s, it was just a matter of time before their attention turned to the Irvine Coast and the possibilities for development.

In his oral history, Watson recalled the initiation of the process and some of the activities that ultimately led to an initial coastal plan that proved dead on arrival, an innovative and sincere effort to obtain consensus from a disparate group of stakeholders, and yet another lawsuit from Joan Irvine Smith:

> We did a general plan for the coastal sector of the ranch, about 35,000 acres. We showed most of its land as yellow colored, the land use language for residential, along with the appropriate amount of commercial and schools and other things.
>
> By the early 1970s we began to get serious about the coast and started a planning program; we hired some consultants to stimulate ideas on potential uses on the coast—once you get past general planning ideas you have to start being specific.
>
> In our general plan we had indicated the coast had the capacity for as many as 50,000 dwelling units. All that was saying was that the 10,000 acres on the coast, at five housing units per acres, which was a relatively low but common density at the time, and you come up with 50,000 dwelling units. You do that in the early planning stages for a very specific reason; historically, most communities have underestimated the size of ultimate development and have not properly sized the basic infrastructure to serve it. So, we decided it would be better to make a mistake on the high side than on the low … and when we got into specific planning, we could identify the project densities of the various land uses.[3]

Watson's oral history alludes to the seismic social and political upheaval that would impact the coastal planning process as it started—the birth of the national environmental movement. Earth Day, the Santa Barbara oil spill, the company's ongoing battle over Upper Newport Bay—all would coalesce into a new frame of reference that redefined how residents reacted to developer plans for new housing, offices, or shopping centers.

Watson and his fellow planning professionals saw a giant swath of yellow on maps as something of a rough draft that would ultimately be refined, and 50,000 units as just a placeholder, only a way to determine street widths and sewer capacity. To the average citizen, however, the visual image on the map combined with a huge number of houses far exceeding those in Newport Beach, Irvine, or Laguna Beach *together* evoked reactions of disbelief and fear.

The 50,000 homes figure haunted the planners throughout the entire coastal process, creating a negative image and feeling that could never fully be explained away.

But Watson and his colleagues couldn't anticipate how their initial estimates would eventually turn on them as they took the next step in the coastal planning process; a 1969 visit to coastal communities in Europe that shared the same climate and geography as the Irvine Coast.

Watson, company president William Mason, vice president of planning Richard Reese, and two lower-level planners set out to examine the coastlines of Portugal, Spain, France, and Italy. Also accompanying them was Adam Krivatsy, a San Francisco planner whose firm had been consulting on coastal planning.

> We first flew to Lisbon, then to the south of Portugal visiting the many coastal resorts and old towns. The entire length of the Irvine Coast was very similar to the coast area of Portugal. From there we went to Spain, toured all the resorts along the Spanish coast, again visiting old towns and resorts. Then we drove to Barcelona, then along the French Riviera, to Nice.[4]

It was the last leg of the trip along the western coast of Italy, and especially his stay in Portofino, that gave Watson an inspiration for a tourist center at Crystal Cove.

The tiny fishing village, with its brilliant-colored hotels and homes surrounding a modest harbor, had enchanted many previous visitors. In the 1960s, Portofino was enjoying what Italians called the *La Dolce Vita* period—its harbor filled with yachts, restaurants, and hotels with movie stars and VIPs, stalked by the paparazzi. Travel writers rhapsodized in their descriptions of the scene, universally agreeing the charms of the village were unmatched.

Watson thought of Crystal Cove as the right place to create something like what he had seen in Italy:

> I suggested we build a sort of Portofino-like community. Also, I said that to show the importance of public contact to the ocean, we should run a public sidewalk or path all the way from Newport Beach to Laguna Beach along the top of the cliff.

Watson says the trip also,

> ... influenced me on how to think about that narrow portion of land that was between Pacific Coast Highway and the ocean. I believed by then that without question, we were not going to be able to build below the high bluffs and the water even though the company owned the land from the high tide mark inland.
>
> So, I convinced the company right from the beginning we should contain our development to the top of the bluffs and dedicate all the beach areas and the faces of the bluffs to the public. Then what I suggested is on the bluff top create a mixture of residential development, probably mostly townhouses,

low scale so that it would not interfere with the view of the ocean from the highway, which was a very precious thing from the public point of view.[5]

The company retained other consultants to stimulate ideas for coastal planning.

> ... but mostly it was in-house planning ... (at that time) from Pacific Coast Highway inland, which was the bulk of the land, we thought of primarily as residential development. But by the early 1970s, the Coastal Commission has come along, and the coast is a place attracting the attention of very different groups with very different views as to what to do with it.[6]

In an attempt to organize disparate views—public and private—into what could result in a consensus plan for the Irvine Coast, the company took the daring step of opening up the planning process by establishing a planning entity called The Irvine Company Multi-Agency Planning Program, known as TICMAP.

In addition to the neighboring cities on the coast, there were state, federal, and local agencies that would have an official say in development approvals, as well as private interest groups representing environmental and civic constituencies. In all, 20 organizations were invited to participate.

Watson was careful at the outset of the process to structure a roadmap to (hopefully) a conclusion that began with the company's plan.

> My style of doing (TICMAP) is: we're not going to start from scratch. We're not going to all sit around together and say, what should we do? The Irvine Company is going to come to you with a plan; to stimulate the ideas, here's what we think it should be. And I felt pretty comfortable about what we were coming up with (and) I'd convinced the company they ought to give up part of their land to have a public sidewalk area along the bluffs, and that the company was endorsing that idea.[7]

The TICMAP process ground on for almost two years. Watson describes a roller coaster of progress, then setbacks, compromises, and accommodations, but never the ability to reach the elusive goal of genuine consensus.

While TICMAP was able to contain debate on coast planning issues within something of a controlled structure, other forces were swirling throughout the county and the state, roiling the atmosphere like currents in churning seas.

Primary among them was the Coastal Act, passed by state voters in 1972, setting up regional commissions that would oversee coastal development, plus a statewide commission with jurisdiction over decisions made by the regional commissions. With commissioners all appointed by elected officials, the initial months and years of Coastal Commission oversight were a learning process for everyone involved. Establishing protocols for decision making, hiring staff, setting up guidelines for the inevitable appeals all combined into a bureaucratic Gulag.

Seven environmental organizations had been invited into the TICMAP process, including heavyweights like the Sierra Club and the Planning and Conservation League. They brought sophistication and their own planning and legal resources to the table, as well as memberships in the tens of thousands. Locally, the Laguna Greenbelt was also a player. The Greenbelt was founded with a largely provincial focus on Laguna Beach but was expanding its examination of developments well beyond the city. Finally, a new group had been organized specifically to lobby on the Irvine Coast plan: Friends of the Irvine Coast. Fern Pirkle, who had cut her advocacy teeth in the mid-South as a League of Women Voters organizer, proved to be an articulate and efficient leader, eventually signing up thousands of local members.

And then there was Joan Irvine Smith.

As Watson described, leaving some portion of the coastal property in public ownership was a critical element in the overall Irvine Company strategy for obtaining government permission to develop. But as the planning progressed, it became evident to Watson and others that TICMAP wasn't going to work, and the company should submit what it had come up with to the County of Orange and hope for the best. But the company's idea of selling the coastal strip from Pacific Coast Highway to the bluff to capture some revenue went forward. After reviewing an appraisal of $13 million for the land, the company received approval from its board of directors to approach the state of California and offer the land at half the appraised price to encourage completion of the transaction.

Joan Irvine Smith voted no at the board, and as was usually the case, was out-voted. And as was usually the case when that happened, she filed a lawsuit to stop the sale, calling it a massive giveaway of company resources. She pointed out that the sale price worked out to about $4,000 an acre. In contrast, just up the coast in Huntington Beach, the state parks department had paid $250,000 an acre for parcels next to the pier.

Smith also repeated an allegation she had made in the past that her father, James Irvine Jr., "had in 1931 resolved a case before the Board of Tax Appeals in Washington D.C. by agreeing to give the (coastal) land for a federal park."[8] (Smith appears to be the only person who knew about this deal—there is no other mention of it anywhere in Irvine Company or other histories and if it happened, it took place two years before she was born.)

A judge granted an injunction preventing the sale, and the case went to trial in West Virginia, where James Irvine, Jr., had incorporated the Irvine Company in 1894.

Watson's memory of the trial is less than positive: "I remember spending three days in a hot courtroom, with no air conditioning—I will always remember that. They had no modern techniques. They had a woman taking (the testimony) shorthand, which took years to get transcribed."[9]

In the end, while the company achieved a local approval for a coastal plan showing an ultimate population of around 39,000 people, it was all too evident that moving it forward into the state coastal commission process was futile. The plan went into limbo.

By the summer of 1977, the new owners of the Irvine Company were reshaping the company. Watson and several other senior executives had departed, and a cohort of managers had been hired to replace them. And as the new Irvine Company had been incorporated in Michigan, the West Virginia lawsuit became moot. It would be several years before the company resurrected the coastal planning process, hewing to a strategy that included sale of the immediate coast for public use, combined with a dramatic downsizing of overall development.

In the meantime, company employees—from secretaries to vice presidents—enjoyed what must have been the most magnificent employee benefit in Orange County: private access to the Irvine Coast.

As part of their orientation, new employees received a key, which opened a locked gate a few yards inland from Pacific Coast Highway on a narrow dirt road. Once through the gate, parking was available on a grassy bluff near the path that led to the beach. And there it was, four miles of empty beach, just for Irvine Company personnel.

The beach was not only a fantastic perk, but it was also something of a leveler, as bodysurfing or splashing along the shoreline with someone in board shorts instead of a Brooks Brothers suit brought a touch of humanity to what could otherwise be an atmosphere of formality in the office.

(Author's note: The title of this chapter comes from a phrase invented by Tom Murphine, managing editor of *Daily Pilot*. He often used it to describe the coastal communities the paper served; it seems especially appropriate for the Irvine Coast.)

Notes

1. Various histories describe the Irvine Coast as six or eight miles long. Measured from Irvine Cove to the northern edge of modern Corona del Mar, this is an approximately accurate calculation. For this book, the authors describe the property as it existed in 1960, undeveloped between Irvine Cove and Corona del Mar, about four miles along the coastline.
2. "History of the Crystal Cove Area," Crystal Cove State Park (California State Department of Parks), accessed November 6, 2021, www.crystalcovestatepark.org/history-of-the-area/.
3. Raymond L. Watson and Ann Lage, *Planning and Developing the New Town of Irvine California, 1960–2003: Irvine Company President, 1973–1977, Walt Disney Company Chairman, 1983–1984* (Regional Oral History Office, the Bancroft Library, University of California, Berkeley, 2005) 312.
4. Watson and Lage, *Planning and Developing*, 312.
5. Watson and Lage, *Planning and Developing*, 314.
6. Watson and Lage, *Planning and Developing*, 315.
7. Watson and Lage, *Planning and Developing*, 317.
8. Joan Irvine Smith, *A California Woman's Story* (Irvine, CA: The Irvine Museum, 2006) 112.
9. Watson and Lage, *Planning and Developing*, 320.

22 Town and Gown

It was an auspicious beginning for the new university that warm June 20, 1964.

No less than the President of the United States and the governor of California would be present to commemorate the occasion, along with an array of University of California dignitaries, local leaders, and the first chancellor of the young campus, Daniel Aldrich.

Looking out at the desolate and dusty hillside, where the foundations of five buildings comprised the entirety of the new campus, Aldrich said from the humble beginnings there, "...shall rise an institution of higher education devoted to ... giving opportunity to qualified youth to mature intellectually, morally, aesthetically, socially and vocationally." Aldrich vowed that, "Irvine is not conceived as an isolated academia but as an institution that plays an active role in the transfer of learning to life."[1]

UC President Clark Kerr was equally optimistic. After thanking everyone from the Irvine Company to faculty and local leaders, he predicted that "in the years to come, a university campus of truly monumental proportions will arise here."[2]

President Lyndon Johnson, just seven months in office and running for election in November, sounded a cheerleading tone, listing national problems and assuring that solutions would follow. Perhaps the bare hills reminded him of his native Texas, as he declared in closing: "I know something about this state. I know something about the West ... I know you have the concern, the caring and the commitment to get the job done."[3]

(According to a 1989 article in the Los Angeles Times quoting Brad Atwood, UCI's first public affairs staffer, "... Kerr and Regent Ed Pauley, an old political crony, persuaded (Johnson) to make an appearance in 'Goldwater country.' Ground had already been broken at UCI with appropriate ceremonies, so UC administrators dreamed up an event they called a 'site dedication' for the President of the United States."[4])

Present at the ceremony was Aldrich's youngest child, Stuart. While tagging along with his father afterwards, he recalled that the chancellor was approached by a serious looking man. "He asked my father, 'what are we going to do to control the students?'

"My father looked puzzled by the question. He said to the man, 'well, they are young adults.'

DOI: 10.1201/9781003226291-23

Figure 22.1 At the UC Irvine campus dedication on June 20, 1964, President Lyndon Johnson is flanked by Chancellor Daniel Aldrich on the left, UC President Clark Kerr on the right, and California Governor Edmund G. "Pat" Brown on the far right.

(UC Irvine Library, Special Collections and Archives)

"The man repeated his question—'how are we going to control them?' My father couldn't answer."[5]

The man with the concerns was Newport Beach chief of police James Glavas. His city was just over the hill from the campus, and many students were moving onto Balboa Island and the Balboa Peninsula.

Aldrich had little inclination that day to worry about real or imagined student conduct on the shores of Newport Beach—he had a university to build and staff.

UC Irvine was one of three new branches of the University of California founded under the administration of Clark Kerr; since 1960, he had pondered the question of how to structure the academic philosophy of each new campus.

As Kerr examined Irvine, he thought back to the Morrill Act, passed in 1862, which created what came to be known as the Land Grant colleges. The federal law gave states a gift of 30,000 acres for each of its congressional seats to establish colleges with a curriculum focused on agriculture and mechanics.

In a 1968 interview with former UCI history professor Samuel McCulloch, Kerr recalled asking himself:

> ... suppose instead of being created in the 1860's, if (the law) was established in the 1960's, how would we do it? How should the campus be tied to the community as the community has changed over a century? And how would it be tied with new technology? The land grant concept came along with the idea of technology going into industry, schools of engineering, etc. So (we had) this idea of the land grant institutions of the 1960's versus the 1860's. The idea was to make (UC Irvine) a highly concentrated campus using technology to tie it together.[6]

Kerr had translated a 100-year-old academic approach into a modern application; now he needed someone to lead the campus in that direction.

Kerr had previously hired Aldrich (he referred to him in his interview with McCulloch as "Danny") to head the university's agricultural division. Aldrich had been working at the UC Davis campus when Kerr moved him into the system's administration.

Kerr thought Aldrich would be a good match for Orange County and his vision of UC Irvine as a modern land grant institution. "He was a person who had a real knowledge of academic life, but who would perhaps be able to work with the Orange County community, just by his personality—the All-American boy— than almost anyone I could think of."[7]

(Apparently Kerr didn't fully appreciate how fast the Irvine Company was moving away from farming and into city building, as he told McCulloch he also thought Aldrich's background in agriculture academics would bring him "better rapport with the Irvine Land people (getting the name of the company wrong as well) who'd been identified with agriculture."[8])

So, Kerr was surprised when Aldrich turned down his offer to become chancellor of the new campus.

Aldrich told Kerr he had some "personal" aspects of his life that he believed would prevent him from doing the job well. Kerr initially accepted the explanation, but soon became curious. Aldrich was married, had children, a spotless reputation—what was the problem?

The problem was drinking; Aldrich was not only a teetotaler, but he also didn't allow liquor in his home. How could he host the innumerable events required of a chancellor when serving and consuming liquor were anathema to his personal values? Kerr argued that it was a minor problem if a problem at all. Surely, he told Aldrich, you have so much going for you as a man and an academic leader you can get over this.

Aldrich relented and accepted the position. Kerr was extremely pleased, and often cited his selection of Aldrich as one of the principal reasons the new campus grew into such a success. The incident also gave Kerr a continuing opportunity to tease Aldrich whenever he would see him at social events, greeting him with a smile and the words, "well Dan, drunk again."[9]

Aldrich's personality was something of a contradiction. Well over six feet tall, he was lean and trim, and had a head of closely shorn, graying hair that gave him an air of formality and a bit of rectitude. Aldrich carried his Down East accent with him, a reflection of his native New Hampshire. A first impression of the new chancellor could be a bit intimidating.

But Aldrich loved students and loved to mix with them. In UCI's early years, a tradition developed of challenging the chancellor to an arm-wrestling contest. There he would be, seated at a table in the square in the front of the library, the sleeves of his white, starched shirt rolled up to his elbows, grimacing with sweat across from a student 30 years his junior. Aldrich almost always won; he was a talented athlete who competed in track and field events in senior games well into his 60s, throwing the javelin, the discus, and shot putting. Aldrich also had a sense of humor, albeit a bit dry, and he was not above making fun of himself if the occasion called for it.

Aldrich made the rounds of the campus on a regular basis and became a familiar figure, stopping to talk with his young charges, challenging their views, sympathizing with all the vicissitudes common to life on a university campus.

Students and staff who were there in the early days of the campus invariably have stories about Aldrich's devotion to his role—official and unofficial. Diana Janas had decided to attend UC Irvine after Aldrich spoke at her high school class in Corona del Mar. A year later, she had joined a group of students developing an honor code for the new school. "How many times, as a freshman, do you sit on the floor eating guacamole with the chancellor … discussing ideas related to honor?"[10]

Figure 22.2 Daniel Aldrich in the 1960s.

(UC Irvine Libraries, Special Collections and Archives)

Jack Lockhart worked in the facilities unit at UCI. He recalled that Aldrich,

> … knew and addressed all employees by their first name. I would often see
> him walking in the park, with a bucket and a pair of snips to pick up trash.
> He would also prune the sapling trees. One day I scolded him about picking
> up trash: 'you have a grounds crew to do that.' He replied, 'I know that Jack,
> but this is my campus.'"[11]

Scott Wood, a public relations officer at UCI, recalled walking across campus
with Aldrich, who mused on one stroll through the park, "when I retire, I want to
come back as a gardener. Give me one hundred feet of hose and wheelbarrow and
I'll have this place in great shape."[12]

Within a few years the campus newspaper and many students began to refer to
Aldrich as Chancellor Dan. (So did the faculty and staff, with greater discretion.)
If he didn't like the label, he never let on. Most people who knew him believe he
probably did.

UC Irvine welcomed 1,589 students and 179 faculty and staff upon opening in
September of 1965.

Photos of the occasion show what could be mistaken for initial construction
of an outpost on Mars; a handful of buildings plopped in the middle of a bar-
ren landscape at the top of a rise with no other signs of civilization in sight.
Landscaping was minimal and the architecture was far from College Traditional
of brick walls covered in ivy. Instead, William Pereira had chosen a stark, mini-
malistic look, long on white concrete and short on decorative flourishes.

Despite its remote location, the new university rooted itself into its gifted land
and set out to fulfil Clark Kerr's prediction of greatness.

Oral histories of the time with faculty and staff members brim with hope, imagination, and enthusiasm. Like Ray Watson's experience as a young planner facing
the blank slate of the Irvine Ranch, the newly appointed deans of schools and the
faculty they would recruit recognized their once in a lifetime opportunity to mold the
academic philosophy of a new university and those who would implement its vision.

Kerr and Aldrich tapped trusted colleagues from within the UC system for
senior positions, including future chancellors Jack Peltason and Ivan Hinderaker.
In turn, the senior academics found faculty in California and beyond to staff the
new departments. When the professional lure of starting on the ground floor of
the new campus wasn't enough, Peltason employed the climate gambit, sending
postcards of scenes from the beaches of Corona del Mar to snowbound potential
recruits on the East Coast.

As UCI was an entirely new institution, there were unparalleled opportunities to
throw off tradition and fashion bold, untried approaches to a college education. One
was a new approach to what would be expected from students in terms of behavior.
With Aldrich's assent, the concept of *in loco parentis*—the university acting in the
role of parents for students absent from their parents—was downplayed; students
would be expected to make their own decisions. Aldrich also allowed co-ed dormitories at the new school, a move that drew flak from some county residents.

A great deal of consideration was given to how academic departments would be set up, and what subject areas would be established. Kerr had struggled with whether a humanities department should be created at UCI, lamenting in an interview with McCulloch that at UC Berkeley, the humanities department had grown so large that no dean could possibly administer it effectively. Aldrich and the newly hired deans debated similar questions. Out of their thinking came a new venture with the creation of a department of Information and Computer Science, and the Psychobiology Department, which combined biological, cognitive, and neuro sciences.

Not every new idea worked. Robert Gentry, who worked for decades at UCI in student affairs, heard Aldrich speak at a convention of student affairs professionals, vowing not to hire specialists for such student affairs areas like financial aid, or housing. Aldrich planned instead to have faculty members—in addition to teaching—handle those duties. Gentry told Aldrich it was a terrible idea, and indeed, it failed. Gentry said that Aldrich recognized the error and subsequently embraced student affairs as critical to the success of the campus and beefed up the professionalism of the staff.

The academic innovation that UCI is best known for is the School of Social Ecology, which has grown from what was originally an academic major of the same name.

Professor Arnold Binder was the father of social ecology on the campus. A psychologist, he had been drawn into real world experimentation and interaction in a variety of subjects, primarily criminology. Binder believed that students needed to study the interaction of human beings and their environment, whether it was in a tropical forest or a gritty urban neighborhood. Social Ecology students took classes in many different courses, seeking a common thread of understanding in the fundamental question of how humans and organizations make decisions, interrelate, and ultimately find meaning in doing so. As part of the major, students had to get off the campus and into communities for up to 100 hours every quarter to collect and analyze information and experience.[13]

Binder achieved significant success and notoriety by developing a diversion program for youthful offenders, an attempt to intervene early if a juvenile was arrested or detained for an offense. The program was well-received by Orange County law enforcement, bringing credibility to Binder, the new social ecology program, and the new university.

While Aldrich and his deans were looking inward, a variety of programs aimed at connecting the university to the larger community were initiated.

University Extension was well underway in 1965 when the campus opened. Started in Orange County in 1959 under sponsorship by the University of California at Los Angeles (UCLA), the extension program offered classes and lectures to anyone willing to pay the modest fees. In addition to instruction themed to traditional classroom subjects, Extension specialized in certificate classes, offering people in fields that were more technical than academic a recognition that they had achieved greater proficiency by studying at Extension.

Extension initially began offerings off site, but once UCI opened it moved into regular classrooms at night, which brought thousands of people to the new campus who otherwise would likely have not visited. As the years passed, the Extension program sponsored what became another UCI innovation, the Women's Opportunity Center. The center specialized in helping women experiencing life transitions such as divorce or career/motherhood issues. Impressively, a building for the center was located on the campus and built with off-campus donations. Over the years hundreds of women from all parts of the county received assistance and counseling there.

Town and Gown, which began with the wives of faculty and administration members, started organizing in 1963 and incorporated in 1965 as the campus opened.[14]

The goal of Town and Gown was simple: bring members of the community into contact with spouses of the university leadership and faculty to explain and promote the value the new university had to offer Orange County. Jean Aldrich, wife of the chancellor, took an early role in organizing the group along with Frosty Gerard, whose husband was dean of graduate studies.

Ten women involved in the early years of Town and Gown gave oral histories in 2012, recalling their memories of the time. Three of them cited the Orange County political climate as a reason to reach out to other women in the area.

Jean Aldrich: "Orange County was very conservative ... and anxious about what kind of community the university might attract." France Campbell: "We knew about the negative reactions from local organizations that were opposed to having a public campus in Orange County. It was openly said that another UC campus would bring in foreigners, Jews and communists." Suzanne Peltason: "People in town said they'd like to meet some of us (faculty wives). They said, 'we hope it's not like Berkeley, which was experiencing free speech and riots...'."[15]

Town and Gown grew quickly, attracting a large contingent of faculty wives and a smaller number of community members. A primary strategy employed to generate and sustain enthusiastic membership was the creation of interest groups, such as music, theater, book discussions, and one especially popular with East Coast wives who had relocated to a coastal campus—beach walking.

Soon Town and Gown was raising funds for student scholarships. And a long-term benefit of membership was negotiated when Town and Gown gave $1,000 to help build the University Club; all future members of Town and Gown got preferred parking at the facility.

Since forming in 1965, Town and Gown has raised more than $800,000 for student scholarships.

When an impressive group of business, government, and community leaders in 1965 empaneled themselves into an organization dubbed Project 21 to promote economic growth, UCI was quick to join the effort. Aldrich was named to the 20-member board of directors and recruited faculty and staff at the university to lend time and expertise. After months of study and analysis, six separate reports were written, with heavy input on the Open Space and Transportation elements from UCI participants.

A small but consequential UCI program that also drew people to the campus was the Farm School, established in 1969 on a vacant section of the sprawling campus.

As its name implied, the Farm School used the natural environment, including domestic farm animals, as a key ingredient in its curriculum, which at its core was not much of an organized learning system at all. The director of the school believed that children would thrive in an unstructured environment with minimal instruction. Fifty children aged 5 to 12 gathered each day in three old Irvine Company farm buildings that had been refurbished into classrooms.

Hundreds of children, many the offspring of faculty and staff, attended the Farm School during the 38 years it was open. According to one middle school educator in Irvine, Farm School students entering their schools were almost always well-prepared. (A smattering of students whose parents were not affiliated with the university attended the Farm School, including the children of a high-level Irvine Company executive and those of a senior editor at the Orange County edition of the *Los Angeles Times*.)

The new student body at UC Irvine did its part to help put the school on the map when it chose what was then—and still is—the most unusual sports mascot in the nation.

Two members of the water polo team—one of the new university's first sports—are credited with organizing the campaign to make the Anteater the official symbol of school athletics. The pair were inspired by a comic strip that was popular at the time: "B.C." The strip featured cavemen, dinosaurs, talking ants, and, yes, an anteater.

Coaches and administrators were not enthused, but their reluctance emboldened the student body to rally around the whimsical character. Soon cries of "Zot," the sound the comic strip animal made when nabbing his prey, were heard at games, as well as more ribald chants such as "give 'em the tongue," and "right in the ear, right in the ear, zot!"[16]

The student body made it official with a vote on November 30, 1965, enshrining the anteater as the new school's athletic symbol. Soon images of the anteater were appearing all over the campus and being attached to student institutions like the school newspaper (known for a time as the Anthill).

In 1970, students organized an open house and Spring festival they christened the Wayzgoose. The origination of the name is obscure; in Old English it refers to a celebration tied to St. Bartholomew's Day, something that was never referenced in any documentation of the UCI event. However, the students who made it all happen were apparently enthralled by the medieval connection—a highlight of the event revolved around reenactments of knightly battles, complete with swordplay and faux suits of armor. More traditional festival elements included food booths and games for children.

Wayzgoose was usually held the weekend just before Spring Break when the weather in Southern California was at its best. Hundreds of students took part, some in the jousting, some in the eating and drinking, others just watching. While the greater off-campus community was invited, and the event was publicized, community attendance was sparse (the authors attended several Wayzgoose events and didn't see many other non-students in the crowd).

But festive events and comical mascots couldn't overcome the national and international events of the mid-1960s and early 1970s that were darkening the mood of students throughout the United States, including on the temperate shores of Orange County.

A year before UCI opened, the best known and most notorious academic institution in the state was the Berkeley campus of the University of California.

The campus had erupted into a series of student demonstrations protesting the university's ban on political activities on campus. The rule was discreetly ignored in some instances, but most activist groups simply moved their tables and signs outside the university border into the city of Berkeley. When that action was also prohibited, a student named Mario Savio organized what became a series of marches and gatherings that escalated into violence, as much from police brought in to restore order as from students on the barricades.

Dubbed the Free Speech Movement, the turmoil became front page news across the state. For Ronald Reagan, seeking the governorship, the student dissent presented a readymade issue to campaign on, which he did skillfully; it would propel him to victory over Pat Brown in 1966. And while a new chancellor installed at the campus acceded to the Free Speech demands, it wasn't enough to quell rising resistance to the Viet Nam war. During the 1968–1969 school year at Berkeley there were six major demonstrations, 22 days of street fighting, and 2,000 arrests.

Aldrich and the new staff understood such student and faculty activism was not likely to go over well in the county where their new campus was taking shape.

Orange County in the mid-1960s was just beginning to grow out of some of the more radical elements of right-wing conservatism that had flourished there a decade earlier. The John Birch Society was still strong, but the extreme allegations of its leaders (President Eisenhower was a communist, as an example) were causing its ranks to decline. James Utt, a local member of Congress, was increasingly viewed as ineffective and erratic. Walter Knott continued to fund anti-communist forums and new organizations promoting free enterprise, but with less fervor as he aged.

The ultra-Libertarian *Santa Ana Register* continued sympathetic editorial coverage of anti-communist and fundamentalist activities and individuals, and the weekly *Newport Ensign* was filled with columns full of right-wing rhetoric. Only the *Daily Pilot*, whose publisher had been an ardent supporter of UCI, could be counted on to treat the university fairly. (*Los Angeles Times* established a separate Orange County edition in 1968. The arrival of the paper added a new level of sophistication to news reporting in the county.)

Students at UCI were feeling the impact of political and social forces swirling through the nation. The Viet Nam war was ramping up and hundreds of young men were being killed and wounded—the threat of the draft was increasingly foreboding; in Chicago in 1968, the Democratic Convention devolved into street riots as anti-war protestors clashed with police; Robert Kennedy and Martin Luther King were gunned down, as were students at Kent State. And while it didn't salve most of the psychic wounds, there had been some relief and escape in the Summer of Love in nearby San Francisco in 1967.

Documentation of the anti-war movement at UC Irvine by McCulloch in his book, *Instant University*, and in a research paper published in 2012 by Rebecca Huey, present a compelling case that UCI's student response to the war was measured and almost entirely peaceful.[17,18]

Huey credits the nature of the student body, the newness of the campus, and the cooperative atmosphere between students, faculty, and staff as a principal reason UCI remained calm. McCulloch made similar arguments, but also cited the continuing personal involvement of Aldrich as a critical element in maintaining order at the campus.

Which is not to say the campus and student body was uninvolved. Students for a Democratic Society (SDS) had an active chapter at UCI and organized regular demonstrations. Robert Gentry complained in his oral history interview that the student newspaper, the *New University*, paid too much attention to SDS and inflated its role relative to other anti-war activities.

A large national anti-war demonstration took place on October 15, 1969, the Moratorium Against the War. At UCI thousands of students, faculty, and community members gathered at the campus to hear speakers; students created a Moratorium Bulletin to educate others about the impacts of the conflict and held special classes examining military action in Viet Nam.

Throughout the entire time, according to McCulloch, Aldrich made it clear to the students that he supported their right to speak out, organize, and demonstrate, so long as they did not engage in violence or destruction of property. His commitment to the students was a key element in the relative calm that accompanied virtually every anti-war action at the campus, McCulloch argued.

Aldrich's forbearance would be tested at three high-profile events during the same timeframe; he dodged the public relations bullet at the first two, but the third would cause lasting damage.

The UCI students had formed a government and student activities association that promoted events of interest to the small student body, including sponsoring speakers. The students selected several individuals to visit the campus; two were guaranteed to provoke controversy—Black Panther Party leader Eldridge Cleaver and admitted communist Angela Davis.

Cleaver was free on bail in September 1968, and was making the rounds of California campuses, speaking on racism, Black Power, police brutality, and a host of other anti-Establishment topics.

The day before his scheduled speech at UCI, the *Daily Pilot* street edition pulled out the largest typeface in its print box with the screaming headline: DEATH THREATS SHADOW CLEAVER'S UCI SPEECH. Cleaver had skipped a scheduled appearance the day before at the Riverside campus of the university due to a phone death threat. His parole officer was quoted in the paper saying Cleaver had "mixed emotions" about the threat, but was ultimately philosophical, telling him, "... well man, if I don't get killed there I'll get killed somewhere."[19]

Cleaver was one of three speakers at a forum titled "Racism in America." He did not disappoint the dozens of students in attendance. Referring to Black people, he declared that, "… we're going to be free, or nobody is free. Let's make the pain democratic. I don't want to hear no more crying in the ghetto and laughing in the white suburbs." Noting another part of his comments, the *Pilot* headlined the story as CLEAVER ASSAILS 'PIGS' AT UCI LECTURE.

Aldrich fended off attacks on the event as best he could, arguing for free speech. He would have somewhat better luck with Angela Davis.

She visited the campus just over a year later, on October 9, 1969. Davis had achieved a level of fame and notoriety in the late 1960s by speaking out against the Viet Nam war and in support of feminist issues. She was articulate and attractive; unlike Cleaver's rhetoric that smacked of confrontation and violence, she was philosophical and reasoned, but no less passionate.

More than 400 students crowded into a lecture hall that had been searched by campus police after a bomb threat was received. Press access to the hall was banned, but a *Register* reporter joined more than a thousand students listening on loudspeakers outside the building.

External reaction to the Davis appearance is reflected in the university's records, which contain dozens of angry, outraged letters from individuals and organizations pummeling Aldrich, the campus, and the UC system for allowing a communist on campus. State Senator John Schmitz was especially incensed, writing to his constituents that WE MUST CUT OFF THE UNIVERSITY'S FUNDS UNTIL IT CLEANS HOUSE.[20]

There was internal reaction to Davis' appearance from the UCI Faculty Senate, and it was angry as well. Davis had been hired, fired, rehired, and then fired again as an assistant professor of philosophy at UCLA. The reason: she was a communist. This was too much for the UCI faculty to ignore, and after a spirited meeting of the faculty senate they voted to sue the UC Regents over the issue.

Aldrich tried to forge a middle course. Questioned about the situation at a meeting of the Newport Harbor Chamber of Commerce, he explained that university policy forbade communists from being employed, but that Davis had the right to appeal the decision

In a few days the Davis appearance was forgotten, but the fact she had been welcomed to speak at the university would be resurrected a year later when two prisoners staged a murderous escape attempt at the courthouse in Marin County, just north of San Francisco. The pair were affiliated with the Soledad Brothers, a Black activist group. Davis was implicated when it was discovered that she owned a gun used in the escape. She was subsequently tried and acquitted of charges related to the incident, but it stained her reputation for decades.

The crushing blow to UCI's reputation for reasoned, non-violent student dissent took place in the early hours of October 26, 1970.

Across the street from the entrance to the campus there was a large trailer that housed a branch of the Bank of America. Whether it was the bank's role in providing financial services for the federal government, and by association the military, or because it was the most convenient symbol of the Establishment near the university, it was set afire and badly burned.

It was the third Bank of America branch burned in recent months, one at UC Santa Barbara, another in the northern Orange County city of Placentia. Spray painted on the side of the building and still visible after the fire was the catch-all leftist slogan popular of the time, All Power to the People.[21]

In a national context, it was a modest event. Just two weeks earlier in Chicago the Weather Underground launched three days of violent rioting, including the bombing of a statue of a policeman. Dozens of people were injured, including a police officer whose neck was broken. The rioting marked the beginning of a three-year series of bombings across the United States carried out by the group that came to be known as the Weathermen.

(The year 1970 had already been a trying one for Aldrich. University records retained by his office for the period are filled with outraged correspondence from cities, Republican organizations, and elected officials, and the humorously named TIRE committee [Tired Taxpayers Indignant about Radicals in Education] from Newport Beach. Even the PTA of Sierra Elementary School in Santa Ana had a complaint. Aldrich dutifully replied to each letter with reasoned comments on university policy and procedures affecting free speech and student and faculty behavior.)

The fire at the bank proved to be an ill omen for the future of the development project planned that the Irvine Company called University Town Center.

****

The plans that William Pereira had drawn up for UC Irvine and the community adjoining it showed a seamless connection between the two.

What Pereira labeled the Town Center would be joined directly across Campus Drive at the entrance of the campus with a large pedestrian bridge. A few hundred feet on either side of the bridge, two-lane roads would also connect the campus and the Town Center.

In Pereira's vision:[22]

> The University Town Center is destined to serve as the focus for social, cultural and commercial activity within the University Community. This will be no ordinary regional shopping center with vast parking areas and colossal markets. It will not compete with Irvine Center. The plan, which has evolved is shown on the facing page and is influenced by early towns in Europe and America where shops, civic buildings, offices and housing are blended into an intimate scale.
>
> This 110-acre development is linked together by an interesting local street. By varying the building line, as well as the width of the automobile route, the path this street follows is broken into a series of related spaces and plazas. A transit vehicle on the planned loop road will give easy and convenient

connection to other main centers of activity. Much of the brick-paved spine will be shaded by awnings or structures as well as full-grown trees. Such diverse elements as fountains, exhibit areas, outdoor sales areas, small kiosks, children's play areas, etc., will add charm and interest to the town.

Located within the pedestrian center is the principal town square. Close by is the civic group, varied retail shops, restaurants, offices, etc. The square permits accommodation of large gatherings of people for such varied activities as band concerts, market days, political rallies, etc.

Because close-in residential developments add to the vitality and interest of the town a number of these have been introduced. It is proposed that this housing be interesting and varied, catering to inhabitants who enjoy the life and activity of the inner town. This housing would also be extremely desirable for shop owners, university oriented people, artists, retired persons, professional people, etc. For many there would be no need for car ownership. The hillside apartments minimize grading problems and will add architectural variety and appeal to the town.

By extending waterways from the Upper Bay to the town center and University, transportation by water would create a strong physical tie between the University and the many interesting developments all along the Bay. A hotel with a first-class restaurant is proposed near the lake and park, offering boating and golf privileges to guests. Small and attractive parks of approximately a half-acre are proposed throughout the town center, forming focal points for offices, apartments, etc. A district parking system is also proposed to maximize the advantages to merchants, residents and employees.[23]

What was built in the initial element of University Town Center was a shadow of the lofty portrait of the key section of the "city of intellect" that Pereira designed.

There was a single, two-story commercial building at the site. It housed the Spritzgarten, a beer and wine bar, and several office suites, including one occupied by the University Interfaith Foundation. There were also a few retail outlets. When the City of Irvine incorporated, it took over most of the office area as City Hall.

What is meant by "the essential character of a university town" turned out to mean different things to different people.

Many Irvine residents had attended colleges and universities all over the United States. Being part of a new community linked closely to a new university was, for many of them, a big reason why they moved to Irvine. If they came from a large—or small—college on the East Coast or the Midwest, their vision of a college town might have meant Ann Arbor, where the giant University of Michigan blended into Ann Arbor at virtually every corner of the campus. Harvard and Cambridge similarly bled into each other's neighborhoods, and at Yale, while the campus was more compact, it bordered a local cemetery on one side and city hall on the other. And nearly every East Coast and Midwest college town was a virtual arbor, verdant with massive trees.

California was a different story.

The oldest campus of the University of California was at Berkeley. While it climbed onto and into the hillside to create an upper boundary almost exclusively academic, at the base of the hill the school spilled into the city of Berkeley along Telegraph Avenue.

Telegraph Avenue in the 1950s was staid and Establishment. That all changed by the time Pereira was proposing his quintessential college town for UC Irvine.

Rag Theater, a blog that chronicles the heyday of the Berkeley scene, offers this description:

> Starting in the mid-1960's, Telegraph Avenue—where the sidewalks teemed with street vendors, musicians, politicos, runaways and the down and out— became shorthand for the cultural whirlwind of Berkeley. For conservatives, a stage set for 'the greatest freak show on earth.' For more sympathetic observers, it offered a 'rag theater' of great poignancy—a refuge that while inspired by idealism, often made for hard living in practice.[24]

Rag Theater's observation was generous. Others familiar with the area would have added the abundance of stray dogs, street beggars, and drug addicts on hand. Telegraph Avenue did have a thriving commercial district oriented to student needs, including three independent bookstores, coffee houses, and a collection of restaurants serving dishes from every corner of the world.

As far out, groovy, and sometimes dangerous as Telegraph Avenue was to Berkeley, Westwood—adjacent to the campus of UCLA—offered a smattering of the urban benefits in Pereira's vision of Town Center. Little more than an assemblage of food outlets, record stores, and student-themed shops squeezed into a 12-block area between the campus boundary and busy Wilshire Boulevard, Westwood became just another edge of the sprawl of Los Angeles that flowed toward Santa Monica and Beverly Hills.

The campus of UC Santa Barbara was built miles from the downtown core of the sophisticated and quiet city where it was located, which was just fine with the locals. UC Santa Barbara would create its own town center in campus-adjacent Isla Vista, where many students lived and partied next to the Pacific Ocean.

Ray Watson wanted the Irvine Company to plant a flag in Town Center by building its headquarters there:

> I thought it should be (there). I was a planning guy, there were the real estate guys, and the agriculture guys. President Charles Thomas let the debate go on between us. I made my arguments that I knew it wasn't as good a commercial location (as Newport Center), but we were the Irvine Company, and it would show a strong symbol to other prospective businesses that this is a good location to work. And we ought to show that strength by building our headquarters there.
>
> Thomas bought my arguments, presented it to the board of directors, and they approved the site, but with reservations, because university campuses

were experiencing political turmoil ... but Thomas said 'yes, I think it's a good idea.' But before it was announced to the world the Bank of America was firebombed.[25]

And, according to Watson, "that ended the discussion. (Irvine Company headquarters) immediately reverted back to Newport Center."

The company's decision, Watson noted,

> ... eliminated one prospective magnet that would have been very important to strengthen Town Center. Some years later, the university began exploring where to build their student union. Chancellor Aldrich, after discussions with me, openly favored in the Town Center, not on the campus. Again, it would have been another reason to bring students across the bridge (which was not actually built until 1984) into the Town Center. (The students) overwhelmingly voted for it to be on campus, so another leg of this unique idea of town and gown got eroded.[26]

There were plenty of more professionally enticing and potentially profitable projects competing for the Irvine Company's attention at the time: Fashion Island's exciting array of shops and restaurants, new office buildings at Newport Center, signature housing neighborhoods of University Park in Irvine, and looming on the horizon, what was anticipated to become the company's masterpiece—Woodbridge.

Fourteen months after the Bank of America blaze, Robert Dannenbrink arrived at the Irvine Company with degrees in planning and architecture. He had worked at the city of Los Angeles and at Gruen and Associates when he heard about the Irvine Ranch and what was underway. The potential to work at a place that was actually "building a city" appealed to him.[27]

Dannenbrink was assigned to the internal company team charged with planning University Town Center. The team had a strong and enthusiastic leader in William Watt, who led the company's apartment building division. But the heart of the project was commercial, and in Dannenbrink's recollection, the company executives assigned to University Town Center were unfocused. "The commercial people on the team were new every year," he recalled, making it difficult to maintain continuity and focus.

Dannenbrink said over the long months he drew more than 50 different sets of sketches and drawings as the project meandered through the internal review process, searching for the combination of planning principles, design elements, and landscaping that would make it come alive.

A *New Worlds* magazine article published in mid-1976 catalogued all the major developments the company was working on, most in the glowing terms the company-owned publication usually employed to promote them. But even *New Worlds* had to acknowledge the problems that were impacting University Town Center.[28]

Describing it as, "... another project a lot of people are impatiently awaiting ... (University Town Center) has already begun to emerge on the land, but only some hints of it."

The existing two-story office building was described as the project's "oldest occupant," and bravely predicted it was, "… fairly representative, in microcosm, of things to come. Packed into it are a campus bookstore, small shops," the city offices, and those of the Irvine Ranch Water District. "It is a very busy place, and it has a rich array of offices (and) so will the rest of the fifty acres that will surround (it)," the story added hopefully.

> That is a key element of the Town Center village plan. Its central area is envisioned as a distinctly urban place, fifty acres of busy and bustling human activity—a small scale 'downtown.' In the heart of the smallest of all of Irvine's villages will be malls, plazas, fountains, and walkways intermingled with two- and three-story buildings housing shops, services, and commercial business of all sorts … there would be room too, for public buildings.[29]

In one of the many versions of the project, planners mentioned the concept of locating residences above retail or commercial uses on the ground floor of the building. The quaint idea, so radically at odds with the company's other suburban offerings, was embraced by several city councilmembers. Long after the company had discarded the idea as impractical and unprofitable, it was inevitable that during a zoning meeting, someone would plaintively ask what happened to homes above the shops? Company officials could only smile or cringe, then try to change the subject.

The *New Worlds* article also referenced the Campus Valley Shopping Center, which was about a quarter of a mile from the Town Center parcel. Campus Valley had been built to serve two audiences: students in nearby dorms and residents of Turtle Rock, another half mile down Campus Drive. The company had originally planned to build the center in Turtle Rock proper, but residents objected to more traffic. Building Campus Valley damaged the potential success of the budding "small scale downtown" by creating competing business opportunities that might have otherwise located in University Town Center.

Eventually, a commercial project did emerge at University Town Center, but it lacked coherence and sparkle. Dannenbrink noted that trying to mix a commercial element immediately next to higher-density housing never generated much enthusiasm from the company commercial executives charged with its creation. The vision, he said, "just got watered down and watered down" as time passed.[30] The company also gave up on the strong pedestrian links between the housing and businesses, unconvinced that people would use them.

In his oral history, Watson bemoaned other problems University Town Center experienced. In addition to losing the company headquarters and the university student union, the City of Irvine never built its permanent city hall at Town Center, he said:

> So, when you take those magnets away from it, what do you have left? Pretty soon you're left with yogurt shops and so forth. Then people say,

'we need to do something about the Town Center to make it vibrant.' The reality is, you can spend money on remodeling buildings and making them look good, but some merchant still has to come in there and sell enough yogurt to pay the rent.[31]

Watson also noted a problem that continues to this day at University Town Center—lack of parking. Students trying to avoid paying for parking on campus instead sneak into the lots at Town Center. Security patrols trying to prevent it have been somewhat successful, but not entirely.

Another glaring omission at University Town Center, from the day the campus opened across the street, was the pedestrian bridge, a key element in the Pereira plan.

The only way for students, faculty, or staff to reach Town Center was to cross at one of two small roads from the campus. For a student with just an hour between classes, the extra ten minutes' walk going to and from the signaled crossing to Town Center shops kept many students away. The same could be said for staff on a short lunch or coffee break. (To the horror of university and city leaders, students regularly jaywalked across Campus Drive rather than use the signalized crossings. That no one was killed remains a tribute to the gods of fortune and the agility and speed of youth).

From a business standpoint, in 1965 when there were just 1,500 people on the new campus, spending millions of dollars on a bridge made little sense. But as the university grew, the lack of direct access was clearly impeding the potential for commercial success at University Town Center. Watson left the company in 1977, and Town Center was at the bottom of the list for action by the new owners. Moreover, when it became clear that the city and university were not willing or able to help fund the cost of finally building the pedestrian bridge, there was a spirited debate within company management about the potential expenditure.

The bridge was finally built in 1984, almost 20 years after the university opened; the Irvine Company paid for it.

Watson's comments in his oral history make clear his disappointment with the outcome at University Town Center. Ironically, the main physical recognition in Irvine of Watson's contributions to the city is the bridge between UCI and University Town Center, dedicated in 2005 in his honor as the Ray Watson Bridge. (Watson also has a plaque at the City of Irvine Wall of Recognition at city hall.)

(Daniel Aldrich's service as chancellor is remembered at UCI as well—the administration building is Aldrich Hall and the park in the center of the campus that he loved so much is named in his honor, Aldrich Park.)

Notes

1. Daniel G. Aldrich, "Remarks of Chancellor Daniel G. Aldrich, Jr. at Dedication of University of California at Irvine", June 20, 1964 (Special Collections and Archives, UC Irvine Libraries). http://ucispace.lib.uci.edu/bitstream/handle/10575/5918/as-004_b057_f006_004.pdf.?sequence=17.
2. Clark Kerr, "Remarks of President Clark Kerr at Dedication of University of California at Irvine", June 20, 1964, (Special Collections and Archives, UC Irvine Libraries). http://ucispace.lib.uci.edu/bitstream/handle/10575/5918/as-004_b057_f006_005.pdf?sequence=18.

3. Lyndon B. Johnson, "Remarks of President Lyndon B. Johnson at Dedication of University of California at Irvine", June 20, 1964, (Special Collections and Archives, UC Irvine Libraries.)

4. *Los Angeles Times*, June 24, 1989.

5. Jean Aldrich and Stuart Aldrich, "Oral History Video" (AS-179) (Special Collections and Archives, UC Irvine Libraries, 2015).

6. Samuel McCulloch, "Interview with Clark Kerr," in *Samuel C. McCulloch Oral Histories* (AS-033) (University Archives, UC Irvine Libraries, 1969) 10.

7. McCulloch, "Interview with Clark Kerr," 12.

8. McCulloch, "Interview with Clark Kerr," 12.

9. McCulloch, "Interview with Clark Kerr," 13–14.

10. Samuel C. McCulloch, "Interview with Diana Janas," In *Samuel C. McCulloch Oral Histories* (AS-033) (University Archives, UC Irvine Libraries, 1969) 19.

11. Jack Lockhart and Jason Valdry, "Oral History Video" (AS-179) (UCI Stories Video Oral Histories Collection, UC Irvine Libraries, University Archives 2016). https://calisphere.org/item/ark:/81235/d8rz59/

12. Scott Wood, interview by C.M. Stockstill, June 15, 2021.

13. Samuel McCulloch, "Arnold Binder Interview," in *Samuel C. McCulloch Oral Histories* (AS-033) (University Archives, UC Irvine Libraries, 1989).

14. *UCI Town and Gown Trailblazers: The Women Who Built Town and Gown – 1963–1980* (Irvine, CA: Town and Gown Oral History Committee, 2013).

15. *UCI Town and Gown Trailblazers*, 13, 19, and 38.

16. J. Wilson, "The Making of a Mascot," *UCI News*, November 18, 2015.

17. Samuel C. McCulloch and Clark Kerr, *Instant University: The History of the University of California, Irvine 1957–93* (Irvine, CA: University of California, 1996).

18. Rebecca Huey, *Protest in Practice: The University of California Irvine's Place in the Anti-Vietnam War Movement from 1965–1970* (Research Paper for UCI Humanities Core – Spring, June 6, 2012).

19. "Cleaver Assails 'Pigs' in Power at UCI Lecture," *Daily Pilot*, September 27, 1968, 1.

20. Author's recollection.

21. Raymond L. Watson and Ann Lage, *Planning and Developing the New Town of Irvine California, 1960–2003: Irvine Company President, 1973–1977, Walt Disney Company Chairman, 1983–1984* (Regional Oral History Office, the Bancroft Library, University of California, Berkeley, 2005) 204.

22. In August 1961, William Pereira's firm submitted to the Irvine Company a revised draft of a master plan for the Irvine Ranch. The 108-page leather bound folio was entitled *The Irvine Ranch Master Plan (Revised Draft)*. The plan included the location for a town center adjacent to the UC Irvine Campus on page 92, described the town center on pages 92 through 94, and included a conceptual site plan exhibit on page 95.

23. William L. Pereira, *The Irvine Ranch Master Plan (Revised Draft)* (Los Angeles, CA: Pereira and Associates, August 21, 1961) 93.

24. "Telegraph Avenue," *The Berkeley Revolution*, accessed November 12, 2021. http://revolution.berkeley.edu/view-archive-by-place/telegraph-avenue.

25. Watson and Lage, *Planning and Developing*, 204.

26. Watson and Lage, *Planning and Developing*, 343–344.

27. Robert Dannenbrink, interview by H.P. Oliver and C.M. Stockstill, January 4, 2021.

28. *New Worlds Magazine*, June–July 1976, 108.

29. *New Worlds Magazine*, 110.

30. Robert Dannenbrink, interview by H.P. Oliver and C.M. Stockstill, January 4, 2021

31. Watson and Lage, *Planning and Developing*, 344.

23 Joan Redux

Joan Irvine's life was recast in the 20 years between ascending to the board of directors of the Irvine Company and bringing the charitable foundation that controlled it to its knees.

Adrift at 18 after graduating from an exclusive girl's school, she debuted into Pasadena society at the prestigious Las Madrinas Ball, then married for the first time at 19. She was a mother a year later, divorced soon thereafter.

Joan's public profile went national in 1957 after she married Russell Penniman. *Sports Illustrated* published an article chronicling their primitively extravagant honeymoon in South America. When she divorced Penniman two years later, her reputed wealth and her often-mentioned blond beauty attracted coverage from Los Angeles newspapers.

It was, after all, the 1950s. Cities near the Irvine Ranch each had a Miss Tustin, Miss Newport Beach, or Miss Santa Ana. Grand openings of new stores or shopping centers invariably featured a pretty girl to cut the ribbon with ceremonial scissors, beaming among the crowd of middle-aged men looking on with appreciation.

Joan's appearance reflected the feminine image of the day. She was a beautiful, trim young woman with natural blond hair and blue eyes. She dressed well and looked stunning in her wardrobe. It was the unusual news story about Joan that did not describe her as blond, pretty, shapely, or all three.

In her autobiography, Joan said that on the advice of *Daily Pilot* publisher Walter Burroughs, she hired a publicist.

Frederick "Chip" Cleary was a successful Hollywood press agent. He had cut his teeth at the *Hollywood Reporter* after World War II, then joined a publicity agency; Desi Arnez was among his clients. Cleary moved to Newport Beach in 1958 to indulge his passion for sailing, but he wasn't ready to quit working, and signed on with Joan to help create a positive profile befitting a young heiress.

Cleary quickly applied himself to the task, and beginning in 1960 and continuing through 1961, Joan Irvine's story was appearing in newspapers all over the nation.

Cleary must have called in some favors from his show biz past to score a photo spread in *Look* magazine in September 1961, that featured "Joan Irvine—Golden Girl" on her horse rounding up cattle and appearing domestic at her home. A year earlier, it was the Inside Society section of the *San Francisco Examiner* headlining

DOI: 10.1201/9781003226291-24

its story on Joan with, "When Joan Irvine Burt Battles, She Doesn't Pick on Pipsqueaks!"[1] (At the time Joan was married to Richard Burt—some papers used her married name, others not.)

Joan traveled the local speaking circuit during this publicity blitz, with appearances at the Newport Harbor Chamber of Commerce and Tustin Women's Club. In a *Los Angeles Times* Society Section profile, "the tanned, athletic Mrs. Burt looks like a *Field and Stream* version of Grace Kelly."[2] Another paper described her as "a Junoesque 27-year-old with beauty, brains, millions of dollars and a fierce devotion to the Irvine Ranch," adding, "she loves a good fight."[3]

Cleary hired a freelance writer to pen a profile of Joan, building on the beauty angle but also describing her as a "corporate executive," presumably a nod to her seat on the board of directors of the Irvine Company. Wire services picked up the story, and it appeared in newspapers in Texas, Iowa, Washington, Pennsylvania, Missouri, Ohio, and Florida.

While Cleary was framing a portrait of Joan as a mid-century Girl of the Golden West, battling the James Irvine Foundation, she was also raising two young boys. There are few references to Joan's years of motherhood in her autobiography or in any of the dozens of magazine and newspaper articles written about her during this time. An exception was in a 2001 profile in *Orange Coast* Magazine, when she told an interviewer she had an easy time raising her sons because "they liked the same things I did growing up; fishing, hunting, surfing, boating and flying."[4]

In an oral history, her first son, James Swinden, remembers his mother's love of animals as an important part of their lives. As a girl, he said, Joan had a pet skunk, which she delighted in taking to formal events. She also corralled a young coyote at the Irvine Ranch and returned it to Beverly Hills to raise—until it escaped into the hills. Joan also had a parrot and Mynah bird and dozens of dogs throughout her life.[5]

Swinden tells an especially entertaining story about a seal rescue that led from Laguna Beach to San Marino.

A friend of his had turned up at the house in Irvine Cove with a sick seal. Joan tried to find a veterinarian but failing, called the family doctor in Santa Ana, who made the long drive to attend to what she had described as a "houseguest." Arriving to find the seal, the doctor gave him a shot of penicillin as Joan "sat on its head to keep it from biting the doctor."

Swinden continued: "She gets the idea she is going to take it back to our pool in San Marino." Upon arrival, Joan backed the car into her driveway to guide the seal into the pool, it hops out and goes hopping down the street. So here she is, eight months pregnant with my younger brother. She grabs a lasso ... runs after the seal, lassos it, pulls it back ... and puts it in the swimming pool.

> Well, the seal lived in the pool for several months. My grandmother (was) horrified ... because my mother would be in the pool swimming with the seal. She would actually take fish, put them in her bikini top, and feed the seal. She would also take me swimming with the seal, I was maybe four years old.[6]

Swinden claims credit for naming the seal: Torpedo. Friendly to its human benefactors, Torpedo chased the milkman and postman, "just like a dog. The long and short is, the seal got pretty domesticated and would hop up in the house and watch television with you." Ultimately the pool man refused to service the pool because the seal's excrement was fouling the filter.

Joan rented a U-Haul to take the now larger seal ("he ate 20 pounds of fish a day") back to Irvine Cove, where he was dumped on the sand in front of the ocean and lumbered into the waves. "For about two years after that there was a seal that used to body surf with us in the waves, and you always kind of imagined, well, maybe that was the seal," Swinden said.[7]

Swinden would see his father on weekends and on summer vacations, he said in his oral history, but the rest of his time he was with his mother.[8]

In 1963, Joan uprooted the family and moved to Middleburg, Virginia to join her fourth husband, Morton "Cappy" Smith. Swinden remembers the abrupt transition of going from "being a kid on the beach and having a lot of free time, to working on a horse farm and not having a lot of free time."[9] Like many other children in the area, he attended a boarding school.

After three marriages in just over a decade, Joan appeared to find balance in the union with Smith. Amateur psychologists will theorize that in marriage, Joan had been searching for the father she lost at age 2, finding him in a man 18 years her senior. He is quoted as saying "I was the only husband who set limits for her." Her mother agreed, quoted in the *Los Angeles Times* seven years after their wedding that, "Cappy provided the maturity her earlier marriages lacked."[10]

Friends and acquaintances who knew Joan in Middleburg describe a woman of charm and elegance who knew how to throw a party.

When not busy with Cappy breeding and selling horses, Joan was known for organizing "interesting, well thought out dinner parties," remembered Mrs. Winston Guest, who described herself as a friend of Joan's for 20 years.

The story of Mrs. Guest gives a glimpse of the type of people Joan was socializing with during her Middleburg days. Known as C.Z., Guest had spurned a blueblood Boston childhood for the nightclub stage in New York City at the tender age of 22, followed by a visit to Mexico City where Diego Rivera painted a portrait of her in the nude. Like Joan, she found the equestrian world a few years later when she married Winston Guest, a champion polo player and heir to a steel fortune. Mrs. Guest appeared on the cover of *Time* magazine in riding gear in 1962 but lowered her profile as the politics and values of the 1960s delivered a backlash against the leisure class.[11]

By 1977, however, Mrs. Guest was delivering a full-throated defense of the wealthy in an interview with Sally Quinn of *The Washington Post*, with such comments as, "... if you have money and servants then you are helping somebody. If the rich didn't spend money the country would be in worse shape than it is today." She also had the answer to why a recent political scandal had occurred: "... if Nixon had had proper breeding, Watergate would have never happened."[12]

Joan was living in Virginia but her ties to California remained strong. She traveled back to her Emerald Bay home to attend Irvine Company board meetings and enjoyed shopping for artwork and antiques with her mother. She also was reported to indulge in luxuries like a trip to San Francisco just to enjoy dinner at a favorite Chinese restaurant, or a visit to Rodeo Drive to freshen up her designer wardrobe.

From the time she joined the Irvine Company board of directors, Joan had continued to hammer on the board of the James Irvine Foundation in the press. But her strongest attacks came in wave upon wave of lawsuits litigated by a law firm and attorney who became intertwined with her and her mother for decades.

Her step-father, Judge Thurmond Clarke, recommended that she retain the Los Angeles law firm of Loeb and Loeb to represent hers and her mother's interests. Loeb and Loeb had been in business since the early 1900s and had a long list of clients in the entertainment field. It also represented wealthy families like the Gettys. Joan's wealth and notoriety made her a natural fit for the firm. Two attorneys were assigned to her and her mother: Howard Selvin, a senior litigator, and a younger one, Howard Friedman.

Friedman was an understudy to Selvin, but within a short time had emerged from the wings to the role of leading man on the main stage of Joan and her mother's ongoing drama of business and personal conflict.

In a lengthy epilog to Joan's book memorializing her mother, Friedman wrote about his long association with mother and daughter.[13]

Friedman said that in addition to directing the list of legal actions he undertook on behalf of the pair, he provided counsel:

> ... involving adoption of the master plan for the Irvine Company, the decision to convey undeveloped acreage to the University of California for ... UC Irvine, the opening up of the company to a broader range of developers ... the organization of the City of Irvine and numerous other major policy matters ...[14]

Friedman continued:

> I believe that when the history of Orange County is written covering the past forty years, the roles of Athalie and Joan in influencing the company toward constructive citizenship and effective planning will be among the highlights recounted in such a history. Their influence was a product of their farseeing vision for the company, their steadfastness of purpose in asserting their points of view and in maintaining appropriate litigation strategies designed to accomplish constructive ends.[15]

Friedman added that:

> Athalie and Joan manifested an intelligence and devotion to hard work not characteristically part of the popular perception of the role of women during those years. They were the vanguard of non-confrontational feminism in the

best sense of the phrase. Though encountering repeated rebuffs and scorn for not maintaining a more passive feminine role, they were ultimately able to command attention and respect for what they were seeking to accomplish.

I have represented numerous companies and individuals faced with challenges over the years. I have never encountered any clients, male or female, with a better capacity to understand issues, to do homework, and to maintain prudent postures ...[16]

Friedman's association with Joan, her mother, and the Irvine Ranch no doubt enhanced his reputation and enriched him personally (estimates of the amount of money Joan spent on lawsuits ranges into the multiple millions of dollars). He was, however, aside from the Irvine connection, a well-respected member of the legal community in Los Angeles, as well as a dedicated supporter of Jewish causes locally and nationally. He was the first person from the western United States to serve as chair of the American Jewish Committee, and for 18 years served chairman of the Skirball Cultural Center in west Los Angeles.

Los Angeles attorney Douglas Mirell who worked at Loeb and Loeb with Friedman, remembers him as "a giant, physically large, but more important, he had a presence in the courtroom that was palpable. He was someone who—if he was on your side—was capable of getting people to rethink their views."[17]

Friedman, Mirell said, "... was a supremely prepared and confident advocate. If you had a 'bet the company' case, Howard Friedman was the attorney you hired."

Friedman's win/loss record on Joan's behalf was less than stellar in terms of absolute numbers, but on a couple of major issues, his wins were significant; perhaps the most important was stopping the sale of a substantial share of the company to an out of state developer in the late 1950s. And Friedman was a key player in her long and complex campaign to change the tax code affecting charitable foundations, which started the legal avalanche that ultimately forced the James Irvine Foundation to relinquish control of the Irvine Company.

In 1970, when she should have been basking in the glow of the Tax Reform Act victory, Joan was instead gearing up to enter the incorporation campaign for the City of Irvine. It was far from her finest hour, as her opposition to citizen involvement and activism came off as self-serving and elitist. Home life was also beginning to fray, and by 1976 she and Cappy had divorced. Around 1978, Joan departed from the sophisticated life of Middleburg and its wealthy residents to return to California full time.

It was during these years the psychic seeds were planted that would eventually yield a bitter harvest of paranoia, suspicion, and fear in her daily life. And while what appeared to be a personal and professional victory was on the horizon, reaching it took a lasting toll on her family, friends, and on her.

Notes

1. *San Francisco Examiner*, April 18, 1960, 21.
2. *Los Angeles Times*, July 2, 1961, 120.

3. *Sioux City Journal*, July 9, 1961, 21.
4. *Orange Coast Magazine*, August 2001, 166.
5. "An Oral History with James Swinden." California State University, Fullerton. LAWRENCE DEGRAFF CENTER FOR ORAL AND PUBLIC HISTORY, MCAS El Toro Oral History Project, 2012.
6. "An Oral History with James Swinden."
7. "An Oral History with James Swinden."
8. "An Oral History with James Swinden."
9. "An Oral History with James Swinden."
10. "An Oral History with James Swinden."
11. E. Nemy, "C. Z. GUEST, Beauty Who Rose to Top of New York Society, Dies at 83," *The New York Times*, November 10, 1983. www.nytimes.com/2003/11/10/nyregion/c-z-guest-beauty-who-rose-to-top-of-new-york-society-dies-at-83.html.
12. Sally Quinn, "C.Z. Guest: The Rich Fight Back," *The Washington Post*, May 1, 1977.
13. Jean Stern, *Reflections of California: The Athalie Richardson Irvine Clarke Memorial Exhibition*. (Irvine, CA: Irvine Museum, 1994) 153–154.
14. Stern, *Reflections of California*, 153–154.
15. Stern, *Reflections of California*, 153–154.
16. Stern, *Reflections of California*, 153–154.
17. Douglas Mirell, interview by C.M. Stockstill, May 15, 2021.

24 Buying Time

The countdown had begun for the James Irvine Foundation.

Passage of the Tax Reform Act of 1969 would have immediate and long-term impacts on how the foundation operated and disbursed money. It was likely it would be forced to begin paying income taxes on its multi-million-dollar holdings, and its annual giving would have to meet a new standard.

Those issues could be handled with relative ease. The most ominous question was how and when the foundation would be required to reduce its holdings of Irvine Company stock.

The foundation, its trustees, and attorneys had put up a valiant fight during consideration of the law. Records of the hearings are filled with details of the foundation's governance, finances, and its symbiotic relationship with the Irvine Company. Loyall McLaren, nearly 80, flew across the country to duel with Wright Patman, Wilber Mills, and other members of the House of Representatives who wanted to know more, more, and more about the machinations and motivations of the non-profit that controlled more than 93,000 acres of prime California real estate.

But the momentum for reform, combined with the deep-pocketed and glamorous advocacy of Joan Irvine Smith, were impossible to overcome. Along with hundreds of other foundations, the James Irvine Foundation was forced to plot its future under new and uncertain circumstances.

The law became official in the final days of 1969. In the year that followed, the bureaucracy that would interpret and administer the monumental changes for the non-profits slowly heaved into action.

Thus the 1970 annual report for the foundation could state that many new provisions in the law, "… are quite complex, and we are advised it will be some time before we can expect detailed interpretations and regulations from the Treasury Department."[1]

The following year, according to the 1971 annual report (the foundation's fiscal year ran April 1 to March 31), little had changed. "To date, the Treasury regulations necessary for interpretation and implementation of many provisions of the Act have not been adopted." In the meantime, the foundation continued to dole out millions of dollars in grants to colleges, hospitals, schools, and other charitable organizations throughout California.[2]

DOI: 10.1201/9781003226291-25

The annual report language was likely written with one person in mind.

Joan Irvine Smith had been widely acknowledged as the individual most responsible for driving the legislative stake in the foundation's heart. A year after the new law's passage, she was busy opposing the incorporation of the City of Irvine as well as scrutinizing the company's coastal plans in anticipation of yet more litigation.

Joan was also keeping her eye on the foundation, and in October 1972, she was raising objections to the value of Irvine Company stock the foundation had ordered appraised to comply with the Tax Reform Act.

The previous week the foundation had released the appraisal, valuing its total holdings at $103,375,000 and setting the price of an Irvine Company share at $22.50. Joan was beside herself at the news. As reported in the *Orange County Register* on October 11, 1972:

> ... Mrs. Smith maintained that she has learned from the county assessor's office that the market value of the Irvine Company is $697,878,200. The total would be $777,362,000 she said, if 49,000 acres of the company's 83,000 acres were not in an agricultural preserve ...
>
> ... she said she had been advised that the alleged appraisal of company assets was made by a New York City banking company and that the total consists of three pages and is based solely on the earnings value of the Irvine Company.
>
> ... she charged that the (James Irvine) foundation is attempting to perpetrate a fraud not only upon the federal government, but also upon the people of California who are the beneficiaries of the James Irvine Foundation.[3]

The foundation had made its first move in its campaign for survival 14 months earlier when it filed a lawsuit in Los Angeles Superior Court against the state of California.

The lawsuit listed five issues of fact that it sought the court's opinion on:

1 Could the foundation's indenture of trust be amended to allow the foundation to comply with the new law?
2 Could James Irvine's order that the foundation retain control over the Irvine Company be changed to allow divestiture of Irvine Company stock?
3 Could James Irvine's order that Irvine Company stock be administered as a block be changed to allow marketing of company stock all or in part?
4 Could the indenture of trust be changed in all respects to comply with the Tax Reform Act?
5 Were California laws applicable to the indenture and articles of incorporation of the foundation?

The questions all revolved around a key provision in the governing documents of the trust that JI had created, providing that the trust "shall hold a controlling voice" in Irvine Company affairs and administer its stock holdings in the company "as a unit and without division or segregation thereof." In essence, the foundation sued the state in a friendly lawsuit asking it to grant the trustees the legal authority to override governing instructions in the trust so it could comply with the new federal law.[4]

But then the foundation added a final request, a legal Hail Mary that, if granted, could have given the foundation a powerful weapon for survival: a constitutional challenge to the Tax Reform Act itself as it applied to charitable foundations.

The staff lawyer representing the state, Deputy Attorney General Carl Boronkay, objected to the final pleading, but Superior Court Commissioner Maurice J. Hogan allowed it and set a trial date for the following July.

Reporters covering the proceedings asked foundation attorney Howard Privett to justify the challenge to a federal law that had been passed in large part to deal specifically with charitable foundations. He argued that the interests of everyone involved were the same, and that all should agree to a settlement.

Privett made a more detailed argument defending the need for the lawsuit a few weeks earlier in Washington D.C., part of a long, contentious, and at times bitter series of accusations and counter arguments between him and Joan Irvine Smith.

The Ways and Means committee was listening to dozens of representatives of foundations who had come to the nation's capital to explain how they were—or were not—complying with the Tax Reform Act of 1969. On April 9 and 10, 1973, Chairman Wilber Mills and 24 of his colleagues took their seats upon the dais of the committee's hearing room to consider if the law they had written a little more than three years earlier was achieving its desired effect.

Joan was more than willing to offer her opinion. She said the James Irvine Foundation was trying to avoid its legal obligations to give away more money and to divest its holdings of Irvine Company stock.

She began by labeling the lawsuit Privett was defending as underpinned by, "… calculated, bad faith motives … a charade." She continued: "Through these and other devices (foundation chair Loyall McLaren) and the foundation trustees intend to prolong their absolute and dominant control of the Irvine Company."[5]

Joan continued with her familiar theme that the price of Irvine Company stock was wildly undervalued and that the dividends were too low. It was a self-serving argument—as a stockholder, what she claimed was an artificially modest return translated into less income for her. However, she argued, the miserly return also lowered the amount of money the foundation could donate each year.

Joan used County of Orange property tax records to bolster her claim that the stock was undervalued; Privett argued that the unique nature of the stock— privately owned and therefore not traded on public markets—made it difficult to value. He challenged Joan's assumptions about present and future earnings based on the company's revenues and pointed out to the committee that from 1968 to 1973, Joan had received more than $4 million in dividends from her stock (about $29 million in 2022 dollars). He also noted that if Irvine Company stock was sold, there could be significant capital gains tax liability, which would impact its value.

Then Joan got personal, attacking foundation trustees Edward Carter and John S. Fluor, accusing them of self-dealing to the advantage of their businesses. She railed at the salaries paid to Irvine Company senior executives and accused the company of taking out loans to build office buildings, which required more employees to be hired to manage them, further diluting revenues and stock payouts. The foundation's loan to develop the Big Canyon Country Club came under fire, as well as a land lease involving William White, whose mother was Myford Irvine's second wife.

Joan's testimony made a lasting impression on Privett's daughter Pamela, who had come to Washington D.C. with her mother, sister, and father and attended the hearing. Pamela—now an attorney in Los Angeles—recalled that:

> ... it got quite fiery on Mrs. Smith's part. She did some name calling and was quite theatrical, and at age 12 I'll admit I was alarmed by it. My mom had to explain to me later in the ladies' room that Mrs. Irvine Smith didn't really mean the things that she said about my dad, she was just grandstanding to make a point.[6]

After what must have been hours of testimony, Rep. Joel Broyhill interrupted Joan to ask, what do you want?

She was forthright: "To force the foundation to divest, to begin to sell the (Irvine Company) stock, to register it with the Securities and Exchange Commission and begin an active registration (for a) sale with a purchaser for the stock they own." She went on: "what concerns me is (the foundation) is going to encumber the entire property ... when they do, we (individual stockholders) are going to be in real trouble."[7]

Forcing a public sale of the foundation's stock was the key to Joan taking control of the Irvine Company. If dozens of investment funds and individuals purchased 100, 1,000, or 100,000 shares of the 4.5 million shares outstanding, the 22 per cent she and her mother owned would provide a strong platform to form a majority.

Joan concluded and turned the witness table over to Privett. It was all too familiar for the 43-year-old attorney—he had been contending with her for years.

Methodically, Privett dismantled each of the allegations Joan had made, citing her habit of making charges with, "... half-truths and innuendos." In summary, he said that,

> Mrs. Smith has been litigating with (the foundation) for 15 years, and it is no pride to me as a lawyer to say I have never lost a lawsuit to her. The reason is because she is wrong in her facts and makes incorrect assessments of the law.[8]

Privett then allowed himself his own opinion of Joan Irvine Smith's motivations.

"I submit Mrs. Smith is pursuing ... her own personal interests.... these things which she has said are colored not by a desire to benefit charity, but in service to her own personal interests."[9]

Pamela Privett watched her father with fascination and pride:

> My Dad was my absolute hero growing up and I'd never heard anyone say
> anything negative about him ... and I couldn't understand why he was just
> sitting there, in an utterly relaxed pose wearing his semi-amused smile while
> this beautifully dressed and perfectly turned-out woman accused him of
> things. I learned a few lessons that day for sure.[10]

Privett's testimony before Ways and Means had been preceded by his appearance
before the Committee on Banking and Currency, chaired by Wright Patman,
who led the attack on the foundation during the hearings on the Tax Reform Act
of 1969. Patman even made Privett swear an oath that his testimony was truthful,
something no other witness that day had been subject to. When another attorney
representing the foundation asked Patman why Privett was being singled out, he
simply said that "someone" had requested it. Joan, perhaps?

Patman probed the death of James Irvine in Montana, nearly 26 years earlier,
asking the kind of questions only the chairman of a committee could get away with.
Regarding JI's actual demise, he noted that it happened while JI and others were
fishing. But Patman speculated (with no indication he had any evidence), hadn't JI
and the anglers just had a big meal "... and then immediately after the meal, they
went fishing? Isn't that unusual? Don't they take a nap and rest or something before
further activity?" Patman then wanted to know if JI and Brad Hellis had been fishing from a boat. Privett explained that they had been in a stream, wearing waders.
Patman finally let go of JI's demise, but not before musing, "... well, the whole thing
is unusual, right after a big meal they go fishing in the middle of the day."[11]

Patman then turned to the other notorious Irvine family death, Myford Irvine.
The sordid details of Myford's suicide were revisited, with Privett pleading igno-
rance of specifics as to how the actual deed was accomplished. Details of two
autopsies performed on the unfortunate Irvine son were recounted. Other committee members began to object to Patman's grilling of Privett. Just what was the
point, they asked?

But Rep. Frank Annunzio leapt to Patman's defense. He offered a comment
some might have found surprising from an Italian American representative from
Chicago, but he offered it nonetheless:

> I mean this is a tax-exempt foundation. When you were interrogating the
> witness, I was really amazed. I was almost ready to write another book on the
> rise of *The Godfather*. We are dealing with the taxpayer's money here. We are
> talking about millions and millions of dollars that are being exempted and
> would probably go to the Treasury.[12]

Privett was asked again to defend the foundation's position that it needed the full ten
years provided in law to sell its Irvine Company stock, especially since other foundations were shedding their stock holdings. Apples and oranges, Privett argued—Irvine
Company stock was privately held and not traded on the public markets.

The hearings concluded, shifting the story back to Orange County.

In June 1973, the Irvine Company was predicting there would be no immediate sale of company stock by the foundation. John Newman, the chairman of the company board, allowed that it might be 18 months or longer before a sale might take place. Board member Keith Gaede, Joan's cousin by marriage, told the *Register* that Newman had discussed the potential of a secondary stock offering to any minority owner that might be interested.

A month later, Joan scored a major victory when the Los Angeles Superior Court ruled that the foundation could sell its Irvine Company stock to conform to the Tax Reform Act of 1969. But Howard Privett popped any celebratory balloons Joan might have been tossing by predicting that the foundation would take 12 to 15 years to dispose of the stock.

According to the *Register* article on the court ruling, "Lyndol Young, attorney for Joan predicted that sale of the stock in small amounts, instead of all at once, reduced the possibility that another party could acquire more than 22% of the stock."[13]

(Young was 78 in 1973. He was no stranger to representing celebrities: in 1927—six years before Joan was born—he was counsel to Lita Grey Chaplin in her divorce proceedings against silent film legend Charlie Chaplin. A few years later he represented Charles Duell, the fiancé of actress Lilian Gish, in a lawsuit involving the pair. By the time he was affiliated with Joan, his practice appeared to deal largely with estates and trusts.)

Fourteen months passed before the penultimate chapter in the struggle between Joan and the foundation began. Let her tell the story: "In November 1974 ... my attorney, Mr. James Brown, happened to talk with another attorney at a social gathering (who) remarked that he was representing a client who was merging with the Irvine Company."[14]

The suitor was the international energy giant, Mobil Oil. Joan wasted little time in filing a lawsuit to prevent the sale. Three months later a temporary injunction to halt it was issued in Orange County Superior Court, giving Joan and her legal team time to mount a defense.

Joan continued her story:

> What motivated the trustees of the James Irvine Foundation to fight for years in court to try and eventually make a 'sweetheart' deal with Mobil Oil instead of complying with the law in 1971 by an orderly divestiture of Irvine Company stock ...?[15]

The answer, she said, was explained in a *Wall Street Journal* article, which reported that:

> ... the deal was brought to the foundation by ... John Simon Fluor, a former chairman of Fluor Corp., an Irvine (Foundation) trustee, and a business contact of Mobil chairman Rawleigh Warner Jr. The price raised eyebrows: it worked out to $23.50 per Irvine share, whereas an appraisal of Irvine done

for the IRS in 1973 put the value at $35.65 (and) a financial advisor to the (California) attorney general testified at the current trial that the market value of the company is more than $400 million.

(Details of Fluor's involvement were never clarified; he died in September of 1974).

Former Irvine City Councilmember John Burton, who worked at Fluor, recalled that the Fluor Corporation itself considered purchasing the Irvine Company stock. Another source claims that Fluor paid Wall Street heavyweight Benjamin Lambert $180,000 to evaluate a potential sale. (Lambert would make another appearance in the story in 1977.)

Joan also pointed out that Morgan Stanley, which had been retained by the foundation to advise on the disposal of the stock, was a Mobil Oil underwriter, reinforcing the *Wall Street Journal's* comment that, "... (the deal) has some earmarks of a cozy arrangement."[16] Morgan Stanley had also been the source of the appraisal of Irvine Company stock that led to the $24 per share valuation.

The foundation struck back in February 1975, with a civil suit against Joan confirming—without naming Mobil Oil—that it was negotiating "with certain American companies" to sell its Irvine Company holdings. According to the *Register* article on the suit, the foundation said in its legal documents it had, "... secured informal and tentative commitments in principle on most of the material terms of a transaction ..." at a price of about $24 per share.[17]

At the same time, the California attorney general's office waded into the legal proceedings.

California law gives the attorney general the responsibility to regulate charitable trusts and those who raise funds for charities. Deputy Attorney General Yeoryios Appallas argued that the foundation's proposed sale of company stock to Mobil Oil was, "... highly questionable." He joined Joan in asserting the $24 per share price was, "... considerably below the fair market value of the stock."[18]

Ten months after filing the lawsuit to block the deal, Joan formulated a complicated offer for the foundation and the company to consider: it called for the foundation to swap its 54.5 per cent company interest for whatever portion of the Irvine Company's ground leases that would yield $10.5 million in annual revenue for the foundation.

At the time, the company controlled more than 5,000 ground leases for homes and commercial properties.

Joan's offer went further. It proposed that the Irvine Company issue warrants to the foundation for its stock at $24 per share, with the warrants to be held by the financial firm underwriting the issuance. The warrants could be redeemed within five to seven years after the foundation retired its controlling interest in the company in exchange for the leases.

Then, if the stock was placed on the public market and sold, the foundation would be able to receive funds more than $24 per share, with the original $24 going back to the company. Joan argued that her plan would also provide tax benefits.

Irvine Company and foundation lawyers made short work of her offer, which they declared dead on arrival.

Joan was running out of time. It had been 11 months since she filed her lawsuit; the trial on the merits of her legal arguments had begun a few weeks earlier. Her attorneys could slow the pace as much as possible, but not indefinitely. On November 20, 1976, as a bidding war had begun, she offered to buy the Irvine Company stock from the foundation for $24 per share. As an incentive for the foundation, as well as to give her time to raise the money, she proposed that the stock sale be conducted on an installment basis. Such an arrangement, she said, would allow the foundation to continue to control the company until she obtained a majority of the shares.

Her offer went nowhere. In fact, a few days later, on December 9, the James Irvine Foundation was reviewing a five-page written offer from Mobil, according to foundation board meeting minutes.

The fight for the Irvine Ranch had become national news, attracting the attention of two men—one on Wall Street, one in Detroit—who were personal friends and business partners. They sensed an opportunity, which—as the saying goes—favors the bold.

Notes

1. *Annual Report – 1970* (San Francisco, CA: James Irvine Foundation, 1971).
2. *Annual Report – 1971* (San Francisco, CA: James Irvine Foundation, 1972).
3. *Orange County Register*, October 11, 1972.
4. "Irvine Foundation to Question Legality of '69 Tax Reform Act," *Los Angeles Times*, May 10, 1973, 5.
5. U.S. Congress. House. Committee on Ways and Means, *General Tax Reform (Testimony from Administration and Public Witnesses): Public Hearings Before the Committee on Ways and Means, House of Representatives, 93rd Congress, First Session, March, April and May 1973* (Washington, D.C.: U.S. Government Printing Office, 1973) 5915.
6. Pamela Privett, interview by C.M. Stockstill, June 15, 2021.
7. U.S. Congress. House. Committee on Ways and Means, *General Tax Reform*, 5944.
8. U.S. Congress. House. Committee on Ways and Means, *General Tax Reform*, 5953.
9. U.S. Congress. House. Committee on Ways and Means, *General Tax Reform*, 5962.
10. Privett, interview, June 15, 2021.
11. U.S. Congress. House. Committee on Banking and Commerce. *Tax Exempt Foundations and Charitable Trusts: Public Hearings Before the Committee on Banking and Commerce, House of Representatives, 93rd Congress, First Session.* (Washington, D.C.: U.S. Government Printing Office, 1973) 275–276.
12. U.S. Congress. House. Committee on Banking and Commerce. *Tax Exempt Foundations and Charitable Trusts*, 280.
13. *Orange County Register*, October 11, 1972.
14. "Advertising Supplement," *Los Angeles / Times/Santa Ana Register*, November 11, 1977.
15. "Advertising Supplement," 1977.
16. "Advertising Supplement," 1977.
17. *Santa Ana Register*, February 22, 1975, 1.
18. *Santa Ana Register*, February 12, 1975.

25 Schout's Honor

When Alfred Taubman reached Robert Schout, his vice president of marketing was playing football in a suite at the Waldorf Astoria in New York with John Reed, the chairman of Citibank, and a couple of other executives from large financial institutions.

Taubman asked impatiently, "Why are you doing that?"[1]

Because, Schout answered, you asked me to start getting close to other banks in case the Taubman Company needs additional lines of credit. And don't worry, we're playing football with biscuits from this morning's breakfast.

Taubman was curt. "Meet me tomorrow morning in San Francisco at my apartment. I want you to buy the Irvine Ranch."[2]

A day before, Taubman had received a call from Charles Allen Jr., a principal at the boutique New York City investment bank Allen and Company. In a world of outsized and brash financiers jousting loudly with one another on Wall Street, Allen and Company was, by design, an anomaly.

Low key, low profile, the firm avoided the headline-making Big Deals, preferring to identify opportunities with potential long-term value. Allen and Company would make a modest investment, usually around 10 per cent, then bring in trusted partners to accumulate the necessary capital to complete the transaction. The Allens did this again and again, a strategy that Herbert Allen Jr. in 2004 described in a *Fortune* magazine article as, "... circles around circles of investing." *Fortune* explained, "... by that he means that when an attractive place to put money surfaces, the firm invests, its people invest, Allens personally invest until the mind reels at sorting things out."[3]

Allen had a tip for Taubman; fly to Los Angeles and find a man named Colonel John Gottlieb, a longtime friend of Allen's, who would provide an introduction to Joan Irvine Smith.

In his autobiography, *Threshold Resistance*, Taubman wrote that he had been following Mobil Oil's effort to purchase the Irvine Company. "I had long admired Irvine's state of the art master plan," he noted. Arriving in Orange County, he and Joan connected. "I was impressed with (her) the minute I met her. You could sense her determination and love for the ranch. It was also clear that she was one tough woman."[4]

DOI: 10.1201/9781003226291-26

Figure 25.1 Retail magnate A. Alfred "Al" Taubman in 1978.

(Detroit Free Press)

Colonel Gottlieb disappears from almost every subsequent account of the epic contest that traces its genesis to his connection with Charles Allen Jr. However, according to Schout, Gottlieb remained deeply involved in the transaction and received a payment from Allen and Company for his efforts (language in the actual sales agreement confirms Schout's assertion).[5]

The Colonel, as he liked to be called, graduated from West Point and was a World War II veteran reportedly assigned to the transportation section of the Army, a business he continued in after the war in Chicago, as well as managing interests in pinball machines and commercial laundries.

It was in the laundry business he made the acquaintance of James R. Hoffa, president of the Teamsters Union.

According to one of more than a dozen articles in the *Los Angeles Times* in 1962 that delved deep into the machinations of the Teamsters union pension funds, Colonel Gottlieb was a regular beneficiary of loans from the fund for land developments. Hoffa didn't deny the affiliation, he embraced it: "I have known Colonel Gottlieb for more than thirty years. He was one of the first business owners to sign a contract with the Teamsters."[6]

In addition to being identified publicly in the *Times* as connected to Hoffa, an FBI field report dated January 11, 1962, detailed the activities of a Teamster official in Los Angeles connected to Gottlieb, noting that the two were partners in land deals.[7]

There is no record of any criminal activity by Gottlieb or charges related to the pension funds or anything else. A visitor to the Gottlieb home in Beverly Hills during the 1960s described him as a man with a sweet disposition, well dressed, and carrying an air of quiet authority, but otherwise nondescript. "He was a nice looking, middle aged Jewish man you wouldn't look twice at," the visitor recalled.[8] Gottlieb died in 1984.[9]

("Gottlieb was known in Beverly Hills as the 'candy man,' a reference to his habit of passing out candy to his numerous friends and acquaintances."[10])

Taubman's selection of Schout to investigate the potential value of the Irvine Company reflected the trust the two had developed since Schout joined Taubman's company not long after law school.

Schout said in a 2021 interview that he and Taubman bonded because they both, "... grew up in a ghetto." In Taubman's case it was not really a ghetto in the restrictive sense, but, as he noted in his autobiography, a tight knit group of 60 Jewish families in Pontiac, Michigan, where his family had moved when he was 4.

Taubman's father brought the family from Iowa to Michigan to find work in the automotive industry. After doing so, he opened fruit stands in the area and began building homes. The family did well until the Great Depression hit, plunging the elder Taubman into debt when homeowners went bust. "Lean years ensued ... but Taubman recalls that experience drove home a hard lesson ... pay off your debts." His father paid every dime back to the bank.[11]

At age 11, Taubman made his debut in the retail business that would eventually define his commercial life when he went to work as a clerk in a discount store in downtown Pontiac.

Schout came from Zeeland, a community of immigrant and first-generation Dutch not far from Pontiac. He learned his ABCs, he recalled, from reciting Bible verses ("A is for Adam ..."). Schout's membership in the North Street Christian Reformed Church became the foundation of his life. No matter the press of business, he never worked on Sundays, often taking a red eye to be home and attend church.

(Schout had good reason to be home. He and his wife Janet, over the course of their 58-year marriage, adopted 14 children, most of them American Indian, Hispanic, or Black, and many with developmental difficulties. Twelve of the children survive and have given the Schout's 38 grandchildren and two great-grandchildren. During their marriage, in addition to raising their children, Janet Schout worked as a nurse.)

As Schout flew across the country to meet Taubman, he was in the service of his employer as well as an unofficial, off the books affiliate.

Schout had prospered in his role working for Taubman as a marketing executive (his official title) as well as someone Taubman could trust to round up cash for the company's increasing needs to expand its retail empire, which at its peak included 26 malls in 19 states. Most of the Taubman holdings were high-end marketplaces with impressive features that promoted profits and were expensive to maintain. Finally, Schout was Taubman's trusted utility player, a man who could be thrust into sensitive situations and be counted on to perform with skill and discretion.

But Schout also had a handshake arrangement with Allen and Company. As Allen had fed the potential Irvine Company deal to Taubman (as well as making loans to him in the past), so Schout was always on the lookout for a business opportunity he thought the Allens would find attractive—circles around circles.

In Schout's retelling of the Irvine Ranch purchase, it was Allen and Company that was behind the deal—Taubman was recruited to become the public face of the transaction and to help the Allens find additional investors.

To get the process going, Taubman and the Allens needed to determine the value of what they would be trying to purchase. It was an enormous task, as at the time the Irvine Company had a vast array of holdings including land, office buildings, residential and commercial land leases, apartments, boat slips, retail centers, and a reservoir. The company was private, so there were no 10-K reports that could be easily accessed and analyzed. Where to begin?

Taubman and Schout decamped to Orange County with a couple of attorneys in Taubman's employ to meet with representatives of the Touche Ross accounting firm and get their take on the financial web of Irvine Company assets. After a few hours of discussion, Taubman flew back to Detroit and told Schout to figure it all out.

Schout was not impressed with what he was hearing from the accountants. But he had a plan.

Schout knew that the Irvine Company had a large line of credit with the insurance giant Aetna. He also had a contact who could convince Aetna to disclose the financial data it had accumulated over time to justify the potential to make multi-million-dollar loans for company projects. He and Jerry Howie, an appraiser for L.W. Ellwood Company, hopped on a helicopter to the Aetna offices in Los Angeles and returned with five large banker's boxes of paperwork.

For the next four days, almost non-stop, Schout and Howie pored through the Aetna files, Schout using nothing more than his trusty Hewlett Packard calculator. Before passing out on the last day from exhaustion, Schout recalled that he found four key factors that he considered critical to the company's value.

First was the water and sewer system installed by the Irvine Ranch Water District, which extended to almost every acre of the ranch that was buildable. The debt for all that pipe was issued by a public agency, and as such was relatively cheap as opposed to what a private owner would have to pay. Moreover, as the land was developed, the responsibility to pay it off was transferred to homeowners and owners of commercial properties. So even though the Irvine Company still owned a great amount of property, as the ranch developed, the financial burden of paying for the infrastructure would diminish.

Second was the relative value of the land leases, which in Schout's analysis were very low compared to the market. He found similarly low values on commercial leases, leading to the conclusion shared by others—notably Joan Irvine Smith—that the company (and its controlling faction, the James Irvine Foundation) had worked to minimize profits.

Third was the fact that many properties the company owned had little or no debt on them, giving a new owner tremendous potential to raise cash.

Finally, Schout saw the same phenomenon company executives had seen a decade and a half earlier: a surge of humanity and accompanying commercial activity from the greater Los Angeles basin bearing down on the borders of the ranch. This place, Schout thought, is going to increase in value for a long, long time.

Looming over Schout's calculations and the plans of Taubman and the Allens was Mobil Oil.

Mobil had already firmed up a serious set of negotiations with the James Irvine Foundation when Joan's lawsuit had thrown a legal monkey wrench into the process. Nevertheless, while the legalities continued, Mobil inched closer and closer to a handshake deal with the foundation that could be consummated if the legal decision went the right way.

Indeed, records of the James Irvine Foundation show that in March 1976, the foundation trustees had determined, "... it is in the best interests of the foundation," to accept Mobil's offer and directed their lawyers to "bind Mobil" to terms of sale and present it to the board at its September meeting for approval.

Three months later, Mobil had tweaked its offer, minutes of the foundation noted, but it was still deemed acceptable, and the September target date remained intact.

Mobil's interest in the Irvine Company, most people believed, was as an opportunity to expand its land development business.

At the time, other oil companies had a great deal of cash in reserve; some were looking to diversify. Mobil had already set up a subsidiary, Mobil Oil Estates, which in 1973 had purchased 1,500 acres of land alongside the San Francisco Bay to develop what became Redwood Shores. Gulf Oil had been one of the original investors in the New Town of Reston in Virginia, and in Houston, a new community called The Woodlands was taking shape in 1974 with the financial backing of oil millionaire George Mitchell. And a few years after the Irvine Company purchase was completed, the community of Coto de Caza in the foothills east of the ranch would get a large infusion of cash from Chevron Land.

Robert Schout never believed Mobil wanted the Irvine Company for its land development potential; the reason, he believed, was a pipeline.

The pipeline was owned by El Paso Natural Gas. It ran alongside the right of way for the Santa Fe Railroad that traversed the Irvine Ranch. The pipeline was empty and had been for some time. Mobil, Schout thought then—and still does today—wanted to use it to ship crude oil.

In Schout's retelling, Mobil was outflanked by the Environmental Protection Agency (EPA) decision to forbid oil to be offloaded from tankers at the Port of Los Angeles. He believes Mobil had a plan to offload somewhere on the Orange County coast and get the oil into the El Paso pipeline, where it could be distributed at points east. Further, Schout believes, Mobil had calculated what it would bid for the Irvine Company against what it would cost as an alternative to build a pipeline in Panama to accomplish the same goal.

Mobil's initial discussions with the James Irvine Foundation were still underway in late October of 1976 when a new suitor for the Irvine Company showed up with an attractive financial bouquet.

The Canadian firm Cadillac Fairview (CF) had been formed in 1974 with the merger of a construction company, Cadillac, and a developer of retail centers, Fairview Company. The company was valued at $2 billion and owned 16,000 apartments, 35 shopping centers, and ten million square feet of office space. Cadillac Fairview also had access to deep pockets—the Bronfman family owned about one-third of the company. (The Bronfmans had built a fortune in the distilling business.)

Cadillac Fairview had started looking to expand into the United States just two years after the merger. According to a case study on the company published by the Rotman School of Management at the University of Toronto in 2013.

> John Daniels, CF's executive vice president … encouraged CEO Ephraim Diamond to look at the Irvine Ranch. CF had never developed a property of such scale in Canada, let alone in the United States, but Daniels felt the location and size of the ranch made it ideal for development.
> … Diamond assessed the ranch by conducting research that included frequent site visits … studies for due diligence and pro-forma analysis.

Diamond calculated that if the company could develop 1,000 acres of land annually for 20 years, it could afford to pay $280 million. "Eager to make the purchase, Diamond arranged for financing with four banks to support an offer of $265 million … $145 million in cash, and $120 million in notes."[12]

Confident of his analysis, Diamond made a bid of $265 million on October 24, 1976.

The foundation had noted Cadillac Fairview's interest in early October and had given their attorney permission to ask the court for a recess in the lawsuit with Joan should a better offer materialize. The foundation liked what they saw from Cadillac Fairview, voting at their last meeting in October to accept the Canadian firm's offer, which in addition to pricing, was accompanied by a seven-page term sheet.

Before the agreement could be consummated, Mobil countered at $273.5 million.

(Leo Kolber, who was president of Cadillac Fairview, wrote in his autobiography that Taubman had approached him to discuss partnering on the deal, but nothing came of it.[13])

As the action heated up, Taubman knew it was time to make a play. Using an acronym of SMBH&Z761 (a combination of the initials of the Taubman law firm and the number of corporations it had formed), Taubman called Schout and told him to enter a bid of $225 million cash plus additional compensation in the form of lease exchanges and notes that brought the total offer to $285.6 million.[14]

The problem was timing. The bid was due at the Orange County courthouse at 3 pm. Taubman had called shortly after noon. An official form required to enter the bid document was only available at Howard Friedman's law office in downtown Los Angeles.

Schout was prepared. He had a helicopter waiting at Orange County Airport.

A series of events worthy of a Keystone Kops movie began with Schout and an associate climbing into the chopper and making a beeline for downtown. However, the pilot and Schout had neglected to find a place to land. They spotted a landing pad on top of a building a few blocks south of downtown proper. Alighting, they were met by a group of armed guards there to protect Occidental Petroleum building owner Armand Hammer.

A conversation ensued and money changed hands. Schout and the pilot remained on the roof while his associated went on foot to Friedman's office and grabbed the paperwork.

Now it was a race to Orange County. With nowhere to land in downtown Santa Ana, the pilot recalled a friend who owned a Porsche dealership in Anaheim with a large parking lot where the chopper could safely descend. He'd even have a car waiting, the pilot assured Schout.

Once on the ground, the friend and promised car were missing. With the deadline looming, Schout clambered over a six-foot fence and located a car on the lot with keys in the ignition. He raced to the courthouse and ran into the front door. "I had no idea where to go, but then I saw Joan standing in the doorway of a court hearing room."[15] Schout delivered the highest bid submitted to the court that day, with moments to spare.[16]

Taubman and Allen were no strangers to high finance and boardroom intrigues, but they now found themselves in an arena far from home with sophisticated opponents who had hundreds of millions of dollars available to toss on the table—a table everyone in Orange County would be watching. Mobil was a household name, Cadillac Fairview a feisty newcomer. Just who were these guys from Wall Street and … Detroit?

Taubman and the Allen made a critical strategic move. They asked Joan Irvine Smith to join their consortium, promising her that if they prevailed, she could buy back into their Irvine Company ownership group. With the Mobil offer, Joan would have either ended up with cash or Mobil stock. She would have been rich but would no longer have any connection to the company she had spent her adult life trying to obtain. With Taubman and the Allens she wouldn't have control, but at least she'd have a seat at the table—a table without the presence of the hated James Irvine Foundation. She agreed to come aboard.

The partnership with the famous heiress who bore the name of the company and its founders added luster to the consortium, as well as strong local credibility. Her money would help too. But Taubman and Allen knew they needed more stature and more money; Taubman knew where to find both.

Notes

1. Robert Schout, interview by H.P. Oliver and C.M. Stockstill, July 27, 2020.
2. Schout, interview, July 27, 2020.
3. Carol J. Loomis and Patricia Neering, "Inside the Private World of Allen & Co. Putting a Premium on Personal Ties, This Family Firm Thrives in the Land of the Giants," *CNNMoney* (Cable News Network), June 28, 2004. https://money.cnn.com/magazines/fortune/fortune_archive/2004/06/28/374371/index.htm.
4. A. Alfred Taubman, *Threshold Resistance* (New York, NY: Harper Collins, 2009) 49.
5. The Max Fisher Papers at Wayne State University contain a copy of the sales agreement between the James Irvine Foundation and Taubman–Allen–Irvine. See *Max M. Fisher, 1908–2005*. Walter P. Reuther Library, Wayne State University (n.d.). https://reuther.wayne.edu/taxonomy/term/1955.
6. "Local Teamster Loans Detailed," *Los Angeles Times*, May 17, 1962. Articles on Teamsters Pension Funds from the *Los Angeles Times* were reprinted at the request of Rep. Alphonzo Bell Jr. in the Congressional Record, 87th Congress, Volume 108, Part 15 covering dates from September 18 to November 27, 1962.
7. The connection between Col. Gottlieb and the Teamsters is referenced in an FBI memorandum. U.S. Dept. of Justice, FBI Memo 124-90044-1036. Agency file 63-7145-15. (Released under the John F. Kennedy Assassination Records Collection Act of 1992 44 USC on November 14, 2017) (January 11, 1962).
8. Anonymous source.
9. Anonymous source.
10. "'Candy Man' John O. Gottlieb Dead at 86," *Los Angeles Times*, February 26, 1984.
11. R.J. King, "Taubman, Take Two," *DBusiness Magazine*, December 13, 2018. www.dbusiness.com/business-features/taubman-take-two/.
12. Madison Issacman, "Building a Legacy: Lessons from Cadillac Fairview's First Leader," Rotman School of Management, University of Toronto, 2013, 17.
13. Leo Kolber, *Leo: A Life* (Montreal: McGill-Queen's University Press, 2003) 105.
14. Robert Schout, interview by H.P. Oliver and C.M. Stockstill, July 27, 2020.
15. Schout, interview, July 27, 2020.
16. The Taubman group bid totaled $285.6 million and consisted of $225 million of cash plus lease exchanges and notes.

26 Wise (and Rich) Men from the East

It was good to be a friend of Al Taubman.

Friendship meant a bond of warmth and caring, often lasting for decades. It meant lively and intelligent conversations about the finer points of business—especially retailing, but also about history and artwork. It meant visits to exotic locales and meals at some of the best restaurants in the world.

And for the closest friends—all of whom were wealthy—it meant the opportunity to achieve even greater riches.

Such was the case for the four men who joined Taubman in his contest to acquire the Irvine Company.

First among equals was one of Taubman's oldest friends, business partners, and mentors: Max Fisher.

Like Taubman, Fisher was self-made. Raised in the tiny town of Salem, Ohio, Fisher's size and talent on the football field led him to Ohio State University on a scholarship. Obtaining a degree, he moved to Detroit to work with his father's petroleum recycling business, then founded his own company operating service stations throughout the Midwest. Fisher and Taubman's lifetime relationship began when Taubman was hired to spruce up Fisher's Speedway brand of service stations. He did such a good job, Fisher retained him for others and their relationship deepened.

Fisher was a very wealthy man in 1968 when Detroit exploded in racial rioting, driving the already economically depressed city deeper into social and political malaise. Fisher became the chairman of New Detroit, a collaboration with economic leaders (including Henry Ford II) that attempted to find a way out of the urban ills afflicting the city. Black members of New Detroit praised Fisher's sympathy to racial issues and his even-handed approach to leading the coalition.

For the next decade, Fisher labored to breathe new life into the city; photos of meetings with Fisher and political or business leaders often show Taubman at his side. During the mid-1970s the pair formed a partnership called Riverfront Associates to build a large apartment complex on the Detroit River. Like a similar venture they had invested in with Henry Ford II it was a loser, costing the pair an estimated $30 million over 15 years.

DOI: 10.1201/9781003226291-27

While Fisher maintained an interest in business ventures after essentially retiring from active management responsibilities in 1963, his passions revolved around Jewish life and the state of Israel, as well as national and international politics.

The list of Jewish organizations that Fisher supported is monumental. International, national, regional, and local entities promoting Jewish causes received hundreds of thousands of dollars from Fisher and his family. He also served them in positions of leadership, usually as president or chairman.

Fisher was a generous and active supporter of Israel, using his wealth and influence to align himself and other Jews with the Republican Party. His long relationship with Michigan resident Gerald Ford was enhanced when Ford became president. In an obituary written by the *Oakland News* in March 2005, it was reported that Ford and Secretary of State Henry Kissinger once summoned Fisher to the White House to help heal a diplomatic rift with Israel over the diplomatic relationship between Egypt and the United States.

Max Fisher liked what he heard from Al Taubman about the Irvine Company, and when Taubman asked him to invest, he agreed, receiving 500 shares of the new company. He divided 250 shares between his wife and daughters and retained the other 250 for himself.

****

Taubman was just 24 years old when he met Milton Petrie. He tells the story in his autobiography:

"Petrie was a big wheel in retailing. Starting with a single hosiery shop in 1932, he had essentially invented the women's specialty store business in America and knew a great deal about how to design and build stores." Taubman was meeting with Petrie to pitch a new store design, and he was nervous.[1]

"What was wrong with the basic design his company had relied on so successfully, and what did a junior draftsman half his age know that he didn't?"

Taubman explained his analysis of the standard Petrie store, why he believed it was inefficient and how his design would eliminate "threshold resistance."

Petrie asked Taubman what he meant by threshold resistance. "The physical and psychological barriers that stand between your shoppers and your merchandise ... the force that keeps your customer from opening your door and coming in over the threshold."

"What followed seemed like the longest silence in my life ... all I could think about as Petrie stared at the blueprints was how I was going to tell my fiancé I had been fired. But that's when those glorious words came out of his mouth: 'This better work kid. It's your ass if it doesn't.'"[2]

Petrie's rise in commerce began on shaky ground. After going bankrupt in 1937 when his first chain of big city discount women's clothing stores went under, Petrie turned his focus to the suburbs and the new phenomenon of the mall, a style of development that Taubman was designing, building, and operating with increasing success.

Petrie stores with names like *Rave, Stuarts, Jean Nicole*, and others found their way into Taubman malls like hands into a glove. Both men prospered. As the years passed, they became neighbors in New York City and Palm Beach and their friendship grew.

Petrie had a reputation for avoiding credit and hoarding cash, so when Taubman came looking for an investor in the Irvine Company acquisition, spending $10 million wasn't a problem—he was in.

****

There are few names in American industry more famous than Ford.

In 1976, Henry Ford II, the grandson of the creator of the assembly line and modern automobile manufacturing, was just months away from ending his 31-year run as president of the storied company.

Derided as a playboy in his youth, he was being groomed for the executive suite when World War II turned the massive Ford plant at River Rouge in Michigan into part of the American "arsenal of democracy," building war machines instead of sedans. Ford had joined the Navy at the start of the war, but when his father Edsel died suddenly in 1943, he was summoned back to Detroit to assume control of the company and direct the war production effort.

Founder Henry had taken back the reigns of the company but was deemed by Secretary of War Henry Knox to be too senile and in ill health to function in such a critical wartime role. With help from Henry Ford II's mother—she threatened to sell her stock unless he was promoted—Ford II became president. His first moves were bold: he fired Harry Bennet, a notorious anti-labor enforcer for the company, then invited the United Auto Workers to renegotiate their contract.

Ford II directed the process to take the company public in 1956, and for the next two decades presided over the best (Mustang) and worst (Edsel) Ford auto offerings.

Ford II's personal life had its ups and downs as well, including divorces, affairs, drunk driving arrests, punctuated by executive suite drama with Ford leaders including Lee Iacocca. Through it all, Ford II persevered, often using what his obituary in the *Los Angeles Times* concluded, "... in many respects, was his life theme: never complain, never explain."[3]

Taubman doesn't pinpoint the precise time he met Ford II, but it is likely Max Fisher was involved, as photos of Ford II and Fisher are prominently featured on Fisher's history webpage. And Ford II was the principal promoter of the Detroit Renaissance in 1971—a $500 million project that Taubman and Fisher invested in. As is the case with everyone he approached on the Irvine deal, Ford II is described by Taubman as "my good friend," and like the others, Ford II joined the team.

(Ford took a tour around Newport Beach a few years later with Martin Brower, then the director of public relations at the Irvine Company. Brower reported that Ford was astonished by Newport Beach home prices.)

****

The business friendship network produced another investor for Taubman, courtesy of Max Fisher's service on the board of United Foods.

Howard Marguleas had grown up in the produce business, first in the San Francisco Bay Area, then in the California's fruit and vegetable heartland, the Central Valley. When Fisher made the approach on behalf of the Allens and Taubman, Marguleas was a well-known and respected agricultural innovator residing in the Coachella Valley.

Marguleas surely knew about the Irvine Company's holdings in the Imperial Valley, just a few miles further south of the headquarters of his company, Sun World. Marguleas had founded the company in 1975 with Carl Sam Maggio, another grower. Soon Sun World was producing tons of table grapes, lettuce, and marketing some of the specialty crops that Marguleas had developed earlier in his career like seedless watermelons and yellow and red peppers.

Robert Schout said in his 2020 interview that he and Joan Irvine Smith flew from Orange County to Palm Springs to meet Marguleas and Maggio during the bidding war. Schout, recently arrived from Michigan and dressed accordingly, recalls the stifling heat more than details of the meeting, but Joan must have given the nod for Marguleas to join the consortium, or at least didn't object.

Bringing in Marguleas was a wise decision for Taubman, whose knowledge of farming was likely limited to his father's fruit stand business.

In 1976, agriculture was still an important part of Irvine Company operations. There were 5,300 acres of citrus and 3,200 acres of row crops. Tenant farmers were managing 4,100 acres of row crops and there were just over 1,000 acres in nurseries. It was understood that if the consortium was successful, Marguleas would have responsibility for squeezing whatever money was possible from the Ag operations.

Taubman had succeeded in transforming his allies from a group of Detroit Rodney Dangerfields to a business and finance All Star team.

Waiting in the wings was a local homebuilder who would become the final partner to help fund Taubman and Allen's longshot bet against Mobil Oil.

Notes

1. A. Alfred Taubman, *Threshold Resistance* (New York, NY: Harper Collins, 2009) ix–x.
2. Taubman, *Threshold Resistance*, ix–x.
3. "Henry Ford II Dies, Led Auto Firm 35 Years," *Los Angeles Times*, September 30, 1987.

27 Going All In

With new partners and more money, Al Taubman and Charles Allen were prepared to go all in on the bidding for the Irvine Company.

Taubman, however, sensed the need for a sophisticated and seasoned financial coach to help structure the complex and increasingly expensive deal.

He turned to Benjamin Lambert, the founder of Eastdil Realty in Manhattan.

Lambert had risen from selling fabrics from a rolling cart in New York's garment district to a position at the investment bank of Eastman Dillon. While there, he conceived the idea of forming an investment bank that would specialize in real estate. Lambert nurtured an atmosphere of collaboration at Eastdil, and famously bragged that while other companies had brokers, Eastdil had trusted advisors.

Taubman was unaware at the time, according to Robert Schout, that Lambert already knew quite a bit about the Irvine Company. "Ben was paid $180,000 by Bob Fluor to evaluate the Irvine Company" for possible purchase, Schout said in a 2020 interview.[1]

Schout was in New York searching for lenders. He was in the office of Teacher's Insurance Company and was about to be thrown out for the impertinence of asking for a $350 million loan, he said, when Lambert found him and told him to come to his office.

Lambert told Schout when he arrived that he had concluded the Irvine Company was not worth more than $150 million. "You have to get Al out of this deal," Schout remembers Lambert telling him. Schout disputed the valuation and told Lambert the Eastdil staff he sent to California to gather information were lazy; "… they stayed at the Newporter Inn, then drove around, that's all."[2]

Schout launched into a recitation of his own analysis for Lambert, citing the immense value of the existing and future infrastructure on the ranch courtesy of the Irvine Ranch Water District, plus the value of the thousands of ground leases the company held. Just then, Schout said, Donald Bren called Lambert, who recounted Schout's analysis of the company's value. According to Schout, Bren backed him up.

Bren told Lambert and Schout he had substantial financial commitments to personally purchase the company, but the bidding had already exceeded his

DOI: 10.1201/9781003226291-28

capacity—he needed a partner. Lambert found Bren persuasive and told Schout to return to California to meet him.

Bren started his homebuilding career with a $10,000 loan for a spec house on Lido Isle in Newport Beach. In 1963 he and two partners formed the Mission Viejo Company and set out to create a master planned community on 11,000 acres of land owned by the O'Neill family. Like the Irvines, the O'Neills were descendants of a pioneer family that had acquired ranches in southern Orange County.[3]

Bren stayed at Mission Viejo for four years, then returned to his homebuilding company, which he sold to International Paper (IP) in 1970 for $34 million. When the real estate market slumped a couple of years later, IP had a change of heart and Bren bought his company back for $22 million.[4]

Schout recalls his first memorable glimpse of Bren: tall, handsome, and trim, Bren fit the image of what Schout believed would be an appealing local partner for Taubman and Allen. And he had $100 million in financing already lined up. Schout called Taubman and told him, "I've found our guy."

"Who is it?" Taubman asked.

"Donald Bren," Schout said.

"Why?" was Taubman's retort.

"Because Al, you and I look like a couple of gangsters from Detroit. This guy looks like he came from Hollywood."[5]

(Schout—who bears a resemblance to the actor Phillip Baker Hall—sometimes in conversations with unsuspecting West Coasters adopted the mock-threatening persona of "a guy from Detroit." Taubman was a bit overweight and slightly jowly but had a warm smile and was always immaculately dressed—few people would have mistaken him for a gangster.)

Taubman told Schout to offer Bren 35 per cent of the deal. Schout returned to the meeting room and motioned for Bren to join him. In the hallway, Schout said he looked at Bren and said, "… shake my hand, I am going to make you one of the richest people on the planet."[6]

****

The value of land leases is a subject that repeatedly comes up in the retelling of how the complicated analysis of the Irvine Company's value was determined.

Michael Meyer was working for the accounting firm of Kenneth Leventhal at the time. Leventhal had been retained by Cadillac Fairview to do a financial analysis, but once they dropped out, Taubman brought Leventhal aboard his team. Meyer recalled in a 2020 interview that he and other Leventhal employees did a "paper build out" of the ranch but found the leases a challenge to interpret and value accurately.[7]

Unsubordinated ground leases were not popular with banks at the time, Meyer recalled. Moreover, he said, there were so many different leases with different terms, potential lenders viewed them as having risky title, further complicating the potential to value them as collateral for the loans the Taubman group would need.

Meyer offered an example of one lease that exemplified the value challenge.

Ford Aeroneutronic had a long-term ground lease for its property near Eastbluff that upon examination, Meyer concluded was a "sweetheart deal." Taking a standard capitalization rate for the lease value, Meyer came up with $1 million. He knew, however, the actual value was probably $10 million. Meyer reached the same conclusion that others had argued in the past—under the management of the James Irvine Foundation, the company had been operated to minimize taxes and financial statement income.[8]

In addition to the value of the leases, there was the issue of how long some of them lasted, and the payment terms.

There were hundreds of the leases on land that homes were built upon. They ranged from waterfront mansions on Newport Bay to modest town homes in University Park. The lease term was usually 99 years but included a revaluation provision; at about halfway through the term the lease payment would be revised based on the new assessed value of the land.

For reasons lost to history, the implications of this element of the leaseholds were never fully analyzed or acknowledged as a potential downside to the transaction. A few years later the consequences would become very, very evident to the new owners.

****

When it became apparent the company would be sold, Ray Watson and his senior management team were providing information to potential buyers about the company's holdings and finances, as well as lobbying them:

> Our interest in management was to keep the company together ... we were devoted to the idea of being community builders. If they (the foundation) had anybody that might be remotely interested, besides giving them information about the company, we would go on a sort of selling crusade of why it's beneficial to do it the way we were doing it.[9]

Watson and the managers were also following the sales process for personal reasons—what will happen to us?

Mobil's initial offer to the foundation—the only one viable at the time it was made—was a stock for stock trade, which would have made it a tax-free transaction for the Irvine family; as a non-profit, the foundation would not pay any taxes.

While such a transaction would have been favorable for Joan from a tax standpoint, it would not have fulfilled her desire for total control of the company. In Watson's view, that was why she sued to stop the sale to Mobil.

Watson's stature within and outside the company was becoming more and more apparent to Mobil, Taubman, and Joan Irvine. All were beginning to look beyond the hard financial figures and consider if a company without Watson at the helm would be able to achieve the kind of business success each desired as a new owner.

Joan made the first move. She called Watson and asked him point blank: "…are you staying at the company after it sells?" Watson demurred, telling her it would depend on who the new owner was.

"She says to me, 'you have to stay, you're the most important person in the company'." (Watson's smile is apparent in his oral history, "…that's the first complimentary term I'd ever heard from her.")[10]

Joan sent her lawyers to explain to Watson the deal previously described in Chapter 27: the company itself would buy the shares owned by the foundation using the value of the leaseholds.

Watson observed that her plan was akin to stock repurchase, which was like buying your stock back. What did that do? It elevated her to the majority shareholder.

Watson told the lawyers that given Joan's disagreement with almost every action the company had taken under his leadership, he had a tough time reconciling the thought of continuing as president with her as the controlling owner. No problem, the lawyers said, she will give you her proxy vote for the next five years.

Except, they added on critical issues. Which are what, Watson asked? No answer from the lawyers.

Watson explained that before he could genuinely consider her offer, the company management had to find out if the company had the financial strength to indebt itself to buy the stock back. Independent financial advisors were retained.

> Their conclusion: we are financially strong enough to do this. The other shareholders were asking me: 'Are you going to stay?' The foundation said they'd consider selling.
>
> So, I called for a meeting of all the shareholders, and presented the finding that a buyback was possible. It's up to you as shareholders. This is your company. You have to decide whether you want to buy back the foundation's stock.
>
> The first question was from Bill White (a family shareholder), who said, 'Will you stay?' And I said, Mrs. Smith has made me a very generous offer. I appreciate it, but I have spent many years here in which she had not agreed with my management. And then in fairness to her, since she will now be in control, she needs to have a president of her choice, and I don't believe the history shows I am that person.
>
> As we were walking out of the room, her lawyers came to me and said, 'You just killed the transaction.' I think what happened was that the banks had said that (Watson staying) was a condition.[11]

By late March of 1977, the bidding landscape had come down to Mobil and the Taubman–Allen–Irvine consortium. During the preceding weeks rumors had popped up repeatedly in Orange County business circles about mysterious other suitors sniffing around the process. A South African group was alleged to be making a play but never surfaced. Given the state of world wealth, a regular rumor had Middle Eastern interests about to drop millions into the pot. (Minutes of the James Irvine Foundation reference an unsolicited proposal for purchase of their shares from the Trust for Public Land. There was no description of the offer, and it was rejected.)

Irvine City Councilman Bill Vardoulis suggested that the City of Irvine purchase the Irvine Company, issuing public debt for the purpose. City Attorney James Erickson gently dissuaded Vardoulis away from the proposal.

And at an Irvine City Council meeting, company senior executive James Taylor had wrapped up a presentation when Mayor David Sills asked innocently:

"Well Jim, who owns the Irvine Company today?"

Taylor deadpanned his reply. "If it is Tuesday, it must be Mobil."[12]

Taylor got a big laugh from the audience because for weeks the *Daily Pilot* had been covering the bidding contest on the front page of every edition. Day after day, as each new bid was announced, the *Pilot* kept score, gleefully marking the rising price of the lands and properties in Newport Beach and Irvine that were so familiar to its readers.

The high stakes auction was pushing aside news like Ronald Reagan's surging campaign for the Republican presidential nomination, the trial of county supervisor Robert Battin, charged with misuse of campaign funds, and Patty Hearst entering a plea in her trial. Even the bloody murder of a UCI coed—the kind of story *Pilot* editors could always be counted on to play up—took second place to the seesaw bidding.

Then in early May the gloves came off.

Full page ads appeared in the *Wall Street Journal*, *The New York Times*, *The Washington Post*, *Houston Post*, and *Houston Chronicle*. "Why Are Oil Companies Telling Congress They Need More Profits to Explore for Oil?" was the headline in each of the ads.

"Why is Mobil Corporation investing substantial cash reserves in real estate development ventures throughout the United States in their foreign-based subsidiary?" the text in the ad asked. Then the ad got specific: "Why is Mobil now considering additional major real estate investments such as the 70,000-acre Irvine Ranch in Southern California?"[13]

The first ads were signed by the Committee for Energy Resources, with an address in Washington D.C. The ads listed one G.H. Hunt as chairman of the committee. A subsequent ad showed a man's back facing the camera with the headline, "Is Mobil Turning Its Back on America During the Energy Crisis?"

G.H. Hunt was Gary Hunt, a 28-year-old California law student who had formerly served as executive director of the California Republican Party. He was also an employee of Donald Bren.

Hunt was a combination of extraordinary intelligence and limitless energy. Raised in the California high desert community of Lancaster, he aspired to a career as a YMCA director based on his teenage experience at the local Y branch. But after college he discovered the rough and tumble world of California politics and was soon immersed in California Republican Party intrigues and policy issues as a staffer to a Republican State Assemblyman and a Member of Congress.

Hunt and Bren had met in the aftermath of the 1974 gubernatorial campaign of Houston Flournoy, who had barely lost to Jerry Brown—Bren had been Flournoy's finance chairman. Bren and Hunt were meeting with others to address the leftover campaign funds and debts.

In Hunt, Bren saw raw political talent and the willingness to engage in the retail elements of California politics—glad-handing elected officials, schmoozing big donors, rubbing shoulders with grassroots activists—all the things about politics Bren disliked.

It was Hunt, according to Robert Schout, who conceived the idea of the ads "and convinced Bren to go for the jugular" and attack Mobil.

Mobil was not amused. A May 7, 1977, article in the *Los Angeles Times* reported a Mobil spokesman commenting,

> If the purpose of the ads was to interfere with the bidding process, there might be some ethical questions raised. We were shocked, especially in view of the stature of some of the people involved, he said, referring to the members of the Taubman-Allen-Irvine group, which includes Henry Ford II and New York financier Charles Allen, Jr.

Bren took the blame. "Bren emphasized in a prepared statement Friday that, although he took part in financing the advertisement, no other member of the Taubman-Allen-Irvine group was a participant or contributed funds to the committee," the *Times* reported.[14]

The ads had no impact on the bidding. On May 9, Taubman—who was making the day-to-day decisions on the bidding, which by now was strictly measured in cash—raised the offer by 25 cents per share, for a total of $309.25 million. (Watson noted in his oral history that in the early period of the bidding, the Taubman group had repeatedly made bids that combined cash and different forms of debt, and each time the value of the bid was discounted by the James Irvine Foundation. When Mobil went to cash, Taubman and his allies were forced to do the same.)

For the next nine days the bidding intensified, every bid seen and raised by each of the two combatants. Taubman was enthused, circling the huge Mobil bull like a toreador with sword raised, preparing for the moment of truth.

> I will always remember fondly the daily phone calls with my sons ... during the manic, high stakes bidding war. They always wanted me to counter Mobil's offer and would encourage me with a spirited mix of well-thought-out rationale and youthful optimism ... their competitive juices were flowing, and so were mine (the sons were 24 and 19 at the time).[15]

In his autobiography, Taubman describes the final bid:

> Mobil's president, who was handling the bidding personally, gave us his full and last shot on May 18 at $40 per share, or $336.6 million. My small bump of ten cents to $40.10, or $337.44 million, ended the bidding on May 19. We were notified the next day that Mobil had withdrawn ...[16]

The headline in the *Daily Pilot* told the story: "Now It's Taubman-Allen-Irvine."[17]

Then came the money.

Months earlier, before the bidding contest began, Taubman had contacted bankers at Wells Fargo in California to discuss financing. Taubman had done several deals in California and had borrowed from Wells Fargo—he was a trusted customer. On the East Coast, Taubman had a relationship with Chase Bank for the same reason. After hearing his analysis of the value of the Irvine Ranch, both banks agreed to become part of a consortium that would join forces to provide the money. At that point, no one was sure just how much money would be needed.

In his autobiography, Taubman said he, the Allens, Fisher, Ford, Petrie, and Joan Irvine had agreed to capitalize the partnership at $100 million (Bren had not joined at that point). The remainder would be borrowed from the banks, and could be as much as $300 million, Taubman estimated.

The magnitude of the numbers underscored what Taubman and his allies had been up against. Mobil had reported profits of $382 million in 1975 and $434 million the following year. And Mobil had a great deal of cash on hand—just two years after losing the Irvine Ranch bidding, Mobil paid $737 million in cash for an oil company owned by International Paper.

In addition to Wells and Chase, the banking group now included Security Pacific, First National Bank of Boston, Bank of New York, Seattle First National, Citibank, Bank of America, and Manufacturer's Bank of Detroit.

The bankers were willing to loan $240 million of the $337.44 million purchase price, leaving the new owners the responsibility of finding $100 million. They did so by issuing subordinated debentures in the amount of $75 million, essentially taking a second loan on their new company. Subordinated debt is not guaranteed and is second in line for repayment—if the whole deal cratered, the bank loan would be repaid first. Michael Meyer also said in his 2020 interview that a couple of months after the deal closed, Prudential, the huge insurance company, stepped in to pay the new owners $120 million, guaranteed by the value and revenue of the Irvine Company's ground leases. So, in Meyer's analysis, "... the buyers really only paid $20 million in cash."[18]

Prudential had been teed up as a potential lender early in the process. Schout said that he and Claude Ballard, who had made loans to the Taubman Company in the past, had driven around the ranch to assess its value. Schout must have convinced Ballard the risk was worth it, and he came through for Taubman and his team after the sale closed.

With the money in hand, the new owners drafted the sales agreement memorializing the terms of the purchase from the James Irvine Foundation. It ran to 47 pages, filled with legalese and financial terminology. Among the highlights:

- The foundation promised that all Irvine Company properties "were not adversely affected by fire, earthquake, flood or mudslide"
- Touche Ross and Coopers and Lybrand would review all the company's financial records
- The buyers would receive a copy of the company's current business plan, mortgages, a list of all leases and rents, a list of all employees making more than $40,000 per year, employee benefit plans and contracts, balance sheets, and a "true and complete statement of the assessed value of Irvine Company lands," as well as a list of any pending land sales.[19]

It took two months to wrap up the due diligence. On July 22, 1977, the new owners assembled in a room in the Los Angeles offices of Wells Fargo. "I had never seen so many lawyers, bankers and boxes of documents in one room in my life," Taubman recalled in his autobiography.[20]

Then, a last-minute glitch. Taubman explained:

Charlie Johnson of Wells Fargo pulled me into a small private room and informed me that there was an unexpected snag. Some years earlier, Don Bren had sold his company to International Paper (IP) ... things didn't go as anticipated, so Don bought back his company, granting International Paper certain warrants to buy back in if they wished.

Don was a partner in Taubman-Allen-Irvine as an individual. But the clever folks at IP wanted Bren's company, in which they still had the right to fifty percent ownership, to hold the interest in the ranch, thus setting up the opportunity for IP to get into the deal. They were holding up the assets Bren had pledged for our deal without their blessing.

Wells Fargo representatives in New York were frantically trying to work something out with IP and Bren's lender, Bank of America, to no avail. Sensing that we were at an impasse, Charlie proposed (that) Wells Fargo would extend me the credit for Bren's portion of the equity. That would allow us to close on schedule ... At the very last minute, Bren worked out a $5 million payment to IP ... and the closing went forward without a hitch.[21]

Schout had a different memory of the tense, final weeks and days of the bidding war. Four or five times during the process, Schout said, Taubman got cold feet and in Schout's words, "... nearly blew up the deal." The reason, Schout said, was that the dollars were getting so big, Taubman became concerned about his ability to raise the money. Taubman's retail empire was feeling the negative effects of swings in the national economy, Schout said, and he was under pressure from other lenders who held debt on his malls. Schout said that he and Charles Allen talked Taubman off the ledge and kept the deal together.[22]

Once the transaction concluded, the ownership of the Irvine Company was as follows:

Donald Bren	35.00%
Alfred Taubman	15.00%
Max Fisher	10.00%
Allen and Company	10.00%
Milton Petrie	10.00%
Henry Ford II	4.00%
Joan Irvine Smith and Athalie Clarke	10.00%
Howard Marguleas	2.00%
Keith and Linda Gaede	3.00%
William Wheeler	0.03%
James Irvine[23]	0.03%

The percentages in the table do not reflect shares received by Peter Kremer, the new company president. Schout says that Benjamin Lambert received one share.

****

For the remainder of his life, Taubman reveled in telling and retelling the story of *How Al Taubman Outsmarted Mobil Oil.*

He told it in speeches, he told it in interviews, he told it in gatherings, large and small. It even made it into his obituary. And why not? It was a great story. And it was true.

In his autobiography, Taubman explained that "when we completed our initial appraisal (of the value of the Irvine Ranch) it was clear to us that Mobil was trying to buy the company on the cheap."

Taubman believed Mobil was looking at the ranch as an industrial business, while he and his partners saw it as real estate deal. "I was also sure they were assessing the value of the company using their conventional corporate earnings per share basis."

> Here's how Mobil probably saw it: the Irvine Company had earned approximately $10.9 million after taxes in fiscal year 1974–75; it was not out of line to offer nineteen to twenty times earnings, or about $218 million … their offer on the table when we got interested was $192 million. The Irvine Company's earnings had been growing at about 10 to 12 percent annually, which gave Mobil confidence that the deal would contribute to their own financial results. Clearly, they had room to go higher.
>
> But how high were we willing to go? We looked beyond earnings per share and appraised value of the opportunity on the basis of land value and real estate development upside, which led to a significantly higher present-day valuation, at least $400 million. If we played our cards right, we could outbid Mobil and still get the ranch at a huge discount to its value.[24]

Like a military commander preparing for battle, Taubman tried to anticipate how Mobil would array its troops and what strategy it would choose—a massive full-frontal assault? A series of probes and then a flanking attack? Would it go for broke on a single charge, or would it keep a battalion or so in reserve?

Taubman correctly predicted that Mobil's bidding would be determined by hard numbers. He believed that "based on the Irvine Company's 1976 year-end earnings of $17.9 million, the maximum bidding authority granted by Mobil's board would be approximately nineteen times earnings, or $340 million. We were betting Mobil would quit before reaching that ceiling."[25]

Taubman's analysis was right. Mobil's last bid was $336.6 million, just about $3 million below the ceiling he had predicted. Taubman outbid them by a dime and took home the prize the next day.

Taubman's victory is impressive on its face—outmaneuvering one of the largest and most sophisticated corporations in the world. Moreover, it played out not behind closed doors in a boardroom, but in full view of the public as breathlessly reported by the local and national press.

But Taubman's achievement is even more impressive as the internal meeting minutes of the James Irvine Foundation for the time period reveal the frantic roller coaster ride he was on, soaring to a potential sale one moment, then plunged into stomach churning depths the next.

The foundation records show that Mobil was the clear favorite during the months-long process; twice Mobil was all but declared the winner by the foundation board. Just five months before the bidding concluded, the foundation had evaluated the competing offers on the table and ranked them as follows:

1 Mobil all cash offer
2 Mobil offer of cash plus notes
3 Cadillac Fairview offer.

Without even giving it a ranking number, the offer from Taubman and Allen was judged "least attractive."[26]

A month later, the Taubman team was nearly disqualified from the entire process when their offer was received a day late. Apparently, the foundation took pity on Taubman, commenting that "notwithstanding tardiness in submitting its offer, (it) was found to be unsatisfactory in several respects."[27]

Four months later, Taubman's group was still in contention, but the terms it was offering continued to be unacceptable to the foundation. On April 13, 1977, the foundation president was authorized by the board of trustees to inform Taubman his latest offer was lacking, but they gave him the chance to correct it.

And Taubman would not be deterred. On April 16 he was on the phone to foundation attorneys making last minute oral changes to the fine points of the deal, promising to memorialize them in writing the next day, which he did. The same day, what appeared to be the deciding factor in swinging the balance to Taubman took place when foundation president Morris Doyle talked with Earnest

Arbuckle of Wells Fargo bank, at its headquarters just down the street from the foundation offices in San Francisco.[28]

Arbuckle assured Doyle of one of California's oldest and strongest banking institutions, continuing interest in being part of the Taubman team and its offer to purchase the foundation's Irvine Company shares.

That was good enough for the James Irvine Foundation. The trustees voted to stipulate that Taubman's offer was the best one available and should be accepted.

In addition to showing what a come-from-behind victory Taubman achieved, the minutes of the James Irvine Foundation for the period also dispel any speculation that Mobil Oil received special treatment or inside assistance in the bidding process.

When the foundation learned of the potential for competing offers for their Irvine Company shares, they told their attorney to alert the judge in the case so the legal proceedings would not interfere with bidding and the possibility of receiving greater value; when offers that exceeded those of Mobil were received, the foundation trustees voted to accept them; when one bidder pressured the foundation to conduct the bidding process using sealed bids, the trustees refused, arguing correctly that a public process would generate higher bids.

Mobil may have entered the sale process as the favorite suitor, but in the end, the foundation chose what they determined was the best deal for the foundation.

****

A month before the sale of its Irvine Company stock was officially complete, the James Irvine Foundation was returning to business at its annual meeting. J. Robert Fluor was elected to the board; a payment of $220,000 was authorized to the McCutcheon law firm for services rendered, and $5,564,000 in donations were approved, the largest: $2 million to the University of Southern California for its School of Urban and Regional Planning, the smallest $10,000 to the Academy of Welders for equipment.

At its last meeting of 1977, the foundation sadly noted the death of Loyall McLaren in October, remembering in a resolution his "fortitude and determination" in leading the foundation, and noting for posterity "their appreciation of (his) wisdom, wit, courage and gentlemanly character ..."[29]

The trustees voted to pay their lawyers another $400,000 for their efforts during the bidding war, bringing the total for the year to $620,000, equivalent to about $2.9 million in 2022 dollars.

Then, flush with cash from the sale of the Irvine Company stock, the foundation made additional donations of $3,642,480 (about $16.8 million in 2022 dollars) to dozens of schools and charitable organizations up and down the state of California.

Notes

1. Robert Schout, interview by C.M. Stockstill and H.P. Oliver, July 25, 2020.
2. Schout, interview, July 25, 2020.

3. Gary Hector, "America's Richest Land Baron," *Fortune*, August 27, 1990. https://archive.fortune.com/magazines/fortune/fortune_archive/1990/08/27/73941/

4. Hector, "America's Richest Land Barron."

5. Schout, interview, July 25, 2020.

6. Schout, interview, July 25, 2020.

7. Mike Meyer, interview by C.M. Stockstill and H.P. Oliver, August 7, 2020.

8. Meyer, interview, August 7, 2020.

9. Raymond L. Watson and Ann Lage, *Planning and Developing the New Town of Irvine California, 1960–2003: Irvine Company President, 1973–1977, Walt Disney Company Chairman, 1983–1984* (Regional Oral History Office, the Bancroft Library, University of California, Berkeley, 2005) x.

10. Watson and Lage, *Planning and Developing*, 391.

11. Watson and Lage. *Planning and Developing*, 392.

12. "Irvine Co. Worth Over $315 Million?" *Daily Pilot*, March 16, 1977.

13. "Builder Admits Helping Pay for Ads Critical of Mobil," *Los Angeles Times*, May 7, 1977.

14. "Builder Admits Helping Pay for Ads," 1977.

15. A. Alfred Taubman, *Threshold Resistance* (New York, NY: Harper Collins, 2009) 53.

16. Taubman, *Threshold Resistance*, 53.

17. "Now Its Taubman-Allen-Irvine," *Daily Pilot*, May 21, 1977, 1.

18. Meyer, interview, August 7, 2020.

19. Taubman-Allen-Bren-Irvine. Purchase Sale Agreement for Shares of the Irvine Company, May 1977 as found in the Max Fisher Papers (Box 252) at the Walter P. Reuther Library at Wayne State University, Detroit, MI.

20. Taubman, *Threshold Resistance*, 53.

21. Taubman, *Threshold Resistance*, 54.

22. Schout, interview, July 25, 2020.

23. James Irvine is the son of the deceased Myford Irvine.

24. Taubman, *Threshold Resistance*, 50.

25. Taubman. *Threshold Resistance*, 52 and 53.

26. James Irvine Foundation, Minutes, December 1976.

27. James Irvine Foundation, Minutes, January 1977.

28. Schout, interview, July 25, 2020.

29. James Irvine Foundation, Minutes, December 1977.

28 Ray Departs

As the bidding war for the Irvine Company intensified, Ray Watson began to reflect on his career there: what he had achieved, and what might lie ahead.

Watson had enjoyed a steady rise to the presidency of the company.

As a young planner, he had impressed Charles Thomas with his ability to articulate and simplify the complexities of large-scale planning issues and to convince others of the company's wisdom in implementing them. William Mason felt the same way, and it became apparent to both men and the people who worked for them that Mason and Watson had achieved a bond that went far beyond the professional.

The Mason–Watson partnership solidified in 1966 when Mason became president of the company and Watson was named vice president of land development; when the company reorganized two years later, Watson became senior vice president.

Seven years later, Mason died of a heart attack, just 54 years old.

Watson was next in line according to company bylaws, but there was no guarantee that he would be selected for the top spot. To no one's surprise, he was.

Watson was president of the Irvine Company for just four years; that time, plus his previous service as a senior executive responsible for many of the day-to-day operations of the company, forged a reputation that has lasted for decades, especially among the men and women who worked with him at the company, and who interacted with him at cities, the county, the state, the university, and in the world of planning and development.

Those who worked with and for Watson recall a person they trusted, respected, and admired.

A principal reason for Ray Watson's success at the Irvine Company was who he was.

Watson was a likeable man with a positive outlook and personality. He was informal, approachable, and genuine in his dealings with fellow employees, consultants, and even those on the other side of the table in negotiations or discussions.

Ray Watson was always referred to as Ray. And while there was no one else at the company with the same name, the shorthand among employees was universal

DOI: 10.1201/9781003226291-29

in identifying the man at the top—it was never Mr. Watson or the president, it was simply, "Ray."

Watson didn't have to cultivate informality, he was informal. He often wore a short sleeve shirt, slacks, and loafers. For occasions that called for it, he wore a sport coat. It was rare to see Watson in a suit.

Watson's informality could extend into another person's space. William Watt recalled that Watson would sometimes join him and others at a café for lunch and engage in discussions about company projects. One day, Watt said, he opened a bag of Fritos to have with his sandwich. Before long, he noticed his Fritos supply was diminishing—Watson was helping himself to Watt's Fritos.

The Frito filching aside, Watt remembers Watson's management style as inclusive: "He knew where he was headed, but he wanted to bring everyone along." Watt said one of the key lessons he learned about leadership from Watson was, "… if you have a good process, people will buy-in because process is designed to get their input and as a result, buy-in comes naturally."[1]

And while he didn't invent the concept known as Management by Walking Around, Watson excelled at it and enjoyed it. More than one former employee describes a similar scene: sitting in their office chair reading a report or drafting a memo, "… you'd look up and there in the doorway is the president of the company." "What are you working on?" Watson would ask, and depending on the answer, would invite himself into the office.[2]

Dan Beals had been working at the Irvine Company for only a short time as a new personnel manager when he ran into Watson on a Saturday. He was at his desk when Watson knocked on his window and motioned him outside. "I know you personnel guys have all the keys," Watson told the startled Beals; Watson had forgotten his office keys and asked Beals to let him in.[3]

Engaging employees informally and unexpectedly both flattered them and authenticated them as people with something valuable to offer the organization—after all, it was the president of the company who was interested in their efforts.

Watson enjoyed not only asking employees about their work, but also challenging them. In his oral history, Watson recalled the early days of his career when he found verbal sparring enjoyable and a productive way to stimulate meaningful interaction with people:

> I can remember … enjoying while you are bantering away, engaging the person next to me in a sort of cocky way saying, 'OK, what are we going to debate today? You pick either side; I don't care what it is, and I'll take the other side.' I just enjoyed the verbal dialog.[4]

With more junior employees, Watson might tone down his inquiries, but if the employee was able to match his verbal and intellectual assertions, the debate would go on.

Watson's willingness to be provocative was reinforced by a business consultant the company had hired to evaluate the strengths and weaknesses of individual executives. He recounted the incident in his oral history:

> As for me, the consultant said, 'do you know that you intimidate some people in the company?' I had never had anybody say that to me before.... I realize I am very competitive verbally, but I didn't think of that as intimidation. I asked the consultant, 'what should I do?' And his answer—I'll never forget it—he says, nothing. I said, what do you mean? He says, 'because that is how you got to where you are. The only thing you need to do is make sure you hire strong people, as strong as you, because a strong person cannot be intimidated.'
>
> And it was very good advice ... I remember discussions I'd have with an executive, and he would sort of back away and I'd get very irritated, and I'd say, 'don't back away. Kick me in the rear end, hit me, do anything but I don't want anybody backing away. Don't give up. How do we ever resolve a thing unless we get it all out there?[5]

Watson had enjoyed more than a decade of satisfaction as he climbed the corporate ladder to the spot as chief executive, but the final two years wore on him.

When word reached the company that Mobil had dropped out of the bidding and the Taubman consortium had won, Watson's reaction was "thank God it's over. By that time, I was sick and tired of it. It was hard on the employees and hard on the company. I was just glad it was over."[6]

By that time, Watson had already decided to resign. "It was just time for me to go. You can get saturated with the job very easily—I was seeing the same thing over and over again."[7]

If Watson had any second thoughts, they were dispelled after reading the company bylaws the new owners were adopting: Taubman would become chief executive officer, Watson would stay on as chief operating officer. "I thought, OK, they want a token president. They want to use my reputation with the community and I'm not going to have the same voice I had before. That was hard for me."[8]

Watson kept his views private. In public, he was positive. He authored a column in *Irvine World News* after the sale was announced and assured the readers that the new owners had already achieved great success in real estate development and could be counted on to continue that record in Orange County

He stayed through the two-month due diligence but departed the day escrow closed to make way for Peter Kremer, the new Irvine Company president. Watson had worked for the company for 17 years.

Joining Watson in the exodus were company executives Lanny Eberling and Thomas Wolff. Together with Los Angeles businessmen William Lund and Donald Albrecht they formed the Newport Development Company. For the next five years, the company developed a variety of projects—condominiums, a medical office, an industrial park, and a small subdivision of single-family homes.

At the same time, Watson was invited to sit on the boards of Pacific Mutual, a life insurance company that had moved its headquarters to Newport Beach, and the Walt Disney Company.

The Disney connection—begun to mine Watson's real estate expertise for the Disney developments in Florida—would propel him into the most contentious chapter of his business life as chairman of the board of the company.

Watson served at Disney during a prolonged, bitter, and very public boardroom conflict involving the Disney family, greenmailing speculators, and warring management factions. The months-long assault left a trail of broken bodies and reputations while paving the way for the ascension of Michael Eisner to the Disney leadership post.

Watson escaped intact, and a few years later would find himself back at the Irvine Company as an adviser to another new owner facing issues that Watson found very familiar.

Notes

1. William Watt, interview by C.M. Stockstill and H.P. Oliver, July 8, 2020.
2. Robert Dannenbrink, interview by C.M. Stockstill and H.P. Oliver, January 4, 2021.
3. Daniel Beals, interview by C.M. Stockstill and H.P. Oliver, December 14, 2020.
4. Raymond L. Watson and Ann Lage, *Planning and Developing the New Town of Irvine California, 1960–2003: Irvine Company President, 1973–1977, Walt Disney Company Chairman, 1983–1984* (Regional Oral History Office, the Bancroft Library, University of California, Berkeley, 2005) 351.
5. Watson and Lage, *Planning and Developing*, 363.
6. "A Ray of Home, One Year Later," *Forum 50 Magazine*, July 1978, 11.
7. "A Ray of Home, One Year Later," 11.
8. Watson and Lage, *Planning and Developing*, 388.

29 Villains No More

Largely by Joan Irvine Smith, two men have been painted as villains in the saga of the Irvine Ranch.

One was the general manager of the ranch. He had grown up with the Irvine family in San Francisco, was recruited to work on the ranch as a field hand and had risen to oversee its entire operation. He had the trust of James Irvine II and the respect of his sons.

His name was William Bradford Hellis.

The other was a businessman whose expertise in accounting and taxation was recognized by peers in California and across the nation. He served with distinction both in and after World War II. Critically, his acumen was so apparent to James Irvine II that he entrusted the fate of his property to this individual he had known since early in the 20th century.

His name was Norman Loyall McLaren.

****

Hellis was targeted by Joan and her mother shortly after Joan joined the board of directors of the Irvine Company in 1957. In her autobiography, she recounted that after her lawyers investigated company books, she determined that a land deal involving Hellis, the company, and a real estate broker was "improper."

When Joan's lawyers served the two with subpoenas, she said,

> … they both immediately agreed to a partition of the properties they held with the Irvine Company in the Imperial Valley. Hellis resigned from the James Irvine Foundation and Irvine Company board of directors. However, he continued his role in the company's management until May 1959.

(Foundation records show that for a time, Hellis was retained by the foundation as a paid consultant after leaving the Irvine Company.)[1]

In public testimony before the House Ways and Means Committee in March 1969, Joan Irvine Smith repeated her story about the alleged improper land deal. Then she went further, all but accusing Hellis of foul play connected with the death of her grandfather.

DOI: 10.1201/9781003226291-30

The Ways and Means Committee hearings gave Joan a forum to continue her attacks on the James Irvine Foundation and its chairman, Loyall McLaren. Ever since joining the Irvine Company board, Joan and McLaren had been trading insults and verbal brickbats, usually in the local Orange County press, but sometimes in papers with a statewide audience like the *Los Angeles Times*. And in the multiple lawsuits Joan had filed where accusations—however virulent—were protected by privilege, she targeted McLaren repeatedly.

Now she was testifying on a national stage, and she repeated her frequent complaint that McLaren acted like a dictator as chairman of the foundation, using what she described as ruthless tactics and strong-arm methods. Unlike Hellis, who withdrew from the battle, McLaren soldiered on, remaining on the foundation board, and clashing repeatedly with Joan until a few months before his death in October 1977.

****

His family's choice of a home in San Francisco proved providential for Brad Hellis.

The Hellis home was just three doors down from the Irvine family, whose two sons, James and Myford, were close to Brad's age and became playmates, then fast friends.

Hellis was 13 when the 1906 earthquake struck San Francisco. His memories of the event, given more than 70 years later in his oral history, were vivid:

> I had difficulty opening my bedroom door, as it was wedged by fallen furniture … the family got outside, and there were several aftershocks. We could look out over the city and see the collapsed dome of city hall … here and there puffs of smoke were rising.
>
> Streams of refugees from the burning parts of the city on the flats below passed our house on the way to Golden Gate Park … they pushed carts or anything with wheels or casters on it, including beds piled high with clothing or personal treasures…. Everyone contrived some sort of kitchen in the street in front of the remaining homes. Soldiers and civilian guards inspected the homes, and where space was sufficient, additional people were lodged with you.
>
> The fires raged for days, and in an attempt to check it, many buildings were dynamited. Before this was done store doors were thrown open and mobs of people were permitted to carry off whatever they needed or could carry … Food was obtained by lining up for single items like bread, meat, or vegetables. In order to get enough, everyone—including your enforced guests—would go out foraging and return to put it together for a meal.
>
> Aside from the fire, some of the effects of the earthquake were startling: streets and streetcar tracks twisted into waves. Some buildings, like the Fairmont Hotel, the Emporium Palace Hotel and the Call Building survived structurally though gutted by the fire.[2]

Shortly after the earthquake, the Hellis family moved to Pasadena and were invited to visit the Irvine Ranch in nearby Orange County. This and subsequent summer visits doing work between school terms sealed for Hellis what would become a lifetime connection to the Irvine family and the Irvine Ranch.

Hellis left his studies at UC Berkeley due to his father's death and took a job with the Mortgage Guarantee Company in Los Angeles. But his summer work at the ranch had impressed general manager C.K. Krauss, who offered him a full-time job. Hellis was concerned working at the ranch might lead to conflict with the career plans of James Irvine Jr., but by then Jase, as he was known, had graduated from college, married his first wife Madelaine, and had taken a job in advertising that required him to travel all over the state. Hellis applied himself to his new role, which included, "... driving or riding over the ranch daily, checking tenant farmers, estimating yields, counting crops, and collecting rent."

Hellis notes that his nickname at the time was "Count du Sack," a reference to one of his most onerous jobs—counting sacks of beans, grain, and hay bales.[3]

By then Jase had returned to the ranch and was installed by his father into a cottage in the citrus orchards. He and Hellis were soon teamed up by James Irvine II to learn to operate and manage the ranch. "Mr. Irvine indicated that my services would be more valuable if I could handle his dictation and correspondence, and have more accounting training," Hellis signed up for an accounting class in Santa Ana, commuting there on horseback. "Eventually Jase and I alternated jobs for six months; when I was not in the fields I was in the office."[4]

Two events in 1933 solidified Hellis' future as ranch manager. Jase was stricken with a recurrence of tuberculosis and could not work. Then the general manager of the ranch died unexpectedly. Hellis stepped into the role on what he called an "ex officio basis." Jase died two years later and Hellis became general manager as well as secretary of the corporation.

In the Cal State University Fullerton oral history, Hellis gave page after page of recollections on the workings of the Irvine Ranch, with particular emphasis on water supply, the lifeblood of the entire operation. Hellis displayed a sophisticated and detailed understanding of obtaining and directing water from the hundreds of wells that had been drilled on the property.

There were also the mundane and even humorous responsibilities shouldered by the general manager of the large ranch. County historian Jim Sleeper's voluminous files include dozens of pages from Hellis' notebooks, revealing more than one lengthy, handwritten letter from a woman complaining about the treatment of sheep and their (in her view) incompetent shepherds, proposals for spraying citrus orchards, with detail down to the number of tent coverings, gallons of spray and labor ($3.75 an hour in 1938). There was also a request from a popcorn vendor to set up a stand during the summer on company land adjacent to Balboa Island. Hellis accepted his proposed fee of $10 for the privilege.

Hellis also understood the role that water agencies would play in the county and spoke with authority on his efforts and others in creating the Metropolitan Water District of Orange County, the water wholesaler for the giant Metropolitan Water District (he served on that board as well). And according to Robert Glass Cleland's *The Irvine Ranch*, Hellis conducted the critical negotiations that led to the ranch obtaining access to Colorado River water.[5]

In addition to agriculture issues and operations, Hellis also mentioned several land developments the Irvine Company had sponsored or participated in. He clearly had a deep and sophisticated understanding of the scope of the ranch's business ventures, as might be expected from someone whose title was general manager.

Hellis was also involved in community and business organizations in greater Orange County and Southern California. He was a member of the board of governors of Chapman University, a small Christian private college in Orange, and was a director of the Bank of Santa Ana, the Santa Ana Savings and Loan, and the Lincoln Club, the major funding arm of the county's Republican political activities.

A wing of the Santa Ana Community Hospital was named in honor of Hellis; he supported the Boy Scouts of America and the Santa Ana Boy's Club. The pallbearers and honorary pallbearers at his funeral in 1975 included some of the county's most prominent citizens.

Was Hellis the beneficiary of business dealings with either JI, the Irvine Ranch, or both? Probably so. In his oral history, Loyall McLaren said that while JI paid low wages, for trusted associates he would sometimes cut them in on business ventures he thought would prove lucrative.

And in A.J. McFadden's oral history, he recalls selling properties on the Irvine Ranch he owned and cites a similar sale of around 200 acres of land owned by Hellis in the same timeframe. This is consistent with reports that JI gifted small properties to tenant farmers on the ranch he considered especially loyal. Hellis certainly fit the standard of loyalty.

At one point in his oral history, Hellis was asked about the James Irvine Foundation. He politely declined to answer the question or anything about the foundation. He did, however, have something to say about his relationship with James Irvine II:

> My association with him for 33 years as an employee and the contact during my childhood certainly gave me an insight exceeding most others. He was a strong character, a fighter, but still a builder, and he had a sentimental side not usually known. We had our battles, but I believe we had a mutual respect for each other. I thought he was entitled to my loyalty to him … but I was not a Yes Man. I differed with him on many occasions … which sometimes caused temporary tensions.[6]

Hellis talked about many people in his oral history, but one person was never mentioned: Joan Irvine Smith.

****

Loyall McLaren and James Irvine II found an affinity for one another because of taxes: JI hated them, and McLaren understood them.

JI was dining at the Bohemian Club in 1919 when he ran into Percy Goode, McLaren's partner at the accounting firm of McLaren, Goode, and Company (founded by McLaren's father). JI complained to Goode of a complex business arrangement that he feared was not being handled correctly by his lawyers. Goode suggested a meeting with McLaren, who was known for his sophisticated understanding of the tax code.

In his oral history, McLaren described meeting with JI and learning the details of the business deal. You're in luck, McLaren said, just last week I researched a very similar deal and discovered how to structure it to minimize the tax bill. JI followed his advice and was both enriched and impressed. Later, Irvine returned to McLaren with another business matter; a company he had a large investment in was liquidating, causing concern about the tax implications. Once again McLaren devised a sale that would lower the tax bill and save Irvine about $100,000. And, McLaren recalled fondly, "... that, of course, was the final fruition of a confidence that extended over all his life."[7]

Loyall McLaren in the early years of the 20th century was making a mark in his chosen career of accounting. In addition to growing the firm in San Francisco, he led efforts to expand, acquiring smaller firms in California and Utah, and brokering a reciprocal work sharing arrangement with a national firm that needed a San Francisco presence.

McLaren shrewdly recognized the substantial potential the establishment of the federal income tax in 1913 would mean for the accounting business. He devoured information from the federal government about the new system and found that his ability to present arguments for clients in clear prose was nearly as important as understanding the fiscal elements of the tax law. Business expanded.

At the young age of 28 he was elected president of the California Society of Public Accountants and just a few years later he had authored an important book on tax accounting. McLaren was also devoting himself to upgrading the standing of the accounting business, traveling to Sacramento to seek legislation that would establish higher standards for accountants to receive the Certified Public Accountant designation.

For the next two decades, McLaren excelled at a pair of intertwined activities: expanding his accounting business and joining and serving as a leader of many clubs. The most prestigious of his memberships were in two San Francisco-based men's clubs whose connections to the business/political establishments of the state and the nation were extraordinary: the Pacific Union Club and the Bohemian Club.

McLaren joined clubs the way other men purchased their neckties. At the end of his life, recounting how club memberships brought him both business success and personal satisfaction, he listed dozens of them all over the United States, mostly men's clubs or country clubs.

At the pinnacle of prestige in the McLaren club universe was the Bohemian Club. Founded in San Francisco by a group of writers and intellectuals, it had transformed into an enclave of privilege, increasingly populated by business leaders. As the years passed, politicians, including presidents, senators, and cabinet members, joined the ranks. The apex of the Bohemian year was the annual summer encampment in the redwood forest at Bohemian Grove in Sonoma County.

The physical location was measured in a few miles, but the emotional and psychological distance from work and politics for this cadre of leaders was better calculated in light years.

While some time in the encampment was given over to serious speeches or presentations from famous guests, boyish hi-jinks account for some of the most memorable legends of these upper crust sojourns, including developing and performing skits with ribald songs, something McLaren reported that he did with regularity and, according to others, with skill.

(The records of the California Historical Society contain dozens of scripts and lyrics for a large-scale, light-hearted musical production presented at each summer's encampment, including credits for writer and musical director. Jack London was among those who scripted a summer encampment play. Some of the titles include "The Bonny Cravat," "The Cave Man," and perhaps most appropriate, "Fools in the Forest.")

As the 1920s roared on and into the Great Depression, McLaren was engaged in what would today be described as networking.

And he was good at it, gathering clients for the accounting firm—some, he noted in the oral history—who remained with the firm for decades. And he was gathering a collection of affiliations for himself, not just because someone was a poker pal from the Links, but because of his business expertise.

In his lifetime, McLaren served as a member of the board of directors of national firms including the Atchison, Topeka and Santa Fe Railroad, Rheem Corporation, Pacific Telephone, as well as the regional airline startup Air California. He was a regent emeritus for the University of San Francisco, on the president's council at the California Institute of Technology and was a director of the San Francisco branch of the Federal Reserve Bank of the United States.

Shortly after the start of World War II, McLaren received a commission as a commander in the US Navy (he was 50 years old) and headed up the Navy Price Adjustment Board. While he would never claim the board's assignment to develop new accounting methods for the Navy had much to do with winning the war, he was proud that the work it did negotiating contracts for the construction of ships and other materiel to support the war effort saved taxpayers millions of dollars. He left the Navy as a captain.

After a brief stint helping with protocol and entertainment accounting for the formation activities of the United Nations in 1945 in San Francisco, McLaren was summoned by President Harry Truman to join a team of seasoned business executives being sent to Moscow to join the Reparations Commission.

McLaren's recollections of his weeks in Moscow and Germany on this assignment could fill a small book. The highlights were that his friend Edwin Pauley (who as a regent of the University of California would play a role in the creation of UC Irvine) led negotiations with the Russians over dividing the spoils of war. McLaren examined artworks and other treasurers recovered from the Germans by the Allies and helped devise an accurate method to catalog them. While accomplishing these duties, there was also time to enjoy other captured treasures that had been larded into the basement of a former resort where he was staying—dining on caviar using beautiful silverware and drinking fine wine from the best crystal.

McLaren told an intriguing tale about the reparations process:

> The most valuable reparations the Russians or the United States received was the spiriting out of Germany and into our respective countries, the great scientists, the great doctors ... there was a tremendous concentration of them ... and this wasn't done by saying, 'have a drink now and we'll get on the train to London.'[8]

Identifying and rounding up the German scientific brain trust, McLaren recounted, was done, "... by a special American group, and they did a very effective, quiet job behind the scenes ... they were academic people, lawyers, industrialists, and to some extent bankers. They were just incognito, I mean, they didn't wear uniforms ..."[9]

And while socializing with his Russian compatriots in the reparations effort, McLaren summoned up memories from a lighter time at Bohemian Grove, composing a parody of *Volga Boatmen* and singing it to the assembled veterans and bureaucrats—no doubt with a healthy serving of vodka. (Songwriting came naturally to McLaren; he and a friend wrote the Cal fight song in 1911 while attending UC Berkeley.)

****

Joan Irvine Smith claimed that between 1935 and 1937, Loyall McLaren had wormed his way into the mind of James Irvine II, persuading him to create the James Irvine Foundation.

As might be expected, McLaren remembered it differently. He recalled that JI came to him in 1936 to discuss estate planning after the death of a friend, someone younger than him. After focusing first on (what else?) tax issues that would impact JI's holdings, McLaren turned to matters he knew JI would find critical.

McLaren suggested the creation of a trust to hold most of the Irvine Company stock after JI's death. It would be the best vehicle, he said, to insure one of JI's most sacred goals—maintaining the ranch in single ownership as far into the future as possible. McLaren had worked with JI long enough to also give him a frank appraisal of the Irvine family, which in his view had significant interpersonal issues and unless prevented from doing so, would fall prey to entreaties from developers to piecemeal away the landholdings to enrich themselves.

The foundation was formed in 1937. JI donated a building he owned in San Francisco, some cash, and a bare majority of the shares of the Irvine Company. McLaren joined a few others on the board and began doling out modest contributions to charities. In 1947, upon JI's death, the foundation asserted its control of the Irvine Company.

McLaren had no misgivings about his role in the matter. He stated it succinctly and clearly in his oral history:

> Under the trust that was created by Mr. Irvine, he gave the responsibility to the directors of the foundation to run the Irvine Company.... which meant that ... and in effect the *foundation delegated to me* the responsibility of running the company, with the understanding that if anything ever arose that was a conflict ... then the foundation directors as a whole would get into things and make a decision. Well, that as a practical matter never came up, so I really had quite a responsibility.[10]

McLaren executed his responsibility for the foundation as he did in his business—with authority. A young associate from his accounting firm, writing in a preface to McLaren's oral history, described him as an aristocrat who played the role. A fellow foundation board member cited his relentless devotion to the James Irvine Foundation.

Unlike Hellis, McLaren had a few things to say about Joan Irvine Smith, both positive and negative, in his oral history. As a condition of donating the history to the Bancroft Library, he stipulated that the comments about her would not become public for 11 years afterward. His comments were:

> Joan Irvine is one of the most talented humans I have ever laid eyes on ... she is still a very handsome woman, but when she was a young person, she was beautiful. She was graceful, she had a natural aptitude for sports ... At the time Mr. Irvine died, if her family had mapped out a career for her, she would be the lady bountiful that would appear and do nice things. She would have been put on the foundation. She would have had more money that any person can possibly spend. She would have been a great heroine down there (in Orange County). She would be one of the most famous women in the United States, and yet this other side of her character just dominated her. Too bad.[11]

Joan's character flaw, in McLaren's view? "She's not strong for anybody but herself. She's the most selfish person I've ever met."[12]

Just six months after giving his oral history, McLaren died at age 86. A bon vivant clubman to the end, his son said that his father was pouring a Scotch and soda when he succumbed.

(After battling McLaren for 20 years, Joan softened slightly after his death. In his obituary in the *Los Angeles Times* on October 26, 1977, she remembered him, "... as a very capable and wily adversary—a brilliant man.")

Notes

1. Joan Irvine Smith, *A California Woman's Story* (Irvine, CA: The Irvine Museum, 2006) 102.
2. Barbara Metz and W. Bradford Hellis, *Recollections of Early Orange County and the Irvine Ranch* (LAWRENCE DEGRAFF CENTER FOR ORAL HISTORY California State University, Fullerton, 1968) 51–52.

3. Metz and Hellis, *Recollections of Early Orange County and the Irvine Ranch*, 54.
4. Metz and Hellis, *Recollections of Early Orange County and the Irvine Ranch*, 8.
5. Robert Glass Cleland and Robert V. Hine, "Chapter 11 – Orchards and Water," in *The Irvine Ranch* (San Marino, CA: Huntington Library, 1984) 144.
6. Metz and Hellis, *Recollections of Early Orange County and the Irvine Ranch*, 62.
7. Gabrielle Morris and Ruth Teiser, *Business and Club Life [of N. Loyall McLaren] in San Francisco: Recollections of a California Pioneer Scion* (Berkeley, CA: Regional Oral History Office, the Bancroft Library, University of California, 1969) 128. https://digitalassets.lib.berkeley.edu/roho/ucb/text/mclaren_norman_loyall.pdf.
8. Morris and Teiser, *Business and Club Life [of N. Loyall McLaren] in San Francisco*, 213.
9. Morris and Teiser, *Business and Club Life [of N. Loyall McLaren] in San Francisco*, 213.
10. Morris and Teiser, *Business and Club Life [of N. Loyall McLaren] in San Francisco*, 239 [emphasis added].
11. Morris and Teiser, *Business and Club Life [of N. Loyall McLaren] in San Francisco*, 144.
12. Morris and Teiser, *Business and Club Life [of N. Loyall McLaren] in San Francisco*, 145.

30 The Big Plans of William Pereira

There are people who believe William Pereira gets no respect. Or at least, not enough respect.

Indeed, the only book devoted exclusively to Pereira's career begins with the complaint that of the four architects selected to grace the cover of *Time* magazine, Pereira "seems to have been largely forgotten."

Author James Steele noted the continuing fame of Frank Lloyd Wright, Philip Johnson, IM Pei, but observed that Pereira has been, "… denied the status now conferred upon the others by the professional and the public."[1]

Steele's book was written in 2002. Fast forward two decades, and in Southern California, other writers and conservationists are sounding similar warnings—Pereira's works are endangered, his reputation and genius fading from memory like his face on the cover of the 1963 *Time* magazine that has been moldering away in the corner of a dusty garage.

Alan Hess, writing in *Orange Coast Magazine* in 2014, lamented in his essay "Erasing Pereira," that elements of the architect's vision at UC Irvine were slowly being either dismantled or ignored.[2]

Hess acknowledged that Pereira's overarching design protecting the natural topography of the university site—and enhanced with the park at its center—remains intact, but cited several instances where new buildings in a variety of styles clash with the modernism that was Pereira's guiding principle for the campus.

Ray Watson contributed a chapter to Steele's book that contains additional perspective on William Pereira's visions for the UC Irvine campus and the master plan for the Irvine Ranch.[3]

****

At least most of UC Irvine is firmly rooted to the ground. In Los Angeles, the decision of the Los Angeles County Museum of Art (LACMA) to raze the existing buildings Pereira designed provoked a virulent protest from the Los Angeles Conservancy, as well as individuals. Their efforts were to no avail, and the new museum will be born in continuing controversy, as some professional and equally passionate amateur architecture critics have heaped scorn on the plans of Swiss

DOI: 10.1201/9781003226291-31

Figure 30.1 Architect and planner William Pereira in the 1960s.

architect Peter Zumther. His design, the critics point out, will cost more than half a billion dollars to build, and result in less museum space than what was torn down.[4]

A Pereira landmark in Orange County is also in danger of being taken down by the federal government.

The Chet Holifeld Building is best known as the Ziggurat. Pereira designed it in the mid-1960s for North American Rockwell, another in his portfolio of large-scale developments and buildings for the ecosystem of aerospace firms in Southern California.

The Ziggurat paid homage to images from Mesopotamia, its concrete platforms built one upon the other like a mystical wedding cake. Rising out of the largely empty plains of the Moulton Ranch a few miles south of Irvine, it was at once futuristic as well as ancient. It remained brooding and empty like a squat Sphinx until 1974, when Rockwell unloaded it on the federal government, where it now houses employees of the Internal Revenue Service and vast stores of records for the National Archives.

In 2020, the government declared it surplus, and an environmental document laying out alternatives for re-use, rehabilitation, or destruction is circulating. Murmurs of concern that another Pereira building could be leveled have been heard locally, but nothing to match the LACMA uproar.[5]

****

It was Pereira's invitation to former college classmate Charles Luckman that initiated the success the two enjoyed in their eight-year partnership, as well as the renown Pereira would achieve later on his own.

In Luckman's telling of their relationship in his autobiography, *Twice in a Lifetime*, it was his business acumen and connections with corporate titans from his previous life as a big-time executive that boosted the small firm into the architectural stratosphere within a few years of his arrival.

Charles Luckman had risen to the pinnacle of American business like a rocket ship. "In 1937, at age 27, he was featured on the cover of Time Magazine as the Boy Wonder of American industry. In 1946, three years after Pepsodent was acquired by Lever Brothers, Mr. Luckman became Lever's president."[6]

But Luckman's relationship with the foreign owners of Lever Brothers led to conflict and his departure from the job that had been paying him $300,000 a year (nearly $3.5 million in 2022 dollars).

While pondering his next move, Luckman received an invitation from Pereira to join his firm in Los Angeles and return to his roots as an architect. Luckman decided to do it.

Arriving at Pereira's tiny office in Los Angeles in 1950, Luckman found that, "… he had about eight men working for him, all wearing the traditional gray artist's smock … reminiscent of the old L'Ecole des Beaux Arts of Paris, with which the University of Illinois architectural school had been associated."[7]

Pereira at this point was hands-on as well. Famed photographer Julius Schulman, who would build a stunning portfolio of work for architects of the era, recalled visiting the office and seeing Pereira with his shirt sleeves rolled up, a green visor on his head, a pencil behind his ear.

(In addition to running his office, Pereira was teaching an architecture class at the University of Southern California. It was the start of what would become a lasting relationship with the Los Angeles private university. Pereira would receive commissions in 1960 and 1966 to create the campus master plan and would design more than a dozen buildings there. His class also paid another dividend; several students who took it ended up working for his firm after graduation, including Gin Wong.)

Luckman thought that,

> … Bill and I would have something unique to sell to clients: the partnership of an architect and a businessman. As a former corporate chief executive,

I could talk to clients on their level, and Bill as a first-rate architect deliver what I could sell.[8]

The two new partners made a handshake agreement—Luckman would not draw a salary for a year, as Pereira didn't have the money and Luckman's previous financial success would easily cover him. Then Luckman found out his architect license from Illinois wouldn't be recognized in California and he would have to take the state test, replete with earthquake engineering requirements unknown in the flatlands of the Midwest and thus not part of the test he had passed years earlier.

Luckman's initial reaction was panic and a bit of partner remorse, but he hired a tutor and passed the exam. He had, he said, returned to his first love, and was eager to dive into Pereira and Luckman and generate some new business.

It didn't take long for the new team to land a major assignment, both in size and prestige.

The Age of Television was dawning in 1950. In addition to recruiting talent and developing the technical expertise for hours of new programming, networks like CBS needed a place to make the magic happen. It soon became apparent that trying to use existing New York City theaters to broadcast a television show was a major headache. A TV show with three bulky cameras on stage, along with yards of electrical cables snaking all over the floor and microphones hanging from the rafters just didn't fit into a space built for the legitimate theater.

Pereira, according to Steele, had been commissioned in 1948 to evaluate theaters in the Los Angeles area for possible conversion or modification to television production. However, Luckman reported in his book that he made the deal in New York City with CBS chairman William Paley that led to the assignment to Pereira and Luckman to design CBS Television City in Los Angeles.

The 25-acre site gave the pair ample room to make a structure that focused on utility.

According to Steele, Pereira designed a studio wing with four large studios and three rehearsal halls. "Dressing rooms ... and space for designing, building ... sets and properties were placed outside ... the studios are divided by a central service corridor which allows an efficient linear flow of sets, props and equipment ... to the stages."[9]

Speaking to *Variety* magazine in November 1952, Pereira and Luckman described their philosophy of design for the new center:

> Our aim was to develop a facility in which the creative elements in television—the actors, musicians, writers, and directors—were provided the best environment for working and projecting their talent; and at the same time design a plant in which entertainment could be mass-produced with enough economy and efficiency to meet the requirements of the management group in reducing operating costs.[10]

The $7.5 million center was a home run for the new partners. Its innovative features were used in subsequent television production centers—the firm picked up several commissions in the years that followed to build television stations across the nation. Moreover, the decades that CBS Television City served as a work horse in the TV business underscored how thoughtful, intelligent, and well-executed design from Pereira and Luckman delivered tremendous value to a client.

CBS Television City was designated as a cultural heritage site in Los Angeles in 2018, and 70 years after making its showbusiness debut, is only now slated for redevelopment, with the firm selected to do the work promising to carefully preserve the spirit of Pereira and Luckman's original intent.[11]

The following year, Pereira and Luckman entered what might be called their airborne era, with commissions to develop master plans for an experimental military airport, a domestic airport, and a space center.

We focus on Los Angeles International Airport (LAX) to the exclusion of Edwards Air Force Base and Cape Canaveral as the LAX project transcended the Pereira–Luckman partnership, as well as because of the enduring connection in California between the architects and what was built (and in 2022, continues to be built).

The proposed new airport to serve greater Los Angeles was touted as the first airport created specifically to serve commercial jet aircraft. As such, the three firms that won the $60 million contract worked together in an atmosphere of the future.

In addition to Pereira and Luckman, two other Los Angeles firms made up the joint venture: Welton Becket, at the time the largest architectural firm in California, and Paul Revere Williams, a pioneer Black architect who had worked in Los Angeles since the 1920s.

Luckman summed up the challenge the trio faced:

> In 1955 we were planning an airport to be constructed by 1960, which was to be large enough for 1980.
> … Sixty planners and architects from our firm worked on behalf of the joint venture, for two years in planning and designing the new airport,
> … Once again, research into the unknown future was the key element in design … we talked with jet airplane manufacturers, conferred with experts in each of the various technologies involved, and then put together the complex, interlocking problems involved in a jet airport.[12]

One of the first futuristic concepts for the new airport was to enclose virtually the entire terminal in a giant glass dome. But cost considerations to air condition such a large space, as well as resistance from airlines that wanted their own terminals, quickly ended that vision.

The design that won out was a group of eight satellite terminals. They were elliptical, allowing airplanes to taxi to the edge of the building; Pereira designed them with future expansion in mind.

To address what Luckman considered the most complex problem facing a modern airport—separating the people from the planes—tunnels were constructed, some as long as 375 to 575 feet. Lighting effects were added to make the tunnels appear shorter.

In an excerpt from a book on architecture in Los Angeles, University of Southern California professor Vanessa Schwartz pointed out that:

> ... although Pereira explained that architecture was a 'series of contrasting spaces which solve specific ... problems,' his work really focused almost exclusively on creating functional spaces. For the airport, he and Luckman defined that challenge as moving people rather than planes. The 'movement of people can be intercepted and diverted by architecture, just as a dam affects a river,' he observed.[13]

The most enduring and iconic symbol of LAX was never intended as such, but over time has transcended purpose and utility to achieve the status as one of the most often cited examples of Pereira's genius.

The Theme Building has been compared to a giant, upside-down flying saucer, as well as one of the Martian attack ships from George Orwell's *War of the Worlds*. Cultural observers note that just a year after the airport was dedicated, similar structures began to appear in the cartoon show *The Jetsons*.

The Theme Building was a structural challenge; it featured parabolic arches 135 feet high that needed to hold up the floating floor that became a restaurant as well as a viewing deck for paying visitors.

The Los Angeles Department of Airports saw the multi-story control tower as the preferred symbol of their newest and increasingly famous air travel center, but the space-age look of the Theme Building relegated the control tower to utilitarian obscurity.

The design parentage of the Theme Building remains a subject of debate. The Pereira faction believes only the master, with his affection for the Space Age, could have conceived such an image and the engineering needed to pull it off. Another faction favors Gin Wong, a former Pereira student who was the director of design for the entire project. A photo of Paul Williams in front of the Theme Building has been raised to urban legend status, although the evidence of his involvement is slim. At present, the leading candidate for Theme Building design creation is James Langenheim, a Pereira–Luckman employee whose initials are reportedly found on the original drawings and who received a letter from Luckman praising his effort on it.

Luckman is rarely given any credit for the Theme Building. Perhaps tellingly, he mentions it in his autobiography in a single sentence.

Another innovative feature of LAX was a dual set of roadways to serve the terminal buildings, one to deliver passengers, another to pick them up. When the airport opened in 1960, there was no upper deck for autos—the city decided the $1.5 million cost was too much. Luckman gleefully notes in his book that the upper deck was added 20 years later at a cost of $121 million.

In 1965, with LAX serving millions of passengers and near capacity, the city went back to Pereira for big picture answers. He conceived the notion of an entirely new, regional approach to air service, creating a mega-airport in Palmdale, more than 30 miles from LAX, where most flights would arrive, and passengers would be whisked into the Los Angeles basin by mass transit. The plan was debated for a few years at City Hall and then abandoned; LAX has become LA's version of the Duomo in Milan, a continuing construction project spanning the political lifespans of dozens of mayors and councilmembers.

In 2023, the airport is scheduled to open a 2.25-mile elevated Automated People Mover system to bring passengers from off-site locations into the airport proper, the fulfillment of a similar plan Pereira and Luckman included in their 1955 proposal.

In 1958, with LAX and several other projects in midstream, Pereira told Luckman he wanted to dissolve the partnership. Speculation for motivation behind Pereira's decision remains fresh in contemporary retelling of the matter, but the only stated reason was Pereira's press announcement that he wanted to limit the number of his future projects.

Luckman paid Pereira for his shares and half of anticipated profits from the projects still underway, then took most of the staff with him to form Charles Luckman and Associates. Pereira formed William Pereira and Associates and set off on a 27-year career that would leave his mark all over the world.

****

The precise number of projects that William Pereira and Associates produced from 1958 to 1985 varies by the historical source, but the consensus total is well over 400.

There was a smattering of private homes, including Pereira's own in Los Angeles, but most assignments were what would be expected of a major architectural firm. Broken down into categories, they include:

- Commercial buildings
- Hotels
- Hospitals and medical buildings
- Schools and college buildings
- Industrial buildings
- Military facilities
- Museums
- Recreational facilities and amusement parks
- Government offices and buildings
- Airports and port facilities
- Large-scale land use plans.

As the workload at William Pereira and Associates grew, so did Pereira's public profile. He had taken a back seat to a degree when the publicity-conscious Luckman was his co-owner, but with Luckman gone, his time in the spotlight expanded.

One aspect of Pereira's public persona that recurs in many chronicles of his career post-Luckman is his appearance. The striking profile, the wavy gray hair, his large, expressive eyes—all were mentioned again and again in a variety of descriptions that boiled down to the fact that William Pereira was one handsome dude.

Pereira had a pair of assistants unique to an architectural firm—his driver and a parking lot attendant. Don Lawson was the driver/valet—he had once worked for actor Yul Brynner. The parking lot attendant was Peter Meria, formerly employed by Frank Sinatra and George Jessel.

The driver accompanied what became one of the principal props Pereira utilized to frame his image as the larger-than-life visionary: a Bentley (observers sometimes mistakenly referred to it as a Rolls Royce).

Consider the recollection of William Banowsky, president of Pepperdine University. Pereira was the master designer for the Malibu campus the university was building on a hillside above the coastal town filled with millionaires and movie stars. There had been a construction problem the day before, and Pereira wanted to know why. Banowsky recalls the visit: "Pereira arrived royally in a limousine and swept into the construction trailer, black cape flowing, lecturing everyone in sight. He warned me that as master architect, he would not be associated with shoddy construction …"[14]

Cape? What serious business executive in 1970 wore a cape?

Dig into the past with those who worked with or for Pereira, and inevitably the cape finds its way into the conversation.

Don Smith worked at Pereira and Associates before later joining the Irvine Company as a planner. He recalled walking into the office one day to find a group of his associates struggling to manhandle a large model of a project into a waiting truck for a client visit. Then, he said, a few yards behind, the elevator doors opened, and Pereira strode forward, sweeping his cape around his shoulders on his way to his waiting Bentley.[15]

There were several theories about the cape. Some said Pereira's days in the Paramount studio inspired him to create a signature look that clients and lesser mortals would associate with his presence. Others found it as a fashion statement to go with the black and white motif of his wardrobe. And then, there was what might have been the obvious explanation: what famous architect often wore a cape?

Frank Lloyd Wright.

****

Pereira was known to friends and associates as someone who studied history and appreciated it. It was not unusual for him to sprinkle speeches or interviews with reflections on planning decisions made centuries before.

For instance, in a 1969 profile that appeared in the *Los Angeles Times*, Pereira cited the ancient cities of Persepolis and Rhodes in the context of travel—caravans for Persepolis and galley ships for Rhodes. Then it was an explanation of why, later, all roads led to Rome.[16]

Three years later, also in the *Times*, when explaining his plan for a Houston shopping mall, he harkened back to a design of Leonardo di Vinci of the Greek city of Adelphi to demonstrate the concept of two-level roadways like the one he and Luckman had designed into Los Angeles International Airport, and finally, Caesar's attempt at traffic management in Rome by banning chariots and trade wagons during various times of the day.[17]

And in 1960, again in the *Times*, as Pereira pondered the design of the Los Angeles County Museum of Art (LACMA), he recalled that Napoleon had opened the former palace at the Louvre as a museum.[18]

Historical research is often cited as one of Pereira's great planning strengths.

His firm was likely one of the few in Southern California to employ—as a vice president—a director of research. Barbara Gray had been educated at Oxford and was an accomplished writer and historian. The pair met when Pereira worked at Paramount. For 30 years she was at his side, delving deep into subjects related to upcoming projects.[19]

Pereira, she said, "... was not interested in creating architectural monuments. Everything the firm did was based on research, regardless of the building type or the location. And research became an especially valuable tool in the foreign projects."[20]

While Barbara Gray was researching, ordering facts and statistics, Pereira—by his own admission—was often thinking and dreaming.

Reading through the dozens of stories about Pereira, most of them flattering, some obsequious, occasionally challenging, a familiar theme recurs—looking deep into the future, analyzing what might be two or three generations hence, and simply ... dreaming.

"I know I'm a dreamer," Pereira told the *Los Angeles Times* in 1969, responding to critics who labeled as "preposterous" some of his ideas like hotels suspended from huge bridges, cities that cascaded down steep hillsides, or urban centers where autos were banned.

"We have to dream, or we won't survive. We have to come up with boldly different concepts for a boldly different future, or we won't have a future to enjoy."[21]

****

Every written word or photographic image that attempts to sum up the professional life of William Pereira must include a single building: the Transamerica Tower in San Francisco.

Soaring 835 feet above the edge of Chinatown and the financial district, the tower is a slender pyramid, rising to a narrow peak from what a critic called a, "... forest of concrete pillars" on a relatively small footprint of land.

Like the parentage of the other iconic Pereira structure, the Theme Building at Los Angeles International Airport, the origins of the pyramid are conflicting.

Bill Stinger worked at Pereira's Los Angeles office for a few months after returning from a long stint in Doha, Qatar, where he was part of a team building the Sheraton Hotel there, and later the master planned city Pereira was designing for the Emir.

Stinger recalls that the model of the Transamerica Tower was shoved into a corner of the office, almost as an afterthought—"it was certainly not on display."

Figure 30.2 Transamerica Tower in San Francisco.
(CoStar)

The story among the staff, he recalled in a 2021 interview, was that the design had originally been done for an office building in Manhattan that was never built.[22]

Gin Wong was president of the Pereira firm when the pyramid was designed, and in several articles about it he is noted as overseeing, supervising, or assisting in its creation.

But it was Pereira who had to face the furor that erupted with the building's design debut in January 1969. When plans were revealed, critics of all stripes began to pile on with varying degrees of outrage calling it everything from an abomination to tasteless.

The city's planning director, Allan Jacobs, fought the proposed design, but along with the city planning commission, was whipped into submission by Mayor Joseph Alioto. Pereira bravely described his firm's design as simple, classical form, and noted that because the building tapered upwards to the pyramid point, it met the city's desire that new skyscrapers block as little sunlight as physically possible on the streets below.

Alioto muscled the project to completion, along with the massive set of buildings just down the street—the Embarcadero Center—and the city's most significant public works project since the Golden Gate Bridge, the Bay Area Rapid Transit (BART) system. San Francisco author Art Peterson attributes Alioto's support for the pyramid to his view of San Francisco as a European city, and the building as, "… our Eiffel Tower."[23]

Once open, like the ugly duckling of the fairy tale, the Transamerica Tower transformed into a graceful white swan on the San Francisco skyline. As the years passed, the detractors diminished and faded away like the city's summer fogbanks. In 2009, *San Francisco Chronicle* writer John King summed up the improved opinion of the building as "an architectural icon of the best sort—one that fits its location and gets better with age."[24]

****

The words James Steele chose in the introduction to his book on Pereira provide a fitting coda to the career of a man who lived and created with style, imagination, and panache:

> (His) projects run the gamut from private homes, department stores, television studios, research facilities, high-rise office towers and airports and entire cities … The dry statistics of such a litany, however, fail to convey the extent to which this work has, by extrapolation, affected the lives of millions of people, the impact it has subsequently had on the careers of all of those involved in helping to create it and make it a realty, or the countless number of people on the periphery who have been touched in some way or another by his contribution.[25]

Notes

1. James Steele, ed., *William Pereira* (Los Angeles, CA: University of Southern California Architectural Guild, 2002) 12.
2. Alan Hess, "Erasing Pereira," *Orange Coast Magazine*, August 2014, 45–58.
3. Raymond L. Watson, "Chapter 3 – Irvine Ranch Master Plan," in *William Pereira*, ed. James Steele (Los Angeles, CA: University of Southern California, Architectural Guild, 2002) 108–139.
4. Sarah Amelar, "Unofficial Competition Seeks Alternative Designs for LACMA as Demolition Begins," *Architectural Record*, April 28, 2020.
5. "Chet Holifield Federal Building, Laguna Niguel, CA," U.S. General Services Administration, August 13, 2017. www.gsa.gov/historic-buildings/chet-holifield-federal-building-laguna-niguel-ca.

6. "Charles Luckman, Architect Who Designed Penn Station's Replacement, Dies at 89", *The New York Times*, January 28, 1999.

7. Charles Luckman, *Twice in a Lifetime: From Soaps to Skyscrapers* (New York, NY: W. W. Norton & Company, 1988) 277.

8. Luckman, *Twice in a Lifetime*, 277.

9. Steele, *William Pereira*, 88.

10. *Variety* magazine, November 1952.

11. R. Vincent, "A $1.25-Billion Overhaul Will Bring Television City into the Streaming Era," *Los Angeles Times*, March 26, 2021.

12. Luckman, *Twice in a Lifetime*, 299.

13. Vanessa Schwartz, "LAX: Designing for the Jet Age," in *Overdrive: L.A. Constructs the Future, 1940–1990*, ed. Wim de Wit and Christopher James Alexander (Los Angeles, CA: Getty Research Institute, 2013) 163–183.

14. Willaima Banowsky, "Malibu Miracle," Pepperdine University Press, 2010.

15. Author's recollection.

16. *Los Angeles Times*, September 14, 1960, 43.

17. *Los Angeles Times*, August 20, 1972, 434.

18. *Los Angeles Times*, July 1, 1969, 21.

19. "Barbara Gray Obituary," *Los Angeles Times*, November 10, 1998.

20. "Barbara Gray Obituary," 1998.

21. *Los Angeles Times*, July 1, 1969.

22. Bill Stinger, interview by C.M. Stockstill, April 8, 2021.

23. Art Peterson, "Transamerica Pyramid." FOUNDSF, 2013.

24. John King, "Pyramid's Steep Path from Civic Eyesore to Icon," SFGATE (*San Francisco Chronicle*, August 16, 2019), www.sfgate.com/news/article/Pyramid-s-steep-path-from-civic-eyesore-to-icon-3277598.php.

25. Steele, *William Pereira*, 12.

31 Reasons for Success

In less than two decades, the Irvine Company transformed an agricultural landscape and business into the most successful New Town in the United States.

The company's planners, managers, and business partners also expanded and solidified the foundation of a commercial organization that would generate massive value for its new owners.

The formula for the success contains several ingredients, each one blended with skill, discipline, and luck.

The first factor, and perhaps the most vital, can be ascribed to the fiscal philosophy of James Irvine II.

He inherited a vast property for which his father paid an average of about $1.62 per acre ($42.21 in 2022 dollars) when he bought out his partners and took sole ownership in 1876.

As time passed, inflation and improvements drove up the value of the land. More important, JI refused to encumber either the land or himself with debt. To pay for most of the substantial capital improvements needed to sustain and expand thousands of acres of orchards and crops (largely related to water), JI sold off parcels of the ranch he considered non-essential to farming. At the time of his death, the Irvine Ranch was virtually debt fee and possessed cash reserves.

In addition to being debt free, the ranch was large—in 1899 it totaled 110,000 acres. There were undoubtedly larger holdings in California at the time, and of course throughout the nation, where places like the King Ranch dwarfed Irvine.

But it was during the period of transformation to an urban setting that the size of the ranch became one of the critical factors in its success.

Compare Irvine to a pair of New Towns underway in the mid-1960s: Columbia, Maryland, and Reston, Virginia. Columbia was about 15,000 acres, Reston just under 10,000. And while perhaps 15,000 to 20,000 acres of the Irvine Ranch was unfarmable or unbuildable, it left between 70,000 to 75,000 acres available to sell or, as JI preferred, to lease to generate income.

The size of the holding and the diversity—geographic and political—was a potent strategic asset for company management.

DOI: 10.1201/9781003226291-32

Three cities eventually governed the bulk of the company's holdings; other land was within the jurisdiction of the county.

For the Irvine Company, it was like joining a poker game while holding three decks of cards to an opponent's one. The company had the ability, if it chose, to sell land for housing, or propose a shopping center, in any of the different jurisdictions (depending on market conditions). Or it could dangle a development that would generate significant sales tax production either as a bonus for other approvals, or as an enticement to promote good will.

Holding more than 90,000 acres of land made it a lot easier as well to donate an extra acre here or there to expand a park, make the alignment of a school site more favorable, or gift land for a specific public purpose that would in turn generate value for company land adjacent or near it. Reston and Columbia didn't have the breadth of opportunity the Irvine Company did in this manner.

The third success-generating factor was the location of the ranch in the path of growth.

After World War II, the megalopolis of Los Angeles was like a giant surging river, seeking channels to direct the flow of new families, businesses, schools, and churches. Northeast of downtown Los Angeles, the San Fernando Valley continued to fill in, to the east, the San Gabriel Valley, and to the southeast, Long Beach and northern Orange County.

By the late 1950s, the bean fields of Huntington Beach and Garden Grove, as well as the citrus orchards of Anaheim and Orange, were being clear cut and plowed under to make way for three-bedroom ranch style homes for sale at no down payment on a Veteran's Administration loan. The surge of humanity continued until it reached the border of the Irvine Ranch. Finding no opening in the solid boundary, growth leapfrogged south and east over the Irvine lands and onto the new community of Mission Viejo, located on property owned by the O'Neill and Avery families.

Eventually, there would be two cracks in the ranch boundary that would funnel and accelerate more people and commerce directly into the heart of the ranch, courtesy of the state of California and the federal government—a pair of interstate freeways, one that would link the northern and southern borders of the entire state, the second an offshoot that would terminate in San Diego.

Developers would maim, bribe, or worse to locate a single major highway on or near their property. On the Irvine Ranch, there were three: Pacific Coast Highway along the western edge of the property connecting Newport Beach to Laguna Beach and eventually, San Clemente; the Santa Ana Freeway (Interstate 5), which started at the Oregon border; and the San Diego Freeway (Interstate 405), snaking from the San Fernando Valley through coastal communities like Santa Monica, Torrance, and Long Beach, then arcing through Huntington Beach, Fountain Valley, and Costa Mesa before passing through the south central section of the ranch and joining the I-5 to form a confluence that would eventually host more than 300,000 passing autos and trucks per day.

In 1960, aerospace giants like Rockwell, McDonnell Douglas, and Boeing were expanding, as was the ecosystem of suppliers that fed material and knowledge into them. All were located west of Irvine and commuting time on the multi-lane I-5 and I-405 was reasonable. A man could leave Irvine and within 20 minutes or so, be at the job. Driving to downtown Los Angeles took longer, but it would be decades until the commute stretched past one hour.

The bulk of Irvine's growth would take place between the two freeways or on either side of them, giving residents incredibly easy access to the vehicular paths to employment, shopping, or recreation. Eventually, the highways would promote and accommodate employment growth at the two major commercial/industrial complexes the Irvine Company had mapped out adjacent to the Orange County Airport and at the junction of the I-5 and I-405 that would become the Irvine Spectrum. In the late 1990s, when that happened, the morning/evening commuting pattern on the two would largely reverse.

The fourth factor of success was the decision to locate UC Irvine on the Irvine Ranch.

As was obvious to anyone familiar with the success the Janss family realized by the growth on their land surrounding the University of California at Los Angeles, prosperity was highly likely to accompany a new branch of the University of California. (Joan Irvine Smith claimed she knew it immediately and had to fight to bring the company managers and trustees of the James Irvine Foundation along with her.)

Ironically, the commercial core at the gateway to the new campus would never achieve the level of economic value William Pereira predicted in his master plan, nor would the residential neighborhoods on either side of it.

The values that would later blossom forth for the Irvine Company on the acreage nearest the campus would occur more than 15 years after the campus opened. The new owners of the company, with sophisticated insights into the market for research and development facilities, realized that creating a partnership with university scientists and researchers could pay tremendous dividends for decades, even if some of the improvements (initially paid for by the company) were transferred to university ownership.

Following the start of construction on the new campus, the company built two new residential villages that drew buyers who found proximity to a UC campus of genuine value, socially and intellectually. And while the laid back, funky lifestyle of Laguna Beach and Balboa Island appealed to some UCI faculty and staff, others found University Park and Turtle Rock in Irvine equally inviting.

From 1965 onward, UC Irvine would educate thousands of young men and women, some of whom found jobs and homes in Irvine and other growing neighborhoods in Orange County, a steady flow of well-educated humanity that coursed into the county's growing population. (In 2018, these factors and others would realize Pat Brown's only half-facetious desire to see Democrats like him elected in large numbers in Orange County.)

Finally, UC Irvine put Irvine on the map of state and national consciousness in a positive fashion.

Up until the Free Speech Movement at UC Berkeley in 1964, the University of California was the nation's preeminent system of public higher education. UC Berkeley was home to Nobel Prize winning scholars and scientists, the state's most prestigious law school, and the super-secret Lawrence Livermore Lab, site of high-level national security research and development.

As Harvard was to the centers of political and financial power on the East Coast, Berkeley was to California's younger elite (as was Stanford) producing three governors, federal judges, architects (Ray Watson, '51), writers, doctors, and scientists. And while its academic cache would never match Berkeley's, the south state sister campus of UCLA has produced its share of notable alumni, which skewed to athletes and entertainers, but also includes two mayors of Los Angeles and a Nobel Prize winner in chemistry.

UC Irvine was one of three new campuses that joined the UC system between 1960 and 1970. And while the unrest in Berkeley—compounded by the cultural and political explosions of the late 1960s—would tarnish the system's standing to a degree, in Orange County some enlightened political and business leaders understood the value of a UC campus in their community and would agree among themselves to nurture it with financial and intellectual support, to the benefit of the entire county, but especially to the city and company that shared its name.

The fifth factor underscoring the Irvine Company's road to success was the company's ownership, another indirect (and likely unimagined) consequence of James Irvine II's decision to create a charitable foundation with a carefully pro-scribed set of contributions criteria.

The trustees of the James Irvine Foundation took control of the Irvine Company in 1947, following JI's death. After that the only stockholders of the Irvine Company who directly benefited from increased profits were members of the Irvine family who had inherited shares of the company from JI. But the family were minority owners. The foundation's instruction from James Irvine's trust was clear: keep the Irvine Ranch in single ownership to the degree possible and manage its business prudently.

Implicit in that admonition was to make a profit, but for the foundation, the more money it received just meant it had more to give away.

By 1960, as Irvine Company management began to gear up in earnest for the transition from farming to urbanization, the only significant pressure to increase profits and dividends was coming from Joan Irvine, who by then had been clash-ing with the foundation for three years. But Joan faced three counter pressures. First, company managers were balancing the need to accumulate precious capital reserves to pay for infrastructure to serve the land the company wanted to sell or lease for commercial or residential use. Second, it was clear that new polit-ical leadership at the county was pushing for higher property taxes on Irvine Company land. The company was able to buy some time by placing some acreage in a tax-sheltered agricultural preserve, but as other land was developed, larger property tax bills were inevitable.

The third roadblock to greater riches for Joan was the foundation, which was asserting its authority on the company (McLaren and fellow trustee A.J.

McFadden had placed themselves on the company's board of directors) and was in no mood to shower Joan with more money; she would only use it to hire more attorneys and find new reasons to sue them.

Thus, Irvine Company management until 1977 was essentially free of the typical tyranny of constantly increasing pressure from shareholders to grow revenues, profits, and dividends. Did they want to? Yes, realizing the need to fund improvements, hire more staff, and pay for the company's own projects that would in turn generate more income. Were they compelled to? No. And as such, decisions could be made, risks could be taken, and innovations could be considered in an atmosphere free of purely profit-driven oversight.

The final element of success was the human factor.

Historians who examine the birth of the United States often focus on the extraordinary assemblage of intellect that gathered in Philadelphia for the Constitutional Convention that hot summer of 1787 to forge the foundation of what would become American democracy.

And while Ray Watson and his colleagues at the Irvine Company would have never considered themselves the equals of Hamilton, Jefferson, Madison, or Franklin, there is a comparison that can be made with a real degree of credibility.

For as much as an appreciation of history, philosophy, economics, and belief in religion underscored the motivations of the Founding Fathers, equally compelling was their humanity—their frailties, ambitions, rivalries, and egos—that also shaped the outcome of the debate and compromise that would lead to the writing of the Declaration of Independence and the Constitution.

We can only speculate which Founding Father William Pereira might have compared himself to (wise elder statesman Benjamin Franklin? The commanding aura of George Washington?), but the importance of his presence and advocacy for what would become the master plans of UC Irvine and what became the City of Irvine cannot be understated.

Describing someone as larger than life has become a cliché, but in Pereira's case, it seems appropriate, given the number of times people who worked with and for him used that phrase or similar words to describe him.

Pereira was also blessed with strong and convincing powers of persuasion. Watson called him one of the best salesmen he had ever met, recalling how he could command a roomful of people within moments of entering it.

It was Pereira's salesmanship that would bring together the trustees of the James Irvine Foundation, the shareholders and managers of the Irvine Company, and the regents of the University of California to conclude that it was in the best interest of ALL of them to accept a donation of land for the new university on the Irvine Ranch.

Most popular histories of this process fail to illuminate the personal hurdles that had to be overcome on both sides to achieve success. Myford Irvine resisted entreaties for the land donation more than once. He didn't even want the family name on the university, according to some reports. A.J. McFadden initially felt the same way. There is evidence that Governor Pat Brown was leaning to a site in La Mirada in

Los Angeles County because of connections to real or potential political allies. And had Norton Simon been a more thoughtful or conniving boardroom player, his strident opposition to the Irvine site might have delayed or killed the sale entirely.

Pereira had officially left the playing field when he split off from Charles Luckman, whose new firm took the initial work they had both done on an evaluation of potential new UC campus site and completed it for the regents. But perhaps sensing the enormous prestige of creating both a new university and a new town from a blank canvas, Pereira remained involved. He huddled with UC president Clark Kerr, advised Walter Burroughs and Joan Irvine on strategy to create community support for the Orange County campus, and obtained a direct commission from the Irvine Company to plan the new community that would surround the university—and got the job of designing the new campus as well.

In Watson's view, it was Pereira's vision, charisma, and salesmanship that directly led to the historic agreement between the Irvine Company and the University of California.

The other human factor at work was collected in and around the Irvine family mansion.

It was a relatively young group of professionals who had been asked to tackle the monumental assignment of creating a new community on thousands of acres of farmland and orchards.

Ray Watson was just 34 when he arrived, joining men like Al Treviño (28), Lanny Eberling (26), Warren Fix (24), Donald Cameron (28), and William Mason (41). In his oral history and writings, Watson mentions more than once that the challenge before the group was something that none of them had ever faced in their young careers.

However, moderating the challenge was the opportunity—a once in a lifetime opportunity as Watson had explained to his wife—that would likely never be duplicated for any of them.

It was also in large part a team with no history to constrain it, no hidebound traditions, rulebooks, or artificial standards in the way of creative thinking. Watson notes that a lot of untried concepts were examined, rejected, tried, considered: "We were working for a company that had no idea how to build a new city."

In the end, for these men, the challenges and hurdles drew them together and forged a common purpose. It was a joy to come to work every day, Lanny Eberling remembers, because, "… we were doing something important; we were on a quest."[1]

And it would be a quest like no other, with results like no other: the transformation of the Irvine Ranch.

Note

1. Lansing Eberling, interview by C.M. Stockstill and H.P. Oliver, July 20, 2020.

Development on the Irvine Ranch in 1977

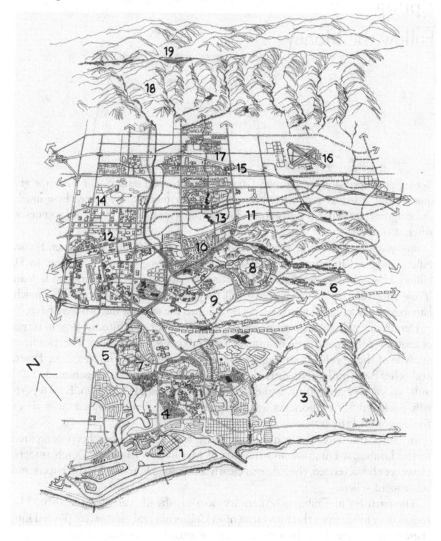

Figure 31.1 Bird's eye view looking northeast from above the Pacific Ocean showing development within the 1899 boundary of the Irvine Ranch as of 1977 with the freeway routes highlighted.

Legend: 1) Newport Bay, 2) Balboa Island, 3) San Joaquin Hills/Irvine Coast, 4) Newport Center/ Fashion Island, 5) Upper Newport Bay, 6) San Joaquin Hills, 7) Eastbluff, 8) Turtle Rock, 9) UC Irvine, 10) University Park, 11) I-405—San Diego Freeway, 12) Irvine Industrial Complex, 13) Village of Woodbridge, 14) Marine Corps Air Station, Tustin, 15) I-5—Santa Ana Freeway, 16) Marine Corps Air Station, El Toro, 17) Village of Northwood, 18) Lomas de Santiago hills, 19) Irvine Lake.

Image hand drawn by Robert Dannenbrink, Jr, FAICP in June 2021, and digitally edited by Jason Baesel and H. Pike Oliver in July 2021.

Epilog
Follow the Money

When conversations in Orange County turn to real estate, the niceties are quickly discarded to get to the bottom line: how much did you pay, how much did it appreciate, what is it worth, and most important—how much did you make when you sold it?

Five years after the 1977 sale, Donald Bren bought out Taubman, Fisher, Petrie, Allen, and Ford in a transaction that valued the Irvine Company at close to $1 billion. Howard Marguleas retained his stock for another 11 years, and while Joan Irvine Smith and her mother agreed to sell, they contested the price (it would be much later before a Michigan judicial referee determined the amount the two were paid).

Details of just how much money each of the investors put into the deal in terms of cash or debt guarantees is difficult to establish 45 years later. The headline analysis of their profits from sources like *Fortune* magazine, *The New York Times*, and other news outlets consistently claim that Fisher and Petrie each made $100 million on a $10 million investment, Taubman around $140 million. Ford reportedly pocketed $19 million. As was their habit, the Allens remained quiet about the outcome of the transaction.

In real estate lore, the acquisition of the Irvine Ranch has been compared to the Louisiana Purchase and the sale of Manhattan Island to Dutch traders. However characterized, the sale was clearly a financial bonanza for the buyers and subsequent sellers.

The partners in Taubman–Allen–Irvine were already very, very wealthy. The profits they made from their investment in California real estate were poured into their bank accounts and in some cases, reinvested for even greater gain.

All but one of the investors have died, and it is instructive to consider how they defined their legacies.

****

Alfred Taubman, who died in 2015, had perhaps the most difficult challenge to rebuilding his reputation. He had been convicted of price fixing in 2002 and served ten months in a federal prison in connection with his management of the Sotheby's auction house. Taubman purchased Sotheby's in the fall of 1983, shortly after selling his Irvine Company shares to Bren.

Upon his release, Taubman returned to Detroit to a hero's welcome at a lunch organized by Max Fisher. In attendance was the city's mayor, a former governor, the president of the University of Michigan, and a host of other business and community leaders.

Taubman spent the next 13 years promoting his beloved Detroit, tutoring his sons to continue their management of the Taubman Company, and giving away some of his fortune. In his lifetime he gave $154.7 million to the University of Michigan, including $45 million for the Taubman College of Architecture and Urban Planning, the remainder to health care, medical research, and the arts. The Taubman name is a familiar one on buildings throughout the huge campus. Taubman also gave $50 million to the Detroit Institute for the Arts.

Taubman created a foundation in his name. In late 2019, its managers predicted that when Taubman's estate was settled, the foundation would receive $200 million.

Perhaps the epitaph on Taubman's grave best sums up his view on life. It says, "make things better, not just different."

****

Max Fisher gave away millions of dollars during his lifetime, with Jewish causes, Detroit revitalization, and a host of other local and national needs on the list of beneficiaries, including $20 million to his alma mater, Ohio State University. One of his best-known donations, $10 million to the concert hall where the Detroit Symphony performs, earned him the honor of having it named for him and his wife. The Max and Marjorie S. Fisher Music Center has since become known to Detroiters as simply, "the Max."

Fisher died in 2005, and like Taubman, created a foundation bearing his name. The foundation's "founders and families shared Jewish values that life's purpose is found in service to others."[1] In 2018, the Max Fisher Foundation had assets of $262 million, and distributed $14 million in gifts.

****

Milton Petrie died in 1994. In his lifetime he had contributed millions to the Metropolitan Museum of Art, the Sloan Kettering Institute, and to several Jewish charities in the United States and Israel. Petrie also made contributions to individuals—his will listed 383 people who received from $5,000 to $15 million, including a police officer who had been paralyzed while injured on duty.

In 2018, the Carroll and Milton Petrie Foundation had $83 million in assets and gave $6.5 million away. According to the foundation's website, it focuses its efforts to benefit families and individuals from low-income and marginalized communities in New York City

Carroll Petrie, Milton's widow, created her own foundation after inheriting a share of his estate. The Carroll Petrie Family Foundation, headquartered in Santa

Fe, New Mexico, promotes animal care and the environment. In 2018, it had $263 million in assets and made gifts of $5.1 million. Carroll Petrie died in 2015.

****

Howard Marguleas didn't create a foundation before his death in 2017 but was remembered as someone who made philanthropy an important part of his life, giving away millions of dollars to health care, youth development, and educational causes all over California. His obituary contained a long list of charitable organizations he had either given to or helped to organize and nurture.

****

While CEO of Ford Motor Company, Henry Ford II served on the board of the Ford Foundation for nearly 30 years, helping it grow to a giant in the philanthropic field. Ford didn't always agree with everything the foundation did, and in his resignation letter reminded the academics who benefited from the foundation's generosity that all of its assets were the fruits of capitalism, largely created by his grandfather's automobile.

Ford died in 1987 at age 70, his estate valued at $350 million. His will provided that his wife, Kathleen DuRoss Ford, would receive an annual annuity from the estate, and upon her death, the remainder would be divided among his six grandchildren. Du Ross Ford died in May 2020.

****

An internet search reveals a single large contribution from Charles Allen Jr., $15 million to Columbia Presbyterian Hospital in New York City in 1986. There is a Charles C. Allen Jr. Family Fund embedded within the Delaware Community Foundation, but its records do not identify the amount in the fund or the donations from it.

****

Joan Irvine Smith died in December 2019. Donald Bren turned 90 in May 2022. Their philanthropic histories will be described in a subsequent publication.

****

The story of the transformation of the Irvine Ranch would be incomplete without an examination of the James Irvine Foundation. Formally incorporated on January 1, 1937, the foundation held its first annual meeting on May 5 of that year in San Francisco. The board members were Katherine White Irvine (JI's wife), Myford Irvine (his son), N. Loyall McLaren, A.J. McFadden, Paul Dinsmore, William H. Spaulding, and James Scarborough.

Scarborough was an Irvine Company attorney, Spaulding an attorney in San Francisco. McFadden and Dinsmore were longtime friends of JI, and McLaren was his trusted finance and tax advisor. Irvine himself decided not to join the foundation board as a voting member but attended many of its meetings.

Irvine endowed the foundation with initial gifts of shares in the Irvine Company and the Moraga Company, which owned hundreds of acres of farmland in Contra Costa County. In December of 1937, Irvine added gifts of $5,000 in cash and a half interest in a building he owned in downtown San Francisco.

For the next ten years, Irvine's pattern of giving continued, cash contributions coming late every December, plus interests in buildings, either in whole or in part. Charitable donations began as well, starting with $1,000 and continuing in similar amounts. During World War II the foundation purchased war bonds and donated to war-related charities. JI increased his cash donations substantially during the war, giving nearly $90,000.

The death of James Irvine II in August 1947 turned the foundation into the controlling manager of the Irvine Company and all its holdings. The foundation swiftly asserted control of the company, installing Myford Irvine as president.

After Myford's death in 1959, the foundation appointed four of its members to seats on the board of directors of the Irvine Company, beginning 18 years of turmoil, legal actions, accusations, and counteraccusations with Joan Irvine Smith, culminating in 1977 in the forced sale of the foundation's Irvine Company stock.

With approximately $200 million in its treasury following the sale, the James Irvine Foundation adopted a moderate investment policy and set out to grow its assets while continuing to fund dozens, then hundreds, of charities that met the definition of need in the indenture of trust created by James Irvine II. Over the next 40 years, some of California's best-known and respected business and community leaders were selected by the board to guide the foundation.

In 2021, the James Irvine Foundation, with offices in San Francisco and Los Angeles, had amassed an astounding $3 billion in assets, allowing it to make contributions totaling $109 million in 2020.

The foundation's current giving strategy focuses on three areas: Fair Work, Better Careers, and Priority Communities.

Fair Work aims to ensure greater fairness and opportunity for workers who earn low wages; Better Careers invests in innovative, high-impact organizations serving Californians seeking middle-skilled jobs; Priority Communities is a multi-year investment to create and promote more good jobs and promote community progress in the California communities of Fresno, Salinas, Riverside, San Bernardino, and Stockton.

In less than a century, the agricultural bounty of the Irvine Ranch and its subsequent value accrued by real estate development led to the creation of one of California's largest charitable organizations.

We believe James Irvine II would be pleased with the outcome.

Note

1. Max & Marjorie Fisher Foundation, April 13, 2021, https://mmfisher.org/.

Bibliography

2007 Long Range Development Plan. UC Irvine Campus Physical and Environmental Planning, 2007.

"A Brief History of Reston Virginia – Founding Principles." Reston Museum. Reston Historic Trust. Accessed July 15, 2020. www.restonmuseum.org/restonhistory.

"A Ray of Hope, One Year Later." *Forum 50 Magazine*, July 1978, 11.

"A University Campus and Community Study." William L. Pereira & Associate. May 1960.

"About Us." Newport Bay Conservancy. Accessed November 11, 2020. https://newport bay.org/about-us/.

"Advertising Supplement." *Los Angeles Times/Santa Ana Register*, circa Fall 1977.

Aldrich, Daniel G. "Remarks of Chancellor Daniel G. Aldrich, Jr.at Dedication of University of California at Irvine", June 20, 1964. (Special Collections and Archives, UC Irvine Libraries.)

Aldrich, Jean and Stuart Aldrich. "Oral History Video" (AS-179) Special Collections and Archives, UC Irvine Libraries, 2015.

Amelar, Sarah. "Unofficial Competition Seeks Alternative Designs for LACMA as Demolition Begins." *Architectural Record*, April 28, 2020.

"An Oral History with James Swinden." California State University, Fullerton. LAWRENCE DEGRAAF CNTER FOR ORAL AND PUBLIC HISTORY, MCAS El Toro Oral History Project, 2012.

Annual Report – 1970. San Francisco, CA: James Irvine Foundation, 1971.

Annual Report – 1971. San Francisco, CA: James Irvine Foundation, 1972.

"Barbara Gray Obituary." *Los Angeles Times*, November 10, 1998.

Benson, C. S. *Charles S. Thomas Memoir.* Claremont, CA: Claremont Graduate School, 1976.

Birmingham, Stephen. *California Rich: The Lives, the Times, the Scandals and the Fortunes of the Men & Women Who Made & Kept California's Wealth.* Guilford, CT: Lyons Press, 2016.

Brigandi, Phil. "1953 Boy Scout Jamboree." OC Historyland. Accessed August 10, 2020. www.ochistoryland.com/jamboree.

Brower, Martin A. *Orange County Jew.* Bloomington, IN: Authorhouse, 2010.

Brower, Martin A. *The Irvine Ranch: A Time for People.* Bloomington, IN: Authorhouse, 1994.

"Builder Admits Helping Pay for Ads Critical of Mobil." *Los Angeles Times*, May 7, 1977, 12.

"'Candy Man' John O. Gottlieb Dead at 86," *Los Angeles Times*, February 26, 1984.

"Celebrating Woodbridge's 40th Anniversary." *Reflections*. Woodbridge Village Association, March 2016.

"Charles Luckman, Architect Who Designed Penn Station's Replacement, Dies at 89", *The New York Times*, January 28, 1999.

"Chet Holifield Federal Building, Laguna Niguel, CA." U.S. General Services Administration, August 13, 2017. www.gsa.gov/historic-buildings/chet-holifield-federal-building-laguna-niguel-ca.

Cleland, Robert Glass and Robert V. Hine. "Chapter 11 - Orchards and Water." In *The Irvine Ranch*, 116–127. San Marino, CA: Huntington Library, 1984.

Cleland, Robert Glass and Robert V. Hine. *The Irvine Ranch*. San Marino, CA: Huntington Library, 1984.

"Cleaver Assails 'Pigs' in Power at UCI Lecture." *Daily Pilot*, September 27, 1968.

Coblentz, William. *San Francisco Lawyer, California Higher Education, and Democratic Politics: 1947–1998, an oral history conducted in 1997–1998* by Leah McGarrigle, Regional Oral History Office, the Bancroft Library, University of California, Berkeley, 2002.

"Creator of Irvine Foundation Dies." *Los Angeles Times*, October 26, 1977, 52.

Curwen, Thomas. "Wizard of Irvine." *Orange Coast Magazine*, June 1996.

Daily Pilot, December 3, 1970.

Dewane, Shawn. "A History of the Orange County Water District." Orange County Water District, 2014.

Domhoff, G. William. *The Bohemian Grove and Other Retreats: A Study in Ruling-Class Cohesiveness*. New York: Harper & Row, 1974.

Feldman, Martin. "Beating Goliath." *Orange Coast Magazine*, December 1996.

"Files of the San Joaquin Fruit and Investment Company and Frances Mutual Water Company." Santa Ana, CA: Orange County Archives, 1970.

Friends of Mammoth v. Board of Supervisors. 1972, 8 Cal. 3d 247, 502 P.2d 1049 Cal. Rptr. 16 4 ERC 1593 (1972). Supreme Court of California.

Goff, Karen. "Virginia Senator Tim Kaine is Clinton's VP Candidate." *Reston Now*, July 22, 2016. www.restonnow.com/?s=Bob+took+a+state.

Golany, Gideon. *Innovations for Future Cities*. Westport, CT: Praeger, 1976.

Gould, Stephen. *Arthur J. McFadden Oral History. LAWRENCE DEGRAAF CENTER FOR ORAL AND PUBLIC HISTORY*, California State University, Fullerton, 154b, 1970.

Haldane, David and Jean O. Pasco. "John Schmitz; Former Right-Wing Congressman from Orange County." *Los Angeles Times*, January 11, 2001.

Hector, Gary. "America's Richest Land Baron." *Fortune*, August 27, 1990. https://archive.fortune.com/magazines/fortune/fortune_archive/1990/08/27/73941/.

Heller, Elinor Raas. *A Volunteer Career in Politics, in Higher Education, and on Governing Boards*, in two volumes, an oral history conducted 1974–1980 by Malca Chall, Regional Oral History Office, the Bancroft Library, University of California, Berkeley, 1984.

"Henry Ford II Dies, Led Auto Firm 35 Years." *Los Angeles Times*, September 30, 1987, 1.

Hess, Alan. "Discovering Irvine." *Places Journal*, October 2014.

Hess, Alan, "Erasing Pereira" *Orange Coast Magazine*, August 2014.

Hinderaker, Ivan. *Draft Provisional Academic Plan*. Irvine, CA: University of California, 1962.

"History." The James Irvine Foundation. Accessed May 4, 2021. www.irvine.org/about-us/history/.

"History of the Crystal Cove Area." Crystal Cove State Park. California State Department of Parks. Accessed November 6, 2021. www.crystalcovestatepark.org/history-of-the-area.

Hitt, Patricia Reilly. 2016. *From Precinct Worker to Assistant Secretary of The Department of Health, Education and Welfare: Oral History Transcript/and Related Material, 1977-1980*. Berkeley, CA: Bancroft Library, Regional Oral History Office.

Huey, Rebecca. *Protest in Practice: The University of California Irvine's Place in the Anti-Vietnam War Movement from 1965–1970* (Research Paper for UCI Humanities Core – Spring, June 6, 2012).

Hurd, Megan. "Malibu Miracle." *Pepperdine Magazine*, April 16, 2010.

"Inclusion Area Sales Agreement." *Land Agreements between the University of California and the Irvine Company* (AS-090) Special Collections and Archives. The UC Irvine Libraries, 1964.

"Irvine Co. Worth Over $315 Million?" *Daily Pilot*, March 16, 1977.

"Irvine Company Property Sales." In *James Irvine Foundation Meeting Minutes*. San Francisco, CA: Irvine Foundation, 1964.

"Irvine Foundation to Question Legality of '69 Tax Reform Act." *Los Angeles Times*, May 10, 1973, 5.

Irvine Ranch Water District. *District Records*. Irvine, CA.

Irvine World News, January 8, 1970.

Irvine World News, July 19, 1973.

Irvine World News, October 9, 1975.

Irvine World News, June 11, 1976.

Irvine World News, December 9, 1976

Issacman, Madison. "Building a Legacy: Lessons from Cadillac Fairview's First Leader." Rotman School of Management. University of Toronto, 2013.

James Irvine Foundation Meeting Minutes. San Francisco, CA: Irvine Foundation.

Janss Investment Co. v. Walden, 196 Cal. 753 (1925).

Jepsen, Chris "O.C. Answer Man: Who was Irvine's Culver Drive Named for?" *Orange Coast Magazine*, November 9, 2016.

"Jewish Orange County Timeline," Orange County Jewish Historical Society, 2016.

Johnson, Lyndon B. "Remarks of President Lyndon B. Johnson at Dedication of University of California at Irvine", June 20, 1964, (Special Collections and Archives, UC Irvine Libraries.)

Johnson, Robert A., and Charlene Riggins. *A Different Shade of Orange: Voices of Orange County, California, Black Pioneers*. Fullerton, CA: California State University, 2009.

Johnson, Scott. "William Pereira." *L. A. Forum*, no. 7, 2015. http://laforum.org/article/william-pereira/

Kerr, Clark. *The Gold and the Blue: A Personal Memoir of the University of California, 1949-1967*. Berkeley, CA: University of California Press, 2003.

Kerr, Clark. "Remarks of President Clark Kerr at Dedication of University of California at Irvine", June 20, 1964, (Special Collections and Archives, UC Irvine Libraries.)

King, John. "Pyramid's Steep Path from Civic Eyesore to Icon." SFGATE. San Francisco Chronicle, August 16, 2019. www.sfgate.com/news/article/Pyramid-s-steep-path-from-civic-eyesore-to-icon-3277598.php.

King, R. J. "Taubman, Take Two." DBusiness Magazine, December 13, 2018. www.dbusiness.com/business-features/taubman-take-two/.

Kling, Rob, Spencer Olin, and Mark Poster, eds. *Postsuburban California: The Transformation of Orange County Since World War II*. Berkeley, CA: University of California Press, 1991.

Kolber, Leo. *Leo: A Life*. Montreal: McGill-Queen's University Press, 2003.

Lage, Ann. *Phillip Berry Oral History: A Broadened Agenda, A Bold Approach. Regional Oral History Office, the Bancroft Library*, University of California, Berkeley, 1984.

Levey, B. "Robert E. Simon Jr., Real Estate Visionary and Creator of Reston, Dies at 101." *Washington Post*, September 21, 2015. www.washingtonpost.com/business/robert-e-simon-jr-real-estate-visionary-and-creator-of-reston-dies-at-101/2015/09/21/28271a6a-6094-11e5-8e9e-dce8a2a2a679_story.html.

"Local Teamster Loans Detailed." *Los Angeles Times*, May 17, 1962, 2.

Lockhart, Jack and Jason Valdry. "Oral History Video." (AS-179) University Archives, UC Irvine Libraries, 2016. https://calisphere.org/item/ark:/81235/d8rz59/

Loomis, Carol J. and Patricia Neering. "Inside the Private World of Allen & Co. Putting a Premium on Personal Ties, This Family Firm Thrives in the Land of the Giants." CNNMoney. Cable News Network, June 28, 2004. https://money.cnn.com/magazines/fortune/fortune_archive/2004/06/28/374371/index.htm.

Los Angeles Times, September 14, 1960.

Los Angeles Times, July 2, 1961.

Los Angeles Times, July 1, 1969.

Los Angeles Times, August 20, 1972.

Los Angeles Times, June 24, 1989.

Los Angeles Times, February 26, 1990.

Los Angeles Times, July 1, 2001.

Luckman, Charles. *Twice in a Lifetime: From Soaps to Skyscrapers* (New York, NY: W. W. Norton & Company, 1988)

Lynch, Kevin. *The Image of the City*. Cambridge, MA: MIT Press – Joint Center for Urban Studies, 1960.

Madrigal, Alexis. "Pipe City." Oakland Museum of California, August 10, 2013. https://museumca.org/story/pipe-city.

Mallory, Mary. "Hollywood Heights: William Pereira, Entertainment Architect." *The Daily Mirror* (blog), April 13, 2020. https://ladailymirror.com/2020/04/13/mary-mallory-hollywood-heights-william-pereira-entertainment-architect/.

Mason, William R. *William R. Mason Papers*. Corona del Mar, CA: Sherman Library and Gardens.

Mason, William R. *William Mason to Irvine Company Employees*. Newport Beach, CA, December 18, 1970.

Max M. Fisher, 1908–2005. Walter P. Reuther Library, Wayne State University (n.d.). https://reuther.wayne.edu/taxonomy/term/1955.

Max & Marjorie Fisher Foundation, April 13, 2021, https://mmfisher.org/

McCulloch, Samuel C. "Interview with Clark Kerr." In *Samuel C. McCulloch Oral Histories*. (AS-033) University Archives, UC Irvine Libraries, 1969.

McCulloch, Samuel C., and Clark Kerr. *Instant University: The History of the University of California, Irvine 1957–93*. Irvine, CA: University of California, 1996.

McCulloch, Samuel C. "Interview with Diana Janas." In *Samuel C. McCulloch Oral Histories*. (AS-033) University Archives, UC Irvine Libraries, 1969.

McCulloch, Samuel C. "Walter Burroughs Oral History." In *Samuel C. McCulloch Oral Histories*. (AS-033) University Archives, UC Irvine Libraries, 1974.

McCulloch, Samuel. "Arnold Binder Interview." In *Samuel C. McCulloch Oral Histories*. (AS-033) University Archives, UC Irvine Libraries, 1989.

McCulloch, Samuel. "Jack Peltason Interview." In *Samuel C. McCulloch Oral Histories*. (AS-033) University Archives, UC Irvine Libraries, 1989.

McCulloch, Samuel. "Robert Gentry Interview." In *Samuel C. McCulloch Oral Histories*. (AS-033) University Archives, UC Irvine Libraries, 1989.

McCulloch, Samuel. "Jean Aldrich Interview." In *Samuel C. McCulloch Oral Histories*. (AS-033) University Archives, UC Irvine Libraries, 1990.

McCulloch, Samuel. "Suzanne Peltason Interview." In *Samuel C. McCulloch Oral Histories*. (AS-033) University Archives, UC Irvine Libraries, 1990.

Metz, Barbara and W. Bradford Hellis. *Recollections of Early Orange County and the Irvine Ranch. Lawrence de Graaf Center for Oral History*, California State University, Fullerton, 1968.

Moffitt, Leonard. *Community and Urbanization in Orange County*. Langson Library, UCI Special Collections and Archives, 1964.

Moon, Vicky. *Middleburg Mystique: A Peek Inside the Gates of Middleburg, Virginia*. Sterling, VA: Capital Books, Inc., 2001.

Morris, Gabrielle and Ruth Teiser. *Business and Club Life [of N. Loyall McLaren] in San Francisco: Recollections of a California Pioneer Scion*. Berkeley, CA: Regional Oral History Office, the Bancroft Library, University of California, 1969.

Nelson, Carl R. *A History of Water Resources Development on the Irvine Ranch, Orange County, California*. Irvine, CA: Self-published, 2009.

Nemy, E. "C. Z. GUEST, Beauty Who Rose to Top of New York Society, Dies at 83." *The New York Times*, November 10, 1983. www.nytimes.com/2003/11/10/nyregion/c-z-guest-beauty-who-rose-to-top-of-new-york-society-dies-at-83.html.

New Worlds Magazine, June–July 1976, 108–110.

"Now Its Taubman-Allen-Irvine." *Daily Pilot*, May 21, 1977.

Oftelie, Stanley. *Shaping Orange County*. Fullerton, CA: Tesoro Publishing, 2020.

Olin, Spencer. *Oral History of UC Irvine Faculty and Staff*. (AS-145) Special Collections and Archives of the UC Irvine Libraries, 2006.

Orange Coast Magazine, August 2001.

Orange County Register, October 11, 1972.

Orange County Register, July 22, 2013.

Pace, Eric. "Norton Simon, Businessman and Collector Dies at 86." *The New York Times*, June 4, 1993.

"Penniman Divorce Case." *Los Angeles Examiner*. February 3, 1958.

Pereira, William L. *The Irvine Ranch Master Plan (Revised Draft)*. Los Angeles, CA: Pereira and Associates, August 21, 1961.

Peterson, Art. "Transamerica Pyramid." FOUNDSF, 2013.

Pinsky, Mark, and George Frank. "Irvine Co. Weekly Performs a Delicate Balancing Act: Credibility, Power to Influence Are Goals of Irvine World News." *Los Angeles Times*, May 29, 1988. www.latimes.com/archives/la-xpm-1988-05-29-me-5312-story.html

"Population.us." Orange County population. Accessed November 7, 2021. https://population.us/county/ca/orange-county/.

Quinn, Sally. "C.Z. Guest: The Rich Fight Back." *The Washington Post*, May 1, 1977. www.washingtonpost.com/archive/lifestyle/1977/05/01/cz-guest-the-rich-fight-back/3f34cd3d-7535-43a1-bae5-608e0fd14620/.

Rindge, Frederick Hastings. *Happy Days in Southern California*. Budapest, Hungary: PublishDrive, 1898 (original publication date).

Ringrose, Kathryn. "Roger Revelle Interview." In *UC San Diego Oral History Project*. San Diego, CA: University of California, 1985.

Rubens, Lisa, and Elizabeth Castle. *Gerson Bakar, Real Estate Developer and Philanthropist*. Regional Oral History Office, Bancroft Library, University of California, 2007

San Francisco Examiner, February 9, 1958.

San Francisco Examiner, April 18, 1960.

Schwartz, Vanessa. "LAX: Designing for the Jet Age." In *Overdrive: L.A. Constructs the Future, 1940–1990*, ed. Wim de Wit and Christopher James Alexander, 163–183. Los Angeles, CA: Getty Research Institute, 2013.

Shelley v. Kramer. 334 U.S. 1. 68. (May 3, 1948)

Siedenbaum, Art. *Los Angeles Times*, April 24, 1977.

SI Staff. "Sporting Start for a Marriage." *Vault* (blog). Sports Illustrated, July 22, 1957. https://vault.si.com/vault/1957/07/22/sporting-start-for-a-marriage.

Sioux City Journal, July 9, 1961.

Smith, Joan Irvine. *A California Woman's Story*. Irvine, CA: The Irvine Museum, 2006.

Stamp, J. "James W. Rouse's Legacy of Living Through Better Design." *Smithsonian Magazine*, April 23, 2014. www.smithsonianmag.com/history/james-w-rouses-legacy-better-living-through-design-180951187/.

Steele, J., ed., *William Pereira*. Los Angeles, CA: University of Southern California, Architectural Guild, 2002.

Stein, Mimi. *From Precinct Worker to Assistant Secretary of the Department of Health, Education and Welfare*, oral history transcript and related material, Hitt 1977–1980: Hitt, Patricia Reilly, 1918. Edited by Robert H. Finch. Bancroft Library, Regional Oral History Office. Accessed November 8, 2020. https://archive.org/details/precinctworker00hittrich.

Stern, Jean. *Reflections of California: The Athalie Richardson Irvine Clarke Memorial Exhibition*. Irvine, CA: Irvine Museum, 1994.

Stewart, Jocelyn Y. "Gil Ferguson, 84; Conservative Served 10 Years in State Assembly." *Los Angeles Times*, May 9, 2007.

Sudjic, Deyan. *The 100 Mile City*. San Diego, CA: Harcourt, Brace, 1993.

Taubman, A. Alfred. *Threshold Resistance*. New York, NY: Harper Collins, 2009.

Tereba, Tere. *Mickey Cohen: The Life and Crimes of L.A.'s Notorious Mobster*. Chicago, IL: Independent Pub Group, 2012.

"Tax-Exempt Foundations and Charitable Trusts: Their Impact on Our Economy (Fifth Installment)." US House Select Committee on Small Business. Subcommittee Chairman's Report to the Subcommittee No. 1 – Volume 5. Washington, DC: US Government Printing Office, April 28, 1967.

"Telegraph Avenue." *The Berkeley Revolution*. Accessed November 12, 2021. http://revolution.berkeley.edu/view-archive-by-place/telegraph-avenue.

The American Broker and Business Man: A Distinct Cyclopedia of 1921. Chicago, IL: American Blue Book Publishers, 1921.

"The History of Active 20-30 US & Canada." Active 20-30 United States and Canada®. Accessed February 6, 2022, www.active20-30.org/history-us-canada.

"The Legendary 'Cappy' Smith Dies." *Equisearch*, July 17, 2002.

"The Man with a Plan." *TIME* 82, no. 10, September 6, 1963.

"The Middleburg Hunt." www.middleburghunt.com/history.html.

Thomas, Charles S. *Personal and Business Files*. (MS.R.003) Special Collections and Archives of the UC Irvine Libraries, 1946–1966.

UC Irvine Campus Physical and Environmental Planning, *Long Range Development Plan* (2007).

UCI Town and Gown Trailblazers: The Women Who Built Town and Gown – 1963–1980. Irvine, CA: Town and Gown Oral History Committee, 2013.

U.S. Congress, House. Committee on Ways and Means. *Hearings on Tax Reform, Tax Exempt Foundations* February 19-20, 1969.

U.S. Congress, House. Committee on Ways and Means. *Subject of Tax Reform: Hearings Before the Committee on Ways and Means.* 91st Cong., 1st sess. February 21, 1969. www. tinyurl.com/ytymxtsy.

U.S. Congress, House. Select Committee on Small Business. Subcommittee Chairman's Report to Subcommittee No. 1. "Letter of Transmittal." *Tax-Exempt Foundations and Charitable Trusts: Their Impact on Our Economy.* 90th Cong., 1st sess., April 28, 1967. tinyurl.com/2p89878n

U.S. Congress, House. Select Committee on Small Business., Subcommittee Chairman's Report to Subcommittee No. 1. *Tax-exempt foundations and charitable trusts: Their impact on our economy. (Fifth installment)* Report to Subcommittee No. 1, 90th Cong., 1st sess. Washington, DC: U.S. Government Printing Office, April 28, 1967.

U.S. Congress. House. Committee on Banking and Commerce. *Tax Exempt Foundations and Charitable Trusts: Public Hearings Before the Committee on Banking and Commerce, House of Representatives.* 93rd Cong., 1st sess. Washington, DC: U.S. Government Printing Office, 1973.

U.S. Congress. House. Committee on Ways and Means. *General Tax Reform (Testimony from Administration and Public Witnesses): Public Hearings Before the Committee on Ways and Means, House of Representatives.* 93rd Cong., 1st sess., March, April and May 1973. Washington, DC: U.S. Government Printing Office, 1973.

U.S. Dept. of Justice, FBI Memo 124-90044-1036. Agency file 63-7145-15. (Released under the John F. Kennedy Assassination Records Collection Act of 1992 44 USC on November 14, 2017) (January 11, 1962).

U.S. House Select Committee on Small Business. *Tax-exempt Foundations and Charitable Trusts: Their Impact on Our Economy (Fifth Installment), Subcommittee Chairman's Report to the Subcommittee No. 1 – Volume 5.* US Government Printing Office, April 28, 1967.

Variety magazine, November 1952.

Vincent, R. "A $1.25-Billion Overhaul Will Bring Television City into the Streaming Era," *Los Angeles Times*, March 26, 2021.

Watson, Raymond L. "1960: A New Era," in *Raymond L. Watson Papers.* (MS.R.120) Special Collections and Archives of the UC Irvine Libraries, 2006.

Watson, Raymond L. "Chapter 3 – Irvine Ranch Master Plan," in *William Pereira*, edited by James Steele, 108–319. Los Angeles, CA: University of Southern California, Architectural Guild, 2002.

Watson, Raymond L. *Planning Department Dear Diary (1960–61),* Part 1 in Box 12, Folder 6 1960 October 10–1961 April 28 and Part 2 Box 13, Folder 1, May1–1961 to October 5, MS.R.120. Raymond L. Watson Papers. Special Collections and Archives, UC Irvine Libraries. Irvine, California.

Watson, Raymond L. *Material for an Unpublished Manuscript on Irvine.* Raymond L. Watson Papers (MS.R.120). Special Collections and Archives of the UC Irvine Libraries, 2006.

Watson, Raymond L, "Post University Agreement," in *Raymond L. Watson Papers.* (MS-R.120) Special Collections and Archives of the UC Irvine Libraries, 1992–2005.

Watson, Raymond L. "The University of California's and the Irvine Company's Historic Agreement," in *Raymond L. Watson Papers.* (MS.R.120) Special Collections and Archives of the UC Irvine Libraries, 2006.

Watson, Raymond L. "Upper Newport Bay: Conflicting Visions," in *Raymond L. Watson Papers.* (MS-R120) Special Collections and Archives of the UC Irvine Libraries, 2005.

Watson, Raymond L. "Irvine's Road to Cityhood," in *Raymond L. Watson Papers.* (MS.R.120) Special Collections and Archives of the UC Irvine Libraries, 2006.

Watson, Raymond L. and Ann Lage. *Planning and Developing the New Town of Irvine California, 1960–2003: Irvine Company President, 1973–1977, Walt Disney Company Chairman, 1983–1984.* Regional Oral History Office, the Bancroft Library, University of California, Berkeley, 2005.

"We Called It a Work Holiday: The 1946 Oakland General Strike." Digital Collections: California Labor Federation, AFL-CIO: Proceedings and publications. Accessed November 14, 2020. https://irle.berkeley.edu/digital-collection/oakland/.

"Westridge School for Girls: Lives of Impact Begin Here." Westridge School for Girls | Lives of Impact Begin Here. Accessed November 8, 2021. www.westridge.org.

"William Pereira Obituary." *Los Angeles Times*, November 14, 1985.

Wilson, J. "The Making of a Mascot." *UCI News*, November 18, 2015.

Index

Printed in the United States
by Baker & Taylor Publisher Services